# Concordia University at 50

We would like to begin by acknowledging that Concordia University is located on unceded Indigenous lands. The Kanien'kehá:ka Nation is recognized as the custodians of the lands and waters on which we gather today. Tiohtià:ke/Montréal is historically known as a gathering place for many First Nations. Today, it is home to a diverse population of Indigenous and other peoples. We respect the continued connections with the past, present and future in our ongoing relationships with Indigenous and other peoples within the Montreal community.

# Concordia University at 50

## A COLLECTIVE HISTORY

Edited by
Monika Kin Gagnon and Brandon Webb

with Steven High, Catherine Wild, and Jason Camlot

Published for Concordia University's 50th Anniversary Celebration
by Concordia University Press
Montreal

Unless otherwise noted, all text and photographs copyright the authors © 2024

CC BY-NC-ND

Every reasonable effort has been made to acquire permission for copyright material used in this publication, and to acknowledge all such indebtedness accurately. Any errors and omissions called to the publisher's attention will be corrected in future printings.

Design and typesetting: Associés Libres Design

Proofreading: Saelan Twerdy and Ryan Van Huijstee

Copy editing: Joanne Muzak

Printed and bound in Canada by Friesens, Altona, MB

This book is printed on Forest Stewardship Council certified paper and meets the permanence of paper requirements of ANSI/NISO Z39.48-1992.

Concordia University Press's books are available for free on several digital platforms.
Visit www.concordia.ca/press

First English edition published in 2024
10 9 8 7 6 5 4 3 2 1

978-1-988111-57-5 | Paper
978-1-988111-58-2 | E-book

Library and Archives Canada
Cataloguing in Publication

Title: Concordia University at 50 : a collective history / edited by Monika Kin Gagnon and Brandon Webb with Steven High, Catherine Wild, and Jason Camlot.
Other titles: Concordia University at fifty
Names: Gagnon, Monika Kin, 1961- editor | Webb, Brandon (Graduate of Concordia University), editor. | High, Steven C., editor | Wild, Catherine, editor. | Camlot, Jason, 1967- editor
Description: Includes bibliographical references.
Identifiers: Canadiana (print) 20240428021 | Canadiana (ebook) 20240428048 | ISBN 9781988111575 (softcover) | ISBN 9781988111582 (EPUB)
Subjects: LCSH: Concordia University (Montréal, Québec)—History.
Classification: LCC LE3.M66 C28 2024 | DDC 378.714/28—dc23

Concordia University Press
1455 de Maisonneuve Blvd. W.
Montreal, Quebec H3G 1M8
Canada

*Concordia University Press gratefully acknowledges the support*

*of the Birks Family Foundation, the Estate of Linda Kay,*

*and the Estate of Tanneke De Zwart.*

# CONTENTS

Introduction, *Monika Kin Gagnon* | xiii

Introduction to Oral Histories, *Steven High* | xvii

## FOUNDATIONS

1 The Quiet Revolution and the Creation of Concordia University
*Ronald Rudin* | 3

2 ORAL HISTORIES: The Merger and Its Legacies
*André Laprade, Russell Breen, Jack Bordan, Henry Habib, Nancy Marrelli, Linda Dyer* | 15

3 Planning Concordia's Loyola and Sir George Williams Campuses:
The First 25 Years, 1974–1999
*Dominique Dumont, Rocio Carvajo-Lucena, and Susan D. Bronson* | 25

4 Statement on Tuition Fees in Quebec and Their Impact on Women (2012)
*Simone de Beauvoir Institute, with an introduction by Viviane Namaste* | 41

5 ORAL HISTORIES: Feminist Perspectives
*Maïr Verthuy, Linda Dyer, Elizabeth Morey, Manon Tremblay* | 46

6 The Grey Nuns Mother House: Confronting the Difficult Legacies
*Peter Gossage* | 53

## BUILDING THE INSTITUTION

7 A Brief History of the Faculty of Arts and Science
*Miriam Posner* | 67

8 Expanding Energies: The Faculty of Fine Arts
*Catherine MacKenzie* | 87

9 "All Merged Up": The John Molson School of Business
*Charles Draimin and Christopher A. Ross* | 109

10 Pathways towards Cultural Diversity, Accessibility, and Knowledge Sharing
*Dave McKenzie* | 121

11  The Gina Cody School of Engineering and Computer Science
*Christopher Trueman and Ted Stathopoulos* | 131

12  VISUAL STORY: Memorial Installation Dedicated to Four Concordia Professors (1996)
*Johanne Sloan* | 146

13  ORAL HISTORIES: August 24, 1992
*Donna Whittaker* | 153

14  The School of Graduate Studies: 50+ Years of Cultivating a Graduate
and Research Culture
*Joanne Beaudoin* | 155

15  Research at Concordia
*Jean-Philippe Warren, Julien Larregue, and Vincent Larivière* | 169

16  Building Aboriginal Territories in Cyberspace (AbTeC)
*Jason Edward Lewis and Skawennati* | 179

17  The Transformation of Concordia Library
*William M. Curran* | 191

18  ORAL HISTORIES: Research and the City
*Lynn Hughes, Henry Habib, Maïr Verthuy, Lorna Roth* | 205


## COMMUNITY ACTIVATIONS

19  Early Indigenous Programming and Pedagogies, 1970–1990
*Colby Gaudet* | 215

20  The Poetry Series at Sir George Williams University
*Jason Camlot* | 225

21  History from Below: George Rudé and Montreal as a Radical Crossroads
*Brandon Webb and Matthew Penney* | 235

22  VISUAL STORY: The 1969 Sir George Williams University Student Protest against
Racism: A Curator's View
*Christiana Abraham* | 242

23  These Halls of Ours: Black Student Presence and Black Montreal Youth History
*Annick Maugile Flavien and Désirée Rochat* | 249

24  "We Could Write History": Telling Stories of the First General Unlimited
Student Strike
*Nadia Hausfather and Anna Sheftel* | 261

**25** ORAL HISTORIES: Student Activism
*Zev Tiefenbach, Geneva Guérin* | 273

**26** Breaking the Tape: Track and Field, Cross-Country Running
*John Lofranco and Gavin Taylor* | 279

**27** VISUAL STORY: Sports and Athletics | 288

**28** ORAL HISTORIES: Athletics in Action
*Paul Chesser* | 295

## VIEWPOINTS

**29** Keeping Time with Oscar Peterson: Between Jazz Archives and the Concert Hall
*Eric Fillion* | 299

**30** Reflections on Student Life
*Andrew Woodall* | 309

**31** ORAL HISTORIES: International Students
*Elizabeth Morey* | 311

**32** Concordia's Legacies of 2SLGBTQ+ Student Community Building
*Gregorio Pablo Rodríguez-Arbolay* | 313

**33** Cinema Politica: Twenty Years of Screening Truth to Power
*Svetla Turnin and Ezra Winton* | 317

**34** VISUAL STORY: History of Student Media | 320

**35** ORAL HISTORIES: Student Perspectives
*Philip Authier, Geneva Guérin* | 325

**36** Concordia University and the Loss of Heritage and Housing
*Eliot Perrin* | 329

**37** Concordia Continuing Education: A History of Lifelong Learning
*Kerry Fleming and Ursula Leonowicz* | 335

**38** The Art of Conversation: 20 Years of University of the Streets Café
*Alexandra Pierre* | 339

**39** VISUAL STORY: 30 Things We Love about Concordia (2004) | 342

## SNAPSHOTS

**40** Queer and Sexuality Studies: How Concordia Emerged at the Forefront of New and Vital Disciplines
*Matthew Hays* | 355

**41** The Story of Ethnocultural Art Histories Research (EAHR)
*Alice Ming Wai Jim* | 359

**42** The History of the Otsenhákta Student Centre
*Portia Lafond* | 363

**43** A Short History of Theological Studies and Its Non-confessional Pedagogy
*Gabriel A. Desjardins* | 369

**44** The Thousand and One Adventures of French at Concordia University
*Françoise Naudillon* | 377

**45** A History of the Early Childhood and Elementary Program, 1971–2021
*Ellen Jacobs and Nina Howe* | 381

**46** Leaping across Time: Four Decades of Contemporary Dance at Concordia University
*Silvy Panet-Raymond* | 385

**47** Electroacoustic Studies at the Department of Music
*Kevin Austin* | 389

**48** ORAL HISTORIES: Formations
*Steven Appelbaum, Ira Robinson, Linda Dyer* | 393


## FUTURES

**49** Reimagining Concordia's Future: A Kanien'kehá:ka Perspective
*Kahérakwas Donna Goodleaf* | 399

**50** Afterword
*Anne Whitelaw* | 405


Acknowledgements | 409

Illustration Credits | 411

Public Art Collection and Credits
*Sandra Margolian* | 415

**Marc-Antoine Côté**
*« Montre-moi par où on commence. Dis-le-moi au creux de l'oreille »*, 2020
Aluminum (8.56 x 2.92 x 2.82 metres)
Exterior, Applied Science Hub, Loyola campus

**Kamila Wozniakowska**
*Acer Concordiae* (detail), 2011
Brushed stainless steel, 52 engraved plaques, detail (40.64 x 30.48 cm each)
De Maisonneuve Tunnel, SGW campus

# INTRODUCTION

## Monika Kin Gagnon

**CONCORDIA UNIVERSITY AT 50: A COLLECTIVE HISTORY** celebrates and offers a moment of reflection on the fiftieth anniversary of the merging of Loyola College and Sir George Williams University in August 1974. A privilege of contributing to this book's creation has been meeting a wide array of people from our Concordia community. As a Montreal-born alumna (BA '82) and current (second-generation) faculty member in the Department of Communication Studies since 1998, my own affiliation to Concordia spans over forty years. I've moved through these buildings as a student and faculty member whose father, Charles Gagnon, left Loyola College in the year of the Concordia merger in 1974. I can easily summon childhood flashes from Loyola's Bryan Building, as well as undergrad memories from the sound editing studios. How Concordia has shaped me has brought a certain interest and affection to this undertaking, as an embodied participant observer with what I hope is keen editorial acumen.

Ushering this book to completion has brought a close-up view on many facets of Concordia that I knew nothing about—the unique (and idiosyncratic) cultures of academic faculties and departments, and the scholars and students who inhabit them; as well as the many administrative offices and their staff members who have ensured its smooth operation for the last five decades, many of whom are alumni. With a population of approximately 57,000—7,000 faculty and staff, and some 50,000 students—we are akin to a small city, with all the needs, complexities, and responsibilities that this entails. Concordia's histories and stories tell of this community, and it is our hope that this multilayered book composed of archival documents and photographs, short and long chapters, and extracts from oral histories, will point to this plurality of its voices.

---

MONIKA KIN GAGNON is Professor of Communication Studies and served as department chair from 2020 to 2023. She is author and editor of numerous books and essays, including *Other Conundrums: Race, Culture, and Canadian Art* (2000); *In Search of Expo 67* (2021); and "Before I Made Films I Was Singing" (2022), a conversation with Abenaki filmmaker Alanis Obomsawin.

In our opening section, Foundations, for instance, the merger of two institutions is told from multiple viewpoints and in different rhetorical forms. Professor Emeritus of history Ronald Rudin's researched chapter locates the external political pressures in Montreal and Quebec that necessitated Concordia's formation, while the oral histories of four men who were there draw us into the day-to-day administrative activities needed to logistically bring it into being. Simultaneously, four women's testimonies vividly describe the male-dominated nature of our institution in the 1970s, not untypical of the time, attesting to their lived contestations and the need for Simone de Beauvoir Institute's feminist activism, commencing in 1978, which Viviane Namaste introduces. Other insights in this first section include campus planning's focus on space and acquisitions, as they populated and mapped "Concordia" into the daily life of Montreal by forming two campuses spread out across the city and united by shuttle buses. The history of these formative acquisitions has their own plurality of voices. The eventual purchase of the Grey Nuns Building in 2007, for example, brought with it the vexed legacy of residential school connections examined and scrutinized in the 2015 *Truth and Reconciliation Commission Report*.

If any singular event reminds us that we are located on unceded Kanien'kehá:ka territory, it is perhaps this recent acquisition. It plunges us into the history of the Grey Nuns, certainly, but also the Jesuit Catholic roots of one of our founding institutions, Loyola College, and their own early histories (and the violence) of settler-colonial inhabitation of *this* place. As historian Peter Gossage suggests, it may be precisely in our reckonings with this building that we can examine the truth of our connections to colonialism and other systems of oppression, in order to genuinely aspire for reconciliation. And as Director of Decolonizing Curriculum and Pedagogy Kahérakwas Donna Goodleaf states, it's perhaps only in thinking together, with harmonized Indigenous and Western knowledges that are shared, that we can collectively work our way out of the climate catastrophe we find ourselves in.

As we organized the book into different sections—from Foundations came Building the Institution, Community Activations, Viewpoints, and Snapshots—a

multitude of voices gathered into a polyphony that brought forth different scales of activity and interaction, some institutional and descriptive, others more anecdotal, subjective, and even critical. Archivist Emeritus Nancy Marrelli disagrees with the 1974 merger as the date of Concordia's inception, considering Sir George Williams University's affiliations with the YMCA and even earlier as integral to our formation. Long-time Concordian and current Indigenous Directions Senior Director Manon Tremblay believes the university must radically rethink itself. How you are and will be positioned as you read—as alumni, current student, employee, faculty, or interested reader—will hopefully contribute in some way to shaping Concordia's next fifty years.

The second of six sections, Building the Institution, addresses some formal aspects of Concordia—its four faculties, library, and school of graduate studies, as well as research-related activities. Because of this book's formation as an open call for participation, we admit to certain gaps that are underrepresented; Concordia's research history is one of them and is, without doubt, a wily topic to fully grasp in its multiplicity and amplitude. Jean-Philippe Warren's co-authored contributions and inventive data visualizations offer a glimpse into some aspects of international collaborations and grant-application subject areas. The third section, Community Activations, captures the close connections Concordia's members have had with and within the Montreal community and other self-defined constituencies, including politicized, activist manifestations. The Viewpoints section then extends these to include sharp, enlarged interpretive stories of some activities. Snapshots, offers quite literally that: quick, focused takes on some student centres, programs, and departments. And finally, Futures, casts its vision to the next fifty years. Interspersed throughout you'll read short lively extracts from oral histories, which historian and co-editor Steven High preambles in his introduction that follows. Where there were other lacunae, we turned to the archives for images and documents that helped us fill out some of the things we love about Concordia, including athletics, the 1969 student protest, and the vibrant history of student media. Additionally, you will find running

throughout the book in-situ images from Concordia's public art collection, commenced over fifty years ago and comprised of over thirty installations. (More information about the collection is available near the end of this book.)

*Concordia University at 50* may not resemble traditional institutional histories that weave a single narrative of a university's origins. Instead, this book anthologizes the many stories and viewpoints that make up Concordia. As we reached the final days of assembling the chapters, stories, photos, and artifacts for Concordia's fiftieth anniversary anthology, our cohesion in multiplicity became ever more apparent, attesting to our very name and its roots in concord and harmony, as Ronald Rudin and Henry Habib both describe. This book is a rich and complex testament to the Montreal university that we are, formed by its many constituents, and by the multilingual city and the complex province that are our home. Constructed from a call for proposals in 2022, the book you now hold in your hands was further shaped by our editorial advisory committee and other readers, and nourished by reader reflections and feedback, word-of-mouth recommendations, chance conversations, a writers' colloquium, a second final callout, and our own deep dive into Concordia's Records Management and Archives (RMA) and Library's Special Collections. Drawing on the expertise and knowledge of Concordia archivists, our growing collections offered unique vantage points, including of absences, and rapidly changing archival practices that have made many artifacts accessible on the RMA's Internet Archive pages and YouTube channel, where materials are now routinely uploaded and simple to access. The radical changes to access and circulation of information, research, and archives since the 1970s have dramatically transformed history and memory and how we remember at a milestone anniversary such as this one. *Concordia University at 50* sits somewhere between the past and the future as most fifty-year anniversaries do—with some generations of people present for the original merger in 1974, and others (re)imagining what the future will bring in the next fifty.

# INTRODUCTION TO ORAL HISTORIES

Steven High

**CONCORDIA UNIVERSITY'S** past and present are peopled with stories. Stories of institutional origin, of struggle and contestation, of experimentation and learning, but most of all of community. When we decided to mark the fiftieth anniversary of the unification of our two founding institutions with a book, we wanted this to be more than a top-down institutional history. Our chapters offer a range of interpretative sightlines, but we also wanted to leave space for personal story.

We hired Piyusha Chatterjee, a recent graduate from Concordia's interdisciplinary PhD program, and based at the Centre for Oral History and Digital Storytelling, to conduct a series of oral history interviews with a spectrum of long-time members of our university community. This was, of course, a challenging process, as there were thousands of possibilities. Everyone reading these words has a story too, I am sure.

Oral history, at its best, brings the past to life through the sharing of stories. We learn much about the past, but also what it *meant* to people at the time and in the present. These interviews, therefore, are acts of personal interpretation but also expressions of felt knowledge. They offer much more than eye-witness accounts. Oral histories are subjective, and that is their great strength.

Keeping in mind our commitment to hear voices from the four corners of our university and a diversity of perspectives over time, we developed a list of people to approach. Almost everyone generously agreed to be interviewed on camera. Brandon Webb then came across a series of extraordinary interviews detailing the merger itself, conducted decades ago by Joel McCormick, a former editor of *The Georgian*. Our team transcribed these interviews, too, and a number of those stories are also included in this book. The experiences of the founding generation who, mostly, are no longer with us, are thus woven into the tapestry.

The life history interviews conducted for this book were substantial, ranging from one to three hours. Our interview partners were invited to reflect back on their years at

---

STEVEN HIGH is Professor of history at Concordia where he co-founded the Centre for Oral History and Digital Storytelling. He is the author of many books and articles, including *Deindustrializing Montreal: Entangled Histories of Race, Residence, and Class* (2022), which was awarded the political book prize from Quebec's National Assembly.

Concordia. The interviews gave space for people to speak freely, without preset questions. Each interview was then meticulously transcribed by our team of student research assistants. Transcription is time-consuming work and can be challenging as the spoken and written word are so very different, making transcription an act of translation. The transcriptions were verbatim, which means that they include the "ums" and "uhs" of normal speech as well as the sentences that start, stop, and restart. Most stories are composed in the moment, which makes them roughly worded. Sometimes, however, they come out smooth as silk, a sure sign that the story has been told and retold.

I then went through the hundreds of pages of verbatim transcripts and identified stories for possible inclusion in the book. These excerpts were shared with the editorial committee, who helped us identify the stories that are included here. And finally, I edited the stories for clarity, though every word you see here was spoken and in that order. We lose a bit of the feel of the spoken word, but we gain far more. These are great stories that help us see our university and its history from other points of view.

Everything has a history. Did you know that some wanted the new university to be named after Canadian surgeon and early advocate of socialized medicine Norman Bethune, whose statue now stands in Quartier Concordia? Did you ever wonder how the People's Potato, Concordia's vegetarian soup kitchen, came into being? Or why one of the student newspapers is called *The Link*? Or what it was like for the first generation of women faculty members who broke into the men's world of many departments? Did you know that the 2002 Benjamin Netanyahu visit and its aftermath cemented adversarial relations between the administration and the student union for a period of time? Or how September 11th, 2001, prompted a wave of organizing by Concordia students to counter Islamophobia? Or how our Department of Religion (now Department of Religions and Cultures) sought to decentre the teaching of Christianity early on? Find the answers to these questions and many more in the stories that follow. On behalf of the entire team, I want to thank all of our interviewees for their tremendous generosity.

**Jean McEwen**
*Untitled* (detail), 1966

Painted glass windows, three triptych panels (3.66 x 4.57 metres each)
Mezzanine, Henry F. Hall Building, SGW campus

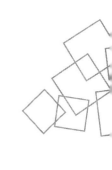

# Foundations

PROVINCE OF QUEBEC

DEPARTMENT OF FINANCIAL INSTITUTIONS,
COMPANIES AND COOPERATIVES

NOTICE OF CHANGE OF NAME

The Minister of Financial Institutions, Companies and Cooperatives gives notice that he has approved special by-law "C" of "SIR GEORGE WILLIAMS UNIVERSITY", incorporated under section 12, George VI, Chapter 91, amended by 8-9 Elizabeth II, chapter 191, changing its name to that of "UNIVERSITE CONCORDIA and its English version CONCORDIA UNIVERSITY", the foregoing pursuant to section 2 of the Special Corporate Powers Act.

Copy of notice recorded the 12th day of September 1974 in

Libro    D-10

Folio    65

of the public record of the Department of Financial Institutions, Companies and Cooperatives.

CERTIFICATE

I certify that the aforementioned is a copy of a notice which was published at page 6012 of the Quebec Official Gazette number 34, dated August 24, 1974, and that copy of this notice was registered on September 12, 1974 in Libro D-10, Folio 65, of the archives of the Department of Financial Institutions, Companies and Cooperatives.

Québec, this twelfth day of September, 1974.

MINISTER

1.1 In 1973 members of Concordia's founding institutions were invited to submit names for the newly merged university. After reviewing a wide range of submissions, Concordia, taken from the Latin *Concordia salus*, the motto of the Ville de Montréal, and meaning "well-being through harmony," was recommended to Loyola's Board of Trustees and the Board of Governors of Sir George Williams University. On September 12, 1974, the Quebec Minister of Financial Institutions, Companies and Cooperatives made the name official.

# THE QUIET REVOLUTION AND THE CREATION OF CONCORDIA UNIVERSITY

Ronald Rudin

## At the Université de Montréal

**THE ROAD THAT LED DIRECTLY TO THE CREATION** of Concordia University began not on the campuses of the two schools that in 1974 would merge to form the institution, but rather at the Université de Montréal.[1] In 1965 Montreal's only French-language university appointed Roger Gaudry as its first lay rector, a clear sign that the central role of religion, and more specifically Catholicism, as a defining characteristic of Quebec society was in decline. Gaudry arrived in his position in the midst of the Quiet Revolution, which saw a secular state take a leading place in the lives of Quebecers, who were in their own right redefining how they saw themselves and their place in the larger world. As Jocelyn Létourneau has put it, there was "the transition from the old-time French Canadians who thought of themselves as conquered, humiliated and demoralized to the new Québécois who were accomplished, entrepreneurial, and ambitious."[2]

In this context, Gaudry played a central role in redefining his university, riding the same wave that would transform other parts of the Quebec educational system, with the decline in the influence of religion replaced with attention to language. As part of the secularization of his institution, Gaudry wanted to end a relationship that stretched back to the late nineteenth century, by which several Jesuit-run institutions were able to define what they saw as an appropriate curriculum for obtaining a university degree. These institutions, the French-language Collège Sainte-Marie and its English-language counterpart, Loyola College, did not have the right to grant university degrees on their own, but, by way of a papal edict from 1889, could provide their students with certificates that could in turn be exchanged for degrees from the Université de Montréal. Students who may have never set foot in that university were able to claim a degree from the institution. This relationship was already viewed by Gaudry's clerical predecessor in 1959 as "a somewhat antiquated convention which

---

RONALD RUDIN is Distinguished Professor Emeritus in the Department of History and the Centre for Oral History and Digital Storytelling at Concordia University. Author of eight books and producer of eight documentary films, Rudin's research has focused on the social, cultural, and environmental history of Atlantic Canada and Quebec.

[was] no longer acceptable."[3] Gaudry ultimately terminated the arrangement, observing later, "I couldn't understand why the Université de Montréal should continue to grant degrees over which it had absolutely no control."[4]

Gaudry and his colleagues ended the relationship with the Jesuit colleges as part of a massive reform of the university's charter in 1967, which set a terminal date for Loyola College (along with Collège Sainte-Marie) to grant degrees via the Université de Montréal. Students admitted after July 1972 would no longer be able to go this route, meaning that the clock was now ticking for Loyola to find some new relationship, if it wanted to continue to offer university degrees, a situation that would ultimately lead to a merger with Sir George Williams University. There is no evidence that either institution would have sought out this merger if Loyola had found the means of granting degrees on its own. Loyola lost this power as part of the secularization of Quebec society, and—as we shall see—the entire process that ultimately led to the creation of Concordia was embedded in the province's highly contentious social and political circumstances in the late 1960s and early 1970s.

## Loyola College Seeks a Charter

Of the two institutions that formed Concordia University, Loyola College was by far the older, having begun as St. Mary's College in 1848 to provide English-language instruction, mostly to Montreal's Irish Catholic community, within Collège Sainte-Marie, before becoming autonomous in 1896 and moving to its west-end campus in 1916.[5] With its independent status, Loyola College set out to obtain a charter that would have allowed it to grant its own university degrees, making it the equal of Quebec institutions such as McGill University and Université Laval (whose branch campus in Montreal would become the Université de Montréal in 1920).

It was probably unrealistic for the Jesuit administrators of Loyola College to believe that they could obtain degree-granting powers, since their counterparts at Collège Sainte-Marie had failed, which led to the papal issuance in 1889 of what was known as the Jamdudum Constitution that created the system for degrees being granted via Université Laval, the only Catholic university at the time. Collège Sainte-Marie became a degree-granting institution in practice, if not in law, and perhaps this was sufficient for its administrators in the late nineteenth century. But the Jesuits at Loyola correctly understood that since they were serving a linguistic minority, it was prudent to have their own degree-granting powers to protect themselves from unforeseeable challenges in the future, a view that turned out to be prescient. In that context, they pushed in 1899 for a charter with all the powers of the full-fledged universities, and a bill towards that end received second reading in the Quebec Legislative (later National) Assembly. However, the rector of Université Laval, unwilling to abandon influence over university-level education in the province,

1.2 Charter Day at Sir George Williams College, March 1948. The charter would be amended first in 1959, when the name Sir George Williams University was adopted, and again in 1974, following the merger. It continues to be the charter under which Concordia operates today.

opposed the bill, which was amended so that Loyola College continued to have the same status as Collège Sainte-Marie.

In the decades that followed, there were various efforts by Loyola to secure degree-granting powers, but none succeeded. For instance, in the 1920s the Quebec government seemed well disposed to create a full-fledged English-Catholic institution, but this was blocked by the archbishop of Montreal, who insisted on preserving the Université de Montréal's monopoly on Catholic university-level education in the city. By the 1960s, as the forces of secularization grew stronger, both Jesuit colleges, Loyola and Sainte-Marie, sought university charters to protect themselves from the changes on the horizon, but to no avail.[6] As a result, the two institutions found themselves vulnerable when the Université de Montréal ended its relationship with them for granting university degrees, leaving them with two options: "either become a CEGEP or disappear by way of merging with another university."[7] In the case of Collège Sainte-Marie, this meant integration into the new Université du Québec à Montréal (UQAM) in 1968, while for Loyola the future was not at all clear in the late 1960s.

# Future of senate in jeopardy

The future of Loyola's highest academic body, the Senate, is in jeopardy, says student senator and LMSA president Gord Clark.

Clark's lament is basically over the fact that the senate has extended its term by a startling four months, unprecedented in Loyola's history.

The main hassle is that it is in the midst of constitutional reform, specifically the recomposition issue, and still has a full backlog of work to complete before calling an election.

Clark said recently that "Senate is at least half a year behind schedule, and if this continues it's going to lose all its credibility at Loyola."

The main problem with senatorial reform is the constitutional issue. It must be approved by both the Senate and the faculty as a whole, opening the way for numerous possibilities of stalemate.

Clark, who is also a member of the committee on elections and privileges, said that when the committee finally makes its report to the senate the main stumbling block will be the question of student representation.

Senate recently voted to allow seven student members in the recomposed senate, along with nine administrators and fifteen faculty.

A clause dealing with student elections to senate states that at least one third of a faculty's population must turn out on election day to make the vote representative. If this standard is not met, another election shall be called.

If the standard is not met for the second time, the report, at present, says "Senate can fill vacant seats." However, indications are Clark alleges that Prof. G. Trudel, of the chemistry department, will interpret the phraseas meaning that senate should leave the seats in question vacant.

"This shows, quite clearly," Clark said, "that Trudel is saying 'we do not want student representation on senate.'"

"It is nothing more than a smokescreen for his blatant desire that students will not have any say in academic policy," he continued.

However, Trudel was unavailable at press time for comment.

"You know," Clark said, "this place never changes, and all this crap lurks in the background. Let's bring it out into the open."

Clark said he anticipates a great floor battle at the next meeting of senate over this issue and said that if it degenerates, and senate is unable to finish its workload, he would much rather see no senate, than one that is so totally against change.

"This kind of thing isn't even debated at places like U of T because they believe that students have a rightful place on all governmental bodies.

"I'd much rather start right back at square one than go through with the farce." Clark said.

Then, should senate come to some sort of an agreement over the constitutional issue, the matter is referred to the faculty community as a whole.

"But the last time the faculty met like that, two years ago," Clark said, "the meeting dissolved into chaos."

"And it really seems," he continued "that Loyola could well be without a senate next year."

# loyola NEWS

Vol. 48, No. 3 - Loyola of Montreal - Wednesday, September 22, 1971

## Estate purchased for intellectual experimentation
### By KEN ERNHOFER

LACOLLE QUE.- College officials have just announced the purchase of a $35,000 country home and estate outside the village of Lacolle near the American border.

The property will be used by the college as a centre "to develop programs to deal with the whole the whole person, including the emotions."

He said the country retreat would have "an experimental program as a resource centre for experimental programs in all departments."

All professors at Loyola, Har-

Lacolle estate.

The property features an oversized six bedroom house with one large meeting room, three small conference rooms, a kitchen and a large foyer.

The building rests on foundations built almost two hundred years ago when the American - British North American border ran to its north. Old cannon placements, on the north side of the foundations are still visible, though popular belief is that they were never used.

The border now officially runs just 150 feet sough of the house and Harman joked at the possibility of it being used as a half-way house for young Americans resisting the draft, though he admitted he did not want to get involved in any political issues.

The property is 320 yards long, and 253 yards wide, and occupies just under 20 acres.

Besides the main house the centre contains two dilapidated barns and what seems to be an old smokehouse.

All buildings are in dire need of repair, and Harman said the $15,000 left over from the grant
Continued on page 2

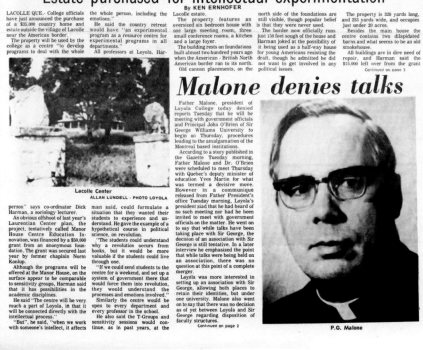

Lacolle Center
ALLAN LUNDELL - PHOTO LOYOLA

person" says co-ordinator Dick Harman, a sociology lecturer.

An obvious offshoot of last year's Laurentian Center plan, the project, tentatively called Manor House Centre Education Innovation, was financed by a $50,000 grant from an anonymous foundation. The grant was secured last year by former chaplain Norm Konlup.

Although the programs will be offered at the Manor House, on the surface appear to be comparable to sensitivity groups, Harman said that it has possibilities in the academic disciplines.

He said "The centre will be very much a part of Loyola, in that it will be connected directly with the intellectual process."

"But", he said, "when we work with someone's intellect, it affects man said, could formulate a situation that they wanted their students to experience and understand. He gave the example of a hypothetical course in political science, on revolution.

"The students could understand why a revolution occurs from books, but it would be more valuable if the students could live through one.

"If we could send students to the centre for a weekend, and set up a system of government there that would force them into revolution, they would understand the processes and emotions involved."

Similarly the centre would be open to every department and every professor in the school.

He also said the T-Groups and sensitivity sessions would continue, as in past years, at the

## Malone denies talks

Father Malone, president of Loyola College today denied reports Tuesday that he will be meeting with government officials and Principal John O'Brien of Sir George Williams University to begin on Thursday, procedures leading to the amalgamation of the Montreal based institutions.

According to a story published in the Gazette Tuesday morning, Father Malone and Dr. O'Brien were scheduled to meet Thursday with Quebec's deputy minister of education Yves Martin for what was termed a decisive move. However in a communique released from Father President's office Tuesday morning, Loyola's president siad that he had heard of no such meeting nor had he been invited to meet with government officials on the matter. He went on to say that while talks have been taking place with Sir George, the decision of an association with Sir George is still tentative. In a later interview he emphasized the point that while talks were being held on an association, there was no question at this point of a complete merger.

Loyola was more interested in setting up an association with Sir George, allowing both places to retain their identities, but under one university. Malone also went on to say that there was no decision as of yet between Loyola and Sir George regarding disposition of faculty structures.
Continued on page 2

P.G. Malone

1.3 In the lead-up to the merger, many Loyola students and alumni were anxious that a potential merger with SGWU would erode its identity. Student paper *Loyola News* voiced these concerns, and in 1971 reported that Father Patrick G. Malone had denied merger talks were taking place.

## Sir George Williams University and the Coming of the Merger

While Loyola College's history was marked by its inability to secure university status, this was not the case for its eventual merger partner. Sir George Williams College was created in 1926 to offer higher education as an extension of the Montreal YMCA (Sir George Williams was the Y's founder), at first providing education, mostly in the evening, to people who were working during the day. In 1948 the college secured full university status with degree-granting powers and was renamed in 1959 as Sir George Williams University (SGWU). Into the 1960s, the downtown university took on the trappings of a modern institution, with numerous departments creating graduate programs and with the construction of the Hall Building, which sported the brutalist architecture so common on campuses at the time, giving it the appearance of permanence that was sorely lacking at Loyola.[8]

To be sure, Sir George Williams was not without its problems: too little space for too many students, no student residences, and no green space; but it also had no reason to be concerned about whether it would exist over the long run. As a result, when Loyola, starting in 1967, was faced with its existential crisis, the response from Sir George administrators was less than enthusiastic. As Michel Despland, a philosophy professor who would play an important role in the merger process, observed, "There was no positive enthusiasm (at Sir George) for the prospect of the merger of Sir George Williams and Loyola."[9] Similarly, Jack Bordan, at the time dean of engineering, recalled that there was some consideration of the merger idea at a deans' meeting "in light of difficulties Loyola was having yet again on getting a charter." Bordan describes how "the idea was simply stonewalled; it was shot down in flames by at least one other member of the Deans Committee. Sam Madras, the dean of science, said at the time, 'Look, we've got troubles of our own enough; we don't need *their* troubles.'"[10]

In spite of this reticence, informal talks began in 1968, according to Despland, because of the encouragement of the Quebec government, which made it clear that "the only option for the two institutions was by working in a unified manner."[11] For his part, André Laprade, who would serve as secretary on the Sir George Williams Committee on Cooperation with Loyola, described how, following a certain initial disinterest, pressure was felt from Quebec City: "It must have been in the meetings with the government over financing that we got wind that they wanted us to take a more positive role. In fact, I think we must've got the message very clear that they expected Sir George to do something rather than just sit and wait."[12]

Successive Quebec governments could hardly remain unconcerned with the situation created by the Université de Montréal's withdrawal from its long-standing arrangement with Loyola College. If it allowed Loyola to become a CEGEP or to simply cease to exist, it ran the risk of alienating the large and vocal alumni, particularly among English-speaking Catholics, who viewed the college as a crucial part of their community. At the same time, with efforts afoot to bolster the French language, there was never any possibility that Loyola would become a university in its own right. With the creation of UQAM in 1968, there were four universities in Montreal, two for each linguistic community. Given the growing nationalist sentiment at the time, creating a third English-language university was unthinkable as it would have provided the linguistic minority with a majority of the universities in the city. Ultimately, a merger of some sort was the only way out for the province.

In that context, Laprade described how "Loyola was out fishing," looking for a partner. They were in contact with McGill, but this was a non-starter when McGill only showed interest in swallowing Loyola to create "a satellite campus in the west end of Montreal," dismissing the idea of maintaining anything of the Loyola identity, with small classes and an emphasis on the liberal arts. There were also talks about Loyola becoming an English component in the Université du Québec system that was just taking shape. But this option floundered when the president of the new province-wide university, Alphonse Riverin, suggested that serious talks could only take place "perhaps in five years," far too late from Loyola's perspective.[13]

While these overtures were being made, and with a nudge from the Quebec government, exploratory talks began between Loyola and Sir George Williams in fall 1968, but from the start it was clear that Loyola, in spite of its weak bargaining position, was ever pre-occupied with avoiding complete absorption. Writing at the time, Laprade described how "merger is not Loyola's favourite pattern of cooperation … We conclude therefore that Loyola College does not see merger with Sir George Williams and the setting up of a new merged institution as being in the interests of Loyola College." He speculated that Loyola's concerns might be allayed if there were a loose federation between the two institutions, but he "fail[ed] to see how this would be in the interest of Sir George Williams." Nevertheless, "we still want to discuss cooperation with Loyola."[14]

In that context, talks continued in 1969 between two professors—Michel Despland, then the assistant dean of arts at Sir George Williams, and Donald Savage, a history professor from Loyola. Recognizing Loyola's sensitivities, they set out to create what they called "the federal university," in which the arts (humanities, social sciences, and fine arts) would be "decentralized in two Arts Colleges, namely (the existing) Loyola College and (a newly constituted) SGWU College." As for the other faculties (science, engineering, and commerce), they would be located entirely in the Hall Building on the Sir George Williams campus, even though there had been teaching in these fields at Loyola.[15]

While Despland and Savage may have believed that they were responding to Loyola's concerns, that was not the view of a high-level Loyola committee on the college's future. The Sir George Williams Board of Governors approved the report shortly after it was distributed, but at Loyola there was a sense that the document was "unacceptable because it reduces Loyola to the status of a liberal arts college. The essence of the proposal involves such a radical change that the basic philosophy and identity of Loyola would be unrecognizable." And when Loyola expressed its concerns, the Sir George Williams administration became "rather cool" towards the merger.[16]

## Quebec Intervenes

And so the clock continued to tick towards the termination of Loyola's relationship with the Université de Montréal at the end of July 1972. Over the previous two years, there had been sporadic meetings on a possible merger with Sir George Williams, but negotiations were going nowhere, that is until the province's Conseil des universités dropped a bomb that ultimately led to the creation of Concordia. The Conseil, an advisory body that reported to the minister of education, conveniently tabled a report that touched largely, although not exclusively, on the future of Loyola College only weeks before the end of the Université de Montréal arrangement. Pulling no punches, the Conseil made it clear that, from its perspective, Loyola's days were numbered: "The government of Quebec cannot approve the entrance of a new institution in the university network unless it is justified by the needs of the population ... The government has, in all instances, refused the transition of Loyola to a full-scale university by not granting the charter that it requested. Therefore, the question today is not when will Loyola become a university, but rather what are the possibilities of its association with another higher education establishment or its integration into it."[17]

Starting from this premise, the report showed the technocrats in Quebec City, the new masters of the province following the Quiet Revolution, working their magic. The document lacked any particular vision for university-level education in English, as it constituted instead an exercise in bean counting. The bottom line was that by the start of the 1980s there would be roughly twenty thousand students attending the English-language universities, while there would be capacity for twenty-eight thousand. There were slightly more than three thousand students at Loyola, so if the college were shut down and its resources absorbed by other institutions, there would still be excess capacity. In this context, the Conseil was sympathetic to the idea of a merger with Sir George Williams if "there will be only a downtown campus."[18] But regardless of whether a merger occurred, the Conseil wanted to see an end to all university-level education on the Loyola campus after June 1975 (which is when the last cohort accepted under the soon-to-be-terminated agreement with Université de Montréal would be graduating), with the result that the buildings at Loyola would no longer be "included in the inventory of physical resources of English universities."[19]

THE CREATION OF CONCORDIA UNIVERSITY  9

The Conseil's report definitely got the attention of Loyola administrators. It finally seemed to penetrate that they would never be getting their university charter, and that even the continuation of university education at Loyola (if not by Loyola College) was in peril. As Russell Breen, then dean of arts at Loyola, put it, "The chips were now down, and it was going to be necessary for us to go for broke."[20] He suggested going to Quebec City to see the minister of education, François Cloutier. But before that meeting took place, in July 1972, Father Breen arranged to get together with Claude Ryan, the highly respected director of Le Devoir, whom Breen had known when both were involved with Action catholique canadienne, a movement dedicated to finding a place for Catholicism in postwar Quebec, of which Ryan was national secretary from 1945 to 1962.

Ryan asked Breen when the meeting with Cloutier was scheduled so that he could publish an editorial in Le Devoir the day before it took place. In his piece, "Why Should Loyola Be a Scapegoat?" Ryan did not deny that the English-language universities had greater resources than their French counterparts (taking into account the linguistic division of the population), but wondered why Loyola had to be the scapegoat. He touted the distinctive nature of Loyola's "university" education and pointed to its increasing role in teaching part-time students (not included in the Conseil's calculations). If cuts had to be made, he wondered why Bishop's University had not been considered, and even suggested that it might be "more realistic to eliminate certain boondoggles at McGill and elsewhere." Finally, he couldn't see what was gained by concentrating all English-language university education in downtown Montreal, when there was the option of "the integration being sought between Loyola and Sir George" as opposed to the "brutal absorption proposed by the Conseil des universités."[21]

As Breen tells the story, when they entered Cloutier's office, Le Devoir was on the minister's desk, opened to the Ryan editorial. The minister assured the delegation that he had no intention of following the recommendation to end university-level education at Loyola, but at the same time wanted to see progress on merger negotiations. Towards this end, he called upon representatives from Loyola and Sir George to meet with him in his office in early August 1972.[22] Within weeks of that meeting, a joint committee from the two institutions (which had been meeting since late 1971) came up with a "model for the new university," which envisioned adapting the existing Sir George Williams charter to create what became Concordia, precluding the need to seek government approval for a new institution. The model also imagined a full range of academic activity on the two campuses, a considerable improvement, from the Loyola perspective, over earlier proposals that would have significantly limited the scope of teaching on that campus.[23]

The model was approved by both the Board of Trustees at Loyola College and the Sir George Williams Board of Governors in November 1972, and in the months that followed the details were fine-tuned, including the selection of "Concordia" as the new name.[24] Then, in early August 1973 the pertinent boards met again, this time to approve the transfer of assets to the new institution, following which the reconstituted Sir George Williams board, now including representatives from what had been Loyola College, had its initial meeting.

While it appeared that Concordia University had been born, the actual birth only took place a year later due to the Quebec government's delay in adopting orders-in-council that would officially change the name and, more importantly, provide provincial guarantees for loans that had been taken out by Loyola College and that would now be assumed by the new university. In the year that followed, for all intents and purposes, Sir George Williams University operated as if it were Concordia, but without the name, with the new board meeting regularly. But behind this appearance of normality, the final act in the merger story once again reflected the social and political tensions in Quebec at the time.

## The Final Act

For the first months following the internal approval of the merger, the Liberal government of Robert Bourassa was reluctant to act during the lead-up to provincial elections to be held in October 1973. Bourassa was facing off with the Parti Québécois, which emerged as its strongest competition and was eager to paint the Liberals as bending over backwards to accommodate English speakers by creating this new university. But even following the election, nationalist elements continued to make their voices heard about the creation of Concordia, only protracting the delay by the Bourassa government to take the final steps. In November 1973 the Association des professeurs de l'Université de Montréal came out strongly against the merger, noting that "in view of the real needs of the Quebec population ... McGill and Sir George Williams provide sufficient facilities for the English-speaking population."[25]

And the way forward seemed no clearer by early 1974 when the government was still weighing its options. Lysiane Gagnon, writing in *La Presse*, observed that "the Department of Education has produced numerous studies over the past six months to determine whether the transfer of the Loyola charter to the new Concordia University could be done by an order-in-council rather than by the National Assembly." Regardless of how the government chose to proceed, Gagnon characterized the merger as a not-very-veiled attempt "to create a third English-language university in Montreal," given that there would be a certain duplication of teaching on the two campuses, resulting in expenditures that would not be available in the French sector. As she put it, "We are looking at an incredible doubling up of services at a time when the universities (and in particular the anglophone universities) are experiencing a decline in enrollments."[26]

1.4 The idea of a shuttle bus service linking the two campuses first originated with the 1969 Loyola–Sir George Steering Committee. The first shuttle service, pictured here as a van in 1978, soon expanded its service times and was eventually replaced by full-sized buses.

Clearly, the order-in-council option had the advantage of being out of the glare of public scrutiny, and ultimately this was the route that was followed in August 1974, almost a year to the day from the internal agreement regarding the merger.[27] But even the conclusion to this story, legally creating Concordia University, was deeply embedded in the combustible politics of language in Quebec at the time. In this regard, it was significant that the Bourassa government moved Bill 22 through the National Assembly in late July, only weeks before the Concordia orders-in-council were approved. The bill established French as Quebec's official language and set limits on exactly who could attend English-language schools, reversing legislation from the late 1960s that had effectively provided parents with freedom to choose their child's language of instruction. With Bill 22, students would have to indicate sufficient knowledge of English to attend an English-language school, resulting in the testing of five-year-olds to determine their linguistic competence.

To cut the legs out from under the increasingly powerful Parti Québécois, Bourassa hoped that Bill 22 would win nationalists to his side, figuring that English speakers would stick with his party anyway. But just to make sure that this was the case, the Liberal government had the opportunity in August 1974 to throw English speakers a bone, by finally taking the steps required to make Concordia a reality.[28] In a sense, it was only fitting that Concordia was, at least in part, born out of linguistic conflict, since the start of this story—the Université de Montréal's termination of its link with Loyola College—spoke to the beginning of the secularization of Quebec's institutions and the decline of connections along religious lines. From start to finish, the story of the creation of Concordia University reflected this major transformation in Quebec society.

## NOTES

1   An extended version of this essay was previously published as "The Quiet Revolution and the Creation of Concordia University," *Historical Studies in Education / Revue d'histoire de l'éducation* 35, no. 1 (Spring/printemps 2023): 49–64.

2   Jocelyn Létourneau, "La production historienne courante portant sur le Québec et ses rapports avec la construction des figures identitaires d'une communauté communicationnelle," *Recherches sociographiques* 36, no. 1 (1995): 9–45. This and all subsequent passages that were originally in French have been translated by the author, with the original French version in the notes. Létourneau described "le passage du Sujet vaincu, humilié et démoralisé (L'Ancien Canadien français) au Sujet accompli, entreprenant et ambitieux (le Nouveau Québécois)" (12).

3   Loyola College, *Brief Submitted by Loyola College to the Royal Commission of Inquiry on Education* (Montreal: Loyola College, 1961), 14.

4   Hélène Bizier, *L'Université de Montréal: La quête du savoir* (Montreal: Libre Expression, 1993), 241. "Je ne voyais pas pourquoi l'Université de Montréal aurait continué de décerner des diplômes sur lesquels elle n'avait pas absolument aucun contrôle."

5   For the early history of Loyola College, see T.P. Slattery, *Loyola and Montreal: A History* (Montreal: Palm Publishers, 1962).

6   The Commission royale d'enquête sur l'enseignement dans la province de Québec made reference to these requests: *Rapport Parent*, vol. 2 (1964), 249, 252.

7   Jean Cinq-Mars, *Histoire du collège Sainte-Marie de Montréal* (Montreal: HMH Hurtubise, 1998), 376. The options were "ou devenir un cégep, ou disparaître en s'assimilant à une autre université." In the restructuring of the Quebec education system in the late 1960s, CEGEPs (Collèges d'enseignement général et professionnel) provided a path towards university education for those so inclined, while also offering professional training for students not intending to attend university.

8   For the history of Sir George Williams College/University, see Henry Hall, *The Georgian Spirit: The Story of Sir George Williams University* (Montreal: Sir George Williams University, 1967); Douglass Burns Clarke, *Decades of Decision: Sir George Williams University, 1952–53 to 1972–73* (Montreal: n.p., 1973).

9   Interview with Michel Despland,1980, Office of the Principal, Concordia University, Records Management and Archives (hereafter RMA), https://archive.org/details/I0010-11-0010.

10  Interview with Jack Bordan, 1980, Office of the Principal, RMA, https://archive.org/details/I0010-11-0006.

11  Denis de Belleval (Directeur de la recherche, Direction générale de l'enseignement supérieur, Ministère de l'Éducation) to Father Patrick Malone (Rector, Loyola College), November 20, 1968, I147/11A, HA433, RMA. "Il n'y avait d'avenir pour les deux institutions que dans un développement unifié."

12   Interview with André Laprade, 1980, Office of the Principal, RMA, https://archive.org/details/
     I0010-11-0014.

13   Loyola College, Interim Report, Joint Board/Senate Committee on Future of Loyola, September
     22, 1970, RMA.

14   André Laprade, Memorandum, March 18, 1969, I147/11A, HA433, RMA.

15   Donald Savage and Michel Despland to Secretaries of Joint Loyola – Sir George Williams
     Negotiating Committee, September 30, 1969, RMA. Attached to their covering letter was the
     text for the "Proposed Federation of Loyola College and Sir George William University."

16   Loyola College, Interim Report, Joint Board/Senate Committee on Future of Loyola, September
     22, 1970, RMA.

17   Québec, Conseil des universités, *Rapport du Conseil des universités au Ministère de l'Éducation
     sur les orientations générales du secteur universitaire de langue anglaise et l'avenir de Bishop's et de
     Loyola* (Québec: Conseil des universités, juin 16, 1972), 8. "Le gouvernement du Québec ne
     peut accepter l'entrée d'un nouvel établissement dans le réseau universitaire que si les besoins de
     la population le justifient ... Le gouvernement a de toute façon refusé la reconversion de Loyola
     en université de plein exercice, en lui refusant la charte qu'il demandait. La question posée
     aujourd'hui n'est donc pas celle de la transformation de Loyola en une université, mais celle de
     l'opportunité de son association avec un autre établissement d'enseignement supérieur, ou de
     son intégration à celui-ci."

18   Québec, Conseil des universités, *Rapport du Conseil des universités*, 30. "On ne conservera que
     le campus du centre ville."

19   Québec, Conseil des universités, *Rapport du Conseil des universités*, 34. The buildings at Loyola
     would no longer be "inclus dans l'inventaire des ressources physiques du secteur universitaire
     anglophone."

20   Interview with Russell Breen,1980, Office of the Principal, RMA, https://archive.org/details/
     I0010-11-0020.

21   *Le Devoir*, July 12, 1972. In his article, "Loyola doit-il servir de bouc émissaire?," Ryan
     wondered whether it might be "plus réaliste d'éliminer certaines boursouflures à McGill et
     ailleurs." He called for "l'intégration recherchée entre Loyola et Sir George" as opposed to the
     "absorption brutale que propose le Conseil des universités."

22   Statement from the Very Reverend Patrick Malone, President of Loyola, July 14, 1972, RMA.

23   "A Model for a New University," Joint Committee Statement on the Establishment of a New
     University, November 8, 1972, I0002 Public Relations Department fonds, RMA.

24   Joint Committee to the Board of Trustees of Loyola and the Board of Governors of Sir George
     Williams University, May 8, 1973, RMA. The name was derived from the motto of the Ville de
     Montréal, "Concordia salus," and had the advantage of being neither English nor French. It was
     selected following a call for suggestions that yielded over 120 ideas. Name Contest, 1973,
     I002.1/18, HA3288, RMA.

25   "U de M Profs Rap Concordia," *The Georgian*, November 30, 1973.

26   Lysiane Gagnon, "Sans bruit, Loyola va devenir une université ... de trop," *La Presse*, March 16,
     1974. She explained how "le ministère (de l'éducation) a multiplié depuis six mois les études
     pour savoir si le tranfert de charte de Loyola à la nouvelle université Concordia pouvait se faire
     par arrêté-en-conseil plutôt qu'à l'Assemblée nationale." She viewed the creation of Concordia
     as an effort "à instituer une troisième université anglaise (à Montréal) ... On assiste à un
     incroyable dédoublement des services à l'heure où toutes les universités (et en particulier les
     universités anglophones) voient leur clientèle baisser."

27   Quebec, Orders-in-Council, 3004-1974; 3005-1974; 3006-1974. The name became legal by an
     official notice published in the *Gazette officielle du Québec* 106 (34), August 24, 1974, 6012.

28   "Concordia: Still Waiting," *The Georgian*, August 9, 1974.

# ORAL HISTORIES: The Merger and Its Legacies

### ANDRÉ LAPRADE, MERGING IN THE IMAGE OF SIR GEORGE

I was the official secretary and coordinator of the Loyola Merger Committee. I think the official title we gave it at the time was, rather than "Merger Committee," we called it the Sir George Committee on Cooperation with Loyola. Now the true story as I remember it now is that Father Malone, at the time that the merger was being talked about, knew of me and knew me, and he developed a very close relationship with me. I think it was based on the fact that being a Catholic, having worked closely with the Jesuits in the renewal of the Catholic Church in the Montreal area, at the time, I'd met Father French and other Jesuits.

---

ANDRÉ LAPRADE was the former Assistant Vice-Rector of Relations and Audit at Concordia University. Prior to the merger between Sir George Williams University and Loyola College he served as secretary and coordinator of the Loyola Merger Committee. This interview was conducted by Joel McCormick in the 1980s.

RUSSELL BREEN was a former Dean of Arts and Sciences at Loyola College. During the merger negotiations between Sir George Williams University and Loyola College he was a strong advocate for retaining Loyola's identity. From 1977 to 1985 he served as Concordia University's Vice-Rector Academic, Arts and Science. This interview was conducted by Joel McCormick in the 1980s.

JACK BORDAN was Sir George Williams University's first Dean of Engineering. He played an instrumental role in merging Concordia University's two founding institutions. Following the merger, he served as Concordia's Vice-Rector, Academic, until his retirement in 1980. This interview was conducted by Joel McCormick in the 1980s.

HENRY HABIB is Distinguished Professor Emeritus at Concordia University who founded the Department of Political Science at Loyola College in 1961. He also served on the Board of Governors since 1971. This interview took place at the Centre for Oral History and Digital Storytelling on December 15, 2022.

NANCY MARRELLI is Archivist Emerita at Concordia University and an author who has written on the history of Montreal jazz. She worked at the university for forty-five years and in 1982 became Director of Concordia Archives, which she led until her retirement in 2010. This interview took place at the Centre for Oral History and Digital Storytelling on November 9, 2022.

LINDA DYER is Professor and Chair of the Department of Management in the John Molson School of Business at Concordia University. She has also served on the President's Task Force on Anti-Black Racism. This interview took place at the Centre for Oral History and Digital Storytelling on December 12, 2022.

*Joel McCormick: Father French being?*

Well, just a Jesuit at Loyola at the time who was active in our parish, which was Jean Brébeuf, Saint John Brébeuf. And that gave me a rapport with Father Malone of trust, openness, respect ... all these qualities and values. Furthermore, my son, Michael, was a student at Loyola. He'd graduated, or he was graduated from Loyola in arts, um, that was one input I had to Father Malone.

He and I, right from the word *go*, had the same chemistry, we wanted the merger to take place. We met privately; I did an awful lot of talking to him about what I called the positive aspects of the merger. I tried to tell him that in my books the coming together of the Catholic community with the Protestant community here would be a new, well, potential for synergistic energy ... So all along behind the scenes I had Paddy [Deuter] really fired up on what this merger could mean to Loyola. And that was fed back to Malone all the time. And that was based on my own background, because I'd come to the university as a consultant to Dr. [Robert C.] Rae at the time, and he knew that I had had merger experience, because I was given the job of merging two major divisions for Northern Electric before coming to the university. So I'd gone through the human torment of bringing together two large organizations and sorting out all the problems of organization people, people aspects and everything else. I felt very comfortable with what was going on ...

*JM: So, you first heard of merger, what happened after that? How were committees struck, how were they formed?*

Well, I don't think we took a positive role at all, because we had heard, indirectly, Loyola was out fishing. They were out fishing for a relationship with McGill, they were out fishing for a relationship with Marianopolis College, they were fishing very strong with the University of Quebec and Montreal, and I guess we were just too proud or something at the time to say, "Hey, let's get down and talk business." We were waiting to see. I think it was a feeling that it would be better if they did find another home, without coming in and upsetting what we had going for ourselves, called Sir George Williams University. We were already a university; we didn't have that concern. I don't think we showed warmth, understanding, and openness at the time when Loyola was really on the hot seat trying to find a home. It seems to me that the process had moved almost to a fait accompli, that Loyola was persona non grata, ... and McGill in fact turned them down as I understand it. Bluntly turned them down, they didn't want them to merge. Or to be involved ...

Father Malone, his primary motivation was he wanted Loyola to become a university in its own right. If he had his way, that's the way he'd want it to be. And it's very understandable ...

Well, put it this way, we have, in my books, created Concordia in the image of Sir George Williams. Whereas I was gonna say use the building blocks, take a tinker toy example, pull all the things apart and start building Concordia University with the strength from both sides into a new university that you can build and grow on, see? And I don't feel like we went to that new route. We skewed it towards Sir George's image, and Sir George way of life, rather than be central, innovative, leadership, open … The opportunity in my mind was to create a new university. But obviously there've been reasons why we decided to build it in the image of Sir George …

I think what he [Malone] was concerned about as well as this question of getting university status, um … the way of life at Loyola and their system of values was almost opposite of what was going on at Sir George. In our growing up, if you will, as a university, as a small group of senior people who were very close to each other, we were very open, we were, I'd say, *professional* in our way of doing things compared to what was going on at Loyola …

*JM: So, following the chronology of the whole merger period, what were the critical points, and why were they critical?*

Well, it's a minor one maybe in the eyes of a lot of people, but we are Concordia today, but it was a painful exercise to choose that name [*small laugh*], you know? It was an emotional thing. And more people spent more energy over trying to find a solution to that question than, let's say, the technical aspects of merging. And I remember it as a highlight, the [*laughs*] name-slaying, you know, that went around, and the reasons for it, and behind the scenes. And the Loyola students saying, "Hey, if we lose Sir George—" I mean, here, the Sir George students saying, "If we lose the name 'Sir George' in our name, well, you know, all our alumni and everything are lost because they have no continuity." And it seemed to be a thing that had no answer to it. But luckily for us, something prevailed after all the debate and discussion that *Concordia* came out the winner. I'd say that was one of the highlights.

## RUSSELL BREEN, LOYOLA COLLEGE'S FUTURE IN DOUBT

Yeah, well I think first of all, if you're going to make any sort of history of the merger, you cannot divorce that from the whole question of Loyola's attempts at trying to get its own university charter over the years. And I think the first time was, I think, in 1897 when Loyola was first founded and separated from Collège Sainte-Marie. When they petitioned Quebec for their own charter, and Quebec was prepared to give the charter, but because of the intervention of the archbishop of Montreal or the ecclesiastical authorities, it was not granted, because he … did not want his Catholic family divided, the francophones from the anglophones, who were then united in the Université de Montréal. Then there were other attempts in the early part of the century then to get the charter, to no avail. But then, more latterly, during Duplessis's regime, Father Brown, who was the rector, attempted to get Loyola its own charter and the response of Maurice Duplessis at the time was, if you had a Loyola graduate who was a leader in the community and who could run under the Union Nationale flag, and be elected, it would be so much easier to have him present it to the cabinet and the cabinet approve it. I think at that particular time it was pretty hard to find any anglophone in the west end [*small laugh*] of Montreal who would be prepared to—

*Joel McCormick: To stand under that banner.*

To stand under that banner. Now, you did have certainly some in the Eastern Townships, for example, the former minister of mines, Robinson, ran as a Union Nationale man and was in the cabinet. But that was a conservative area, but certainly it would be pretty hard to find a Loyola graduate at that particular time who would be willing to run as a Union Nationale representative. When Father Malone came, there were renewed attempts to get the charter, and it looked as though they were going to get the charter. Because, I think it was Lesage [who] had promised the charter to Malone. And, uh, however, this coincided with the growing nationalistic spirit amongst the French Canadians, and politicians then began to realize that it would have been political suicide for any government to grant a charter to another anglophone university in Montreal.

*JM: Did, did Premier Lesage actually renege and say, "I've changed my mind" and no charter, or was it just something that was dropped and not presented?*

I think it was dropped … Loyola [had tried] to establish a new agreement with the Université de Montréal. Well, certainly there were attempts, but you have to understand that this continuance of our arrangement with the Université de Montréal coincided with the decision to eliminate all the classical colleges from their affiliation … And even though Loyola had evolved to such a point that it was really fundamentally different from the other French Canadian classical colleges, in the minds of the people at the Université de Montréal there was no distinction to be made. The second thing was that, at the time that Loyola really made its last bid to get a university charter … you had the famous group of university professors at the Université de Montréal who came out with their document, "L'Université dit non aux Jesuites," and that meant both the anglophone and the francophone. Now, again, it's a very interesting thing that if, for example, the English Jesuits and the French Jesuits really could not seem to be able to sit down and agree on some sort of common front.

　　… In the light of all of these attempts, when Loyola then could no longer expect to get a charter from Quebec, and without the possibility of a new arrangement with the Université de Montréal, then it meant that Loyola had to then seek its future in conjunction with some other university already existing. Now, you had then in 1970 the famous—I think it was 1970—the report came out around the end of June from the Conseil des universités, which recommended that Loyola cease to exist as a university operation. And I remember that very very distinctly because I had just started my vacation when the report came out in the press. And, Malone and I were in touch—I was a dean, the dean of Arts at Loyola at the time—and I discontinued my vacation to return immediately to Montreal and that is when I really felt that the chips were now down, and it was going to be necessary for us to go for broke. And I had suggested, uh, that first of all that we would go down to see the minister of education …

But, I figured that before we go down to Quebec that it would be necessary for us to touch base, I felt, with Claude Ryan, who was the editor of *Le Devoir*, and the publisher of *Le Devoir*. And I remember going down to see him on, I think it was a Monday, and I had a two-hour discussion with him. It made it easier because I had known Claude Ryan, you know, from his early Action Catholic days. And he asked me if I was prepared to get him, or to give him, all the correspondence that went on between Loyola and Quebec. And I said I would consult with the chairman of the board of governors at Loyola, or the board of trustees, and with the president, who was Father Malone. I remember having a meeting with Father Drummond, Father Malone, and Ferrari, who was the administrative vice president at the time. And I strongly urged them that we make available to Claude Ryan the complete dossier. I felt it was a gamble, but it was a gamble that we had to take. And I brought all that documentation down to him and he asked me when our delegation would be going down to Quebec, and I told him, "Thursday morning." He said, "Well, there will be an editorial on Wednesday morning." I remember Tuesday night going to bed and unable to sleep, got up the very first thing in the morning on Wednesday and ran down to the corner kiosk to pick up *Le Devoir*. I felt it was a gamble because Claude Ryan, I had such complete confidence in his integrity that if he had come to the conclusion that this was the right decision, I think he would've said that in his editorial. And, on the other hand, if he had gone in that direction [*laughs*], it would've been …

JM: *Quite a backfire.*

Uh, quite a reflection on my judgement. So, when I picked up *Le Devoir* the headline on the editorial page was "Loyola doit-il servir d'un bouc emissaire?," "Ought Loyola to become a scapegoat?" And it was very interesting, the next day when our delegation went in to see Cloutier and he indicated quite clearly that this recommendation de le Conseil des universités was not acceptable. And as he indicated that he had on his desk *Le Devoir* open to the editorial page … So it meant that it was necessary for us to find our future in an amalgamation or a merger with an already existing university. And this was narrowed down to three: the possibility of developing something with Bishop's, which still had its charter, the possibility of developing an arrangement with McGill, or with Sir George Williams. The McGill one was not taken too serious—the Bishop's merger was not considered too seriously because it was … suffering much pains of insecurity themselves with regards to their own future. An institution that had less than a thousand students and with the anticipation of a further drop of drop in student enrolments was just holding on to its own.

### JACK BORDAN, "NOT JUST ORDINARY CUPS AND SAUCERS"

Well, a very marginal and kind of charming thing was the fact that it was really very much more pleasant negotiating in Malone's office than O'Brien's office. And the reason was a very simple one: the lifestyle on the Loyola campus, despite their penury—which was worse than the Sir George penury—was a hell of a lot more elegant than the office on the Sir George campus. We discussed things in O'Brien's office on Sherbrooke Street. And his secretary would bring in a tray of these things [seemingly indicates something in the room] for coffee, you know? This kind of cup. A plastic cup. And when we got to the Loyola office, we got served by Father Malone's secretary, Viola Soles, a very elegant lady, with a nice tray, with—

Joel McCormick: Real cups and saucers.

Real cups and saucers. Not just *ordinary* cups and saucers, but *real* cups and saucers. They were bone china, or they may not have been; I never turned it over to look. But the impression was.

JM: You wanted to [laughs].

I wanted to, right, right? And at the end of the meeting, Malone would say, "You want drinks, fellas?" And the answer was yes, then he would walk up to a panel that was otherwise unmarked and press it; that thing would open and behind it was this lovely bar, and we drank scotch in crystal glasses. And it was clearly evidence of a different lifestyle. And O'Brien did nothing to change the Sir George behaviour because it would not have been natural to do so. This is an anecdote, but it said something again about the people that we were dealing with.

When O'Brien, immediately after the merger, established an office for the rector on the Loyola campus, went through a two-step to do so. The first office was fairly crumby, but it was the office that Loyola was able to put together and I can only assume it was intended to be not crummy, but intended to be transient. In the following some months later, within the year, I guess, the present office was established. Kind of an up-front office. But one of the things that was put in *immediately*, in the first office, was a separate, private toilet. They carved it out of an adjacent room. Now, it's very comfortable. I happen to have one because this current office of mine is in what had been a lounge. So, I happen to own the only—well, I guess there are two private toilets on the Sir George campus. Subsequently it was designed into this building, many years later, and I happen to own this one. They're very comfortable, a very nice thing to have. But I know for a fact that O'Brien didn't ask for it. But the Loyola buildings and grounds' mentality said it *has* to be. And then when the proper office was established, this up-front one, they provided him with a bar. And I have every reason to believe—we never talked about it—that O'Brien didn't specify that. But it was just *normale*, that he have a private john and a private bar. And we all acquired keys—I turned mine in at the end of May—to O'Brien's bar. I suspect that I was the only one that used it on a regular basis, because it had Coke in it. That's Coca-Cola [*JM laughs*], not the other ... for the record.

Okay, I mean, that's just lifestyle. The other thing about lifestyle was the kind of bowing and scraping of the civil service at Loyola, to senior officers. Which, to me, had *absolutely* nothing to do with what they thought about you personally. It couldn't have. But on my very first visit to Loyola, after merger—I was spending a couple days a week there. One day a week there, I guess—Was the *incredible* amount of bowing and scraping. You walk in and it was, "Good morning, sir. How are you, sir? May I serve you coffee, sir?" And this just *never* happened on the Sir George campus. We didn't set it up that way, and it just didn't happen. People weren't *rude*, they simply didn't bow and scrape.

*JM: Less formal.*

Very *much* less formal. And that's the way, I guess, we wanted it. It could have been set up otherwise, but it wasn't. And I got to the point where I drank more goddamned coffee than you could think of; I had to stop it. I did a very kind of funny thing, to kind of break up this formality. I did something I'd never done before. I'd come in wearing turtleneck shirts when I worked on the Loyola campus. And that was the only time I *did* something that was deliberately planned, to say, "Look, I can't go on this way. I'm going to end up wearing a Roman collar if I do this." And I deliberately tried to cultivate an air of informality, in a *physical* way, because I couldn't do it in these other ways ...

Turning that negotiated *thing* into a reality was, far and away, the more difficult exercise. And very much more the creative exercise. I mean, you can create all sorts of things on paper. They may be good, they may be bad, but they're not worth a tinker's damn unless they work. And if they're rejected out of hand, if they're—they're sabotaged by the day-to-day activity, then it's no longer an act of creativity at all. I think the *creative* thing in this, for me anyway, was *making* the thing work. For seeing to the fact that we *did* end up, that we *have* ended up, with a single university. It was strained and [the] tensions [*laughs*].

**HENRY HABIB,** MERGING OF THE ALUMNI ASSOCIATIONS

There was a certain pressure that we had to negotiate. And I remember I was part of that negotiation and it was difficult because the two institutions were different in many ways. Loyola was a Catholic institution, and Sir George Williams was an institution that catered to part-timers, especially. And, so, merging the two institutions together was problematic at first. But then we succeeded. It was a question of finding a name for the place. At one time they felt that we could combine the names, Sir George and Loyola, something like that, but then they said one of the two institutions would be forgotten. Finally, they felt that the best thing is to call it Concordia as a concord between the two institutions. And it was a symbol from Montreal, there was the arms, the coat of arms. So, finally we accepted the name Concordia and, and fifty years later, here it is, the university Concordia. Which is in a sense a great university, because it was the synthesis of two institutions, two different institutions that merged together and produced the best, the best of Sir George, and the best of Loyola. In a sense we became better and greater by merging together and keeping the traditions of the two institutions. Because the traditions of the two institutions were basically seeping into the new institution. And little by little, department after department merged. And, it took three, four years to bring about the merger of all these institutions. And I remember the president at the time, Dr. O'Brien, who used to be the president of Sir George but he became president of Concordia University, and he asked me to bring together the Loyola alumni association, and the Sir George William alumni association, to merge them into the Concordia alumni association. I think this was one of the most difficult things to do, because the two associations were set in their ways, and he asked me to bring about the merger of these two institutions. It took me two to three months to do that, and successfully, we became friends, the different members of associations. But Dr. O'Brien was wise, he chose me to bring this association together because—whether I deserve it or not—I was always looked upon as a person who was diplomatic, who wanted to bring about conciliation between institutions. And I succeeded in bringing this, and I feel that this was one of the greatest things that I did for the institution, to bring the two associations into the Concordia alumni association.

**NANCY MARRELLI,** ON THE 50TH ANNIVERSARY

This idea of the university being fifty years old really bothers me. The university is not fifty years old. The merger is fifty years old. In fact, I copied out an old message that I had written in 2002, no, 2006, that was worried about this issue when I was director of libraries because I had been asked to look at a founding date for the university because they needed it for some document or other. I established the founding date of the university as [*brief pause, papers rustling*]. Let me just,

I'm gonna read this out, because it's important to get everything right. I had established 1896, and it was September actually of 1896, that we functioned as a separate institution.

Loyola College and Sir George Williams, there were two founding institutions. Concordia is made up of two founding institutions. So let me read this out to you, okay. "On Wednesday, September 12th 1896, at 2084 Sainte-Catherine's Street"—just east of Bleury, where, the Spectrum was, today it's not there anymore—"the English classical course at College Sainte-Marie separated from its parent institution to become Loyola College." Now College Sainte-Marie was a Jesuit institution at the time, French language. In the first year, over 150 students enrolled. And this was as a separate institution, it had been a program of College Sainte-Marie, an English-language program, before then. Meanwhile, not too far away at the Montreal YMCA on Dominion Square where the Sun Life Building now stands, the evening educational program begun in 1851 was expanding rapidly, and in 1926 it too would separate from its parent body and become Sir George Williams College, then university. So, 1896 was when Loyola College became a separate institution, and 1926 was really the separate institutional date for Sir George Williams.

If you're looking for a founding date, it would be the earliest founding date of the founding institutions because those two institutions didn't die and a new entity was born. It grew out of two existing institutions. So, it bothers me that you're sort of sweeping that under the rug and saying that we came into existence in the 1970s. But that's not the reality. You know, in the early days, it was very, very, very important to talk about Concordia. To act like a merged institution. To not try to be Sir George Williams and Loyola College, because of course there were fierce loyalties.

## LINDA DYER, THE FOUNDING VALUES OF CONCORDIA

*Piyusha Chatterjee: So, over the years, what kind of changes have you seen at Concordia?*

Ha ha, now we come down to it, eh? [*Both laugh loudly*] I think that, maybe it's because Concordia's grown, but it's a *lot* more formal and bureaucratic now than it used to be. I think that, because there are fewer and fewer people here who've been here for a long time, I sometimes worry that we're *losing* some of what I saw as being the founding values of Concordia.

*PC: And what was that?*

Well, you know that Sir George started out being an evening school, right? A school for people who had jobs and they would be coming back and taking classes at night in order to get their degree. And I think that openness to people who were regular working people in Montreal, I *think* that *that* is a vital part of who we are, at Concordia. It's still *there*, to a certain extent, but I'm always shocked at the people

THE MERGER AND ITS LEGACIES  23

who don't know about Concordia's history. Which is why I agreed to do this, because I think that people should know about Concordia's history. And so, I think that that immersion in Montreal and the working life of Montreal was really a big part of what made Concordia special.

McGill was a much more international place; people from all over the place coming in. That's what I felt too, at the time: I'm here [McGill], but I didn't really *know* Montrealers [*laughs*]. You weren't really part of the fabric of the city. And this came out when we were doing interviews with people too. You would say to interviewees, you know, "I'm from Concordia and"—"Oh, *Concordia*, yes!" And *everybody* had *somebody* who was part of Concordia, or was, or will be, or *they* themselves were an alumna, alumnus, or an alumni. There was always a Concordia connection, because we were so embedded in the city. I think we're still embedded in the city. But I feel that not enough people *know* that [*laughs*] …

[Today,] I think that things that have to do with reputation, things that have to do with public relations. It's just become so *extraordinarily* cautious, that I feel that it's not the Concordia I used to know. The Concordia I used to know—I remember, I was a fellow of the Simone de Beauvoir Institute for a short while, and there was a woman there who was, I think, a student in women's studies maybe or something related. And she said, "I don't want a master's. I'm not a *man*, I don't want a *master's*" [*laughs*]. You know? And that's where they came up with the … Magisteriate … But nobody talked to the lawyers and the PR people and the this and the that and the other before deciding. I mean, maybe they did, but it happened really quickly, and it *happened*. Whereas now, I don't think that Concordia could do that today. I don't think they *would* do that today. It's just become an *extraordinarily* cautious, *extraordinarily* bureaucratic place.

Editor's note: The excerpts of André Laprade, Russell Breen, and Jack Bordan were part of a series of interviews with administrators and faculty members who played key roles in the merger. The interviews took place in the early 1980s and were conducted by Joel McCormick, who worked at the time in Concordia's public relations department. For more on this collection, see I0010 Office of the Principal fonds, RMA.

# PLANNING CONCORDIA'S LOYOLA AND SIR GEORGE WILLIAMS CAMPUSES: THE FIRST 25 YEARS, 1974–1999

## Dominique Dumont, Rocio Carvajo-Lucena, and Susan D. Bronson

**WHEN THEY MERGED** in August 1974, both Sir George Williams University (SGWU) and Loyola College had a campus with its own distinct history, identity, and challenges: the first comprised two purpose-built pavilions, a series of Victorian townhouses, and several rented facilities scattered within a half-kilometre radius in the heart of downtown Montreal; the second, seven kilometres west, constituted a careful arrangement of custom-designed edifices dating from 1913 to 1973 in the park-like setting of a large property in the midst of a residential neighbourhood. Each campus reflected the very different origins, values, and priorities of the institution that built it.

During the 1970s and 1980s, provincial funding was scarce, Montreal's urban planning priorities lacked direction, and heritage and housing issues were community concerns. Although their 1974 union forced them to confront these issues together, those responsible for planning the SGW and Loyola campuses continued to work on

---

**DOMINIQUE DUMONT**, architect, is Director of Strategic Planning and Development, Facilities Management and has worked at Concordia since 2003. She has contributed to the planning of many development and renovation projects and to the acquisition of several properties, and since 2020 has been leading the preparation of the second master plan for the SGW and Loyola campuses.

**ROCIO CARVAJO-LUCENA** is an architect on Concordia's Strategic Planning and Development team, Facilities Management. She is working on Concordia's second master plan, several planning and renovation projects, and a pilot project to decarbonize the campuses. Before joining Concordia, she was involved in projects in Canada, the US, Spain, and Mexico.

**SUSAN D. BRONSON** is an architect specialized in heritage and historic research. Since 1980 she has contributed to these fields through professional practice, teaching, research, and work with professional organizations and community groups. She is responsible for over one hundred studies on Montreal properties and ensembles, including Concordia's Loyola and SGW campuses.

3.1 Hall Building under construction, circa 1965. View from Guy Street and De Maisonneuve Boulevard (then Saint-Luc and Burnside).

separate expansion plans until 1979, when they made a joint funding request targeting their most pressing need: library facilities for both locations. When this request was finally approved in 1985, their attention focused on the detailed planning of these projects and their multiple impacts on existing facilities.

It wasn't until the 1990s that the university began campus planning as a single institution: the decade started with a mission statement and ended with an ambitious master plan that recognized both the shared vision and distinct identities of the two campuses, setting the scene for Concordia's continued growth into the twenty-first century.

### Sir George Williams Campus, 1974–1990[1]

The downtown location of the SGW campus was the direct result of Sir George Williams College's mission, since its founding by the YMCA in 1926, to offer accessible general education and vocational training to working men and women. The college occupied part of the YMCA's headquarters on Drummond Street and nearby rented spaces until the Norris Building was constructed as an addition to the YMCA in 1956 and extended in height from 1959 to 1961. When SGW amended its charter in 1959, however, it was already clear that these facilities could not accommodate the rapidly increasing enrolment projections for the next decade. After considering other locations, it was agreed that, despite the expense and unpredictability of downtown real estate, the campus should be close to students' workplaces, and that a large new building was required to meet government norms.

At the time, Montreal's downtown, like others throughout North America, was being transformed in the name of modernism. In an attempt to ease traffic congestion in the late 1950s, the city razed dozens of Victorian townhouses (mostly converted into apartments, rooming houses, and commercial spaces) and early twentieth-century apartment buildings to extend Burnside Street (later De Maisonneuve Boulevard West) between Stanley and Guy Streets. Speculators continued this trend by buying ensembles of small properties and replacing their older buildings with large high-rises or parking lots.

SGWU followed suit in 1962 when it purchased about twenty townhouses and apartment buildings on Bishop and Mackay Streets north of Burnside Street for demolition. The Henry F. Hall Building (H), inaugurated in 1966, represented both a testimony to Montreal's modernist era during the optimistic years leading up to Expo 67 and the coming-of-age of SGWU as a reputable institution of higher learning. Designed "from the inside out," its state-of-the-art laboratories, classrooms, theatre and art gallery, and its modern cafeteria, offices, service spaces, and parking garage created a campus within a building. Like most new constructions of the 1960s, the concrete-panel-clad, twelve-storey megastructure made little attempt to integrate with its context, made up mostly of small, three- to four-storey traditional masonry edifices.

In 1964 the YMCA began to purchase more townhouses north of the Hall Building for SGW's new library. A few years later, when the university gained administrative and financial independence from the YMCA, the Hall Building and these properties were transferred to the former and the Norris Building, still owned by the latter, was rented to SGWU for a dollar a year until 1973. By then, it was expected that a new library complex, which now included classrooms and other facilities as the Norris Building had to be vacated, would be complete.

In the meantime, while SGWU grappled with uncertain enrolment projections and was engaged in merger negotiations with Loyola, Sir George planners were exploring options for the new library complex. The university acquired the remaining townhouses north of the Hall Building and began purchasing others on the west side of Mackay Street. In April 1974, five months before the creation of Concordia

University, SGWU submitted a funding request to the provincial government for its new facilities, with sketches of four options: a new ten-storey construction north of the Hall Building; a new ten-storey construction on the west side of Mackay Street; new seven-storey constructions on both sites; and an infill project combining the front sections of the townhouses on both sites with small high-rises.

As these options were being developed, Montreal's heritage movement was starting to make itself heard. Citizens were concerned by the ongoing demolition of converted Victorian townhouses, which offered affordable downtown housing and created unique, human-scaled streetscapes. Appalled by the approval, by both the City of Montreal and the Ministry of Cultural Affairs (MAC), of the 1973 Van Horne mansion demolition, they began working together to pressure municipal and provincial authorities to protect the city's heritage. New groups such as Save Montreal began waging an effective media campaign. In their view, all four of SGWU's options were unacceptable from a heritage perspective, because they involved demolition and loss of affordable housing.

Many Concordia students and staff members shared these concerns and wanted to work with the community. An opportunity to do so arose in 1974–75, when the potential sale of the nearby Grey Nuns property led to a developer's proposal to conserve its recently classified chapel but replace its historic motherhouse, other buildings, and gardens by a dense mixed-use ensemble with towers.[2] Save Montreal and Concordia developed a counter proposal involving the restoration and renovation, for university purposes, of the motherhouse and chapel, the conservation of most of the gardens and the construction of a few carefully located and proportioned structures for library stacks and facilities that could not be accommodated in historic buildings. Neither project was pursued, however, as the Grey Nuns decided to remain in their home for the time being.[3]

In the meantime, however, the university was paying large sums to rent the Norris Building and several other locations. In 1979, after considering options for its new library and classroom facilities on various parking lots near the Hall Building, it purchased the largest one, located on De Maisonneuve Boulevard West, south of the Hall Building and west of Bishop Court, a 1905 apartment complex that the university had restored and renovated to house administration offices in 1976. As the façades and courtyard of Bishop Court were classified and its "protected area" included the future library site, both the city and the MAC had to approve the project's design.

In addition to parking lots, the site had five buildings, including the Royal George Apartments, an eight-storey edifice built in 1912 with a white terra cotta façade. For technical reasons, the city and MAC eventually conceded in 1983 to the demolition of all the structures, except the front section and façade of the Royal George, which were to be sensitively integrated into the new complex. The provincial

3.2 An aerial view of the Loyola campus, circa 1978.

government announced funding for the project in 1985 and, although a handful of remaining tenants and a local architect organized a series of successful delay tactics to block the project, the final proposal was approved by municipal and provincial authorities in 1988.

The massive four- to nine-storey J.W. McConnell Building (LB) comprised volumes of varied heights and hues in response to the different characters and scales of the three streetscapes of which it was part. A central atrium, recalling the north-south lane that once divided the site, provided a lofty, light-filled spine around which the interior was organized and a fitting backdrop for its custom-designed art installation. The lower and street levels housed the bookstore, cinema, art gallery, and student services; levels two through four, the library; and the upper floors, various departments (and future library expansion space). With the long-awaited inauguration of the new building in the fall of 1992, Concordia not only acquired a leading-edge library facility but full independence from the YMCA, as the lease of the Norris Building could finally be terminated and the SGW campus was now focused around the Hall Building.

### Loyola Campus, 1974–1990[4]

Unlike the SGW campus, the Loyola campus, a large property at the western end of the quiet residential neighbourhood of Notre-Dame-de-Grâce, boasted green space, several new buildings, large parking lots and room for expansion in 1974.

The property had been purchased in 1900 by Loyola College, created in 1898 following the separation of the French- and English-speaking divisions of the Jesuit Collège Sainte-Marie, which had offered classical and commercial education to Catholic boys since 1848. Cultivated as a melon field, it was then surrounded by other agricultural properties in the process of being subdivided into residential lots; the Canadian Pacific Railway line defined its southern limit, and the new western extension of Sherbrooke Street was about to divide it into two parts.

It wasn't until 1912, when Loyola College's building on Drummond Street was too small, that a master plan was prepared for the site. Like all designs for the Jesuit community, it was approved by the order's authority in Rome, who ensured the stylistic appropriateness, high quality, and durability of all constructions. Limited to the area north of Sherbrooke Street West and including properties not yet purchased, the design showed a formal arrangement of pavilions and cloisters in the English collegiate Gothic style around two landscaped quadrangles. The new campus, dominated by the towered Administration Building facing Sherbrooke Street West, was to be realized gradually, as funding became available.

Construction of the first three buildings began in 1913. The Refectory (RF), the Juniors' Building (later the Loyola High School Building and then Concordia's Psychology Building, PY), and the first three floors of the Administration Building (AD) were completed in 1916. Following the First World War, several trees were planted, including those along Sherbrooke Street, to commemorate Loyola students and alumni lost in combat. The fourth floor and tower of the Administration Building were added in 1921 and 1927, respectively.

By the 1920s, it was clear that adjustments to the 1912 master plan were required to meet the evolving needs of the growing college. The first Arena (PS), not foreseen in 1912, was constructed on the east side of the campus in 1924. The Chapel/Auditorium (FC), hidden behind the Administration Building in the plan, was erected in a prominent position beside it in 1932. And the Central Building (CC) replaced a cloister linking the Administration Building to the Refectory in 1947. By 1948 the Loyola campus, while incomplete, constituted a harmonious ensemble of English collegiate Gothic pavilions in a natural landscape with mature trees and gardens.

The late 1940s and the 1950s represented a transitional period for Loyola College as increased funding was received from government sources. In an ongoing but unsuccessful attempt to obtain university status, it expanded its curricula by introducing science, business, and engineering courses. Enrolments increased, lay professors were hired, and women students were admitted. Loyola High School and Loyola College became separate entities, and the former became the owner of the Juniors' Building and the north playing field.

In 1954 new buildings still had to be approved by the Jesuit authorities in Rome, but updated guidelines allowed modernism to be embraced. Between 1959 and 1973, Loyola College inaugurated several modern pavilions with state-of-the-art equipment to accommodate its rapidly growing registrations: the Drummond Science Complex (later CJ), situated west of the Administration Building, in 1962; Hingston Hall (HA, HB, HC), at the northeast corner of the campus, in 1962; Vanier Library (VL), near the southeast corner, in 1963; the Athletic Complex (later RA), south of Sherbrooke Street West, in 1967; the Bryan Building (later part of SP), on the west side of the west quadrangle, in 1968; and the Student Centre (SC), north of Vanier Library, in 1973. Three other modern constructions not owned by Loyola College were erected on the campus by the Jesuit community: the Saint Ignatius of Loyola Church, on the west side, in 1967; the Jesuit Residence (later JR), near the northwest corner, in 1969; and a major addition to the Loyola High School Building (later PY) in 1969. Despite their modern expression and materials, the siting and massing of these new constructions respected the intentions and principles of the college's 1912 master plan. By 1973 Loyola College also owned and rented buildings for residences and other purposes outside its main campus.

After the creation of Concordia University in 1974, campus planning continued. While the SGW planners were exploring the development of the Grey Nuns property, those responsible for the Loyola campus were examining options for its expansion and development.

Completed in January 1976, the Loyola Campus Planning Study proposed that Concordia acquire, in phases, the properties that were part of the main campus but belonged to others: the Jesuit Residence (JR), the Loyola High School Building (later PY), and Saint Ignatius of Loyola Church. In addition, to regularize the campus shape and increase its area, it recommended the purchase of about a hundred residential properties between the north limit of the campus and Somerled Avenue, as well as a handful of others on Belmore Avenue and West Broadway Street, and the demolition of their homes.[5] The study also proposed the demolition of "dysfunctional old buildings" on the campus, including the Old Arena (PS) and two converted apartment buildings at the southeast corner of Sherbrooke Street West and West Broadway Street,[6] and the sale of two university-owned buildings east of the campus.

Finally, the 1976 Planning Study showed several new constructions on the expanded campus:[7] new sports facilities south of Sherbrooke Street West; an eastward extension of the Vanier Library; and unidentified new buildings at the north side of the west quadrangle, east of the Loyola High School Building and north of the east-west roadway and former north property line. All buildings were connected by passageways, including a north-south link extending from De Maisonneuve Boulevard West to Somerled Avenue, and a "main plaza" flanked this link north of the east-west roadway.[8]

While unwilling to approve property acquisitions and new constructions for Concordia University in the 1970s and early 1980s, the provincial government did invest in universal accessibility improvements to the Loyola campus. But the other pressing problem of the Loyola campus in the 1980s was the inadequacy of the Vanier Library and the Science Library (the circular annex of the Drummond Science complex), both too small and obsolete. The university proposed to combine them by extending the Vanier Library to the southeast and redesigning its expanded interior to meet new requirements, provide natural light in study areas, and integrate an artwork. The raised entranceway was to be replaced by an accessible and more welcoming entrance to the north.

Funding for this project and the new library facility for the SGW campus was announced in 1985. Following consultations with neighbours to the east, the project was approved by the City, and the expanded Vanier Library (VL/VE) was inaugurated in 1989.

The library design was underway when Concordia decided to build, with its own funds, a 570-seat concert hall for its music program and other uses. This building, situated behind the Student Centre and north of the Vanier Library, shared the new entrance of the latter. Designed with advanced acoustics and lighting systems, the Concert Hall (PT), later named in honour of Oscar Peterson, was inaugurated in January 1990.

Three other projects were realized on the Loyola campus at the end of the 1980s: an additional floor was added to the Drummond Science Building (later CJ) from 1985 to 1989; the former Science Library was converted into an up-to-date amphitheatre for the University Senate, inaugurated in 1990; and second-hand concrete bleachers were installed for the football field in 1988.

Finally, between 1989 and 1991, Concordia and Loyola High School exchanged properties: the former acquired the High School Building (later PY) and the north playing field, and the latter two buildings at the southeast corner of Sherbrooke Street West and West Broadway Street, which it replaced by a new school in 1991–92. Following this transaction, Concordia owned a large pavilion that provided additional space for expansion.

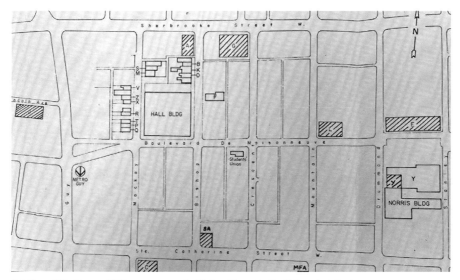

3.3 Plan of Sir George Williams campus in 1974, with rented buildings hatched.

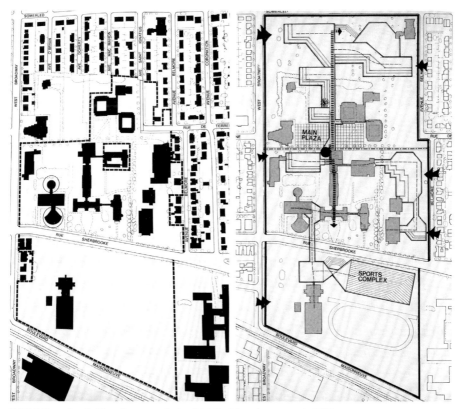

3.4 Existing plan (left) and proposed plan (right) of Loyola campus in 1976.

### Towards a Two-Campus Master Plan, 1990–1999[9]

The 1990s constituted a period of reflection, re-evaluation, committee work, and consultations aimed at articulating Concordia's identity, consolidating its academic and physical resources, and setting its goals for the future. The recession and period of political uncertainty leading up to the 1995 sovereignty referendum saw a decline and then a plateau in enrolments. After the narrow victory of the *non* side, however, economic and political stability gradually returned, and the university's targeted development of specific academic programs sparked a steady increase in registrations. This optimistic trend was combined with renewed government support and encouragement to replace leased locations by property acquisitions and new constructions. The 1990s, which began with Concordia's first mission statement and ended with its first master plan for both campuses, represented a turning point in Concordia's strategic planning history.

In 1990 the rector established two committees: one was to draft a mission statement for Concordia University and the other to develop the *Strategic Space Plan* for its two campuses. Preliminary versions of both documents were to be subjected to consultation with faculty, staff, and students before their finalization and adoption in 1991.

Presenting the new vision of the university as a single institution, the final version of the mission statement did not mention its two founding institutions or its two campuses. It emphasized its character as "an urban university which is responsive to the needs of a diverse student population as well as to the bilingual and multicultural environment in which it resides." It also identified other unique characteristics, including its "broad-based, interdisciplinary approach to learning," and highlighted its priorities, such as inclusion and "superior teaching supported by the best possible research, scholarship, creative activity and service to society."[10]

The final version of the *Strategic Space Plan* was limited to the definition of "seven principles of strategic planning," including prioritization of academic concerns over departmental preferences, inclusion of the entire university community in discussions, respect of government norms, avoidance of duplication of resources, reinforcement of disciplinary and functional affinities, adoption of an efficient and constructive approach to the university's two-campus reality, and enhancement of the environments of both campuses.[11] Although the preliminary version of this plan, presented to the university community in March 1991, included a scenario for relocating some departments from one campus to the other in order to consolidate academic and physical resources, several individuals expressed concern that they had not been consulted earlier and opposed the proposed moves, in particular those from downtown to the Loyola campus. It was ultimately agreed that further consultation would take place before the development of scenarios involving departmental moves.

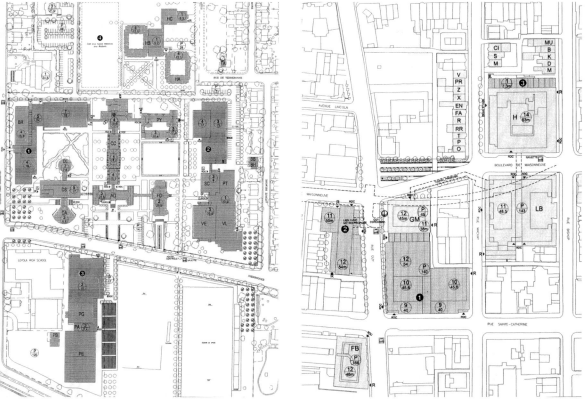

3.5 The 2000 master plan for the Loyola campus.

3.6 The 2000 master plan for the Sir George Williams campus.

In the meantime, however, Concordia had to determine the uses of the additional space on both campuses that would become available in 1992. The former Loyola High School Building and its addition would be renovated for the Psychology Department (PY), until then scattered in several buildings on both campuses, and the upper levels of the J.W. McConnell Building (LB) would house various departments that needed a home following the vacation of the Norris Building. These decisions implied moves of several departments and services, mostly within the SGW campus.

During the gradual recovery of economic and political stability that followed the 1995 referendum, it became clear that Quebec universities—including anglophone institutions, such as Concordia University—could play a key role in shaping the province's future development in the new, technology-based economy. For the first time since the merger, Concordia was instructed, in October 1996, to replace its rented facilities downtown by property, and the provincial government was ready to finance acquisitions.

Due to the recession of the early 1990s, the timing of this directive was opportune. Both buildings and recently vacated land were available for sale near the Hall and McConnell Buildings. In 1997–98, the university purchased two towers—

PLANNING THE LOYOLA AND SIR GEORGE WILLIAMS CAMPUSES 35

the 1991 Faubourg Building (FB) and the 1965 Guy-De Maisonneuve Building (GM)[12]—and two large properties: the vacant site of a defunct development at the southwest corner of Guy Street and De Maisonneuve Boulevard West, and the partially vacant site of an abandoned property on the north side of Sainte-Catherine Street West between Mackay and Guy Streets; the latter site included a 1938 art deco complex composed of the former York Cinema and Lancaster Apartments.[13]

As it was negotiating the acquisition of these four downtown properties in 1997–98, Concordia undertook, in consultation with the university community, two major planning exercises that set the stage for its first master plan: the *Long-Term Space Plan*, which examined options for departmental distribution on both campuses, taking into account new properties downtown, and a proposal for the revitalization of Loyola campus. In addition to other recommendations, both studies concluded that the pure science departments—until then dispersed throughout different buildings on both campuses—should be consolidated on Loyola campus and that a new science complex should be built to create an innovative learning environment that would optimize the synergy between different scientific disciplines. It was also agreed that other departments of the Faculty of Arts and Science already at Loyola campus (Communication Studies and Journalism, Psychology, and Performing Arts) should remain there, enhancing the diverse interests of its student body and educational offerings, and have new facilities.[14]

This position implied that the expanded SGW campus would accommodate the Faculty of Business and Administration (the future John Molson School of Business), the Faculty of Engineering and Computer Science, certain departments of the Faculty of Fine Arts (Studio Arts, Art History, and Art Education), and the remaining departments of the Faculty of Arts and Science (Humanities and Social Sciences), although some courses in the latter disciplines would still also be offered at Loyola campus. New downtown facilities were planned for the Faculty of Business and Administration, the Faculty of Engineering and Computer Science, and part of the Faculty of Fine Arts. Finally, the proposal also included residence facilities on the Loyola campus, new sports facilities on both campuses, and additional space for student activities and services, as well as meeting areas for students and professors on both campuses.

The *Long-Term Space Plan* was presented to the university community in October 1998 and, after adjustments, was approved on the eve of Concordia's twenty-fifth anniversary in 1999. A summary of the university's plans, priorities, problems, and needs was submitted to the Quebec government in October 1999, along with a funding request for new construction, renovations, maintenance, and operations. The rector's accompanying letter confirmed Concordia University's many contributions to Quebec society and reported that its registrations in science, engineering, and computer science were expected to rapidly double as the proposed up-to-date facilities would allow the expansion of academic offerings in these fields.

Over the next two years, the *Long-Term Space Plan* was transformed, in collaboration with the City of Montreal, into the revised urban design of each campus that constituted Concordia University's first master plan. The scheme respected the seven principles of 1991, the strategic academic priorities established since, the recommendations for revitalizing Loyola campus, and the unique character of each campus. In 2001 two municipal bylaws were adopted to facilitate approval of the proposed new constructions.

## Conclusion[15]

Some of the proposed projects of Concordia's first master plan for its two campuses were realized, others were cancelled, and a few were postponed as academic priorities evolved, unforeseen development opportunities arose, and new projects were pursued. Over the last twenty-five years, both campuses have witnessed the construction of innovative new pavilions: the Engineering, Computer Science and Visual Arts Integrated Complex (EV, 2005), the John Molson School of Management (MB, 2009) and the Learning Square (LS, 2019) downtown, and the Richard J. Renaud Science Complex (SP, 2003), the Centre for Structural and Functional Genomics (GE, 2011), the PERFORM Centre (PC, 2011), and the Applied Science Hub (HU, 2020) at Loyola. We've also seen the updating, renovation, and restoration of existing and recently acquired buildings: the Grey Nuns Building (GN, 2007– ), the Guy-De Maisonneuve Building (GM, recladding 2011), the Faubourg Sainte-Catherine Building (FG fifth and sixth floor 2012, FG basement 2015– ), and the Grey Nuns Annex (GA, 2014) downtown, and the Communication Studies and Journalism Building (CJ, 2005) at Loyola. Finally, new properties for future expansion, notably on Guy Street and De Maisonneuve Boulevard West, have been acquired, and a series of landscape and public art initiatives have led to the creation of Quartier Concordia and Quartier Loyola, reinforcing the university's identity and its relationships with its two very different contexts. These projects have allowed the strategic expansion of the academic curricula to address current challenges and have led to the hiring of specialized new professors and the attraction of an ever-increasing number of talented students.

In 2015 Concordia's 1991 mission statement was updated in the form of nine strategic directions to reflect its twenty-first century reality and align its learning opportunities with the aim of tackling significant contemporary societal challenges. These orientations, along with a series of studies conducted between 2016 and 2023 on multiple facets of the two campuses—heritage, landscape, sustainability and environment, mobility, for example—provided the tools necessary for the development, in collaboration with the university community, the local community, and the City of Montreal, of Concordia's second master plan, to be unveiled on the eve of its fiftieth anniversary.

**NOTES**

1     This section is based on parts 1, 2, and 3 of Susan D. Bronson, *Histoire de la stratégie de la planification et du développement du campus Sir-George-Williams de l'Université Concordia, Montréal, 1926 à 2022,* a comprehensive study realized for Dominique Dumont and Rocio Carvajo-Lucena, Strategic Planning and Development, Facilities Management, Concordia University, December 2023. All archival and other sources can be found in I0135 Facilities Management fonds, Concordia University, Records Management and Archives, hereafter RMA.

2     At the time, the Grey Nuns property was bound by Guy Street to the east, Dorchester Street West (now René-Lévesque Boulevard West) to the south, Saint-Mathieu Street to the west and Sainte-Catherine Street West to the north; it included the building later known as Faubourg Sainte-Catherine.

3     As it turned out, Concordia University acquired most of the original Grey Nuns property (with the exception of certain floors of the Faubourg Sainte-Catherine, FG) in phases, decades later.

4     This section is based on parts 4.1 through 4.4 of Susan D. Bronson, *Étude préalable à l'évaluation patrimoniale du campus Loyola de l'Université Concordia, volume 1, parties 1 à 4, version finale,* a comprehensive study realized for Dominique Dumont, Strategic Planning and Development, Facilities Management, Concordia University, December 2016 (I0135 Facilities Management fonds, RMA).

5     It is unlikely that the acquisition of all of these residential properties was ever discussed with the neighbours.

6     These two apartment buildings were eventually demolished and replaced by the new Loyola High School in 1992.

7     The proposed expanded campus, according to the 1976 study, was bound by West Broadway Street to the west, Somerled Avenue to the north, Belmore Avenue to the east, and De Maisonneuve Boulevard West to the south.

8     Although the purchase and demolition of the homes north of the existing campus and of Saint Ignatius Church were not pursued, a few properties on the east and west side of the campus, as well as the Jesuit Residence (JR) and Loyola High School (later PY) properties, would eventually be acquired. Of the proposed new constructions, only two were realized, in modified form: the Vanier Library was expanded in 1989 (without demolishing the residential properties east of it) (VE, VL), and a new science building (SP) was erected at the north and west sides of the quadrangle in 2001–03.

9     This section is based on parts 5 and 4.5 respectively of the following two studies, Bronson, *Histoire de la stratégie*; Bronson, *Étude préalable.*

10    "Concordia University Mission Statement (as approved by SCAPP on March 19,1991) (as approved by Senate 3 May 1991)," US-91-2-D10, https://archive.org/details/1991-05-03-concordia-university-mission-statement/page/n1/mode/2up.

11    Jos. Charles Giguère, "Basis for Discussion of the Final Report of the Strategic Space Planning Committee and of Space development Scenarios for Concordia University, October 21, 1991," Supplement, *Concordia's Thursday Report,* October 24, 1991, S1–S8.

12    These two buildings had already been rented by the university during the 1990s.

13  After several studies by different heritage experts, the city and the MAC agreed in 2001 to the demolition of the 1938 art deco complex, which had been left empty and unheated for a decade before Concordia bought the property and was in a state of advanced deterioration. Fragments of the buildings and their décor were, however, integrated into the new construction that replaced them.

14  Following the construction of the new Richard J. Renaud Science Complex (SP), which integrated the 1968 Bryan Building, in 2003, the Communications Studies and Journalism Department was housed in the refurbished and expanded Drummond Science Complex (CJ) in 2005. It was also proposed that the Old Arena (PS) be replaced by a new building for the Performing Arts Department and that the Student Centre (SC) be transformed for the Music Department, but these projects were not pursued.

15  This section is based on parts 5 and 4.5 respectively of the following two studies, where these projects (with the exception of recent developments on the Loyola campus) are described in detail: Bronson, *Histoire de la stratégie*; Bronson, *Étude préalable*. An illustrated summary in English of the first fifty years of Concordia's planning history is provided in Dominique Dumont, Rocio Carvajo-Lucena, and Susan D. Bronson, *Planning Concordia's Sir George Williams and Loyola Campuses, 1974–2023*, December 2023, I0135 Facilities Management fonds, RMA.

4.1 Poster for the Bread and Roses benefit cabaret for the Women's March Against Poverty, March 8, 1995. In addition to the Simone de Beauvoir Institute, the event was sponsored by the Women's Studies Student Association, the Office on the Status of Women, the Concordia Women's Centre, the Sexual Harassment Office, the Employment Equity Office, the International Student Office, as well as Open City Productions and Librairie l'Androgyne.

# 4 STATEMENT ON TUITION FEES IN QUEBEC AND THEIR IMPACT ON WOMEN (2012)

Simone de Beauvoir Institute, with an introduction by Viviane Namaste

**ESTABLISHED IN 1978**, the Simone de Beauvoir Institute (SdBI) houses Concordia's women's studies program and the interdisciplinary program in sexuality studies. Emerging from feminist scholarship and activisms, the institute has sought to raise critical questions in relation to diverse women's lives. From its very beginnings, the institute has sought to make some waves, using knowledge to create social change. When the SdBI was established in 1978, then Provost Bob Wall declared, "I have no doubt that the women's college will stir up a lot of trouble in the university, but I think that's good—that's a sure sign of health."[1]

The institute is one of Concordia's colleges. Established in the late 1970s, the colleges were modelled on a traditional liberal arts education: small classes, public lectures, and community engagement. Embedded work with local feminist communities is a hallmark of the SdBI, and what distinguishes it from a regular university department.

Rather than offer a broad historical overview of the SdBI—which would inevitably be incomplete as we approach our fiftieth anniversary in 2028—we present instead, one exemplary position statement at the SdBI as a snapshot of a key moment in time. Since 2007 members of the SdBI (students, staff, professors, fellows, and research associates) take public positions on contemporary social issues, particularly those likely to have an impact on women. For instance, the institute has written position statements on the 2007 Bouchard-Taylor Commission, the 2009 Quebec government Bill 94 on reasonable accommodations, and the 2013 Bedford decision on the dangers of Canada's prostitution laws for women.[2]

What follows is the institute's "Statement on Tuition Fees in Québec and Their Impact on Women," released in February 2012. Two pieces of historical context are relevant here. In the first instance, the release of this statement helped nourish the work of the student movement and its mobilization against tuition fee increases. As such, the SdBI sought to bring forth knowledge in dialogue with a social movement.

---

**VIVIANE NAMASTE** is Full Professor at the Simone de Beauvoir Institute.

Second, when we prepared to release this statement, we presented a draft to representatives of Media Relations at Concordia. We were informed orally that in no way would the university assist us in promoting or disseminating our message. We went ahead regardless. We underline this history now so feminists can know and remember an important lesson: universities are often invested in their own positive public relations and may not support women if they feel the reputation of the university could be brought into question.

This contribution to the anthology is rather different than others; that is part of its strength. Readers are encouraged to consider this article not as the definitive history of the SdBI, but as one example of how feminists make some trouble, yoking knowledge and action in an effort to improve women's lives. This statement was chosen for inclusion in this anthology because it stands as an analysis that addresses how economic questions impact women, as well as the differential impacts on women who are less economically privileged. It stands as one feminist attempt to bring knowledge of women's material lives into dialogue with social policy.

## Statement on Tuition Fees in Québec and Their Impact on Women (2012)

Here, we outline our official stance with respect to the Québec government's decision to authorize the increase of undergraduate tuition fees in the amount of $1,625 over the next five years.

### Neoliberal Social Policies and Their Impact on Women

The idea that tuition fees need to be raised so that universities have the appropriate revenues to function is one typical of a neoliberal era. Neoliberalism refers to a social system in which the state plays a diminished role in ensuring that the basic needs of its citizens are met. Neoliberalism is characterized by public-private partnerships, the retreat of the welfare state (social programs such as Employment Insurance), the defunding and deregulation of state institutions, and the shift of service provision from state institutions to community organizations. Neoliberal social policy gives priority to a logic of the economy and cost saving. The decision to authorize the increase in tuition fees is, as such, a neoliberal policy in which the state plays a diminished role in funding post-secondary education in Québec.

Neoliberal policy has particularly negative consequences on women. When, for example, hospitals discharge patients early because of budgetary constraints, it is primarily women who are impacted, through the unpaid care giving work they provide in such cases.[3] Similarly, social policy on raising post-secondary tuition fees in Québec affects women disproportionately.

**Access to Post-Secondary Education for Women and Their Children**
For decades now, feminists have argued that women earn less than men for doing the same work. Recent statistics support this claim: the latest data available from 2008 demonstrate that women still earn 71 cents for every dollar earned by men.[4] Asking individuals to contribute more to their post-secondary education costs, then, affects women in particular. Since women still earn less than men overall, raising tuition fees will impact women first. This is an example of social policy that perpetuates gender inequality.

If we consider the case of single mothers (who still constitute the majority of single-parent families), it is clear that tuition increases will affect not only these women, but their children as well. Eric Martin and Maxime Ouellet, authors of *Université Inc.: Des mythes sur la hausse des frais de scolarité et l'économie du savoir,* argue that a two-parent family would need to allocate 10% of its revenue to fund a BA for one child; in the case of single mothers, however, a woman would need to allocate 18% of her income to ensure her child obtains a BA.[5] Educational funding policy which requires the contribution of individual consumers quietly bypasses the reality that such policy demands more from single mothers. Raising tuition fees in Québec entrenches inequality for single mothers and their children, since they need to allocate more of their income to obtain the same access to state-funded institutions.

**Long-Term Consequences of Increased Tuition Fees for Women**
Some proponents of raising tuition fees contend that, since individuals who have a university education will earn more throughout their lifetimes, they should assume a part of the financial cost. Such proponents use an economic rhetoric, stating that students now need to "invest" in their future.

But again, this argument falls short when we consider that even with a post-secondary diploma, men and women do not earn the same income. On average, a woman with such a diploma will earn $863,268 less than a man with the same diploma over the course of her lifetime.[6]

Suppose that two students—one a man, one a woman—each finish a BA with a debt of $25,000. Each and every month, the woman has to spend more of her income to pay back her debt. Asking individuals to "invest" in their future asks women to pay more, proportionally speaking, than men over their lifetimes. The Québec government is asking women to "invest" in their sustained inequality for decades to come. We reject this kind of neoliberal logic and advocate a system in which access to Québec post-secondary education is equal for men and women—now and in the future.

**Pedagogical Implications of Raising Tuition Fees: Faculty Perspectives**
Objections to raising tuition fees generally focus on the position of students, and with good reason, since they are the ones most impacted. Nevertheless, members of the teaching faculty at the Simone de Beauvoir Institute maintain that raising tuition fees will have negative consequences for teaching and learning more broadly. The more expensive tuition is, the less diversity there will be in the classroom since access is

dependent on financial resources. Statistics Canada reports that "visible minority" women were more likely to be in a low-income situation than non-visible minority women.[7] Similarly, compared to their non-Aboriginal counterparts, Aboriginal women are less likely to have a university degree. In 2006, 9% of Aboriginal women aged 25 and over had a university degree, compared with 20% of non-Aboriginal women.[8]

Members of the Institute understand that diversity is central to the teaching work they do. They see the work of post-secondary teaching as one of preparing students to engage in critical inquiry and dialogue with others, offering them skills and analysis to guide them throughout their lives.

The work of critical pedagogy is facilitated through a diverse classroom. When social policy results in the exclusion of women and people from diverse backgrounds from post-secondary education, the work of teaching is compromised. Ensuring equitable access to state-funded education not only supports students; it is one concrete way to support the work of post-secondary teachers, as well.

**We Have the Financial Resources to Make Equitable Access a Priority**
Public debate on raising post-secondary tuition fees in Québec often assumes that the financial resources do not exist to make universal, equitable access to education a political priority. We contend that, collectively, Québec does have the resources required to ensure that all men and women have equitable access to post-secondary education. A redistribution of resources could make equal access to education possible, as suggested in the following examples:

▪ Bonuses given to managers of *sociétés d'état* in 2010 totalled $105 million.[9]

▪ Imposing licensing fees on mining and industrial manufacturing companies' use of water in Québec could yield $775 million annually ($0.01/litre of water used).[10]

**Summary and Conclusion**
On the question of raising tuition fees for post-secondary education, members of the Simone de Beauvoir Institute underline:

▪ Thinking about women and social policy means thinking beyond so-called "women's issues" such as sexual harassment or daycare. While these issues are important, we also need to understand the way social policies impact women in particular.

▪ Given that women still do not earn the same salaries as men, raising tuition fees means that women will pay more for their education now and in the decades it takes them to pay back their debt. Raising tuition fees perpetuates gender inequality now and in the future.

▪ Increased tuition fees mean there will be a less diverse classroom, which will in turn impoverish opportunities for learning among students and faculty. We advocate social policy which facilitates access to post-secondary education, in order to ensure our classrooms are truly diverse and a rich site of dialogue and exchange.

▪ Social policy which discourages women's involvement in post-secondary education is not good social policy.

▪ Québec has the financial resources required to properly fund post-secondary education and to ensure that women and men can access state-funded education equally. It is time for a genuine debate about how the Québec government should allocate its resources to make equitable access to post-secondary education a political priority.

NOTES

1   David Lisak, *The Gazette*, "Concordia Women's College Is Designed to Make Trouble," May 19, 1978.

2   The SdBI's official statements on various issues can be found online on the institute's webpage: https://www.concordia.ca/artsci/sdbi/about/positions.html.

3   Pat Armstrong and Hugh Armstrong, *Wasting Away: The Undermining of Canadian Health Care* (Toronto: Oxford University Press [Wynford Project Edition], 2010).

4   Gouvernement du Canada, *L'écart salarial entre les femmes et les hommes*, July 29, 2010, http://www.parl.gc.ca/Content/LOP/ResearchPublications/2010-30-f.htm.

5   Eric Martin and Maxime Ouellet, *Université Inc.: Des mythes sur la hausse des frais de scolarité et l'économie du savoir* (Montréal: Lux, 2011), 16.

6   Fédération étudiante universitaire du Québec, "L'éducation universitaire: Un outil pour passer de l'égalité de droit à l'égalité de fait," mémoire de la FEUQ sur le renouvellement du plan d'action gouvernemental sur l'égalité entre les femmes et les hommes, Montréal, 2011, iii.

7   Tina Chui and Hélène Maheux, "Visible Minority Women," in *Women in Canada: A Gender-Based Statistical Report*, 6th ed., catalogue no. 89-503-XIE, Statistics Canada, July 2011, www.statcan.gc.ca/pub/89-503-x/2010001/article/11527-eng.htm.

8   Vivian O'Donnell and Susan Wallace, "First Nations, Métis and Inuit Women," in *Women in Canada: A Gender-Based Statistical Report*, 6th ed., catalogue no. 89-503-XIE, Statistics Canada, July 2011, http://www.statcan.gc.ca/pub/89-503-x/2010001/article/11442-eng.htm.

9   Omar Aktouf, "La marchandisation de l'éducation et le faux alibi de la pauvreté de l'état au Québec," in *Université Inc.*, 143.

10  "Éducation publique et gratuite: Un choix de société cher à Québec Solidaire," *Solidarités*, November 2011, p. A3.

# 5 ORAL HISTORIES: Feminist Perspectives

**MAÏR VERTHUY,** "I WAS THE FIRST WOMAN HIRED, FULL-TIME, IN THE FRENCH DEPARTMENT"

It was Sir George Williams, and I was the first woman hired, full-time, in the French Department. They were in a state of shock. A woman, full-time, the same status as them, in the French Department—excuse me? Was Jim Whitelaw, had he gone insane? Well, there were two that were very pleasant to me but the others they weren't. I mean, because they weren't used to talking to women as colleagues. They were only used to talking to women as their mothers, their sisters, or their mistresses, or whatever, that kind of thing ... I think, I was brought up to be independent and be myself and ... my parents never put pressure on me to get married or date, or anything like that. Get on with your career, get a good job, do good work, think of other people: that was the education I was brought up in. So, I didn't understand what was going on. And then [edited out] ... became chair of the department and he spent three years of his life trying to fire me, thank you very much. It was very stressful because we had just bought a house ...

Besides, I had two daughters and all sorts of other things. It was a very stressful three years. And it was very interesting because the two lefties in the department

---

MAÏR VERTHUY is a Distinguished Professor Emerita at Concordia University who was the co-founder and first principal of the Simone de Beauvoir Institute. She has been inducted into both the Order of Canada and the Ordre national du Québec. This interview took place at University Communications Services Studio on November 7, 2022.

LINDA DYER is Professor and Chair of the Department of Management in the John Molson School of Business at Concordia University. She has also served on the President's Task Force on Anti-Black Racism. This interview took place at the Centre for Oral History and Digital Storytelling on December 12, 2022.

ELIZABETH MOREY has served in multiple administrative roles at Concordia University since the early 1980s. Prior to her retirement in 2011, she served as Dean of Students. This interview took place on Zoom on November 11, 2022.

MANON TREMBLAY is a nêhiyaw iskwêw (Plains Cree woman) and educator. She is the Senior Director of Indigenous Directions at Concordia and in the mid-1990s and early 2000s was the former coordinator of the Centre for Native Education. This interview took place at University Communications Services Studio on October 28, 2022.

defended me [*chuckle*]. And so did people outside the department, because they'd see me at work. You know, people in the Psychology Department and, and in Modern Languages, because Modern Languages had split off at that point … And he just couldn't, he couldn't stand the thought of an independent female. And I wasn't rude or anything, and I just spoke as if I had the same right to speak as other people. Plus, we Welsh speak a lot. But the others, they didn't try to defend me, they were cowardly the way men are frequently, I'm afraid. Not all of them, by a long shot … The minute I won, his attitude changed.

## LINDA DYER, "A BIT OF A GENDER THING HAPPENING"

*Piyusha Chatterjee: One question, I don't know if this would come as a hard question, but in the Faculty of Commerce as a woman and a person of colour, was it more difficult?*

Yeah. When I arrived, there was only one other woman in my department, and she left. So, I would say that [*both laugh quietly*], I would say that gender probably had a big impact. In my department, there was nobody of colour. But … I didn't find that noticeable. But the gender thing, I noticed. Yeah. In one of my first performance evaluations, I was told that I should dress in a more business-like fashion. And I said, "But the other guys, they're wearing jeans and sweaters. I don't see them in suits. Why should I wear a suit?" And I remember the department chair coming to me and saying, "I really apologize for that. The Personnel Committee never should have written that. I will remove it." You know? So, I think there was a—there was a bit of a gender thing happening. It was still fun though.

## ELIZABETH MOREY, THE STATUS OF WOMEN

My next job? I took a year off and then I was invited back by the rector, who was Patrick Kenniff at the time, to be the first advisor to the rector on the Status of Women. So *that* was challenging. That was very challenging [*laughs*]. Trying to address issues of sexism in the curriculum, in behaviours, you know. And we put together an employment equity commission, because the government required universities to start doing something on employment equity, because they'd never done anything. We also set up an advisor on sexual harassment. You know, all these things were set up and they seemed to disappear over the years. We had a policy on sexual harassment. I organized a national conference on sexual harassment, so that people came from all across the country and worked together on putting together templates for sexual harassment policies for their universities.

But, you know, the last couple years when sexual harassment issues came up, all of a sudden people are saying, "Oh, we need a policy," and I'm going, "What happened to the policy from twenty years ago?" [*laughs*]. I don't know. Yeah. It was

a hard job, that one. It was *very* frustrating. Because, you know, trying to address issues of language was *extremely* difficult. You know. And some professors were not very *nice*. Especially when you were discussing language in the English Department; they were not *nice*. And having to deal with issues that came up, of students—
The engineering students at that point had a newsletter that they put out at the beginning of the year that was just completely sexist and racist and disgusting. Just silly little things that came up. At one point, there was something they were selling in the bookstore, I *vaguely* remember. And it had something about "You can beat your wife with this." And I got in touch with the director of the libraries, who was *horrified*, because she's a wonderful woman. And they took it off the shelves. But if there hadn't been someone there to address that, it would have just gone on.

## MANON TREMBLAY, "WE NEED TO CHANGE THOSE SYSTEMS"

My name is Manon Tremblay and I am a member of the Muskeg Lake Cree Nation. But I've lived, and my family has lived, in this region for many, many years. I was born here. And so, we've always lived in and around the Montreal region, but never really in Montreal itself. I first started to live in Montreal when I was a student. I studied linguistics at Université de Montréal, and later, when I started working at Concordia, I also did a major in child studies here as well. I started working at Concordia when I was twenty-seven years old. It was one of my—actually, one of my very first serious jobs out of school. And I started working in Student Services. I took on the position of coordinator of what was called, at the time, the Centre for Native Education. Which has gone through a number of name changes throughout its history and has now become the Otsenhákta Student Centre. And I held that position for fifteen years. So, for fifteen years, I was, I guess, the familiar face for students who were encountering hiccups throughout their academic journeys, or who just were looking for a safe place to be, a place to interact with their peers, to study in peace. The centre offered a lot, and still offers all of these services. And then, after fifteen years ... you know, once you get to the realization that you can do a job blindfolded and there's nothing really challenging coming your way anymore, I was looking for a new challenge, new horizons, and for a while I found that at the University of Ottawa, where I became their senior advisor on Indigenous affairs. And then I went to the federal government, where I worked for a while in Indigenous HR, and then in Indigenous research. And then I came back here. So, I've been back at Concordia for nearly three years; it'll be three years in December. And now I'm there as senior director, Indigenous Directions. I work in the Office of the Provost, and my role is to oversee the implementation of our Indigenous Directions Action Plan, as well as advise and guide senior management on Indigenous issues and matters. That's me in a nutshell.

*Piyusha Chatterjee: I'm wondering, engaging with such institutions, what does it entail? I'm guessing that at this point you are also trying to shift their perspective on certain matters, and sort of also integrate Indigenous perspective, but also dislodging some of the already existing ideas. What has the work been like?*

Yeah, it's called decolonization and, you know, this is a term that started appearing on the landscape about when I was at the University of Ottawa; we were starting to *very* slowly talk about decolonization. And right now, decolonization's the *big* thing across all universities. And that's it. You know, it's challenging those established systems that work for only a minority of people. And trying to explain to people that those systems need to be changed *if*—if we're really, really serious about equity, diversity, and inclusion, we need to change those systems.

**Pierre Blanchette**
*Nacelle,* 2009

Sapele, ebony finish, and anodized blue metal (6 x 15 x 7 metres)
Atrium, John Molson Building, SGW campus

6.1 Grey Nuns Mother House, 2016.

# THE GREY NUNS MOTHER HOUSE: CONFRONTING THE DIFFICULT LEGACIES[1]

Peter Gossage

**LES SOEURS DE LA CHARITÉ DE L'HÔPITAL GÉNÉRAL DE MONTRÉAL**—also known as les Soeurs grises (the Grey Nuns)—date back to the 1730s when a young widow, Marie-Marguerite Dufrost Lajemmerais d'Youville (1701–1771), and some like-minded women chose to devote their lives to charitable work. By comparison, Concordia's fifty-year history is singularly recent and brief. Yet the stories of Concordia University and the Grey Nuns of Montreal intersect in interesting, important, and troubling ways.

In 2007 Concordia purchased a massive piece of downtown real estate from its venerable neighbour. The Grey Nuns were at that time a 270-year-old religious congregation steeped in Catholic faith and settler-colonialist ideology. Their legacies included not only their much-celebrated work with the urban poor but also extensive involvement in Canada's notorious Indian residential school system: a mission that was planned, coordinated, and supervised from the Mother House in Montreal. How should Concordia as a community of scholars, students, and citizens manage the weight of historical memory attached to this building? How can we reconcile the presence of a monument to Catholic missionary zeal and settler-colonialist racism with our university's progressive values and its specific commitment to Indigenous reconciliation?[2] Our university's fiftieth anniversary provides an opportunity to reflect on these difficult questions.

\* \* \*

La Maison mère des Soeurs de la charité de l'hôpital général de Montréal was designed by the prominent religious architect Victor Bourgeau and constructed in several stages between 1869 and 1904. The site was a plot of farmland in the St. Antoine district on the outskirts of the growing industrial city, acquired from the Sulpicians in 1861. When completed, the new Mother House was among the city's largest buildings, occupying an 84,380 square-foot area on the ten-acre site.[3] Architectural drawings prepared by

---

**PETER GOSSAGE** joined the Department of History at Concordia University in 2009 and served as its chair from 2016 to 2019. He is a historian of Quebec society, culture, and institutions, and co-author, with J.I. Little, of *An Illustrated History of Quebec: Tradition and Modernity* (2012).

Sister Saint-Jean-de-la-Croix between 1900 and 1907 show all the spaces in this enormous building, how they were used, and by whom. Over 1,000 people lived in the Mother House at that time, with specific areas reserved for religious personnel (mainly in the east wing) and their impoverished charges (mainly in the west). Within those areas there were rooms reserved for sleeping, eating, working, medical care, leisure activities, and a large central chapel for religious observance.[4]

The private, denominational, and institutional character of Quebec's social-service network at the turn of the twentieth century explains the profusion of massive convent buildings like this throughout the province. Fast-forward into the 1970s and we observe a radically different situation. By that time, the state had taken over from private, mainly religious organizations in the delivery of services to the poor; most social assistance was provided at home in the form of income supports rather than within institutional walls; and the intense religiosity of an earlier era had given way to the secularism of recent times. There was no longer much need for the massive convent spaces of the nineteenth century. So, the Grey Nuns, with their numbers declining dramatically and their social relevance increasingly in question, decided to sell.

Indeed, the nuns came very close to finalizing a $17 million sale and redevelopment deal in 1974–75, a deal that would have seen most of the convent demolished and replaced with a modern high-rise office and commercial complex. Only the chapel, the one part of the building protected at that time under provincial heritage laws, would have been saved from the wrecking ball.[5] Mobilization by local heritage activists, however, led to decisions by the provincial government first to block the redevelopment plan (June 1975) and then to extend heritage protection from the chapel alone to the entire building, indeed to the entire city block occupied by the Mother House (February 1976).[6] In the meantime, another potential buyer emerged. "Concordia University," wrote *The Gazette* in 1975, "has submitted a plan—which must be approved by the Ministry of Education—under which the 1871 greystone would be removed and [the site] used as a campus."[7] But with the 1975 rejection of the skyscraper plan and the 1976 provincial heritage designation, it had become clear that any redevelopment plans must involve the renovation and re-use of the "1871 greystone" rather than its demolition.

Fast-forward again to the opening decade of the new millennium, when Concordia's ambition "to take over the convent for use by its Sir George Williams campus" became a reality.[8] We pick up the story on May 31, 2004, when the nuns accepted Concordia's formal offer to acquire the property for the sum of $18 million.[9] At a press conference the following day, the master of ceremonies pointed to the central role of Jonathan Wener, chair of the real estate committee of the board of governors, in securing the valuable downtown property. Wener himself spoke of negotiations and a process of "preliminary due diligence" that had begun some three

6.2 Library and Archives Canada provides the following description of this striking photograph: "Students and family members, principal Father Joseph Hugonnard, school staff, and Grey Nuns on a hill overlooking the Indian Residential School (trade school) at Fort Qu'Appelle, Lebret, Saskatchewan, May 1885."

years earlier. Starting in 2001, the university hired several architectural and engineering firms to assess the state of the building and the feasibility of a project embracing both the protection of a heritage property and its conversion into usable space for post-secondary education. The focus of that project was to be new facilities for the Faculty of Fine Arts, and architectural drawings were prepared by one of the consulting firms, Cardinal Hardy, and presented at the press conference by the Faculty of Fine Arts dean, Christopher Jackson.[10] The agreement between Concordia and the Grey Nuns, however, was provisional and the university built a further period of due diligence into its initial offer to purchase, which in the event was extended several times. The parties also struck a joint management committee (Comité conjoint de gestion) to deal with a range of issues relating to the building and with the challenges posed by its gradual conversion into a sustainable site for university activities.[11]

A surprising twist to this story came in May 2006 when the director of Public Health Protection for Quebec, Dr. Horacio Arruda, refused the Grey Nuns' application to have human remains removed from basement of the Mother House. The 276 individuals buried in the crypt directly below the chapel are mainly Grey Nuns who had died in the nineteenth century, some of them transferred there from a similar

6.3 Suzy Lake, *The Extended Goodbye #1* (2009) was part of the exhibition *Preoccupations: Photographic Explorations of the Mother House of the Grey Nuns*, curated by Distinguished University Research Chair Martha Langford. The exhibition consisted of commissioned photographs by twelve alumni and retired faculty, which is now installed at the Grey Nuns Mother House. This work is part of Lake's *Extended Breathing* series wherein the artist stands perfectly still to record their breathing for a one-hour camera exposure. Pictured here is Lake, surrounded by the 276 graves located in the basement-level crypt. As Lake describes, "It is impossible to control the slight sway of my upper torso, although my feet remain as crisp as the crypt surroundings. It anchors the nun to her surroundings, but the sway suggests mortality. I am the nun."

crypt below the Hôpital général when the congregation moved in the 1870s.[12] Concordia's offer to purchase contained a provision that all of the bodies in the crypt would be exhumed and relocated no later than 2011: the date at which, in a plan that included a four-stage transfer of the premises, Concordia would occupy that part of the building.[13] The nuns' intention was to move the remains to their cemetery on Île St-Bernard, near Chateauguay. But Arruda's decision scuttled that plan, citing the risk (very low, as he acknowledged) that workers involved in the transfer might become infected with the smallpox virus.[14] In the end, the closing of the sale went ahead on May 15, 2007, with all of the bodies still in the basement, to be sealed in place later on by a fifteen-centimetre-thick slab of concrete.[15] But concerns over human remains certainly had an impact on the complicated agreement finalized that day, which specifically excluded the crypt from the property acquired by Concordia and placed it in the hands of a separate body of trustees. For its part, Concordia retained an option to purchase the space for one dollar should a way ultimately be found for the remaining graves to be removed and relocated.[16]

\* \* \*

The Concordia officials who negotiated the purchase of the Mother House were apparently oblivious to the Grey Nuns' extensive involvement in the genocidal system of Indian residential schools.[17] Beginning in the 1840s and into the 1970s and 1980s, the Grey Nuns of Montreal had participated as teachers, staff, and administrators in the operation of at least nineteen Indian residential schools across Turtle Island.[18] They most often worked in partnership with the Missionary Oblates of Mary Immaculate, the militant French missionary order that "established and managed the majority of church-run Canadian residential schools."[19] As the final report of the Truth and Reconciliation Commission of Canada (TRC) showed, the Oblates' work depended heavily on the inexpensive labour of religious women recruited in Quebec. And the Grey Nuns of Montreal are described in that report as their "preferred partners in missionary activity."[20]

The Grey Nuns of Montreal, in short, were thoroughly committed to the colonizing mission of the Indian residential school system and actively engaged in its day-to-day operations for over a century. They were especially active on the Prairies and in the North, with one school in western Ontario (Kenora), four in Saskatchewan, six in Alberta, seven in the Northwest Territories (including present-day Nunavut), and one south of the US border in Fort Totten, North Dakota.[21] They are closely associated with mission work and residential schooling in the far north, arriving at Fort Providence in 1867 and working there and at other northern settlements for well over a century. After 1955, this work included the operation of a series of large residences or "hostels" built to accommodate children attending federal day schools in communities such as Inuvik and Chesterfield Inlet. Thousands of First Nations, Métis, and Inuit children were subjected to their instruction and their round-the-clock authority over several generations.

Thoroughly documented in the TRC's final report, the tragedy of the residential schools system has gained greater focus and urgency since May 2021, when the Tk'emlúps te Secwépemc First Nation announced the discovery of 215 suspected unmarked graves in an apple orchard near the former Kamloops Indian Residential School in British Columbia.[22] Some of the schools the Grey Nuns helped to run, moreover, have now received international media attention as research with ground-penetrating radar continues to find evidence of unmarked graves in similar locations. These include Blue Quills Residential School near St. Paul, Alberta, where the Grey Nuns of Montreal were active from 1862 to 1970; Qu'Appelle Residential School in Lebret, Saskatchewan, where they worked from 1884 to 1975; and École Notre-Dame-du-Sacré-Coeur in Beauval, Saskatchewan, staffed by Grey Nuns from 1910 to 1971.[23] National Centre for Truth and Reconciliation records indicate that 27 Indigenous children died at Blue Quills between 1901 and 1945, 56 at Lebret from 1890 to 1953, and 52 at Beauval between 1909 and 1961, including 19 boys killed in a dormitory fire on the night of September 19, 1927. But there are strong indications that the actual numbers were much higher.[24]

Information about the extent of the Grey Nuns' historic involvement with Indian residential schools was gradually coming to light in the years surrounding Concordia's acquisition of the Mother House. The Royal Commission on Aboriginal Peoples had reported in 1996, raising awareness about residential schools and making key recommendations that led to the establishment of the TRC.[25] In 1995 the Assembly of First Nations launched class-action litigation that paved the way for the Indian Residential Schools Settlement Agreement of 2006. In this landmark agreement, the Grey Nuns of Montreal were one of forty-eight Catholic entities that acknowledged the harm caused by the Indian residential school system and promised to provide millions of dollars in financial compensation.[26] When it was released in 2015 after an eight-year public inquiry, the voluminous final report of the TRC mentioned the Grey Nuns dozens of times.[27] The congregation was also reported in 2018 to be withholding documents from the TRC and its successor organization, the National Centre for Truth and Reconciliation.[28]

An exploration of the records and testimony collected by the TRC and now held by the National Centre for Truth and Reconciliation gives a deep and immediate sense of the tragedy of the residential school system in Canada, including insights into the Grey Nuns' involvement. Third-generation residential school survivor Joe Whitehawk, for example, remembered the nuns at the Lebret school very well. "We never hear any mention about the nuns," he remarked, near the beginning of his testimony before a sharing panel held in Île-à-la-Crosse, Saskatchewan, during the TRC hearings conducted in November 2012. "You know, they were a vicious lot, quite a few of them. Some of them were nice, but unfortunately some of them were (pauses) ruthless."[29] Whitehawk then described three violent incidents that drew blood and left scars on his face and hands, including one where a sister beat him with a broken hockey stick. He also recounted a shocking incident of sexual abuse he experienced at age fourteen or fifteen while spending a night in the Lebret school infirmary.[30] As a survivor of childhood trauma, Whitehawk provides emotional and deeply disturbing testimony. And his point here is well taken: that it was not only priests and brothers who victimized Indigenous children in Canada's residential schools. The nuns, in Whitehawk's experience of Lebret, were direct participations in the larger project of cultural genocide, in many individual acts of physical or psychological cruelty, and as in his own case, in some shameful incidents of sexual abuse.

All of these materials, furthermore, relate to the involvement of just one "Catholic entity"—les Soeurs de la charité de l'hôpital général de Montréal—in the residential school system. Beginning in the 1840s, however, the Grey Nuns began to expand across Canada and into the United States.[31] Most of these new congregations soon established their autonomy as separate bodies answering to local bishops, while retaining their characteristic grey habits, their devotion to Marguerite d'Youville, and an allegiance to the Mother House in Montreal. Several of these autonomous orders of Grey Nuns were also directly involved in the residential school system. Among the forty-eight Catholic entities named in the Indian Residential Schools Settlement Agreement were separate congregations based in Saint-Hyacinthe, Ottawa, Manitoba, Alberta, and the Northwest Territories, in addition to the Grey Nuns of Montreal. Les Soeurs de la charité d'Ottawa, for example, ran a number of schools in Northern Ontario and Quebec, generally in partnership with the Oblates. And these included the notorious St. Anne's Indian Residential School in Fort Albany on the western side of James Bay, where some of the most shocking abuse reported in the national media occurred.[32]

*   *   *

My own journey as a Grey Nuns scholar began around 1980 when I started the research for my MA thesis on the Grey Nuns' foundling hospital,[33] resumed quietly when I arrived at Concordia from the Université de Sherbrooke in 2009, and took a dramatic turn after 2015 when I learned about the extent of the order's involvement with the Indian residential school system. As a Montreal-born settler historian of English and Irish heritage based at Concordia, I have been thinking, talking, teaching, and writing about the complicated and difficult legacies of the Grey Nuns for some time now. I have done so as an unofficial scholar-in-residence in the Grey Nuns building during a sabbatical leave in 2015–16; as a regular guest speaker, invited by the residence-life leadership to lecture on the history of the Mother House and to lead tours of the basement-level crypt; and most recently as a member of the Exploring Concordia's Colonial Past Committee, reporting to the Indigenous Directions Leadership Council. With this chapter, I invite the broader Concordia community to share in those reflections and to join an ongoing conversation about our campus, our founding and partner institutions, and their connections to colonialism and other systems of oppression.

The legacy of the Grey Nuns is complicated and difficult. The positive side of that legacy is featured in most of the existing commemorative materials, including the federal and provincial heritage designations of the Mother House. Here was a group of women motivated by Christian charity who took on difficult and thankless work with the poor, the marginalized, and the suffering, and who risked their lives to care for Irish immigrants in the fever sheds of 1847, established some of Montreal's first childcare centres for working mothers, and provided careers and leadership opportunities for generations of Catholic women who chose a path other than marriage and motherhood.[34] Since 2007 Concordia has played a significant role in promoting and amplifying these narratives of celebration and achievement—narratives that omit the harm done by colonialism and leave no room for Indigenous perspectives. The federal heritage designation for the Grey Nuns Mother House, for instance, was awarded in 2009, based on a nomination file submitted by the university in April 2008. The narrative it embraces is characteristically heroic, one-sided, and oblivious to the harmful legacies of colonialism. "Since the eighteenth century," we read, "the Sisters of Charity of Montreal (known as the Grey Nuns) have pioneered health care and social services in rural areas, towns and cities across the country and as far north as the Arctic Circle. Their majestic Mother House is a testament to the selfless contributions of this national charitable organization and is a critical marker in the history of the medical and social systems of Canada."[35]

Certainly, the Grey Nuns helped to build the Montreal, Quebec, and Canada we know. But, as we also know, the society they helped build was deeply imbued with racism, including the settler-colonialist ideology that saw an urgent need for missionary work to "civilize" Métis, First Nations, and Inuit children by eradicating Indigenous languages, customs, kinship networks, spiritualities, and ways of life. Concordia has taken some halting steps toward redressing the balance.[36] But deep and consistent engagement with the dark and troubling side of the Grey Nuns' legacy seems essential from the university, in its role as custodian of a historic building that served for over a century as the nerve centre and command post for this extensive and tragic colonizing mission. We first need truth, after all, if we ever hope to achieve reconciliation.

## NOTES

1   My thanks to Annmarie Adams, Monika Kin Gagnon, Colby Gaudet, Ronald Rudin, Manon Tremblay, Brandon Webb, Louellyn White, and participants in the February 2023 authors' colloquium for their helpful and encouraging comments on earlier drafts of this chapter, and to archivists Mylène Laurendeau and Eric Côté for their generous assistance with the sources.

2   Concordia's *Indigenous Directions Action Plan* was released in 2019 and updated in 2021. It is available on Concordia's website: https://www.concordia.ca/content/dam/concordia/offices/idlc/docs/indigenous-directions-action-plan-2021.pdf.

3   See Tania Martin, "Housing the Grey Nuns: Power, Religion, and Women in fin-de-siècle Montreal" (Master of Architecture thesis, McGill University, 1995), 22–23.

4.   Item L082, C, 01, 1, 04: Diverses notes pour servir d'historique et pièces justificatives au relevé des plans et des terrains, 1900; and item L082, C, 01, 1, 05: Construction de la Maison Mère – Cahier de Sr. St-Jean-de-la-Croix, 1871–1901, Archives des Soeurs Grises de Montréal (ASGM). See also Martin, "Housing the Grey Nuns," especially chapter 2, 30–56.

5   Donna Gabeline, "Grey Nuns' Convent to Get Wreckers' Axe," *The Gazette*, November 23, 1974; Donna Gabeline, "Historic Status Planned for Convent," *The Gazette*, December 5, 1974; Phyllis Lambert, "New City 'Wall': Move by Religious Orders Helped Set out Urban Pattern," *The Gazette*, February 10, 1975.

6   Patrick Doyle and Donna Gabeline, "Ministry Rejects Convent Plan," *The Gazette*, June 11, 1975; Yardena Arar, "Grey Nuns' Site Sitting Pretty: One Sweet Battle Is Won in War to Preserve History," *The Gazette*, February 23, 1974.

7   Doyle and Gabeline, "Ministry Rejects Convent Plan."

8   Quotation from "Grey Nuns' Site Saved in Montreal," *Ottawa Citizen*, February 5, 1976.

9   Concordia University's Records Management and Archives (hereafter RMA) provided two boxes of materials (numbers RM22589 and RM22596) relating to the university's acquisition of the building between 2004 and 2007. I draw mainly on those documents for the following discussion.

10   GN-Press Conference, Planning notes for press conference, Tuesday, June 1, 2004, RM22569, RMA. A detailed, confidential prospectus for the Faculty of Fine Arts project dated January 2004 is in the same box, in a file labelled GN-Projet de mise en valeur de la Maison Mère des Soeurs Grises.

11   Various documents in GN-Comité conjoint de gestion, GN-Contamination, GN-Contracts, GN-Coordination meetings, GN-Legal documents, GN-CSST, RM22589, RMA.

12   More specifically, the remains of 232 members and 44 non-members of the religious order are buried in the crypt of the Grey Nuns Mother House. The earliest burials are those transferred from the original Hôpital général and date back as far as 1763. Not counting a single set of ashes interred in 1985, the most recent burial dates from 1961. "Soeurs grises de Montréal inhumées dans la crypte de la Maison mère par nom de famille," and "Maison mère des Soeurs Grises de Montréal: Tableau des autres personnes (NON Soeurs Grises de Montréal) inhumées dans la crypte de la Maison mère par nom de famille," ASGM.

13   GN-Legal, Offre d'achat par l'Université Concordia à Les Sœurs Grises de Montréal pour l'édifice et le terrain situés au 1190-1200 rue Guy, Montréal, article 2.5.14, 9, RM22589, RMA.

14   This risk was determined despite the age of the remains and the availability of a smallpox vaccine for generations. GN-Crypt, Dr Horacio Arruda to Me Michel Fleury, May 25, 2006, RM22589, RMA.

15   An exception was made for Marguerite d'Youville herself. She had been canonized in 1990 and her remains were transferred from a shrine in the crypt to her birthplace in Varennes, Quebec, in December 2010.

16   Information in this paragraph is from GN-Legal and GN-Crypt, RM22589; and GN-Final Offer, RM22596, RMA.

17 The systemic violence of the Canadian Indian residential school system is thoroughly documented and its characterization as a form of genocide is well supported by the evidence. See especially David B. MacDonald, *The Sleeping Giant Awakens: Genocide, Indian Residential Schools, and the Challenge of Conciliation* (Toronto: University of Toronto Press, 2019).

18 This number is based on records provided to me by archivist Mylène Laurendeau in September 2020. Capsule histories of nineteen schools in which the Grey Nuns of Montreal acknowledge their involvement, prepared by Sister Suzanne Olivier between 1996 and 2000, ASGM. More detailed historical narratives relating to seventeen of these schools are available from the archives of the National Centre for Truth and Reconciliation (NCTR), online at https://archives.nctr.ca/.

19 Truth and Reconciliation Commission of Canada, *Canada's Residential Schools: The History, Part 1, Origins to 1939*, vol. 1 of the *Final Report of the Truth and Reconciliation Commission of Canada* (Montreal and Kingston: Published for the TRC by McGill-Queen's University Press, 2015), 29.

20 TRC, *Canada's Residential Schools*, 29, 30.

21 Capsule histories, ASGM.

22 The Kamloops school was run by the Oblates from its inception in 1890 until 1969, apparently without any assistance from a women's religious order. Kamloops Residential School Narrative, April 12, 2004, NCTR archives, https://archives.nctr.ca/NAR-NCTR-128.

23 See ASGM capsule histories for the dates of the Grey Nuns' activity at these schools. For the discovery of suspected unmarked graves, see Murray Mandryk, "Even Sadder than Discoveries are the Abuse Deniers," *The Gazette*, January 17, 2023; Nicole Stillger, "Search Underway for Unmarked Burial Sites at Former Alberta Residential School," *Global News*, August 11, 2022, https://globalnews.ca/news/9053848/unmarked-burial-sites-search-alberta-residential-school/; Pratyush Dayal, "English River First Nation Announces More Findings in Radar Search for Unmarked Graves," *CBC News*, August 29, 2023, https://www.cbc.ca/news/canada/saskatoon/english-river-first-nation-announces-more-findings-in-unmarked-graves-1.6951437.

24 For documented deaths at Lebret, see the National Student Memorial on the NCTR website: https://nctr.ca/residential-schools/saskatchewan/lebret-quappelle/; for Blue Quills, see https://nctr.ca/residential-schools/alberta/blue-quills-sacred-heart/; for Beauval, see https://nctr.ca/residential-schools/saskatchewan/beauval-ile-a-la-crosse/.

25 The *Report of the Royal Commission on Aboriginal Peoples* is widely available in electronic form, including from the UBC Library service: https://collections.irshdc.ubc.ca/index.php/Detail/objects/10780.

26 Ultimately, the forty-eight entities fell $21 million short of their overall $79 million commitment. For details, see Tom Cardo, "How the Catholic Church Was Freed from Obligation to Residential School Survivors," *Globe and Mail*, October 4, 2021. The full text of the 2006 Indian Residential School Settlement Agreement is available at https://www.residentialschoolsettlement.ca/settlement.html.

27 I found sixty-six mentions of "Grey Nuns" or "Sisters of Charity" in *Part 1* of volume 1 alone. TRC, *Canada's Residential Schools: The History, Part 1 – Origins to 1939*.

28 Jorge Barrera, "Some Catholic Orders Still Withholding Promised Residential School Records," *CBC News*, June 1, 2018, https://www.cbc.ca/news/indigenous/catholic-orders-residential-school-records-1.4686472.

29 Video posted to the NCTR website: https://archives.nctr.ca/SP090, at time code 51:00.

30 I have chosen not to reproduce this disturbing testimony, but it is available from the video cited in the previous note, at time code 54:50. The Grey Nuns of Montreal are the only women's religious congregation to have worked at Lebret, which they did until 1975, so it is reasonable to assume that the offending nun was a member of the order.

31 See Tania Martin, "The Architecture of Charity: Power, Religion, and Gender in North America, 1840–1960" (PhD diss., University of California, Berkeley, 2002).

32  See Jorge Barrerra, "The Horrors of St. Anne's: Ontario Provincial Police Files Obtained by CBC News Reveal the History of Abuse at the Notorious Residential School that Built Its Own Electric Chair," *CBC News*, March 29, 2018, https://newsinteractives.cbc.ca/longform/st-anne-residential-school-opp-documents.

33  Peter Gossage, "Abandoned Children in Nineteenth-Century Montreal" (MA thesis, McGill University, 1983); Peter Gossage, "Les enfants abandonnés à Montréal au 19e siècle: La crèche d'Youville des Soeurs Grises, 1820–1871," *Revue d'histoire de l'Amérique française* 40, no. 4 (Spring 1987): 537–59.

34  Micheline Dumont, "Des garderies au XIXe siècle: Les salles d'asile des Soeurs Grises à Montréal," *Revue d'histoire de l'Amérique française* 34, no. 1 (June 1980): 27–55; Marta Danylewicz, *Taking the Veil: An Alternative to Marriage, Motherhood, and Spinsterhood in Quebec, 1840–1920* (Toronto: McClelland and Stewart, 1987). Montreal's Irish community is particularly devoted to the memory of the Grey Nuns. See, for instance, "Irish Famine Exhibit Celebrates Courage of Montreal's Grey Nuns," *The Gazette*, April 11, 2016.

35  "Historic Sites and Monuments Board of Canada, Application for Designation of the Grey Nuns Mother House, Montreal, Quebec, Canada, Submitted April 1, 2008," section A.3 "Criteria," n.p. (4), RMA.

36  Concordia responded to the TRC's report by developing its own *Indigenous Directions Action Plan*, released in 2019 (see n2). One conclusion was that the university should "investigate Concordia's history in relation to colonialism [and] produce a comprehensive report that includes concrete recommendations" (Recommended Action 3.5, 30). Working with a mandate from the Indigenous Directions Leadership Council, religious scholar Colby Gaudet produced such a report in September 2021, devoting over eighteen thousand words to a detailed account of the Grey Nuns' involvement with residential schools in the west and the north. Titled *Exploring Concordia's Colonial Past*, the report is accompanied by a series of recommendations prepared by the university's Indigenous Directions Leadership Council. At this writing (September 2023), the university has yet to release the report or make a public statement acknowledging the harm done to Indigenous children in schools operated and staffed by the Grey Nuns. A ceremony planned for September 29, 2023, timed to coincide with the Orange Shirt Day and the National Day for Truth and Reconciliation, was postponed at the last minute and has been rescheduled for October 2024.

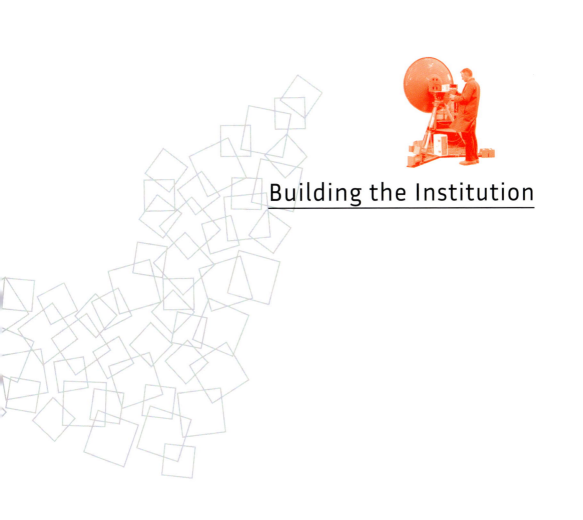

# Building the Institution

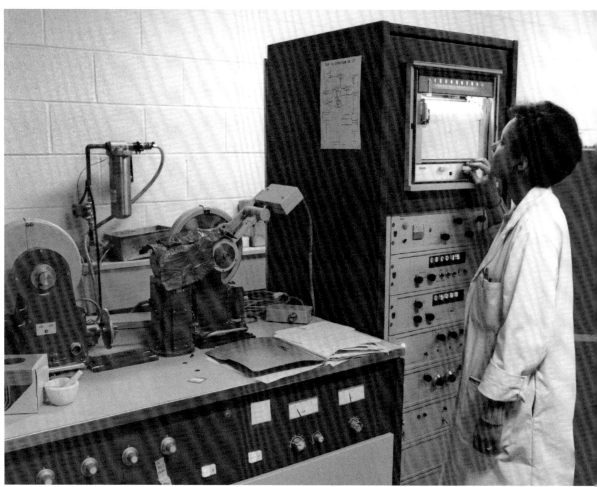

7.1 In this photo chemist Juanita Parris, who completed a MSc in 1987 under the supervision of Professor Georges Denes, works with a powder X-ray diffractometer. This vintage instrument from the 1960s was revived in the mid-1980s, signifying the discipline of chemistry's deep roots at Concordia. At Loyola, distinct courses in the sciences were offered as early as 1921, while at Sir George, chemistry was listed in the first published course calendar in 1934–35.

# A BRIEF HISTORY OF THE FACULTY OF ARTS AND SCIENCE

Miriam Posner

**"Creative Friction": Ten Years of Scholarly Debate**
**LOYOLA COLLEGE AND SIR GEORGE WILLIAMS UNIVERSITY** merged in 1974; however, unlike the Faculties of Engineering and of Commerce and Administration, which merged quickly, a merged Faculty of Arts and Science (FAS) took well over ten years to realize. The question of how and why two traditionally polar opposite and distinct entities, the arts and the sciences, could and should co-exist as one was prevalent throughout and was complex. While it would be an extraordinary task to enumerate all the faculty's turmoils and successes in this brief history, a most humble attempt will be made.

    The strength of the FAS stems from not only its large size and diversity but also an unwavering commitment to traditions embraced by its founding institutions—traditions expressly rooted in meeting the needs of community and in embracing the individual intellectually as a whole via an interdisciplinary and multidisciplinary philosophy of education. As John O'Brien, Concordia's first rector and vice-chancellor, described, the joining of two institutions, "each firmly dedicated to freedom of thought and speech," was expected to come with a certain amount of "creative friction."[1] FAS, without question, did not disappoint in creating a promising future for students and the community at large. Extensive debate focused on understanding the meaning, in a pedagogical sense, of a university education beyond distinct disciplines. Concordia's drive to create a single unified FAS was ahead of its time as demonstrated by recent scholarly deliberations on the necessity of incorporating creative energies explicitly associated with the arts into STEM (science, technology, engineering, and mathematics) to give rise to STEAM (science, technology, engineering, the arts, and mathematics). This and many other similarly oriented initiatives were designed to provide students a well-rounded education for the twenty-first century.[2]

---

MIRIAM POSNER, BSc, MBA, is an alumna and long-serving employee of Concordia. Since being hired in 1974 at Loyola College, she has acquired a broad perspective of university operations through her continuous involvement and service within various levels of the Faculty of Arts and Science and the university.

In anticipation of the merger, Loyola College's Faculty of Science (established in 1942) and its Faculty of Arts consolidated in 1972–73 in the hopes of having a greater voice at the table to negotiate a new arts and science governance structure that would satisfy the needs of the two institutions. Three faculties would be at the table: the Sir George Williams Faculty of Science, the Sir George Williams Faculty of Arts, and the Loyola College Faculty of Arts and Science.

Following three years of intense dialogue post-merger, power struggles, and positional reports, reflecting Concordia's own internal "Quiet Revolution" peppered with controversy, acrimony, bickering, and scholarly deliberations, the merger of FAS seemed to be nearing completion.[3] Demands from Quebec's government to rationalize and merge the university's Loyola and Sir George Williams honours science programs continued to spark debate as to whether there should be a single faculty of arts and science with increased centralization of faculty programs and administration or two separate distinct faculties. These debates consumed Faculty Councils, Senate, and the university's Board of Governors for years. A then surprisingly bold decision to create a system of small units or "colleges" (schools, centres, institutes) within a larger faculty of arts and science suddenly gained wide acceptance for a single faculty. The notion of colleges, initially presented in an academic deans report on the reorganization of the Faculty of Arts and Science to Concordia's Senate in summer 1976, proved extraordinarily helpful in turning the corner towards the creation of a unified faculty of arts and science. The colleges, approved by Senate in spring 1977 and later Concordia's Board of Governors, would be defined by Concordia's realities, and would serve as a means not only for Concordia to differentiate itself from other universities but also to attract new groups of potential students, particularly women and older students at a time when enrolments were declining across North America. The colleges would help solidify the role of Concordia in the Quebec university system and would also minimize the risks of an impersonal, large faculty at a time when large universities were becoming more bureaucratic. Loyola's and Sir George Williams's long histories of emphasizing education for part-time students, while providing quality undergraduate education through innovative structures would remain central to the mission of FAS. Colleges, each with its own principal and physical space, would afford students a personalized learning environment and a broad multidisciplinary educational experience via both traditional and para-academic activities.[4]

Concordia's FAS was finally established on July 1, 1977, and a pilot structure put in place. The new "unified" structure would be comprised of three divisions: the Humanities, the Social Sciences, and the Natural Sciences. Each, led by a divisional dean, would report to a vice-rector academic, arts and science (Russell Breen), one of then two university vice-rectors academic.[5] A fourth division (Division IV), led by a provost (Robert Wall), also reporting to Russell Breen, would oversee the Centre for Interdisciplinary Studies and several smaller units and programs as well as the soon-to-be created colleges.

The creation of the colleges/units was not without its challenges, however. Obstacles included guaranteeing departments the responsibility for curricula while giving newly created colleges/units sufficient input to support their mission and recruiting faculty members or designated fellows whose interests would be diverted from departments and into the Division IV colleges. Although ten to twelve colleges/units were envisioned as part of the reorganization of a new FAS, in testing the waters, an initial decision was made by the university for the creation of four units in September 1978, which included a women's institute named the Simone de Beauvoir Institute to serve as a bridge between the university and the community at large and provide women with essential academic support structures; a Centre for Mature Students, which reflected Sir George Williams's pioneering role in adult education; a college of religious studies (named Lonergan College after Bernard Lonergan, a Loyola student and Jesuit) in an effort to preserve a portion of Loyola's lost identity and minimize declines in enrolment on the Loyola campus; and a Liberal Arts College, steeped in the liberal arts tradition with rigorous course and admission standards. A Science College—focused on sharing knowledge across science-related disciplines and preparing undergraduate students for careers in academia, research, medicine, and the private sector—and a School of Community and Public Affairs—aimed at training individuals to work in government—followed in 1979. Shortly thereafter, an Institute for Co-operative Education, pioneered by the Departments of Chemistry and Biochemistry, Economics, and Mathematics and Statistics, and emphasizing experiential learning through paid work-terms, was formed in 1980, leading the way to the establishment of university-wide co-operative education programs.

More changes were looming. In February 1982 Rector O'Brien implemented a Board of Governors' directive that was driven by budgetary constraints and called for having a single university-wide vice-rector academic, eliminating the position of the vice-rector academic, arts and science. FAS was instructed to re-examine and streamline its administrative structure.[6] The subsequent commissioning of a number of reports and studies led to two more years of turmoil and heated debate within Faculty Council and the Senate, culminating with Concordia's Board of Governors approving a new FAS structure comprised of a single dean and four vice-deans, and with the subsequent elimination of its three divisional deans and provost.[7] On July 1, 1985, Dr. Charles Bertrand was named as the first "super dean" of the faculty.[8] This more centralized structure fostered increased collaborations between the Humanities, Social Sciences, and Natural Sciences sectors, and addressed the needs of the colleges/units previously under Division IV while ensuring the integrity and development of existing programs and disciplines. The faculty's ability to explore and create new interdisciplinary programs was also enhanced, as was its ability to promote academic excellence in research and teaching.[9]

## Highlights: Throughout the Early Years

Despite years of administrative turmoil, financial struggle, and restructuring, FAS never lost sight of its core mission to develop timely curricula and strive for academic excellence. Nor did it waiver from its mission to cultivate community spirit. As a staff member, it is hard for me to forget the summertime baseball games on the Loyola football field, or the excitement of spur-of-the-moment gatherings and coffee breaks with faculty challenging students and staff, and vice versa, where "out of the blue" initiatives were born, some serving as models for other faculties. The development of formalized, pre-legislated faculty-wide safety training in the mid-1980s and teaching assistant orientation training in the early 1990 are but two examples of cross-sector initiatives. The bi-annual David Frosst solstice viewings on the roof of the LB Building was a highlight in the faculty's Department of Geography, Planning, and the Environment. Both campuses were as lively, innovative, and vibrant in the 1970s and 1980s as they are today.

While the construction of new buildings, increased enrolments, increased research, and new programs changed FAS over the years, much has stayed the same with respect to its core mission.[10] The success of the faculty's colleges, centres, schools, and institutes cannot be understated. Strikingly, the Liberal Arts College and the Simone de Beauvoir Institute held a joint reunion in 2003 with over a thousand alumni in attendance. Concordia was one of the first universities in Canada to offer courses in women's studies through the Simone de Beauvoir Institute. The institute remains a leading institution in feminist studies and social justice, honouring the legacy of its namesake as it continues to provide a platform for the critical analysis of gender, sexuality, and women experiences in various social, cultural, and political contexts, while providing interdisciplinary research and community engagement.

The faculty's School of Community and Public Affairs was unique in Canada, providing bilingual undergraduates an opportunity to pursue an interdisciplinary academic program and affording students credited summer work experience as interns in government, organizations, or in the private sector. By 1999 the School of Community and Public Affairs initiated a graduate diploma program in community economic development, the only program of its kind in Eastern Canada and the only one in the country alternating languages between English and French. The Centre for Mature Students, given its effectiveness in the recruitment, retention, and graduation of mature students, was extended university-wide in 1987, moving out of the faculty, and eventually into the university's Centre for Continuing Education in 2007 as the

7.2 The *Thursday Report*, which in 1977 succeeded *FYI* as the main university-sponsored publication, was an important outlet for Concordia news. In this issue from 1984, editors published a letter sent to Rector John O'Brien, expressing opposition to a proposed plan to restructure the administration of the Faculty of Arts and Science.

7.3 The School of Community and Public Affairs was one of several colleges that emerged from restructuring of Faculty of Arts and Science in the late 1970s. Created in 1979, the school hosted its first meeting of the Board of Advisors on November 5, 1980.

Student Transition Centre. By 1986 the Institute for Co-operative Education had established partnerships with departments outside FAS, linking more students with employers; it would become a university-wide institute in the year following. Today, the Institute for Co-operative Education places over two thousand undergraduate and graduate students a year from over seventy academic programs through its flagship, Career Edge (C.Edge), and Accelerated Career Experience (ACE) internship programs, partnering with multinational and small to mid-sized companies in a multitude of fields and sectors, including biotechnology, pharmaceutical, health, finance, accountancy, health, aerospace, engineering, non-profit, government, and others.

A Sports Medicine Clinic, established at Loyola in 1982 by the Department of Exercise Science, was opened to the public, staffed by Montreal-area doctors and physical and athletic therapists, and handled more than six thousand patient visits per year.[11] The clinic currently finds its home in Concordia's School of Health as the School of Health Athletic Therapy Clinic with state-of-the-art facilities and remains an integral resource for the Department of Health, Kinesiology, and Applied Physiology's highly popular and Canadian Athletic Therapists Association–accredited undergraduate program. The program, devoted to training students pursuing careers

7.4 Researchers in the sciences have a long history of sharing lab spaces at Concordia. This picture from 1988 shows physics researcher Shalini Verghese (MSc 1989) performing computer data analysis in H-837, a large lab space in the Hall Building that housed professor Arlin Kipling's Hall effect lab; professor Nelson Eddy's gamma ray lab; and an instrument that Shalini's supervisor, Dr. Shushil Misra, used for electron paramagnetic resonance research.

in the health care of active individuals through high-performance athletes, has seen close to two thousand graduates since its inception.[12]

A Teaching English as a Second Language (TESL) Centre, established at Sir George Williams University in 1973 as an independent academic unit at the request of the Quebec Ministry of Education, had by the mid-1980s earned its place as the largest and most comprehensive teaching English as a second-language centre in Canada. Many of its graduates went on to develop programs internationally (China, Saudi Arabia), and others closer offered TESL off-campus programs to language teachers from St. Jean to Gaspé. In 2001 the centre was dissolved and its programs were formally integrated into the faculty's Department of Education.

The Creative Writing Program, with roots dating back to the 1940s at Sir George Williams, was relaunched in 1968.[13] It was unique in Quebec at the time and has remained a popular program. Clark Blaise, who was a renowned long-time advocate for the literary arts in North America and founder of Concordia's graduate program in creative writing, was one of two creative writers teaching in the Department of English prior to the program's creation; the other was Margaret Atwood. In contrast to the US, creative writing programs were a relatively new and rare phenomenon in

Canada. By the early 2000s, the number of universities offering creative writing programs in Canada had expanded to eight.[14] Over the years, Concordia's students have benefitted from numerous writers-in-residence, including Patrick Lane, Mordecai Richler, Frank R. Scott, Michel Tremblay, Adele Wiseman, Clark Blaise, Irving Layton, Elizabeth Spencer, and Audrey Thomas. In fact, Nino Ricci, author of the bestseller *Lives of the Saints*, received a master's in creative writing from Concordia in 1987.

FAS's Centre for Human Relations and Community Studies, instituted in 1963 to familiarize businesspeople, community leaders, educators, and others with group dynamics and associated decision-making and leadership skills, had established Canada's longest running trainer development program. Today, having provided services to over 375 organizations and delivering hundreds of workshops open to the public, the centre remains one of Canada's most established programs and pivotal in the development of curriculum and academic programs such as the family life education and community service certificate programs, and the master's program in human systems intervention.

In the late 1980s, the faculty's Department of Applied Social Science (now Applied Human Sciences) in collaboration with the Cree School Board jointly administered on-site programs, adapted to the needs of the province's Indigenous people in Northern Quebec. The program to deliver a certificate in community service was extended in 1999 to include students from Kahnawà:ke and Kanesatake. As the faculty's focus on decolonization and Indigenization continued to evolve, a First Peoples studies undergraduate program, after numerous years in development by the School of Community and Public Affairs in partnership with Concordia's Centre for Native Education (now the Otsenhákta Student Centre), was introduced in fall 2010.[15] Today, the program, designed to build bridges towards a mutual understanding of Quebec society and First Peoples, and introduce students to the world of First Peoples (First Nations, Inuit, and Métis), remains paramount in Concordia's efforts to promote and develop Indigenous-led scholarly and community work.

FAS's commitment to graduate studies was noticeable and by the mid-to-late 1980s many of its programs had acquired national and international recognition.[16] By 1995 the number of graduate programs within FAS sat at forty-five, more than half of those offered by Concordia, and with others on their way. Today, the faculty offers more than sixty-five graduate programs.

At the same time in 1985, the faculty's research profile was growing with $4,155,203 in grants and other research awards, highlighted by an Action Structurante grant in the Department of Chemistry, culminating in the creation of the Concordia's Centre for Picosecond Spectroscopy, which, at the time, was at the forefront nanomaterials research, and the Centre for Studies in Behavioral Neurobiology's Fonds pour la formation de chercheurs et l'aide à recherche grant renewal. Concordia

7.5 The Centre for Mature Students, which was established in 1978 with a mandate to carry on the tradition of making education accessible to adults with varying levels of education, regularly hosted talks aimed at a broad public. This event, advertised in *Thursday Report*, featured John E. O'Brien, the founder of Loyola's Department of Communication Arts (now Communication Studies).

had joined universities across North America in the burgeoning field of biotechnology with Concordia's FAS faculty holding patents on bacteria developed for industrial purposes. By 1995 close to 50 percent (or $6,795,670) of grants and contracts awarded to Concordia were in FAS, and the faculty housed numerous research centres, including the Centre for Broadcasting Studies, established in 1981, which also serves as the official legal depository of radio drama scripts and ancillary drama materials of the Canadian Broadcasting Corporation dating back to the 1920s, and since 2002 has housed the Diniacopoulos/BBC World Radio News Collection (1969–1986); the Centre for Research in Human Development; the Centre for Community and Ethic Studies; the Centre interuniversitaire en calcul mathématique algébrique, created in 1989 as North America's first research centre in computational algebra; as well as the Centre for Picosecond Spectroscopy and the Centre for the Studies of Behavioral Neurobiology.[17] Today, over twenty-seven university and faculty research centres and institutes are home to arts and science faculty researchers and provide infrastructure for researchers to mobilize local communities, influence national issues, and engage in global thinking. From 2018 to 2022, grants and contracts awarded to FAS researchers have continued to flourish, totalling over $150 million.

FAS has clearly gained national and international recognition for its teaching and research. The work of Professor Emeritus Jane Stewart of the Department of

Psychology exemplifies this progress. Dr. Stewart is renowned for her research on the neurochemical and behavioural aspects of drug use. Her persistence in the early 1960s to have a sink installed in what was an office space enabled her to conduct experimental research in her field. Ultimately, Dr. Stewart is to be credited, while serving as chair of the department, with the growth and success of experimental psychology research at Concordia and the establishment of its PhD program in the early 1970s, and in 1983 along with three of her colleagues, with co-founding Centre for Studies in Behavioral Neurobiology, which brought together more than a hundred dedicated researchers from Concordia, McGill, and the Université de Montréal to study neural and psychological mechanisms that focused on addiction, motivation, and relapse. Today, the Department of Psychology is internationally recognized as a leader in clinical and experimental research and teaching.

## Budget Cuts: Restructuring, Rejuvenation, and Renovation

As departments began the process of consolidating in the 1980s on one of two campuses, there were challenges and struggles. Space was limited, as were funds. It took close to thirty years for the Department of Psychology's clinical and experimental operations to consolidate under one umbrella on the Loyola campus. Hall Building corridors were converted into office and lab spaces, the Departments of Exercise Science, Biology, Chemistry, and Physics shared lab spaces for undergraduate teaching on the Loyola campus. Loyola's Jesuit hand-crafted lab furniture was reassembled on the Sir George campus to provide undergraduate students with a much-needed scientific instrumentation laboratory, which further brought the two campuses together.

Between 1995 and 1999, FAS and the university faced additional challenges. The provincial government slashed Concordia's funding, similar to other Quebec universities, by about 25 percent. This drop in funding coincided with a planned rebuilding and revitalization of Concordia's campuses.

In 1995–96, FAS, with 45 graduate programs and 118 of Concordia's 182 undergraduate programs, phased out several its programs. The Departments of Geology, Library Studies, and Theological Studies were most impacted, as well as some graduate programs.[18]

The push to explore new initiatives, including a redesigned general degree in arts and science, gave rise to the notion of interdisciplinary clusters or groups of already existing courses around individual themes. Interdisciplinary clusters provided a judicious balance between concentrated study and one's broader interests and served to recruit students and market faculty programs within a tight economic framework. Clusters provided multidisciplinary course content, over and above that already being offered through the faculty's colleges, centres, schools, and institutes, and created opportunities for students to build a strong foundation for furthering their studies

7.6 Professor Jane Stewart, former director of the Center for Studies in Behavioral Neurobiology, shown working in her lab in 1995. A decorated researcher and member of the Order of Canada, Stewart was also named a "Great Concordian" during the university's fortieth anniversary in 2014.

and/or for entering the labour market.[19] Students in the arts could learn the principles of science, and science students could take a cluster of life science courses to prepare them for entry into medical school, or a cluster focused in Quebec culture or the basics of business.

Budget cuts further necessitated a university-wide early retirement program for faculty and staff in 1996, which led to a wave of departures and ultimately to the hiring of a new generation of professors with increased research activities. Replenishing FAS's faculty ranks would take close to ten years to be fully realized. By 1997 FAS had lost 28 percent or 108 members of its faculty complement, and by 2001 it had hired 106 full-time professors, becoming one of the most active faculties in Canada in terms of creating new positions, and with plans to hire another 100 professors over the next three to four years.[20] This influx of research-active professors contributed greatly to the recognition of FAS as a leader, nationally and internationally, with respect to both its graduate and undergraduate programs, and to its reputation for academic excellence. By fall 2001 faculty student enrolments had climbed to their highest level with over 13,000 undergraduates and with increased graduate enrolments; stepped-up marketing and student recruitment efforts resulted in a 60 percent increase of the faculty's international student cohort.

As research and enrolments grew, so too did FAS's need for adequate facilities. To address these needs, the university had initiated a building construction program and campaign in 1995–96 to raise $350 million. The construction of a $85-million Loyola Science Complex (named the Richard J. Renaud Science Complex), the first of the program's milestones, was completed in fall 2003, enhancing the visibility of the sciences within the faculty and the university.[21] With a new generation of professors and new state-of-the-art facilities designed to foster interdisciplinarity and innovation through a multitude of open collaborative spaces, the faculty's research profile continued to expand and mature. Five new Canada Research Chairs were awarded to the faculty in 2004 in the areas of neurobiology of drug abuse; globalization, citizenship, and social justice; development psychopathology; genome evolution; and biological chemistry

The revitalization of the Loyola campus and the faculty continued with a major renovation of Drummond Science Building (now the CJ Building). The "new" CJ Building, with a scheduled opening date in spring 2005, would house the Department of Communication Studies and the Department of Journalism, both with storied pasts. The beginnings of Communication Arts (renamed Communication Studies in October 1976) could be traced back to a Society of Jesus conference in Rome (1963), a papal ecumenical letter that noted the growing importance of media and the need to study it further, and a time when Marshall McLuhan, Canada's own communications guru who once lectured at Loyola College, was jolting academia with his ideas about the impact of mass media in the modern age. In the following year, 1964, Father John O'Brien, returning from Rome, offered an extremely popular and extraordinarily successful communications arts course that could be taken as a substitute for English. Hence, the Communication Arts program and the Department of Communications were born in 1965, graduating Canada's first communications BAs in 1967.[22] Many of the department's graduates have gone on to successful careers in broadcasting and journalism, including Hana Gartner, Carmel Kilkenny, Bob O'Reilly (Radio Canada International), Michel-Claude Lavoie (the Canadian version of *Sesame Street*), sex columnist Josey Vogels, and Me Mom and Morgentaler alumna Kim Bingham. The Department of Journalism, founded in 1975, had a nomad-like past. It was originally located in a Mackay Street annex that housed apartment units before moving to the top floor of an annex (TJ) that housed an elementary school on the Loyola campus to be closer to the Department of Communication Studies, moving once again in 1986 into the Bryan Building and then into Hingston Hall in 2001, along with the Department of Communication Studies, to allow for the construction of the Science Complex while awaiting completion of its new home in the CJ Complex. Montreal-recognized graduates of the Department of Journalism include Daniele Hamamdjian, Jamie Orchard, Andrew Carter, and Maya Johnson, the first Black women to helm an anchor desk at CTV Montreal.

7.7 Faculty members from the Department of Communication Arts shown here in the early 1970s. *From left to right*: Ross Dolinsky, Charles Gagnon, Pat Paris, Don Clark, Father John E. O'Brien, Gail Guthrie Valaskakis, Father Marc Gervais, John Buell. Communication Arts became the Department of Communication Studies in 1976.

With renovations not limited to the Loyola campus, the Departments of Economics, Sociology and Anthropology, Political Science, and Geography, Planning and the Environment moved in 2006 into newly renovated spaces on the eleventh and twelfth floors of the Hall Building on the Sir George campus, providing the much-needed infrastructure to support expanding research activities, new hires, and new academic programs.

Revitalization initiatives continued at Loyola in 2010–11 with the construction of the Genomics Building, which today houses Concordia's Centre for Applied Synthetic Biology, and in 2020 with the construction of a state-of-the-art Applied Science Hub to focus on next-generation collaborative research and training in science and engineering, as well as increased industrial partnerships. It is home to the Centre for Microscopy and Cellular Imaging and the Centre for NanoScience Research and includes facilities for bioprocessing and aquatic research.

7.8 The Drummond Science Complex, picture here in 1988, first opened in 1961. Its modern design represented a departure in Loyola College's buildings and architecture.

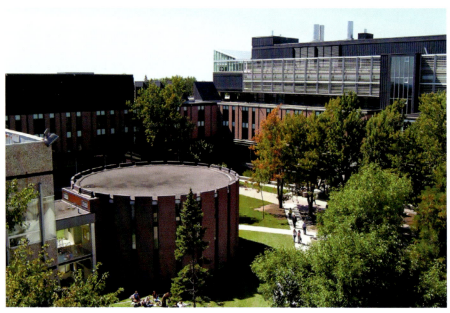

7.9 The Richard J. Renaud Science Pavilion officially opened September 22, 2003. The building design changed the face of the west end of the Loyola campus. The pavilion contains some of the university's most state-of-art facilities and labs.

7.10 Journalism students in the television studio with instructor Paul Gott, 2016.

## Going Forward

The transition to the new unifying administrative structure in 1985, initially implemented as a five-year challenge, has undoubtedly proven to be a success. Today, FAS remains core to the mission of Concordia and continues to operate under the leadership of one dean (Dr. Pascale Sicotte), five associate deans, one vice-dean, and a number of shared governing bodies in meeting today's ever-changing and evolving social, cultural, environmental, and economic demands.

With equity, inclusion, and diversity at the forefront of our university's mission, it will be key for FAS to stay engaged with its communities through various initiatives, whether through the interdisciplinary research activities of the engAGE Centre, which explores creative ways to study age and enhance health and well-being through collaborations with older people, community groups, health care practitioners, and industry partners; the development of innovative curricula such as the major in interdisciplinary studies in sexuality, offered jointly by the Faculty of Fine Arts and FAS with its curriculum spanning a variety of disciplines comprising art history, film studies, history, literature, and others in investigating empirical, theoretical, and creative aspects of sexuality; the research activities of the Faculty's Loyola Sustainability Research Centre or Concordia's Institute for Inclusive, Investigative and

7.11 Professor Steven High with a group of students enrolled in his public history seminar, which was tethered to courses in theatre, art education, and art history. The seminar was focused on the working-class history of Montreal's Pointe Saint-Charles neighbourhood.

7.12 PhD students Scott de Jong and Bipasha Sultana prepare the Ageing + Communications + Technology (ACT) Lab's Escape Room on older adult mistreatment. This was part of the event *B/OLD: Aging in our City* held at Concordia's 4$^{TH}$ Space, May 2019.

Innovative Journalism; Exposcience, a thirty-seven-year-old initiative that brings science and technology out of the classroom and into the community in fostering interest in youth; or through other exciting endeavours.

While administrative structures, curricula, and research initiatives are expected to evolve in response to, and to remain in sync with, the ever-changing social, cultural, technological, political, and environmental demands of the present and of the future, the past fifty years of growth and overcoming hurdles will remind us that opportunities are endless when spirited discussion, bottom-up perseverance, and interconnectedness between disciplines, other faculties, and community partners are encouraged and welcomed.

Concordia's FAS, only one of five combined arts and science faculties remaining in Canada today, including the University of Toronto, Queen's University, the University of Saskatchewan, and the Université de Montréal, will continue to flourish as a leader and powerhouse of scholarship, innovative research, and community engagement given its strengths, diversity, resilience, and demonstrated adaptability to change. Without doubt, a combined Faculty of Arts and Science is best positioned for next-gen learning: "preparing students through real-world, blended and interactive education."[23]

Clearly, the faculty's struggles over the years have been instrumental in its development and its successes, with more in its future!

**NOTES**

1   John O'Brien, "Concordia Begins" (Dr. John O'Brien, Rectors' Address), Loyola Alumnus, September 1974, 1, https://archive.org/details/loyola-alumnus-1974-sept.

2   For more on STEAM, see Martin Braund and Michael J. Reiss, "The 'Great Divide': How the Arts Contribute to Science and Science Education," *Canadian Journal of Science, Mathematics, and Technology Education*, no. 19 (2019): 219–36, https://doi.org/10.1007/s42330-019-00057-7; and Benjamin Miller and Fiona White, "Why Arts and Science Are Better Together," *The Conversation*, June 24, 2013, https://theconversation.com/why-arts-and-science-are-better-together-15004.

3   See Christy McCormick, "Concordia in Review: Merger Near Completion," *Thursday Report* 1, no. 14 (December 8, 1977): 2–3.

4   For more on the reasons behind the creation of the colleges, see the "April 2005" entry description in the Concordia University *Thirtieth Anniversary Calendar, 2004–2005*, Records Management and Archives (hereafter RMA).

5   Division I (the Humanities, Dean W. Aiken) comprised Classics, Communication Studies, English, French, History, Journalism, Library Studies, Modern Languages and Linguistics, Philosophy, Teaching English as a Second Language, and Theological Studies; Division II (the Social Sciences, Dean J. Chaikelson): Andragogy, Applied Social Science, Economics, Education, Geography, Political Science, Psychology, Religion, Sociology and Anthropology; and Division III (the Natural Sciences, Dean M. Cohen): Biology, Bio-physical Education, Chemistry, Geology, Health Education, Mathematics, Physics.

6   See two special editions of *Thursday Report*, September 16 and 28, 1982. The September 16 issue was called "Looking into the Future: Report of the Committee on Planning and Priorities,"

https://archive.org/details/thursday-report-1982-september-16. The September 28 edition was called "Looking to the Future: Phase I Report of the University Mission," https://archive.org/details/thursday-report-1982-september-28-phase-i-report.

7   See, for example, the Breen report, *Comments and Recommendations Submitted to the Council of the Loyola Faculty of Arts and Science on the Future of Science at Concordia*, FYI 3, no. 1 (September 30, 1976): 9–16; and Peat Marwick, *Study on Mission and Strategy for the 80's Report*, December 16, 1982, I0038 Academic Planning Office fonds, RMA.

8   Members of the leadership team included a vice-dean curriculum and administrative affairs (Dr. Denis Dicks); a vice-dean research, space, and technical services (Dr. Paul Albert); a vice-dean student affairs (Dr. F.E. Schlosser); and a vice-dean academic planning (Dr. Gail Valaskakis).

9   For more on the history of FAS and Sir George Williams, see Douglass B. Clarke, "Decades of Decision: Sir George Williams University, 1952–53 to 1972–73," unpublished typescript, Concordia University, 1973.

10  At a glance, in 2023, FAS was comprised of over 850 full-time and part-time faculty members, with over 17,000 undergraduate and 2,500 graduate students, and 267 undergraduate programs and 125,000 alumni worldwide. See Concordia University, Faculty of Arts and Science, "About the Faculty," accessed November 30, 2023, https://www.concordia.ca/artsci/about.html.

11  The Department of Exercise Science was initially created in 1973 as the Department of Bio-physical Education, and has since been renamed the Department of Health, Kinesiology, and Applied Physiology (HKAP).

12  Number of graduates estimated from discussions with Patrice Desaulniers, technical officer, HKAP (March 2023).

13  On the establishment of the new Creative Writing seminar, see *The Georgian* 23, no. 24 (September 20, 1967): 12.

14  For more on creative writing programs in Canada, see Stephen Guppy, "Creative Writing in Canada: A Brief Overview of Degree Programs," *TEXT: Journal of the Australian Association of Writing Programs* 7, no. 1 (April 29, 2003).

15  See *Concordia Journal* 5, no. 18 (June 17, 2010): 2.

16  Programs that acquired national and international recognition, included a master's program in media studies, Quebec's only such program designed for working professionals with experience in media or media-related fields; a master's in public policy and administration, specifically designed for students envisioning a career in the civil service and the only one of its kind being offered in Quebec; a doctoral program in educational technology, the only such English-language doctoral program in Canada; as well as graduate programs in religion and Judaic studies, the department being the first in North America to house an endowed chair in Hindu studies. The Departments of Biology and Chemistry and Biochemistry jointly administered Quebec's only graduate program in ecotoxicology (approved by Senate in 1984) with a focus on living organisms in relation to environmentally impacting social, technological, and economic factors. Other newly developed graduate programs included a doctoral program in religious studies offered jointly by Concordia and l'Université du Québec à Montréal, a master of arts program in child study and a diploma in journalism.

17  For more on the Centre of Broadcast Studies, see *Thursday Report* 5, no. 11 (November 12, 1981): 2.

18  For additional details, see Barbara Black, "Arts and Science Starts Restructuring," *Thursday Report* 20, no. 18 (March 7, 1996).

19  Six clusters, each comprised of fifteen to eighteen course credits, were introduced as a pilot project in fall 1996, and have since been renamed Elective Groups. Expanding to sixteen and open to students in other faculties, they include The Basics of Business; Econometrics and Programming; Health and Lifestyle; Hellenic Studies; Introduction to Life Sciences; Knowledge-Implementation, Networking, and Decision-Making (KIND); Legal Studies,

Management, Marketing, Indigenous Studies, The Planet Earth: Studies in the Environment; Preparing for Success in the Workplace; Quebec Studies; Spanish America; Sustainability Studies; Understanding Western Myth.

20  By 2003–04, FAS had lost close to 200 professors due to both early and regular retirements and had hired 198 new tenure-track professors.

21  The Richard J. Renaud Science Complex features 330 research laboratories and support rooms as well as 100 teaching labs and classrooms, uniting faculty, staff, and students from the Departments of Biology, Chemistry and Biochemistry, Exercise Science (now Health, Kinesiology, and Applied Physiology), Physics, as well as a major component of Psychology. Other units housed in the complex included the Science College, the Centre for Structural and Functional Genomics, the Centre for Studies in Behavioral Neurobiology, as well as several smaller research centres.

22  Today's Department of Communication Studies offers four undergraduate programs: a major and specialization in communication studies, a major in communication and cultural studies, and a specialization in communications and journalism; a one-year graduate diploma program, a master's in media program, and a PhD program (now autonomous, but formerly offered jointly since 1987 with the Université de Montreal and the UQAM).

23  Concordia University, "Next-Gen Student Learning," accessed November 30, 2023, https://www.concordia.ca/next-gen/learning/student_learning.html.

8.1 *stargazing traincrash* dress rehearsal for year-end performance, D.B. Clarke Theatre, April 2016. Dancers: Bradley Eng and Mathilde Loselier-Pellerin. Choreography by Lena Boss. Music by Shertenlaib and Jegerlehner.

# EXPANDING ENERGIES: THE FACULTY OF FINE ARTS

Catherine MacKenzie

*(Images selected with the assistance of David Elliot)*

**IN 1972 QUEBEC'S CONSEIL** des universités approved the fine arts as a major area of development for Sir George Williams University (SGWU), an institution with an unexpectedly vibrant Department of Fine Arts formed eleven years earlier. The merger of Loyola College, with more limited visual and performing arts activities, and SGWU did not include the establishment of a fully-fledged Faculty of Fine Arts (FoFA). Instead, its creation became one of the earliest, decidedly bold decisions taken by Concordia University: fine arts had been treated in a variety of ways inside and outside the Canadian university system, and only two comprehensive university faculties had been created before 1974. Equally bold was the new faculty's rapid development of a rigorous MFA in studio arts and an innovative PhD in art education. Issued was a fierce commitment to graduate studies, counterintuitive for those, including granting agencies, who considered the fine arts as forms of personal expression worthy of undergraduate exploration but not for inclusion in research traditions associated with advanced academic work.

The faculty graduated its first students in May 1975. Spirits were high, with faculty exhibitions and student festivals functioning as bonding events, although settling in absorbed energy. Fine Arts Faculty Council was eventually formalized in 1977 and its members, including students and, unusually, part-time faculty, laboured over pedagogical principles and administrative structures, finally deciding in 1981 for the traditional option of academic departments.[1] All this took place during a scramble to convert a used-car dealership on Crescent Street into a home for undergraduate visual arts, the resulting Visual Arts Building opening in 1979.[2] Still, the faculty was spread across two campuses in owned and rented buildings, some quite rustic,

---

PROFESSOR EMERITA CATHERINE MACKENZIE received her doctorate in art history from the University of Toronto in 1984. Following a decade of administrative activities at Concordia, her academic work focused on feminist art histories, Western representations of racialized "others," and the ongoing impact of art looting under the National Socialists.

separating performing arts units from their visual arts partners for decades. When the former departments were moved downtown in 2009, into purpose-built premises on De Maisonneuve Boulevard, they lost easy access to several facilities. Happily, they benefitted from research labs and exhibition spaces in the nearby Engineering/Visual Arts (EV) Building on Sainte Catherine Street, open since 2005.[3] The east side of that structure had become and remains the third major domicile for visual arts departments. There, a faculty-wide gallery with vitrines reaches out to the thousands who daily spill out of the Guy-Concordia metro station.[4]

Overcoming geography, the faculty found ways early on to fulfil its aspirations, notwithstanding the high costs of much fine arts education. In many areas, small classes, specialized equipment, and creative technical staff helped students translate visions into reality, and administrative staff handled auditions, portfolio reviews, rehearsals, and required internships. Yet early growth in program options was remarkably robust, as the Office of Student Affairs dealt with a growing cadre of full- and part-time students, almost 50 percent of whom listed French as their maternal language. In 1979 alone, modern dance joined music and theatre as the third of the performing arts, while a diploma program in art therapy, a discipline entirely new to Canadian universities, was prepared.[5]

During the 1980s and 1990s, departments continued to unfurl programs. The faculty simultaneously moved across departmental boundaries, true to the nature of artistic practice. Indeed, a course titled The Visual and Performing Arts in Canada became mandatory for all undergraduate students, a decision that, with content modifications, has held since 1996. Pressing social issues propelled cross-faculty innovation, as in 1987 with the minor in women and the fine arts, which incorporated courses from the Simone de Beauvoir Institute, and again in 1994 with the trailblazing HIV/AIDS: Social, Cultural and Scientific Aspects of the Pandemic course, staffed by fine arts and arts and science personnel.[6] According to a former student, Dr. Erin Silver, now at the University of British Columbia, the latter course "instilled the importance of social responsibility, providing opportunities, through community internships and curatorial endeavours, to contribute actively to initiatives serving HIV/AIDS community organizations."[7] The increasing involvement of students (and supervising faculty members) in independent and humanities graduate programs generated many buoyant interdisciplinary projects.

The adventurous 1990s were also taxing for the faculty as pressure to explore new technologies collided with fiscal restraint. A digital film animation stream was introduced in 1996, while programs in digital image/sound in the fine arts, initiated in collaboration with the Faculty of Engineering and Computer Science, started in 1996, with enrolment increases to other programs offsetting costs. More firmly securing the faculty's capacity to address recent technologies was the 2001 formation

8.2 A 1977 exhibition announcement for the first group show of fine arts faculty in which forty-six artists participated. Photos in the poster are by photographer and Fine Arts professor Gabor Szilasi.

of Hexagram / Institute of Research/Creation in Media Arts and Technology, which gathered Concordia and Université du Québec à Montréal (UQAM) fine arts researchers and their graduate students into clusters to address areas such as immersive environments and interactive textiles/wearable computers. In articulating the notion of research-creation—innovative knowledge produced through the combined forces of artistic expression, scholarly investigation, and experimentation—a small group of professors, most from studio arts, enabled Hexagram to access new resources for strategic research. By 2004 funding of some $30 million had been acquired and the faculty soon qualified for its first Canada Research Chair (CRC), Dr. Xin Wei Sha, a joint appointment in New Media Arts with Engineering and Computer Science.[8] Once the EV Building opened, state-of-the-art facilities became available, later inherited by the university-wide Milieux Institute for Arts, Culture and Technology after Hexagram morphed into an international research network.

Hexagram's initial model of physically proximate teams inspired the astonishing number of research communities now hosted in the faculty, not all focused on new

THE FACULTY OF FINE ARTS  89

8.3 A Fine Arts Student Alliance Art Matters Poster from 2001. Created in 2000 by fine arts students, the annual Art Matters festival features two weeks of Concordia student art in professional venues and galleries throughout Montreal. The festival exhibits all art produced by Concordia students: animation, dance, design, film, music, spoken word, theatre, video, and visual art.

technologies. These bring together professors, students, research professionals, and affiliates from other faculties, universities, and external communities. Professors and their students have also become central to Concordia's Indigenous Futures Research Centre (founded 2021),[9] and the many Milieux clusters. In short, the faculty's research culture is an indelible part of what Studio Arts Professor Emerita Lynn Hughes describes as Concordia's "international leadership in research-creation."

Increasingly visible in teaching and research are considerations of sustainability in environmental, social, cultural, and economic realms. Strongly encouraged by student constituencies, the critiquing of hegemonic knowledge-formation systems is seen as urgent. Activities of recent Concordia University Research Chair (CURC) Hannah Claus in Onkwehonwené:ha epistemology (Studio Arts), Dr. Angelique Willkie, CURC in Ecologies of B/black Performance (Contemporary Dance), and Dr. Balbir K. Singh, CRC in Art and Racial Justice (Art History)—along with sharpened recruiting practices, and enhanced outreach and internship activities—signal the desire to ensure authentic inclusivity for important, actionable conversations to come.

The faculty defies capture through generalities. Below are more focused accounts of existing departments.[10] Sadly, that which matters most—the accomplishments of individual faculty, staff, students, who now number over four thousand a year, and alumni—still remain largely invisible. So too does the support of external communities: often it has allowed seven successive deans—Alfred Pinsky, Anthony Emery, Robert Parker, Christopher Jackson, Catherine Wild, Rebecca Duclos, and Annie Gérin—to preserve a hungry enterprise. This chapter simply suggests that Concordia served itself well when it founded the Faculty of Fine Arts and went on to accept its proliferating creative energies.

## Looking More Closely

The strength of the Department of Art Education, guided by the late Professor Leah Sherman's insistence on nurturing genuine artist-teachers, led the 1968–69 Commission d'enquête sur l'enseignement des arts au Québec to designate SGWU as the only English-language university authorized to certify art specialists teaching in schools.[11] This muscle, along with BFA, diploma, and MA degrees in art education migrated to Concordia, and quickly established the faculty's first doctoral program, to this day drawing art education students from around the world.

As Professor Emerita Elizabeth Sacca recalls, "the concept of John Dewey's 'Art as Experience' guided faculty members when practising art teachers turned to Concordia. They sought support for their own development in art, improvements in their teaching, and help in addressing research questions arising from their teaching and art," all challenges embedded in the education the department offered to its students. "Quebec and Canadian students," she continues, "engaged with students

8.4 The remodelled car garage on René Levesque Boulevard between Bishop and Crescent that would become the Faculty of Fine Arts' new Visual Arts Building in 1979.

from five other continents in a rich milieu of give-and-take where faculty's diverse perspectives on art and research ranged from personal inquiry to the scientific. In hindsight, this diversity was a good start, but missed major phenomenon, such as the development of child art in the Black public schools in the US. Attention to Indigenous art in Quebec, Canada, and around the world was limited."

Dr. Kathleen Vaughan, CURC in Art + Education for Sustainable and Just Futures, speaks to the expansive intentions of the current department: "We encourage our undergraduate and graduate artist-teachers to find a way, through research-creation, of knowing, thinking, and feeling through the arts that aims to extend boundaries of knowledge, build inclusive relationships with others (human and other-than-human), and orient the public pedagogies of their creative work towards fostering a more just and sustainable world." In 2018 Dr. Vivek Venkatesh became UNESCO Co-chair in the Prevention of Radicalization and Violent Extremism, an indication of the weighty expectations for the Department of Art Education.

The independent *Journal of Canadian Art History* was created as what became the Department of Art History transited from SGWU to Concordia. As Professor Emerita Sandra Paikowsky, CM, the journal's guide for decades, contends, "it reflects the department's inherited commitment to the field and created a broad national community," occasionally accepting texts from students in the department's pioneering MA program, for many years unique in its focus on art in Canada. The Gail

8.5 Professor Raymonde April, *Quebec City, June 1978* (2016), from the group installation of eleven monumental photographs for the public exhibition *Outre-vie/Afterlife—How Many Seas?* facing the seashore on the Bandra Carter Road bandstand in Mumbai, India. Organized by the Afterlife group in collaboration with What About Art? Mumbai, India.

and Stephen A. Jarislowsky Institute for Studies in Canadian Art (founded in 2001) and the Canadian Women Artists History Initiative (founded in 2008) further engage students and scholars in the field through archival holdings and conferences.

A 1988 overhaul of the major in art history and the major in art history and studio art strengthened the department's profile. Theoretical and methodological issues, such as feminist and gender-based analyses of art and art history were systematically confronted and medium-based offerings ensured stronger support for crafts, new technologies, and eventually photography. Courses on Indigenous art and on the impact of colonialism and racism on the production of Western art and art history were added in 1996. The bilingual interuniversity PhD in art history (1999) and the joint major in art history and film studies (2002) inherited these probative perspectives.

Art history students disseminate insights through student-organized conferences and journals. As Dr. Cynthia Hammond notes, "The department has a long tradition of engaged learning inside and outside the classroom. From 'walking tour' architecture courses to more recent seminars that result in publications like the *Jerusalem Art History Journal*, art historical pedagogy at Concordia is richly interdisciplinary and oriented towards embodied knowledge and professional outcomes." Increasingly, she observes, "students engage with the vitality and politics

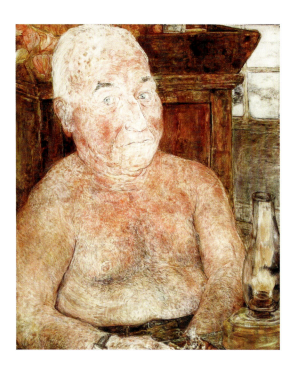

8.6 *Alfie* (1984) by Professor Marion Wagschal. Portrait of Alfred Pinsky, Concordia's first Dean of Fine Arts.

of culture. The Right to the City project (2014–17), for example, brought students into a de-industrializing neighbourhood, asking them to learn with older residents' memories of urban change, and partnered with non-profit organizations to showcase research and creation." Graduated students have tended to be neither timid nor lacking in success in their careers.

Informed by teaching from film studies Professor John Locke, students in 1970 made some two hundred films in the SGWU Department of Fine Arts. Understandably, the new faculty sought a full film mandate. Once obtained, highly competitive programs proliferated: BFA (1977 forward, with streams developed in animation, production, and studies); MFA stream in film production (1988); MA in film studies (1998); and a PhD in film and moving image studies (2008). What since 1999 has been called the Mel Hoppenheim School of Cinema, named for an unstinting benefactor, is currently introducing professionally oriented microprograms, certificates, and diplomas to further Quebec's film industry.

It is easy to construct a dazzling history of awards for faculty, alumni, and student productions, as well as for groundbreaking research in critical analyses of film and moving images. Indeed, Jutra and Academy Award nomination times have long been on the university calendar, as is the student-run year-end screening of films. Arguably this success has been aided by studying films, whenever possible, in their original formats. Dr. Peter Rist, Film Studies, can unfold a series of initiatives, beginning in 1992, that took "full and part-time faculty and students far afield to experience what was not readily accessible otherwise." Cuba, Argentina, and Burkina Faso were visited,

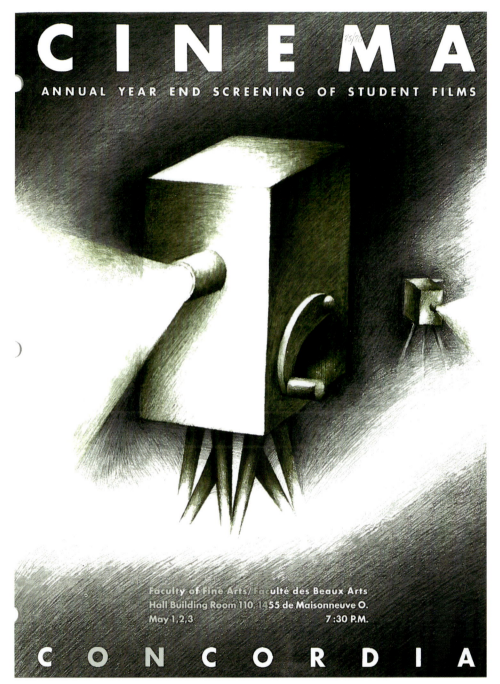

8.7 Cinema year-end screening program cover, 1986.

8.8 Mel Hoppenheim of Cinema PhD students, Patrick Brodie (*left*) and Patrick Brian Smith (*right*) discuss Global Emergent Media Lab initiatives at the annual open house, October 2017. The two co-led the lab's Works-in-Progress Colloquium series in 2017–18.

8.9 Art Hives table at Concordia Student Union Community Street Fair, September 2017. Originally seeded by Professor Janis Timm-Bottos in 2010, Art Hives are inclusive community art studios that welcome everyone as an artist and active contributor to society and culture. This public arts-based therapies and social inclusion initiative is now a network connecting 280 therapeutic, creative spaces in communities and institutions worldwide, positioning Concordia as a national leader in non-clinical campus and community mental health.

8.10 *A Midsummer Night's Dream* performance by the Centre for the Arts in Human Development in the Department of Creative Arts Therapies, February 22, 2011. Since 1996 the centre has been a primary clinical training site for more than three hundred interns providing art, drama, music, and dance/movement therapies for adults with neurodiversity and developmental disabilities. The centre has mounted thirteen original musical shows and involved over three hundred adults and their families since its inception.

relations were opened up with academies in China, and in 2007 an exchange agreement was formalized with Cuba's famed Escuela Internacional de Cine y Televisión.

Production programs tackled digital technologies in the late 1990s. New equipment, editing software, and revised technical support were needed, as were changes to teaching strategies. Marielle Nitoslawska, CURC in Experimental Nonfiction Practices, reflects on this era: "The new millennium inaugurated the category of 'research-creation' with Hexagram prioritizing 'new media' innovation in technology, often to the detriment of cinema and other forms of 'traditional' media that saw technology as a means, not an end." She continues, "When interest in newness waned, research-creation was buttressed with critical theory largely developed by scholars. Today we are on the cusp of another transformation, animated by international discussions around embodied ways of knowing in artistic research. Gone are the binaries of 'new' versus 'old' media." The 2023 restructuring of the MFA in film production to cinematic arts, the awarding of a CRC in Media and Migration to Ishita Tiwary, and the presence of many faculty members and graduate students in interdisciplinary, cross-faculty research clusters such as the Global Emergent Media Lab, directed by CRC in Global Emergent Media, Dr. Joshua Neves, register confidence on the part of those in Canada's largest centre for the practice and study of cinematic arts.

8.11 Professor Charles Ellison and the Jazz Improvisation class II, 2016.

8.12 Professor Barbara Layne working on an AVL Dobby Loom, an early venture into combining art and technology, 1994–95. The loom was first used in an internet project called Fault Lines: Measurement, Distance, and Place, linking looms in Los Angeles and Montreal, organized by Ingrid Bachmann and Barbara Layne. Students can still use the loom for their coursework in the fibres program.

For several years "art hives" on both campuses, guided by creative art therapists and students, have provided Concordians and Montrealers with creation environments designed to relieve stress. This is but one of many consequences of the faculty's 1979 decision to establish offerings in art therapy, initially a diploma and soon afterwards an option in the art education master's program. In 1997, the now-independent MA degree was joined by the MA in drama therapy developed in the Department of Theatre, where students participated in the much-heralded Centre for the Arts in Human Development. Such energies led to the formation of the Department of Creative Arts Therapies (CATS) in 2005 and expedited a partner degree in music (2010), a more recent graduate certificate in play therapy, and ongoing discussions about a dance movement therapy MA. Professor Emeritus Stephen Snow celebrates the "mutual blessing for both the university and the field" afforded by CATS: "Concordia established an innovative, dynamic department which trains students from around the world, implements important research in the field and provides community outreach through its many programs. As a famous British author writes, these therapies represent an 'evolution in healthcare,'" one that is, for example, currently being co-developed with Indigenous partners to provide culturally specific services in urban and remote communities.

8.13 Shelley Spiegel in the Department of Theatre production of Denise Boucher's *Les fées ont soif*, 1981.

Grounded in a graphic design program at SGWU, the Department of Design was established in 1981, and quickly added an undergraduate industrial design stream. Seven years later the departmental name became Design Art, a recalibration having positioned design as a visual and aesthetic discipline with manifold applications. Within that framework, in the second half of the 1980s, design became the first visual area in the faculty to formally address the digital. It implemented a course titled The Computer as a Design Tool and established a small lab, laying the conceptual groundwork for the eventual establishment (in 2000) of a faculty Centre for Digital Arts, now regarded as an essential operation. Not surprising then was the placement of the emerging digital image/sound field under the wing of Design Art in the late 1990s, and another departmental name change, Design and Computation Arts, in 2005. There, the joint major in computation arts and computer science with its foundation in the arts, design, and computer science, and the BFA specialization in computation arts, focusing on gaming, networked societies, and interaction design, have proved highly successful in terms of enrolment, creativity of output, and funding from external sources.

These programs, led by innovative researchers, have been anything but merely technical, and the same applies to the BFA in design art and the MFA in design

THE FACULTY OF FINE ARTS

8.14 Holly Fedida installing her screen print *Disconnecting the Dots* (2016) for the year-end undergraduate student exhibition *Matter of Place*, at FOFA Gallery in 2018.

(introduced in 2016): Professor pk langshaw discerns in these programs "a unique approach to design and technology, focusing on highly conceptual, speculative, and inventive work, embracing technological advancement and innovation, balanced by an emphasis on social, cultural, economic, and environmental sustainability." Co-curated year-end exhibitions display the work of students "mentored to be creative risk-takers, conceptually provocative, innovators, and visionaries."

Urban sustainability has emerged as an explicit departmental concern over the past quarter century, exemplified through a longstanding partnership with Montreal's Dans la rue organization for street youth. Two Concordia University Research Chairs (awarded in 2015 and 2022) are key to Concordia's Next-Generation Cities Institute, Dr. Carmela Cucuzzella, CURC in Integrated Design and Sustainability for the Built Environment, and Professor Alice Jarry, CURC in Critical Practices in Materials and Materiality. They underscore, langshaw argues, "that vibrant cultural production is an essential precondition for a sustainable future since resilient cities are ones in which there is effective symbiotic relationships between city-making and citying, generating designs for urban space as homes for all habitats and inhabitants."

In 1990 an acoustically advanced concert hall opened on the Loyola campus. Later dedicated in his presence to Oscar Peterson, it acknowledged the innumerable

8.15 Concordia hosted the Hemispheric Institute's 9th Encuentro Manifest! in 2014. The nine days of the international Encuentro included performances, workshops, working groups, exhibitions, keynote events, and the Trasnocheo series of late-night cabarets. Performance artist Lois Weaver hosted her Long Table at the Leonard and Bina Ellen Gallery, which creates a dinner table atmosphere as a public forum where only twelve guests seated at the table can engage in discussion. Pictured here are participants in the Long Table, Representing Bodies and Experiences, June 26, 2014.

ways in which the Department of Music had helped sustain a vibrant music culture in Montreal through public performances by its orchestras, bands, choirs, quartets, and solo artists. More than simply a venue or a recording studio, Dr. Charles Ellison views "the Oscar Peterson Concert Hall as a community centre for love, healing, education, musical growth, intellectual growth, and non-judgmental participation in the art of living."

The department has offered degree options in jazz studies since 1983 and electroacoustic studies since 2001, as well as longstanding music performance and theory/composition specializations.[12] One might infer a privileging of genre studies and particular functions within music, but to do so would be to miss the founding ethos of the department, exemplified in Ellison's description of jazz as that which asks people to listen "to all genres of music in embracing our reality as family." This idea is amplified by Professor Emerita Liselyn Adams: "The department, very much a creation of Professor Philip Cohen's dreams, envisioned a music program without the usual fences that herded skills and knowledge into distinct categories, presenting an alternative to traditional conservatories and faculties of music." Stressed, she continues, were "the skills of hearing, composition, theory, history, and performance,

THE FACULTY OF FINE ARTS 101

offering students unprecedented flexibility of access to courses in jazz, electro-acoustics, classical, historical, and contemporary music. Into this challenging culture of 'Yes,' all were welcomed: a strong performer who could not read music, a self-taught composer, an experimenter in raw sound, a specialist in early music, an older student returning to music."

Graduate student energies, for years associated with the diploma in advanced music performance studies, now reside within interdisciplinary programs. There, supported by the diverse research profiles of faculty members, combinatory explorations of music/sound are fostered.

Fashioned in 1996 to oversee undergraduate and graduate programs in Ceramics, Fibres (now Fibres and Material Practices), Interdisciplinary Studies, Painting and Drawing, Photography, Printmaking (now Print Media), and Sculpture, as well as the non-specialized Major in Studio Arts, the Department of Studio Arts overnight became the faculty's largest unit. Embedded within it were energies that had unfolded after the merger, led by the late Professor Alfred Pinsky, a painter who was the first head of the Department of Fine Arts at SGWU and the FoFA's first dean.

The new faculty quickly welcomed new studio "citizens," while advancing its inherited, widely recognized strengths in painting and drawing, printmaking, and sculpture. Photography, released from its "Cinderella" position in 1979, rapidly generated formidable BFA and MFA streams. In 1984 a small crafts component grew into what remains the only full ceramics program in Quebec, as well as a program in fibres whose faculty and students have been important in Hexagram and Milieux clusters. Professor Emerita Kathryn Lipke recalls the "freedom, supported by an international visiting artists program, given at the time of my hire to embrace and develop—as had major museums like the Museum of Modern Art in NYC—fibres and textiles as important art mediums."

Many subsequent changes to studio programs, including the development of challenging art theory courses for BFA and MFA students, responded with great agility to the fluid art world. Professor Leopold Plotek has observed that "the '80s represented a kind of turning away from the abstract modernism of the 1960s and 1970s, opening up to different kinds of figuration, wall painting, graffiti, informal things, pop." No palace revolution was needed because "Pinsky had brought [to Concordia] an enormously varied group of artists."[13] These full- and part-time faculty and their successors have brought national and international acclaim to Concordia through powerful artmaking, while, in classrooms and through studio and exhibition visits, quietly continuing the age-old tradition of working artists passing their insights along to students. In addition to assisting in the formation of generations of acclaimed artists, their efforts have benefited institutions across the country, and within Quebec itself especially the CEGEP (pre-university college and vocational) system. As

8.16 Concordia hosted the annual Congress of the Humanities and Social Sciences in 2010, led by academic convenor Ronald Rudin. 8,880 delegates from seventy academic associations attended the ten-day scholarly event that also included keynotes and cultural events. Professor Owen Chapman unveiled his *Icebreaker* at the FOFA Gallery. A collaboration with Sam Thulin, the pair froze waterproof contact microphones in ice cylinders and connected them to a series of sound processors to create a musical instrument, performance piece, and interactive installation.

Giuseppe Joe di Leo, a BFA Studio Arts graduate and retired full-time faculty member of one of Montreal's CEGEPs, testifies, "for over four decades FoFA grads have helped revitalize aspects of the Fine Arts Program of Dawson College, enhancing the creative spirit and welfare of their students."

Intermedia/Cyber Arts (IMCA), the most recent (2005) program addition to the Studio Arts Department, combined performance, installation, music, sound, video, and electronic arts, a venture in part enabled by Hexagram facilities. The alab, a robotic art lab founded by Dr. Bill Vorn and associated with IMCA faculty, was an instance of what Lynn Hughes has called "the gradual move, for many artists, from more traditional, individual, studio-based practices to collaborative and interdisciplinary ones." Underscoring this phenomenon is the heavy presence of faculty members and graduate students from Studio Arts in Milieux research clusters such as Post Image.

The 2010 creation of the prestigious Claudine and Stephen Bronfman Fellowships in Contemporary Art awarded to graduating MFA studio arts students illuminates the diverse field of production encouraged by the department, with transdisciplinarity given the same credence as work in "traditional" mediums.[14] The Bronfman initiatives underwrite another key feature of the department: from the outset, faculty members, through unsung efforts, have helped students make the challenging transition into meaningful careers. Bronfman fellowships and inventive support mechanisms being developed through the extraordinary 2019 donation from the Peter N. Thomson Family Foundation are adding immeasurably to this commitment.

Born of thriving theatre arts and drama activities at Loyola College and SGWU (overseen, respectively, by Professor Emeritus Gerry Gross and the late Dr. Norma Springford) the Department of Theatre has for decades made highly informed, fearless contributions to the city's theatre worlds. Students, whether prospective actors, playwrights, directors, or production designers, battle exhausting schedules to "learn-by-doing," supported by skilled professional staff. Until 1998 many students also prepared, through the Drama in Education program, to work in community facilities or to obtain teacher certification elsewhere.

At the turn of the millennium, BFA programs began to explore localized, populist, and participatory formats for the theatre arts, exemplified in the lasting ties forged in 2008 with the radical Bread and Puppet Theater of Vermont. Curriculum and degree title changes in 2016 extended definitions further, embracing every activity classifiable as performance. The specialization in performance creation, for example, introduced "a series of hybrid seminar-studio courses on practices such as oral history and performance, Indigenous storytelling, and studies in gender and sexuality in performance." Departmental members bring much to LePARC, the rich Milieux research cluster, alongside partners from Music, Contemporary Dance, Studio, History, English, and interdisciplinary centres.

Expanded terrain is also at the heart of 2023 changes to theatre design. Professor Gene Gibbons articulates how changes made to the longstanding BFA specialization in design for the theatre (established in 1984) promise to enhance its powerful reputation in the field. The earlier program, he observes, "placed great emphasis on the art of design. Students were taught to conceive of a virtual world for the play: only then would the designer consider techniques for producing sets, lights, costumes, props, special effects or soundscapes." As Gibbons further explains, "this emphasis on the art of design over theatre technology set Concordia apart from most under-graduate design programs in North America." Now, with a change in the program title to Scenography, "the intent is to look at the entire scope of live performance. The new program will be inclusive of design processes for theatre, dance, video and film, digital gaming, exhibit work, and performance art, preparing students to participate in the development of new performances from their inception." Its graduates, overtly committed to environmental sustainability, will carry portfolios that "include elements that typically come from directors, cinematographers, dramaturges, theatre directors and even cultural anthropologists, helping to blur the lines among all these professions."[15]

**NOTES**

1   Roy Ostling, "Concordia Spawns New Faculty," *The Concordian* 2, no. 2 (September 1974).

2   *Thursday Report* 3, no. 1 (August 23, 1979): 4.

3   *Concordia's Thursday Report* 30, no. 2 (September 29, 2005): 4.

4   In the 1990s, administration of the Leonard & Bina Ellen Art Gallery was detached from the faculty, making the EV's FOFA Gallery a welcome addition to vibrant student-run galleries.

5   *Thursday Report* 2, no. 30 (May 31, 1979): 12.

6   See *Concordia's Thursday Report* 18, no. 26 (June 2, 1994): 3, as well as Matthew Hays's contribution in this volume.

7   Informal interviews were undertaken with numerous faculty and alumni, whose reflections are included throughout this chapter.

8   For more on this funding, see Frank Kuin, "New Director of Hexagram Welcomes New Partners on Board," *Concordia's Thursday Report* 27, no. 2 (September 26, 2002): 7; on Dr. Xin Wei Sha's joint appointment, see *Concordia's Thursday Report* 29, no. 6 (November 18, 2004): 4.

9   The Indigenous Futures Research Centre was formalized as a university research centre in 2021, founded on the earlier Initiative for Indigenous Futures (2014); see Jason Edward Lewis and Skawennati's contribution in this volume.

10  This chapter does not explore the Department of Contemporary Dance; for more on this department, see Silvy Panet-Raymond, "Leaping across Time: Four Decades of Contemporary Dance at Concordia University," this volume.

11  Leah Sherman, *25 Artists, 25 Years / 25 artistes, 25 ans* (Montreal: Galerie d'art Leonard & Bina Ellen Art Gallery, 2001).

12  For more on the Electroacoustics program, see Kevin Austin's chapter in this collection.

13  Richard Burnett, "Concordia Professor Participates in MAC Showcase," *Concordia University News*, January 29, 2020.

14  *Concordia University Magazine* 33, no. 3 (Fall 2010): 5.

15  The account of the evolution of theatre design is from an unpublished administrative text written by Professor Gibbons, kindly forwarded to me by Professor Ana Cappelluto in an email of January 11, 2023.

**Geneviève Cadieux**
*Lierre sur Pierre,* 2009

Anodized metal on limestone
(51.1 square metres)
North Façade, John Molson
Building, SGW campus

9.1 A view looking south on Drummond Street, with the 1912 YMCA headquarters (*left*) and the 1956 Norris Building (*centre*) in the 1960s.

# "ALL MERGED UP":
# THE JOHN MOLSON SCHOOL OF BUSINESS

Charles Draimin and Christopher A. Ross

**FIFTY YEARS AGO**, the business schools of Loyola College and Sir George Williams University (SGWU) came together quickly and relatively smoothly in comparison to the difficult and drawn-out merger of the separate faculties of arts and of science at SGWU, and Loyola's Faculty Arts and Science. Even so, there were difficulties to be overcome before the merger of these two relatively small business faculties could be declared a success. The merger of these two institutions occurred at a time when there was growing demand for business education in universities. This demand stimulated the call for business faculty with doctoral degrees. The competitive environment in the late twentieth and early twenty-first centuries also saw the alignment of the interest of business schools with that of the business community. The Faculty of Commerce and Administration, now the John Molson School of Business (JMSB), was able to capitalize on these trends.[1]

Loyola College and SGWU were founded in two separate religious traditions—Catholicism and evangelical Christianity—but they grew along parallel paths. Leading up to the merger, each had a business faculty, the Faculty of Commerce at Loyola and the Faculty of Commerce and Administration at Sir George Williams (this was a name change made only in 1970 from the previous name of the Sir George faculty, Faculty of Commerce). On the other hand, during the early days of merger negotiations, the two faculties differed considerably in size. The Faculty of Commerce at Loyola had fewer than a dozen faculty members in 1969–70, whereas, on the eve of the merger,

---

CHARLES DRAIMIN is Professor of accountancy, John Molson School of Business, Concordia University, where he served as MBA director and accountancy department chair. He has presented his research at academic conferences and has co-authored an accounting textbook. He has also been active in the Concordia University Faculty Association, including a term as president.

CHRISTOPHER A. ROSS (PhD, Ivey School of Business), Distinguished Professor Emeritus, Concordia University, has held several administrative positions. He has taught at both the undergraduate and graduate levels and published in conference publications, case collections, and academic journals. He has taught at Caribbean universities and consulted for non-profit organizations and small businesses.

the SGWU Faculty of Commerce and Administration had over forty. Despite Loyola Faculty of Commerce hiring more lecturers over the next three years, the ratio was still heavily weighted in favour of SGWU.

## Origins

In the 1940s, Loyola created faculties of science and commerce offering BSc and BComm degrees. The independence the college had in designing courses and setting examinations for its arts courses, however, was somewhat circumscribed for the science and commerce faculties as the Université de Montréal retained nominal control over courses in these faculties. Over the years Loyola began to adopt a full North American university curriculum. The Faculty of Commerce offered a mix of courses in accounting, economics, and liberal arts. Students were also required to take courses in philosophy, theology, and public speaking as part of their program. By 1972, however, theology and philosophy courses were no longer compulsory; at the same time, the faculty had introduced courses in computer science. By 1974, the year of the merger, the Faculty of Commerce had two departments, Accountancy and Business Administration (this department offered courses in finance, management, marketing, and quantitative methods); four-year undergraduate degree programs were offered. In addition, the faculty offered degrees in economics and computer science. These departments were in the Arts and Science Faculty.

By 1973–74, 1,230 students were enrolled in the commerce program at Loyola while the full-time faculty complement had more than doubled from the late 1960s to keep up with student demand. When accounting for full-time lecturers, the faculty's number of instructors in the faculty on the eve of the merger totaled 34;[2] including two full-time women lecturers, Bernice Wright in economics, and Ulrike de Bretani in business administration, the latter of whom would become the faculty's first tenured woman professor following the merger.[3]

Most of the Loyola instructors in these years had either MBAs or were chartered accountants; several had master's degrees. Loyola's offered four-year bachelor's degrees and, in certain areas, honours degrees, all following a standard North American curriculum. Its graduates were regularly accepted into graduate programs of universities. By the late 1960s, however, the degree-granting arrangements Loyola had with the Université de Montréal, as did all *colléges classiques* in Quebec, were to be terminated under the education reforms being passed in Quebec.

SGWU, by contrast, grew out of evening courses that were first offered by the Montreal YMCA in 1873. Until the 1920s, the institution offered students specialized courses in accounting and other commercial skills such as stenography and commercial mathematics. Its commerce program, first introduced in the late 1920s, graduated two students as part of the college's first graduating class in 1937.[4]

9.2 Planning the Joint PhD Administration tenth anniversary celebration. *From left to right*: students Christiana Demers and Richard Glass, Associate Dean Christopher Ross, Professor Pierre Brunet, and student Louise Côté.

After 1960 there was further evolution: the institution began emphasizing specialized education with a greater reliance on full-time lecturers who were encouraged to pursue graduate degrees. In 1963 SGWU established the three faculties of Arts, Science, and Commerce. The Commerce Faculty launched its MBA program in 1968 and in 1970 changed its name to the Faculty of Commerce and Administration. From the outset, SGWU and its predecessor institutions filled a real void in higher education with its emphasis on providing part-time education. By the 1970s the objective of the business program at SGWU had evolved to a very business focus: "This Faculty is engaged in the education of students for business life … to graduate students liberally educated about business" while providing a solid business education.[5] In 1973 there were 374 students in the MBA program, of which 64 were full time.

By 1974 both business faculties, had full undergraduate commerce programs but only SGWU had an MBA program. There were several other markers differentiating the two institutions, mostly to the advantage of SGWU. There was a higher proportion of faculty holding terminal degrees; SGWU had a university charter, which, despite several attempts over the years, Loyola College had failed to attain; SGWU was larger and had a downtown location. Loyola's small college atmosphere might have been seen as an advantage by some students (and faculty) for those interested in languages and philosophy perhaps, but it would not be seen as a benefit for a business school.

There was a decided emphasis on graduate teaching and research at SGWU that Loyola lacked. Still, the two had been grounded in a Christian educational tradition, and both had as their founding objective to develop the "whole person." But even that was now of little significance: with increasing specialization and the recognition of business as a legitimate area of higher education, the Christian aspect of commerce education gradually disappeared at both schools. Furthermore, the advent of the CEGEP (pre-university college and vocational system) in the late 1960s forced universities in Quebec, including SGWU and Loyola College and, to re-examine and adjust their program offerings. CEGEPs offered courses across the curriculum—in commerce, arts and science, and engineering—forcing universities to modify their offerings in these areas.

Even before the issue of a merger was even thought of, the commerce faculties at both Sir George and Loyola had ambitions to grow and to diversify their teaching programs and other activities. Sir George was somewhat more successful having a head start over Loyola. Its bachelor of commerce was introduced decades before Loyola established its Faculty of Commerce in 1948. Another advantage that SGWU could offer its students was that it was amongst the first institutions of higher education in Canada to offer its courses and programs in the evenings. This represented the beginning of a major social change: people who had to work in their late teens and twenties had an opportunity to enter university and earn a degree by taking courses in the evening. University education would not be just for those whose families had the means to send their children to university. It would be several decades before evening university classes would be available on these terms across Canada. Loyola did have an Extension Department (later renamed the Evening Division), but this was created only in 1957.

The most significant difference between Loyola and SGWU was the possession of a university charter. By 1950 Sir George had one and Loyola did not. Moreover, it was clear after several unsuccessful attempts that Loyola would not acquire a charter. The consequences were evident in the teaching resources available to each of the two institutions. Consider the number of full-time, academically qualified faculty members. Counting only those at the rank of professor—professor, associate professor, and assistant professor—there were, in 1970–71, forty-two full-time faculty members in the Sir George Williams Faculty of Commerce and Administration and just eleven in Loyola's Faculty of Commerce.[6] Both faculties would employ full-time and part-time instructors, but the strength of the teaching faculty must be measured by the number of those with professorial rank. Clearly, of the two commerce faculties, Sir George was, in the early 1970s, larger. Given the reforms of post-secondary education in the 1960s, the only way that Loyola could maintain its university-level vocation would be to link up with a chartered university. SGWU was not the only candidate but, in retrospect, from the point of view of the Loyola Commerce Faculty, it is fair to say that it has worked out very well.

## The Merger

In 1974 and for some time after, there were few obvious signs of the merger: the SGW Commerce Faculty members were still housed in the crowded Norris Building on Drummond Street while at Loyola, Commerce Faculty members remained in the Cloran Building, a small converted two-storey apartment building on Sherbrooke Street opposite the main Loyola campus. To a large extent. instructors taught courses on the campuses where their offices were located. It was not until 1979 that the downtown faculty members moved a few blocks west to more modern quarters in the Guy-De Maisonneuve Building (GM) at the corner of Guy Street and De Maisonneuve Boulevard conveniently right above the metro station. The Loyola faculty members remained in the Cloran Building. When that building was razed for the construction of the now independent Loyola High School, most of the faculty members moved to the Sir George campus downtown. The few who remained were relocated to rented quarters on Sherbrooke Street two blocks east of the campus. It was only in the late 1990s that all members at the faculty were finally united in the GM Building. Some undergraduate business courses continued to be offered on the Loyola campus, but by the early years of the new century scarcely any remained. At a certain point, the critical mass of students interested in taking their classes was lost and so offering classes on the Loyola campus could no longer be justified.

More space had to be found in the GM Building for the last faculty and staff members moving downtown from Loyola as well as for the new hires. At the same time, administrative departments were being moved into the building. Offices were being renovated for them but not for the commerce faculty members. Stories circulated of the air quality in the offices from the poorly maintained ventilation system. Increasingly, faculty and staff complained: it was going on thirty years since the merger. Commerce was a large faculty, yet faculty members were squeezed into second-rate offices. There were just three rooms in the building available for teaching. This is not what anyone expected. They wanted to know when they were going to get their own building.

The issues of offices, the merging of the departments, and rationalizing the programs in the two institutions had proceeded without serious disruption. A merger implementation task force was established with three representatives from each of the founding institutions. Young Loyola faculty members were encouraged to obtain their PhDs and offered generous incentives to do so. Just as important, however, was the rapid development of new academic programs and initiatives, such as the graduate diplomas in institutional administration, sports, and accountancy, as well as the

9.3 In 1982 Concordia hosted the world's first MBA Case Competition. The event would later be renamed the John Molson MBA International Case Competition. Here Concordia students are captured jubilantly celebrating a second place showing in the popular annual event.

creation of the joint PhD program with HEC, McGill, and Université du Québec à Montréal (UQAM).

At the personal level, however, things were not quite so smooth. The merger was generally accepted at Sir George—as the chartered university in this marriage, everyone knew that institutionally it had the upper hand. There was less enthusiasm at Loyola; if there was any adapting to be done, its faculty members sensed that Loyola would have to do the adapting. As things developed, however, there was relatively little application of the heavy hand on the part of Sir George Williams (Loyola's influential alumni probably had a great deal to do with this). In any case, despite some misgivings, there was general acceptance of the merger by most members of the faculty of the Loyola Faculty of Commerce. Apart from anything else, there really had been no choice—it was obvious that rejection of the merger would have meant loss of its university programs and its university students. It would have become a CEGEP if it were not wound up altogether. Not surprisingly, the merger was more attractive to the younger faculty members, especially those who had joined in the early 1970s and who had just a short history and little emotional attachment to Loyola College. Many of the older faculty members at Loyola hoped to maintain the Loyola departments and some wanted Loyola to remain a separate college within the university. But this was not going to happen. A separate Loyola College within the merged university was not in the cards, and separate faculties teaching the same subjects did not make much sense. Merging these units would prove a constant challenge to the administrative skills of the new university's upper administration.

As for resolving the problematic issues that had to be dealt with after the legal merger took place, as far as the existence of two commerce faculties and their departments were concerned, these problems were, in the end, dealt with on an individual basis. Unlike the issue of a separate arts faculty, a science faculty at Sir George, and a faculty of arts and science at Loyola, there was no such difficulty with the two commerce faculties; mergers at the department level began immediately. One complication was that there were five departments at Sir George Williams—Accountancy, Finance, Management, Marketing, and Quantitative Methods—but just two at Loyola: Accountancy and Business Administration. The members of the Loyola Accountancy Department would, of course, join the SGW Accountancy Department. Individually, the members of the Business Department at Loyola would join one of the other four SGW departments, based on their training and experience.

Although the Sir George and Loyola commerce faculties were integrated from the outset, this merger remained a continuing source of bitterness to some of the senior faculty members, especially at Loyola. One, whom we will call Waller, was irritated by the constant reminders of the business school's new arrangements by a member of the Loyola Faculty of Arts and Science, which remained an independent faculty for some time after the merger. "That fellow, Keating (a pseudonym for a member of a department in the Loyola Faculty of Arts and Science)," Waller complained to his accountancy colleagues, "He knows I detest that bunch downtown. 'All merged up, eh?' he says to me, and he laughs, the bastard." This went on for more than a year. Keating knew he could always pull Waller's chain, and he took full advantage. In 1977, however, the merger of the departments of the Loyola Arts and Science Faculty with the corresponding department in the Sir George Faculties of Arts and of Science was finally agreed, creating a single Concordia Faculty of Arts and Science. Not long after, Waller walked across the road to the English department and found his would-be nemesis: "Hey, Keating, all merged up, eh?" There was no response.[7]

Most of the faculty who had initially resisted the merger were eventually reconciled. Not so Waller. Though it was never clear what motivated this animus against his new employer, right up to his retirement, he always had a bad word for Sir George.

### Growth and Development

One of the first formal attempts to interact with the community was approved by the Board of Governors in April 1980 and became operational in November of that year.

This centre had a business advisory board made up of senior representatives of the business community. Faculty members, the university administration, and students were also represented. The objective of the Concordia Centre for Management Studies included research on business, consulting, and business seminars. Unfortunately, the centre was not financially viable and so after eight years, it was closed. It was replaced by the Institute for Executive Education, which offers executive seminars and continues today.

In February 1982, the Commerce Graduate Students Association hosted the first MBA case competition to be held in Canada. The competition was the brainchild of two MBA students. Five universities competed, including McGill and UQAM. In 1983 the competition went national with 16 universities from across Canada competing. In 1992, as part of Concordia's contribution to the 350th anniversary of the city of Montreal, the case competition went international with schools from as far away as New Zealand and Lebanon competing. Concordia continues to host this competition annually.

The executive master of business administration was introduced in 1985. It was the first such degree program in Quebec and only the second in Canada. The program, with classes one day per week, on alternating Fridays and Saturdays, allowed middle and senior managers to continue working while acquiring new knowledge and skills. The aviation MBA program introduced in 1992 followed the executive master of business administration model but was retired after about ten years because of low enrolment. The Goodman Investment Management Program was another innovative venture. The program operated via videoconferencing with students in Montreal and Toronto. Graduates earned an MBA while being trained for the Chartered Financial Analyst (CFA) designation.

In 1992 the faculty established a five-year exchange and training program with the University of the West Indies in Trinidad and Tobago (UWI). It involved the training of potential faculty and the establishment and support of new graduate programs at UWI. Concordia faculty also held visiting appointments at UWI. This program was sponsored and financially supported by the Canadian International Development Agency with a budget of $1 million, at the time the largest externally funded program ever managed by exclusively the faculty.

In 1997 a very important step taken by the faculty, shortly before the change of name, was the successful effort to gain accreditation as a business school by the premier international accreditation body, the Association to Advance Collegiate Schools of Business (AACSB). The Université Laval Business School was accredited in the same year, so Concordia and Laval were the first Canadian business schools to earn AACSB accreditation.

9.4 In 1994 the Faculty of Commerce and Administration hosted Concordia's first annual Women and Work Symposium. Danielle Morin, professor in the Department of Supply Chain and Business Technology Management, is pictured here in May 1998 during its fifth installment.

## The Millennium

In November 2000 there was an important change for the faculty. In recognition of two major donations to the faculty from the Molson Foundation—the first, a $3.5 million donation in 1997, followed by a $10 million in 2004—the faculty changed its name to the John Molson School of Business (JMSB). Still, it was almost another decade before JMSB secured suitable quarters.

Until about the turn of the twenty-first century, the buildings on the west side of Guy Street from the lane behind the TD Bank that fronted on Sainte Catherine Street up to De Maisonneuve were generally old one- and two-storey storefronts. About that time the block had been purchased by a promoter who intended to build a high rise on the lot. At a certain point, the old buildings were razed and excavation began. An opportunity lost, everyone thought. Then all the construction stalled. It was left like that for some time—a large hole, at least three storeys deep. Apparently, the promoter could no longer finance the construction. At this point, the university raised the money to acquire the land and proceed with the design and construction of what would be the Molson Building, the home of JMSB.

The building sits on the southwest corner of Guy Street and De Maisonneuve Boulevard. The building was constructed at a budgeted cost of approximately $118 million and is LEED-certified. It was finally completed in May 2009 and the first classes were held in the fall of that year.

In 2007 the Entrepreneurship Institute for the Development of Minority Communities changed its name to the Institute for Community Entrepreneurship and Development. This institute eventually morphed into the Community Service Initiative with Dave McKenzie as coordinator. Its objectives were broadened and today it works to develop linkages with the wider community (non-profit organizations, social enterprises, small businesses, and governmental institutions) through teaching and learning, research, and community service.

The years 2001 to 2023 witnessed the establishment of research professorships and centres but a major part of the activity centred on rationalization and consolidation of programs and activities. The name change and the subsequent move to the new building somehow forced the school to look seriously at all its programs with the objective of creating greater synergies. The beginning of the twenty-first century and the continued growth in the computerization of business education meant that resources were continually being directed at modernizing and digitizing communication and teaching methods. Thus, programs that were not sustainable in the long run were terminated, other programs were streamlined, and efforts were devoted to identifying external sources of funding for research chairs, professorships, and centres.

Ultimately, the success of all these activities can be measured by the outcomes for our most important stakeholders—our students. We can follow the career of a student: Nicola Stevenson (not her real name). She began her higher education at Loyola in the late 1960s/early 1970s. Shortly after, while working full-time, she took a BA degree in history and English on a part-time basis. Again, after a break, Nicola began an MBA program in the Faculty of Commerce and Administration, part-time for two years, full-time for the last year. During this time, she was a member of the Concordia (MBA) Case Competition Team. The year she completed her MBA degree, she received a limited term contract as a lecturer in the management department of the faculty and she taught in the department for six years. In addition to her teaching duties, she coached in the Concordia Undergraduate Case Competition, and took the team to the finals in the Queen's Case Competition. Subsequently, she moved from Montreal to New York City but maintained her connection to Concordia as a member of the Concordia Alumni Chapter there. She was an active alumna in New York for almost thirty years. Nicola was a real estate stager for twenty years, including ten years as a trainer. She considers her years as a student at Concordia, especially her time as an MBA student and lecturer in management, to be a major asset as a profession stager and a trainer. In the last decade Nicola has volunteered frequently as a judge in the

John Molson Annual Graduate Research Exposition. This competition offers master's and doctoral students in the faculty an opportunity to show posters summarizing their research. People with business experience, such as Nicola, act as judges in the competition. Nicola has been recognized for her skills as a teacher in the John Molson classes and by her professional colleagues as a professional stager. She readily acknowledges the importance of her time as an MBA student and as a teacher in the faculty: "my experience at Concordia in presentation skills and followed by my years teaching certainly were a major asset for me in both aspects of my professional work."

## Conclusion

Between 1974 and 2023 the John Molson School of Business witnessed major changes in its programs, structure, and size. Graduate programs such as the PhD, Executive MBA, the MSc, and graduate diplomas were established in the 1980s and '90s. The AACSB accreditation provided further stimulus to faculty recruiting and student enrolment. The AACSB certification has been especially helpful in attracting applications from international students for places in the John Molson graduate programs. The turn of the millennium saw consolidation that was further enhanced with the construction of the new Molson Building. Other initiatives regarding the environment, women in business, women in the faculty's administrative roles, and community services have contributed to the growing prestige of the JMSB and the city, the province, and beyond.

### NOTES

1   For two historical accounts on the origins of the faculty, see Grace A. Pollock, "History of the Faculty of Commerce at Loyola College: A Business Research Project" (MBA thesis, Concordia University, 1993); and Sophie I. Anand, "The Faculty of Commerce & Administration: A Historical Documentary of Its Origin, vols. 1 & 2, A Business Research Project" (MBA thesis, Concordia University, 1993).

2   See Pollock, "History of the Faculty of Commerce at Loyola College," 64. For a breakdown of total faculty numbers and which courses they taught, see Pollock, "History of the Faculty of Commerce," appendix "Exhibit G."

3   For more on Ulrike de Bretani's career and contributions, see Ian Harrison, "Business School Pioneer Ulrike de Bretani Supports Key Scholarships for Women," *Concordia University News*, February 18, 2022, https://www.concordia.ca/cunews/offices/advancement/2022/02/18/business-school-pioneer-ulrike-de-brentani-supports-key-scholarships-for-women.html.

4   SGW's first graduating class in 1937, which was known as the "Guinea Pigs," included the College's first woman graduate, Rita Shane, and the first two graduates from December 1937. For more on this graduating class, see: https://www.concordia. ca/offices/archives/important-dates/1930-1939.html

5   See *Concordia Undergraduate Calendar, 1975–76*, section 61.4.1, Sir George Williams Campus, paragraph 1.

6   See Sir George Williams University, *Academic Calendar 1970–1971*, 206–16, I0018 Office of the Registrar fonds, Concordia University, Records Management and Archives (RMA); also Loyola College, *General Calendar 1970–1971*, 50–53, I0018 Office of the Registrar fonds, RMA.

7   This story was relayed to the author.

# 10 PATHWAYS TOWARDS CULTURAL DIVERSITY, ACCESSIBILITY, AND KNOWLEDGE SHARING

Dave McKenzie

"We graduated university."
**THESE WORDS WERE WRITTEN ON THE BOARD** of a John Molson School of Business (JMSB) classroom after eighteen Black Montreal high school students completed the first Community Service Initiative (CSI) Young CEO Program in 2015. The students were members of a summer youth co-op led by the Tyndale St-Georges Community Centre in Little Burgundy.

"We graduated university" is a stark contrast to what students told me at the beginning of the four-day program. "Dave, we stand in front of this building every day to take the bus and we never knew that we could come inside."

It's a statement that resonates with me daily. It reinforces my resolve as the founder and coordinator of the CSI to use every available resource to make students feel welcomed and supported as they pursue undergraduate or graduate studies and to reach beyond the classroom, collaborate, and share our knowledge and expertise with community agencies to improve their management and capacity to assist in improving the lives of society's most vulnerable.

Both statements also made me reflect on individual and institutional efforts over the years to create opportunities, access, and support for members of Black, Indigenous, and other visible minority groups in order to acquire a university education. Before CSI, I engaged in two other initiatives—the Black Community Initiative (1997–99) and the Entrepreneurship Institute for the Development of Minority Communities (EIDMC) (2004–07)—that sought to improve these gateways for minority students.

In September 1991, the Concordia University Task Force on Multiculturalism submitted a report titled *Balancing the Equation: Cultural Diversity at Concordia* to Dr. Maurice Cohen, the university's vice-rector of institutional relations and finance.[1]

---

DAVE MCKENZIE, founder and coordinator of the Community Service Initiative, John Molson School of Business, Concordia University, has over thirty years of experience in non-profit governance and management, entrepreneurship, and small business management. He is a servant leader whose positive attitude and tireless energy encouraging others to succeed are infectious.

10.1 Dave McKenzie and a group of MBA students who had recently completed their MBA 661 Community Service projects.

The report was the culmination of research completed over the preceding three years by a multidisciplinary team of faculty and staff. The report focused on educational and informational processes "through which sensitivity towards cultural, ethnic and racial issues may be addressed" and made several recommendations rooted in multiculturalism, equity, and the inclusion of visible minority communities. Faculty and administrators, some of whom represented those minority groups, were also invited to develop innovative ways to balance the equation.

During the 1992–93 academic year, the task force's report was referred to the university community for a response. An implementation Committee on Multiculturalism and Issues of Equity reviewed the community responses to the report. One of the priorities was the establishment of the Advisory Committee on Multiculturalism, which was to be consulted and involved in the development and follow-up of those recommendations. The advisory committee convened in 1995 with Dean of Graduate Studies Dr. Martin Kusy and co-chair Dr. Clarence Bayne. In a memo written to Concordia Rector Dr. Frederick Lowy on December 18, 1996, Dr. Kusy reported on the initiatives taken by the School of Graduate Studies and the

# Black community responds to business seminar

A strong contingent from Montreal's black community came to Concordia for an intensive three-day seminar for entrepreneurs and professionals recently.

The seminar was launched with an evening reception on March 26, and the sessions were held throughout the next two days and the following Saturday.

The 23 participants ranged from young people about to start independent business careers to school principals ready to take early retirement and strike out on a new path.

Seven members of the faculty of Commerce and Administration gave sessions on such topics as financial management and control, conflict management, and current business issues. The three days wound up with presentations by the participants of their own business plans.

The catalyst for the seminar was Decision Sciences Professor Clarence Bayne, Director of the Diploma in Administration and Sport Administration programs and a longtime activist in the black community. He was impressed with the quality of the plans that were presented in the final session.

"Some projects were very elaborate," Bayne said. "There was one ambitious project on health care which took a year to put together and will have start-up capital from Africa. The corporate plan ran to 100 pages." The project would export equipment and home-care services to clients in developing countries, and invest in home care and other health-care delivery services here in Canada.

A typical smaller-scale project was the jewellery business described by a young man. He will design wearable miniature versions of a client's home, or a favourite object.

The seminar was sponsored by Concordia's Minority Institute of the Faculty of Commerce and Administration, and a non-profit community group, the Institute for Organizational Development and Training of the Black Studies Centre.

While the seminar was outreach to a community that needs a stronger business voice rather than a recruiting tool for Concordia, Bayne said that the seminar is bound to have "a significant ripple effect."

Many of the attendees are Sir George Williams or Concordia graduates who are now well placed in the black community. Several were representatives of the Quebec Board of Black Educators, who run PSBGM-accredited summer courses touching about 700 students a year. The success of this seminar, Bayne said, "makes them feel there's a positive, meaningful connection" between Montreal's black community and Concordia.

It wouldn't have been possible, he added, if the participating professors had not accepted only modest honoraria or none at all. They were Professors Bakr Ibrahim (Associate Dean, Human Resources and Administrative Affairs), Robert Oppenheimer (Management), Tom O'Connell (Management), Bill Taylor (Management), Juan Segovia (Accountancy), Chris Ross (Marketing) and Bayne, who is also Director of the Minority Institute.

- BB

Professor Clarence Bayne meets participants at the opening reception.

Professor Bakr Ibrahim leads a workshop on entrepreneurship and small-business management.

10.2 Professor Clarence Bayne of the Department of Supply Chain and Business Technology Management and director of the Institute for Community Entrepreneurship and Development began his career at Sir George Williams University as a part-time lecturer in 1966. Throughout the years, he was a tireless advocate for Black Canadian students as well as those from the wider Black diaspora.

role of the advisory committee.[2] He proposed further action be taken and that a commitment be made to a university-wide recruitment and support program. He also proposed that mechanisms be developed to provide greater access to visible minorities, Indigenous, and Black scholars to enter undergraduate and graduate programs and to raise their rates of retention and graduation.

As a member of the Advisory Committee on Multiculturalism, I was unimpressed with what I heard during a meeting that took place in the spring of 1997. I felt we weren't sufficiently discussing various issues and that the university was not following through on our advice. I said so quite forcefully. My comments caused quite a stir and some discomfort, especially for Dean Kusy.

As I tried to leave the room after the meeting, Kusy stopped me. "Dave, where do you think you are going? You think that you will come here and stir up sh*t and just leave. If you feel so strongly about this, then you do something about it."

Following our exchange, and without my knowledge, Kusy sought funding for a Black community project. Some weeks later, I received a call from Ann Kerby, the director of Advocacy and Support Services. "You have been given to me as a gift," Kerby told me. She then told me to develop a plan for a community project. I went home and worked on a ten-page plan, only for her to demand changes.

"Are you crazy?!" Kerby said. "You and which army are going to do all this work? Go and redo this. Get these ten pages down to one page."

I developed the project name "Black Community Initiative" and wrote a one-page description. I was later hired as the project consultant as part of Kerby's team at Advocacy and Support Services. I did not have a dedicated office space, so I worked from home and spent time in the advocacy offices at both Loyola and Sir George Williams campuses.[3]

Concordia wanted more Black students in the university and to make it accessible to their communities. My role as project consultant was to change the notion of the university as a faceless institution. I began connecting with Black community organizations across the city. I held specialized information sessions in community centres, high schools, and CEGEPs (Quebec's pre-university college and vocational system). The goal was not to wait for persons to come to Concordia for information but to bring information directly to people where they were. Concordia Corners, designated spaces where prospective students could access information about Concordia, were set up in Black community organizations and community centres across the city.

Many Black students coming out of high school and CEGEP don't see university as an option. Some Black students experience a culture shock going from a CEGEP class with fellow students who look like them, to a university class where they might be the only Black person in their class. Black students are likelier to be the only member of their community who went to university, while white students usually come from families with multiple relatives who attended university and graduated.

The Black Community Initiative was a two-year pilot project aimed at making the university more accessible. The pilot project had three main objectives: to recruit Black students to both undergraduate and graduate programs; provide the necessary support and services to retain Black students; and increase the visibility, outreach, and presence of Concordia in Montreal's Black communities. The Black Community Initiative also had secondary but equally important objectives to benefit the wider student population by highlighting the role of students within the university. By focusing on the specialized needs of Black students, the hope was to build a genuine connection with marginalized communities who don't see themselves in universities and later form a more diversified and inclusive campus culture.

I submitted the pilot project report to Dean Donald Boisvert in June 1999.[4] The project was supposed to graduate into the enrolment office, which was being established. Following the project's completion, I was transferred to the Office of the Registrar. While working in the Office of the Registrar, I volunteered with the Minority Entrepreneurship Institute (MEI). I was given the opportunity to work as a full-time employee on contract for the MEI after one year in the Office of the Registrar. I accepted the offer because the enrolment office hadn't been formed yet. It was also an opportunity for me to work on a project that I had a hand in starting.

As a student in the Graduate Diploma in Institutional Administration program at Concordia, I completed the Feasibility and Needs Assessment Study for the Establishment of a Summer Institute in Small Business Management in October 1993. The findings of this research were used to establish the MEI, which later became the Entrepreneurship Institute for the Development of Minority Communities (EIDMC) in 1999 and then the Institute for Community Entrepreneurship and Development (ICED) in 2007.

The MEI was established in the Faculty of Commerce and Administration in 1994. The idea grew out of a confluence of different factors, including the recognition of the systemic discrimination that minority communities face in society at large, the significant representation of minority communities among faculty members, the significant involvement of faculty members in community organizations that facilitate their understanding of the issues and problems members of minority communities face in business and in their daily lives, and the available resources and commitment within the faculty to solve these problems.

The MEI's mission was to provide opportunities for members of minority communities to acquire the knowledge and skills necessary to better their situation and thus improve the economic and social conditions in their communities. The institute achieved its mission by developing, promoting, and delivering non-credit courses and certificate programs as well as customized courses that would assist aspiring businesspersons, professionals, and leaders from visible minority, Indigenous, and Black communities in becoming successful entrepreneurs and decision-makers. The goal was to use entrepreneurship as a way to generate wealth and improve economic conditions in those same communities. The MEI focused on the Cree communities of Northern Quebec and the Black community of Montreal.

In 1996 the Faculty of Commerce and Administration signed an exclusive agreement with the Cree Nations to provide management training programs. The Cree wanted to create a civil service in its territories. The band council was the governing body. They received funding from the federal government through the Department of Indian Affairs as well as royalties from various treaties and they needed to develop the infrastructure to deliver services to their communities. They no longer wanted to rely on non-Cree members to provide those services as it resulted in money leaving the community. Their most educated members would also leave the community to seek higher education and employment. The programs were not in place where they could apply their skills in their own communities and be justly compensated for it.

Across an eleven-year relationship with the Cree Nations of Northern Quebec, we delivered training courses and certificate training programs including community economic development, entrepreneurship, human resource management, conflict management and interpersonal relations, personal finance, and office systems technology to directors of operations, economic development officers, treasurers, benefits counselors, and administrative assistants. We were also a gold sponsor of the Cree Nation of Waswanipi's Business Development Conference in 2005 and 2006. We were supposed to hold the program on the territory of the Cree Nations, but they insisted that the program be held at Concordia because they wanted to be in a university setting. We were obliged to ensure that training materials were culturally sensitive, that all classrooms had windows, and not to schedule training during goose hunting season. "If you want to clear a room full of Cree, just yell goose," Cree Regional Authority Program Manager Alfred Loon said.

In 1999 the MEI changed its name to the Entrepreneurship Institute for the Development of Minority Communities (EIDMC) because Cree members—who had become our biggest sources of business—did not like the name. At the end of the training, participants received a certificate of participation. The certificates had real currency in various Cree communities. They were used to determine promotions and pay raises in the job force.

The program was supposed to graduate into a formal special degree program in business studies for Indigenous communities, but it did not happen. We instead lost an opportunity to build on the trust we had developed. Between 1994 and 2006, the EIDMC worked with Black community organizations by conducting research, and holding courses on leadership, community economic development, and entrepreneurship. The institute developed a Black Community Economic Development program and worked with seven Black community organizations to provide training, technical support, and business counselling to young Black entrepreneurs. They partnered with the Black Studies Centre in incubating entrepreneurs, establishing a computer centre and business library, and archiving Black community history. These efforts were initiated by Dean Christopher Ross and led by Professors Clarence Bayne and Bakr Ibrahim.

From 2006 onward, the EIDMC continued as the Institute for Community Entrepreneurship and Development (ICED) under the direction of Dr. Bayne. ICED is working with three major groups in the Black community: DESTA Black Youth Network, the Quebec Board of Black Educators, and the Black Studies Centre. It uses entrepreneurial training as an integral part of its youth remedial education and development programming.

I left ICED in November 2008 to form the CSI at the JMSB. Earlier that same year, our recruiters noticed that a sizable number of students applying for the JMSB MBA program indicated that they had no interest in working in the corporate sector. As for those who did, they wanted an opportunity to give back to society. This observation, while anecdotal, was unprecedented.

I soon developed an outline for CSI. I wanted to create a platform where the best students, faculty and staff—and, by extension, the JMSB and the university—could work together with community agencies including those providing services to Black, Indigenous, and other people of colour to find solutions for common problems. I wanted the program to be set at the MBA and graduate levels where students could share their expertise while learning, as opposed to the undergraduate level where students were still developing their expertise.

I later presented the outline of the idea for CSI during a meeting with incoming JMSB Dean Sanjay Sharma and all staff members. I had shown up late and the only empty seat was to the right of Sharma's own.

"Nice of you to join us," Sharma said as I entered the room.

After other staff members presented their own submissions and grievances, Sharma looked my way.

"Well, Mr. Late to My Meeting," Sharma said. "What do you have to say for yourself?"

"I have a project that would see the university and the community working closer together and I would love to meet you and discuss it further," I responded.

Sharma was intrigued. We later had a follow-up meeting where we discussed my new initiative further. Sharma then asked me if I knew Alan Hochstein, Concordia's director of the MBA and associate dean of graduate and professional programs. Hochstein had always expressed interest in having me be a part of his team.

"Go see him and tell him that I want to make this happen," Sharma said.

I eventually burst into Hochstein's office and told him what Sharma said.

"David, I know nothing about this," Hochstein said. "If it does not work, it is on you. However, if it works, I am glad I thought of it."

And that is how CSI was born. It continues to grow after 15 years of its existence. Hochstein remains its biggest supporter. He has supervised 100 students as part of the flagship MBA 661 Community Service Elective, where MBA students provide in-depth consulting for credit under the guidance of faculty. Since 2009, 19 faculty members have supervised over 261 students in the completion of 135 projects working in collaboration with not-for-profit organizations and small businesses.

Through our partnership with the Trade Facilitation Office in Ottawa, MBA students act locally and impact globally by providing Canadian market entry studies for small and medium-sized enterprises in the developing world that want to export products into Canada. The Trade Facilitation Office identifies the organizations while we at CSI conduct market entry studies. Since 2010 we have completed 33 projects in 21 countries across South America, the Caribbean, Africa, and Asia.

Through our community roundtable, not-for-profit showcase events and our volunteer and service activities, we have welcomed and worked with hundreds of non-profits and small/medium-sized enterprises. Our community economic development program has allowed us to take the JMSB out of our building and into communities such as Little Burgundy where faculty-trained Black entrepreneurs learn how to become better businesspeople, as well as in the North where Cree managers learned to improve their leadership and administrative skills.

Through the Young CEO program, inner-city high school students across Montreal are welcomed to Concordia each summer to participate in business and leadership development workshops facilitated by students, staff, and faculty who share their expertise while learning and planting the seed in young people that going to university is possible. Over a hundred students participated in the program between 2015 and 2019.

Our biggest success to date has been Isaiah Joyner, then a Black CEGEP student from Little Burgundy who worked as an animator with our inaugural group of high schoolers—the same ones who wrote "We graduated university" on our classroom board. At the program's end, Joyner expressed an interest in enrolling at JMSB. I became his mentor and encouraged him. He was eventually accepted into the bachelor of commerce with a major in finance. He later participated in several university initiatives and received the President's Medal during his graduation ceremony in 2022. He is now in his second year in the JMSB Goodman MBA. He is an example of what the faculty was trying to achieve when it came to balancing the equation. But we still have a long way to go to produce more students like Joyner.

Thirty-three years after formal efforts began to make Concordia University more inclusive for and supportive of members of Black, Indigenous, and other visible minority communities, the work continues today. Black and Indigenous students, faculty, and staff can seek resources and support through the Black Perspectives Office—one of eighty-eight recommendations from the President's Task Force on Anti-Black Racism—as well as the Office of Indigenous Directions and the Equity Office. There is still a dearth of Black male students in the MBA and other graduate business programs, but students of Southeast Asian and Middle Eastern descent now make up the majority. The CSI, through its classroom and external offerings, is an integral component of the MBA and the JMSB. Through the CSI, the JMSB develops more positive and mutually beneficial links with society.

We still have a long way to go. We need to be more intentional about connecting the dots from our past to our present and to our future. This would show that Concordia has been responding and, in some cases, taking the lead in embracing multiculturalism and equity, listening and learning from disadvantaged groups, being inclusive and helping them attain their rightful place in society. Change is slow and incremental, but it is happening. We still strive to balance the equation.

NOTES

1   Concordia University Task Force on Multiculturalism, *Balancing the Equation: Cultural Diversity at Concordia*, edited version of a report to Dr. Maurice Cohen, Vice-Rector, Institutional Relations and Finance, September 1991, I0057 Office of the Provost and Vice-President, Academic Affairs fonds, Concordia University, Records Management and Archives.

2   Dr. Martin Kusy, Dean of Graduate Studies and Research, to Dr. F. Lowy, Rector and Vice-Chancellor, Memo: Diversity in the University, December 18, 1996, author's personal collection. Memo was copied to all the members of the Advisory Committee on Multiculturalism and Issues of Equity.

3   Donald Boisvert, then the dean of students, assigned Kerby to the project. Boisvert was named chair of the Advisory Committee on Multiculturalism in the summer of 1997. The Dean of Students Office was given the responsibility to implement a project for the Black community, leading them to assign the project to Kerby. Kusy secured the funding for the project through the Office of the Rector, the deans from all faculties, the School of Graduate Studies, and Student Services.

4   Dave McKenzie and Ann Kerby, *Black Community Initiative Pilot Project (A Partnership for Excellence and Advancement)*, report to Donald Boisvert, PhD, Dean of Students, Chair, Advisory Committee on Multiculturalism and Issues of Equity, June 1999, I0169 Advocacy and Support Services fonds, RMA.

11.1 Engineering, Computer Science and Visual Arts Complex, west façade, corner Sainte Catherine and Guy Streets.

# THE GINA CODY SCHOOL OF ENGINEERING AND COMPUTER SCIENCE

Christopher Trueman and Ted Stathopoulos

## Beginnings

**THE GINA CODY SCHOOL OF ENGINEERING AND COMPUTER SCIENCE** had its beginnings in the engineering programs of Loyola College and of Sir George Williams University (SGWU). In 1943 Loyola opened the Faculty of Science, and the programs included the first three years of engineering in civil, mechanical, electrical, mining, metallurgical, and chemical engineering. At that time, Sir George offered "Courses for Practical Engineers," which could be credited to the BSc degree. The programs at Loyola and at Sir George prospered. The two schools shared some engineering courses in 1960: Loyola students attended a strength of materials lab at SGWU and Sir George students took a metallurgical lab at Loyola.[1] The first women to graduate in engineering at Loyola were Gabrielle Paul and Loretta Mahoney in 1962. SGWU created the Faculty of Engineering in 1963, with five-year programs in civil, electrical, and mechanical engineering and Loyola created a Faculty of Engineering in 1964. The first bachelor of science in engineering degrees were granted by Loyola College in 1966 in conjunction with the Université de Montréal. SGWU granted its first bachelor of engineering degrees in 1968. A year later the new BEng degree received full recognition by the Canadian Council of Professional Engineers. Master of engineering programs meanwhile were approved in 1965 at SGWU, but not introduced until 1968, the same year doctoral programs were instituted. The first woman to earn a BEng degree at Sir George was Carol Akiko Chang in 1971 in civil engineering. Loyola had a computer science

---

**CHRISTOPHER TRUEMAN** is Professor in the Department of Electrical and Computer Engineering, and has been with Concordia since 1974. His research is in computational electromagnetics. He has investigated electromagnetic compatibility problems involving broadcast antennas and high-voltage power lines, antenna-to-antenna coupling on aircraft, and exposure to radio-frequency fields when using a cellular telephone.

**THEODORE (TED) STATHOPOULOS** is Professor of Building, Civil and Environmental Engineering since 1979. He is a fellow of the Canadian Academy of Engineering, the Institution of Civil Engineers, and the American Society of Civil Engineers and its Structural Engineering Institute. He is the editor of the *Journal of Wind Engineering and Industrial Aerodynamics*.

department prior to 1971, and in 1972 Sir George created their Department of Computer Science and the BCompSci degree.

Following the merger in 1974, the dean of the Faculty of Engineering at the brand-new Concordia University was Clair Callaghan.[2] Loyola's Dean George Joly became the associate dean responsible for engineering activities on the Loyola campus. Students near the end of their program at Loyola took their advanced courses at Sir George and received the Concordia BEng degree. Students near the start of the program at Loyola completed two years of courses on the Loyola campus, then finished their degree on the Sir George campus. By 1979 the two engineering programs had merged and only the first year of engineering courses were offered at Loyola, taking advantage of the classroom space and lab facilities available there. In the early 1980s the first year was moved downtown. However, because of the shortage of space at SGWU, particularly in the Hall Building, some engineering professors' offices and research labs remained at Loyola.

## Evolution of the Gina Cody School

The Gina Cody School's mission has included providing "high-quality and comprehensive undergraduate and graduate curricula, to promote high-calibre research," according to Concordia's undergraduate calendar.[3] Engineering is a rapidly changing field and from its earliest days the faculty has striven to keep our programs current, and to offer new programs to students as new areas of engineering and computer science emerge.

In 1977 the faculty created the Centre for Building Studies, after its founding director secured a Negotiated Development Grant from Ottawa to develop research programs in building engineering. The centre offered graduate degrees including a PhD in building studies, a unique program at that time. In 1989 Gina Cody earned the PhD in building studies, the first woman to do so. With additional financial help from Quebec, the Centre for Building Studies developed the first accredited undergraduate program in building engineering in the country. The Centre for Building Studies was a research centre, but also operated as a department.

Dr. M.N.S. Swamy became dean of the Faculty of Engineering in 1978 and guided the faculty for the ensuing sixteen years. The faculty expanded rapidly in the following ten years, attracting much greater research funding, and increasing the numbers of undergraduate and graduate students.

In 1979 the undergraduate program in building engineering was introduced and became the BEng in building engineering in 1980. Also in 1980 new PhD programs were introduced in electrical networks and systems and fluid control elements and systems. In 1980–81 the Department of Electrical Engineering introduced the first BEng program in computer engineering in Quebec. The program recognized that

11.2 Since the merger, the Engineering Faculty's creative restlessness, combined with technological ingenuity, has demonstrated the tight links between research and practical application. In this photo, an engineering lab from the 1980s shows a plane shell being tested. Today the faculty offers graduate programs in aerospace and aviation engineering.

engineers designing new computer hardware need a different skill set from those working in other areas.

Dean Swamy remarked in 1990 that, over the course of 22 years, the faculty's research funding had increased from $153,000 per year to over $6.47 million per year, which effectively reflects the huge growth in research in the faculty over this period.

Between 1979 and 1990 there were numerous other changes and additions to the faculty attesting to its high demand by students and faculty expertise alike. In recognition of the importance of the programs in the Department of Computer Science, for instance, the faculty changed its name to the Faculty of Engineering and Computer Science in December 1980. And in 1984, the Department of Computer Science successfully introduced a PhD program in computer science. The Department of Mechanical Engineering created a new program in industrial engineering in 1980, and in 1989 created the BEng in industrial engineering. In 1984 Mechanical Engineering added an aeronautical engineering option, recognizing the importance of Montreal as a hub for the aerospace industry. In 1990 the master of engineering (aerospace) degree was introduced. The computer engineering program was revised

11.3 Research collectives like the Electrical Engineering group and Concordia Amateur Radio Club exemplify the school's ethos and spirited sense of competition and experimentation. On the rooftop of the Hall Building one such researcher conducts microwave experimentation research.

in 1986 and became very successful. The department changed its name to the Department of Electrical and Computer Engineering in 1988. Computer engineering has continued to be in high demand since that time, so much so that it is now double the size of the electrical engineering program.

In 1992 tragedy struck when a disgruntled faculty member shot and killed Professors Matthew Douglass, Michael Hogben, Jaan Saber, and Phivos Ziogas. A memorial honouring the deceased faculty members was created in the Hall Building in 1996 (see Sloan, "Memorial Installation Dedicated to Four Concordia Professors," this volume). Dr. Saber especially had been a driving force behind the new industrial engineering program and following his tragic death, the faculty struggled over the following four years to find new leadership. In later years, the program obtained full accreditation and has become very successful.

In the 1995–96 academic year computer science in collaboration with the Faculty of Fine Arts offered students in the computer applications option a major or a minor

11.4 Rector Patrick Kenniff, whose tenure extended from 1984 to 1994, tests out an early version of an experimental off-road vehicle built by engineering students for the Society of Automotive Engineers Baja event. The Concordia club continues to compete in this international competition, operating out of a workspace located in a Hall Building garage.

in digital image/sound in fine arts. Courses include an introductory course in visual and performing arts, courses in multimedia authoring, theory and practice in digital image/sound, and elective courses chosen from design art theory and practice, electroacoustics, animation, foundations in photographic vision, and music.

In 1997 Nabil Esmail became the dean of the Faculty of Engineering and Computer Science. Under Dean Esmail's leadership the faculty began providing financial support for graduate students in the MASc program and in the PhD program. The graduate student support program allowed professors to take on additional students, and the number of the graduate students in the faculty expanded substantially. With more graduate students, professors were able to do more research and attract more research funding. Meanwhile, other changes were afoot and in 1998 the Department of Civil Engineering and the Centre for Building Studies merged. The department had gradually become involved in the new area of environmental engineering, and in the following year was renamed Building, Civil, and Environmental

11.5 Between 1995 and 1999 the US Department of Energy sponsored the FutureCars Challenge, the successor to the Methanol Marathon, which was inaugurated in 1988. Concordia teams thrived in these alternative-fuel competitions over the years and often represented the only participating Canadian school.

11.6 The Troitsky Bridge Building Competition, first inaugurated in 1984, is sponsored by Concordia's Engineering and Computing Science Association and continues to this day. The annual event attracts engineering students from across North America. Students are challenged with designing model bridges with popsicle sticks, toothpicks, glue, and dental floss.

11.7 In 2005 students and faculty in engineering designed and made the self-playing "Robokeith" guitar. *From left to right*: Steve Kiss, Pouyan Haghighat, Omur Kalkan, Andrew Ghattas, Ted Obuchowicz, Konstantinos Vitoroulis, Hadley Myers, Nilandri Roy.

Engineering. In the same year as this consolidation, the cutting-edge software engineering program and the BEng in software engineering were created. This department was subsequently renamed as Computer Science and Software Engineering and has gradually increased in popularity with both the bachelor of computer science and the bachelor of engineering in software engineering in great demand in recent years.

Dean Esmail fostered the creation of the Concordia Institute for Information Systems Engineering in 2004, an interdisciplinary research and development institute encompassing research in telecommunications, software development, electronics, multimedia, aerospace, finance and banking, automotive, manufacturing, building, and construction. The Institute for Information Systems Engineering offers programs at the graduate level in quality systems engineering and information systems security. Given high demand for programs and research in these areas, the institute has grown rapidly over twenty years.

Unprecedented growth led to a shortage of space. Professor offices were scattered wherever space could be found, and even still included some offices on the Loyola campus. To address this concern for space, in 2005, the Engineering and Visual Arts

(EV) Building was completed. After the move to the EV Building, each department was now consolidated and occupied one floor including department professors' offices. Yet, with the rapid increase in the graduate student population and the growing number of professors in each department, space in the new building filled over the following ten years, and the faculty was once again very short of space. Recently, Computer Science and Software Engineering moved to a much more spacious location in a building on Guy Street, alleviating the space crunch in the EV Building.

In 2005 Computer Science revised its joint offerings with Fine Arts and created the joint major in computation arts and computer science. This innovative program combines a comprehensive education in computer science with a complementary set of courses of equivalent value in fine arts, residing across both the Faculty of Engineering and Computer Science and the Faculty of Fine Arts whereby students can receive either a bachelor of computer science degree or a bachelor of fine arts degree. A few years later in 2007, Computer Science started a joint major in data science with the Faculty of Arts and Science, providing a comprehensive education in computer science and in mathematics. Similarly, the program resides in both faculties and students can choose to receive either a bachelor of computer science degree, or a bachelor of science or a bachelor of arts, according to their preferences and aspirations.

Dean Robin Drew assumed the leadership of the Faculty of Engineering and Computer Science in 2008. The faculty worked on developing a program in aerospace engineering and the BEng in aerospace was approved in 2014, a joint program administered by the Department of Mechanical and Industrial Engineering and the Department of Electrical and Computer Engineering. The Department of Mechanical and Industrial Engineering offers options in aerodynamics and propulsion and aerospace structures and materials, and Department of Electrical and Computer Engineering in avionics and aerospace systems. The Canadian Engineering Accreditation Board approved the program, and the first BEng degrees in aerospace engineering were granted in 2016.

Dr. Amir Asif was appointed dean of the Faculty of Engineering and Computer Science in 2015, and under his leadership, the Department of Chemical and Materials Engineering was created in 2017, with a curriculum that trains engineers to find novel ways to solve problems that have a significant impact on everyday life. Faculty members are experts in green chemical processes and the fundamental study of the properties of materials, such as polymers, nanomaterials, and battery materials with an emphasis on the development of sustainable solutions for the energy sector. The new department offers a master's and a doctorate in chemical engineering, as well as a graduate certificate and graduate diploma. An undergraduate program is also under development. Other changes were in 2018, when the Department of Mechanical and Industrial Engineering was renamed the Department of Mechanical, Industrial and

11.8 Women in Engineering (WIE) is a student association at Concordia that provides support and training for female-identifying engineering students. WIE also hosts an annual conference for Montreal high school students who are interested in careers in STEM.

Aerospace Engineering to recognize the importance of the aerospace program and the concentration of aerospace companies in the Montreal area.

In 2021 the Gina Cody School created a new bachelor's degree in computer science in health and life sciences, offered in collaboration with the Department of Biology. The program teaches students the interdisciplinary skills to work on teams involving biology, biochemistry, computing, mathematics, and statistics. Students take the courses in both the computer science core and in the health and life sciences core, and then specialize with electives chosen from health and life sciences and from mathematics.

## Student Life

Engineering students have long engaged in an active student life since the merger, with parades including the Boggermobile being a long tradition. The Boggermobile was a fanciful car carrying "Ye Old Bogge" and was often included in student events. More serious student activities over many years include the Annual Bridge Building Competition, in which teams of four students build a bridge out of popsicle sticks, white glue, and dental floss. The strongest bridge wins! Engineering students also regularly participate in the Great Northern Concrete Toboggan Race wherein teams of civil students from universities across Canada and the United States build toboggans out of concrete with five team members racing them down a ski hill. There is a prize for aesthetics as well as for speed. In 1999 Concordia entered an all-women team. This annual event has been a popular ongoing tradition for many years. The Engineering and Computer Science Association and the Engineering and Computer Science Graduate Association play vital roles in representing students' interests in faculty governance as well as encouraging and supporting the many student societies and initiatives that give the school its character. Student societies are an important venue for networking, experiential learning, and mentoring, and form a crucial part of student support and the social life of the school.

## Research Labs

A research lab brings together professors and graduate students into one space where they can collaborate on a specific area of research. The faculty's first research lab, the Center for Fluid Control, was created at SGWU in 1971. A great many research labs have emerged since then.[4]

In 1979 one of the first post-merger research labs that was established was the Concordia Centre for Composites. The mission of the centre is to conduct research in composite materials with an emphasis on low-cost, high-volume polymer matrix polymer structures. Concordia Centre for Composites has prospered and is now classified a University Research Centre. In 1985 the Concordia Computer-Aided Vehicle Engineering Research Centre was set up, with substantial grants from government agencies and a major contract from Bombardier. The Concordia Computer-Aided Vehicle Engineering Research Centre does fundamental and applied research in safe and efficient transport systems. The centre fosters technology transfer by working closely with industry. Concordia Computer-Aided Vehicle Engineering Research Centre was active for many years and has evolved into the Concordia Centre for Advanced Vehicle Engineering. In 1988 the faculty created the Centre for Pattern Recognition and Machine Intelligence, whose mission was to pursue research in optical character recognition, document analysis, and text processing. Since then, the Centre for Pattern Recognition and Machine Intelligence has expanded into a strong group of professors in the Department of Computer Science and Software Engineering, who collaborate with researchers at Polytechnique Montréal and École de technologie supérieure. This cross-institutional research focuses on pattern recognition, image processing, parallel processing, machine intelligence, and other areas.

The Centre for Signal Processing and Communications was established in 1988 to provide research and development leadership in the areas of signal processing and communication. Dean Swamy was the director of the centre from 1988 until 2011. The centre continues to be an active research hub. In 2011 the university's growing

11.9 A group of students show off their engineering skills with popsicle sticks and marshmallows during the student association's annual high school conference, "WIE Inspire, WIE Empower," March 9, 2019.

11.10 In 2018 engineer and entrepreneur Gina Cody (née Parvaneh Baktash) donated a historic $15-million gift to the Faculty of Engineering and Computer Science. In response to her generous donation the faculty was renamed after her. Here Cody, who was the first woman in Canada to earn a PhD in building studies, poses with WIE students.

commitment to sustainability prompted the faculty to establish the Centre for Zero Energy Building Studies, whose goal is to reduce the environmental impact of buildings while enhancing their safety and comfort. A year later, the Concordia Institute for Water, Energy, and Sustainable Systems, which trains students in sustainable development practice, built on this initiative. Other research labs continue this important work. The Concordia Materials Characterization Program, which is a comprehensive research platform for studying the structural and chemical composition of materials, allows students, researchers, and industry partners to probe complex questions on material structure, from bulk to surface samples, on a scale that ranges from macroscopic to nanoscopic. The Thermal Spray and Surface Engineering Research Centre, which focuses on developing new solutions for advanced coatings with improved resistance to environmental degrading factors such as high temperature, wear, corrosion, and erosion, likewise fosters research that contributes to sustainable practices.

The Gina Cody School of Engineering and Computer Science continues to support research initiatives that tackle problems related to contemporary technology, while partnering with researchers elsewhere in Canada. In February 2022, the federal government appointed the National Cybersecurity Consortium to lead the new Cyber Security Innovation Network. The National Cybersecurity Consortium includes Concordia University, the University of Waterloo, the University of Calgary, Toronto Metropolitan University, and the University of New Brunswick. This Consortium will receive up to $80 million over four years towards a potential total project well above $160 million, including significant cash and in-kind contributions from supporting organizations. As a nation-wide network, the Cyber Security Innovation Network is poised to meaningfully advance cybersecurity across all sectors and in all regions of Canada, opening a new chapter of collaboration on training, research, and development, and innovation in cybersecurity.

Following on the heels of the National Cybersecurity Consortium, Concordia launched the Applied AI Institute, which connects researchers in the Department of Electrical and Computer Engineering, the Concordia Institute for Information Systems Engineering, and the Computer Science and Software Engineering Department. With over ninety-five professors and two-hundred graduate students, the institute collaborates with eight research centres across Concordia's four faculties. Their focus is on three research clusters that address AI applications' social impact, creating deep learning methods for scientific medical imaging, and integrating AI into smart cities, industry and manufacturing, and aerospace.

In April 2023 the federal government awarded Concordia a Canada First Research Excellence Fund grant of more than $123 million, the highest research grant in the history of the university. The grant, which will be distributed over seven years, will support the activities and initiatives encompassed by a project called Electrifying Society: Towards Decarbonized Resilient Communities.

### Engineering in Society

The importance of engineering in society was recognized as early as 1966 in the design of the engineering programs offered by SGWU. In 1970 a formal Social Aspects of Engineering program was established. Courses focusing on the responsibility of engineers to society gained importance within the field and became a requirement for the accreditation of engineering programs. In 2004, the faculty created the General Studies Unit as a formal department to oversee courses in ethics and social responsibility. In 2012 the department was renamed the Centre for Engineering in Society. Its mission is to provide the skills needed for students to become well-rounded engineering professionals who are aware of the public policy, social, and ethical factors that shape our relationship to technology.

### Real-World Working Experience

The experience of working in industry for a semester changes students' perspectives as the material they learn in their coursework is applied outside the classroom. For instance, students in co-op programs hold jobs at commercial companies for three work terms over their program, usually at different companies, which provides the student with a variety of work experiences. To help carry out this real-world experience, in the

11.11 Gina Cody (*middle*) with then Provost and Vice-President of Academic Affairs Graham Carr (*right*) and Chancellor Jonathan Wener (*left*) at 2019 spring convocation.

late 1980s co-operative education programs in building engineering and computer science were founded. A decade later, the faculty extended co-operative studies to include all the bachelor of engineering programs. In 2004 the Concordia Institute for Aerospace Design and Innovation followed suit. The institute connects students with practising engineers in design and innovation in the field of aerospace. Students join the institute in their second or third year of study and complete two aerospace industry work semesters. Some students in the program design a capstone design project drawn from aerospace.

In 2014 the faculty introduced the Industrial Experience Option to offer students not enrolled in the co-op program the opportunity to work in industry for one or two semesters, which allows for their work experience to appear on their transcripts. The Department of Electrical and Computer Engineering has made one semester of industrial experience mandatory in their programs. The Industrial Experience Option was expanded into the Career-Edge Experience or C-Edge option. This program integrates work experience into the student's degree program, and the C-Edge option and associated Reflective Learning course appears on the student's transcript. In the Accelerated Career Experience, students may choose a twelve- to sixteen-month work experience. Work terms are arranged in conjunction with the Institute for Co-operative Education.

### The Gina Cody School

The renaming of the faculty in 2018 to the Gina Cody School of Engineering and Computer Science marked a pivotal moment. After earning her PhD in building studies in 1989, Gina Cody went on to become a successful engineer and business leader. Until her retirement in 2016, she was the chair of CCI Group Inc., and has served on Concordia's Board of Governors and the faculty's Industrial Advisory Board. Her generous donation of $15 million to the university helped fund the creation of over one hundred undergraduate and forty graduate entrance scholarships, as well as supporting the Canada Research Chair in Smart and Resilient Cities and Communities. The renaming of the faculty after a woman engineer was a first in Canada—a fitting honour given Cody's commitment to equity, diversity, and inclusion in science and engineering.

### Women in Engineering

In 2016 the Department of Electrical and Computer Engineering created the Women in Electrical and Computer Engineering Committee, which evolved into the Women in Engineering Committee at the faculty level in 2019. The committee aims to encourage young women to pursue engineering and computer science as a career, to improve the recruitment of female students into engineering, and to foster the retention of these students in the program. Female students at the high school level with a knack for science are often encouraged to take a degree in basic science rather than engineering. Each summer, prospective female students are invited to visit laboratories and meet successful female engineering students and graduates. Engineers of Tomorrow also encourages women from Montreal-area high schools to go into engineering as a career. Students come to the Hall Building and take a tour through various engineering labs, including Solid State Devices, the Human Factors Lab, the Flight Simulator Lab, and the lab run by the student chapter of the Society for Automotive Engineers. A presentation on biomedical engineering is made because of the interest young women have in this area. Visits are also organized to the Building Aerodynamics (Wind Tunnel) Lab and the Solar Simulator and Environmental Lab.

In May 2020 the Women in Engineering Career Launch Experience was created to support female students in the co-op program in building a successful and sustainable career in industry. Role models aim to mentor students with the goal of encouraging confidence, while coaches help students to overcome common barriers to success in evolving industries, and to learn leadership skills, explore career options, and build a professional network. These support initiatives help students develop an understanding of equity, diversity, and inclusion and participate in activities and events promoting the role of women in engineering. As Gina Cody once explained, "I want to support and inspire the next generation of women to pursue their dream and to achieve their independence. Engineering and computer science is for everyone, regardless of gender, ethnicity, or wealth."[5]

## Into the Future

The faculty is well-positioned for the years ahead. The leadership of Dean Mourad Debbabi, who was appointed in 2021, supports the Gina Cody School of Engineering and Computer Science's mission of providing comprehensive, high-quality under-graduate and graduate programs that promote high-calibre research and encourage the development of the profession of engineering and computer science in an ethical and socially responsible manner. In this imaginative environment, top talent will be drawn to the school and will continue the work of turning research into innovative solutions that make a tangible social impact. The faculty's entrepreneurial culture, which values and rewards high-quality research, will empower students and faculty members to turn their ideas into reality, which will lead to meaningful experiential learning opportunities and strong partnerships with organizations in both the public and private sectors. With such firm foundations in place, the faculty will continue to solve the complex and pressing challenges of our time, just as it has set out to do since its beginnings.

### NOTES

1   Douglass Burns Clarke, *Decades of Decisions: Sir George Williams University, 1952–53 to 1972–73* (Montreal: n.p., 1977), 81.

2   This chapter draws from a historical overview of the engineering faculty co-authored by former faculty member Hugh McQueen and former associate dean of student affairs for the Department of Engineering and Computer Science, Doug Hamblin. This unpublished article, titled "Mechanical Engineering at Concordia, Quarter Century of Expansion," is part of the P0258 Hugh McQueen fonds, RMA, currently not available for consultation.

3   *Concordia University Undergraduate Calendar, 2022–23*, 1333.

4   For a list of recent research labs and centres related to the Gina Cody School of Engineering and Computer Science, see the school's "Centres & Labs" webpage: https://www.concordia.ca/ginacody/research/centres.html.

5   See Concordia University, "Women in Engineering – Career Launch Experience (WIE-CLE)," accessed December 2, 2023, https://www.concordia.ca/academics/co-op/students/career-development/women-in-engineering-career-launch-experience.html.

## VISUAL STORY

## MEMORIAL INSTALLATION DEDICATED TO FOUR CONCORDIA PROFESSORS (1996)

Johanne Sloan

*Memorial Installation Dedicated to Four Concordia Professors* was created in 1996 to honour four professors who were shot and killed in Concordia University's Hall Building on August 24, 1992. The entire Concordia community was shaken and traumatized by this violent crime (as alumni and staff member Donna Whittaker in her oral history in this volume recounted). First and foremost, the intention was to honour the Concordia professors who lost their lives. The project was conceived by a collaborative team made up of Eduardo Aquino (artist/architect, MFA 1994), Johanne Sloan (art historian, BFA 1984), and Kathryn Walter (visual artist, MFA 1993) following a competition. The final installation encompasses four granite and aluminum tables, additional concrete seating in the form of miniature Hall Buildings, as well as a neon beacon attached to the wall. The tables resemble picnic tables, but their polished and engraved granite surfaces immediately evoke more durable structures and monuments. Furthermore, each table has the name of a professor, while the Douglass, Hogben, Saber, and Ziogas families provided quotations that were engraved onto the surface of the tables.

At the same time, the installation belongs to the entire Concordia community, in that the grouping of tables, seating, and beacon provides a space of rest, reflection, and conversation at the very heart of the downtown campus. Almost thirty years after its construction, this meticulously maintained commemorative installation continues to fulfill its dual function as a symbolic meeting place: students gravitate to this oasis within the busy life of the university, and once seated they encounter the cherished memory of the slain professors.

When the memorial was inaugurated in 1996, Sara Saber-Freedman spoke on behalf of the families—and her words continue to resonate: "If you seek to honour these men, honour them by living your lives as fully and as well as you can … If you can do that, if the presence of this memorial helps to remind you of these things, then in some measure they will still be with us. That is the finest memorial that we can give them."

---

JOHANNE SLOAN is a Professor Emeritus in the Department of Art History at Concordia University. Her teaching and research have often focused on the art and visual culture of Montreal.

## Matthew McCartney Douglass

(1926–1992)
Professor of Civil Engineering

"If we succeed in giving the love
of learning, the learning itself
is sure to follow."
—Sir John Lubbock

## Michael Gorden Hogben

(1940–1992)
Associate Professor of Chemistry and Biochemistry

"Whoever is a teacher through and through
takes all things seriously only
in relation to his students—even himself."
—Friedrich Nietzsche

### Jaan Saber
(1946–1992)
Associate Professor of Mechanical Engineering

"*Qui tacet consentit.*"
(He who keeps silent, consents.)

### Phoivos Ziogas
(1944–1992)
Chair of Electrical and Computer Engineering

"Phoebus, arise, and paint the sable skies
with azure, white and red."
—William Henry Drummond

Editors' note:

In the wake of the killings, the university launched two independent inquiries, both released to the public in 1994. The first, led by John Scott Cowan and which became known as the Cowan Report, investigated the shooter's employment history at the university; the second, the Arthurs Report, conducted by former York University president Harry W. Arthurs, focused on the ethical standards of research in the Department of Mechanical Engineering and the broader Canadian scientific community. Both inquiries prompted the university to re-examine internal policies and procedures with the aim of creating a safe and civil academic environment for all. In March of that year, representatives from Concordia also presented a 200,000-signature petition to Parliament that called for a ban on the private ownership of guns in Canada. In December 1995 the university reworked its existing code of conduct into a more robust Code of Rights and Responsibilities and, two years later, followed suit with a Code of Ethics after broad consultation with the university community.

## ORAL HISTORIES: August 24, 1992

**DONNA WHITTAKER, "IT JUST BROKE MY HEART"**

Well, tragically one of the biggest memories is the Fabrikant shooting. We had just moved in, as I said, to the library building, and we faced out onto the Hall Building. But, in the year prior to that, Stephen Scheinberg had worked as the CUFA [Concordia University Faculty Association] grievance officer. And I did the typing of the CUFA grievance reports. So I knew what was going on with this Dr. Fabrikant. I mean I didn't know him, I never met him [*sighs*]. But I was the one who was typing up the grievance reports for CUFA. And ... we had moved in June, and this was the end of August. And, I remember being in the office ... and one of our grad students came running in. And he'd been over in the Hall Building, and he said, "There's somebody with a gun and they're shooting." And I looked at Linda and I went, "Oh my god, it's Fabrikant." I knew immediately that it was him. And we, all of us rushed over to the windows. And saw the ambulances and the police cars that all start to arrive and converge on the building. And Linda turned to me, because she knew that Steve was the grievance officer, she goes, "Where's Steve?" And I said, "I don't know." I said, "The last time I—" Well, I mean, I'd seen him earlier in the week where he talked with Michael Hogben, who was the president of the CUFA. He had talked with Michael and they were in the office. I didn't know when Michael was meeting with Fabrikant, but I knew that that was the talk at the time, and that he was, Steve had said to him, "Do you want me to go with you?" And we weren't sure whether Steve, in the end, did or not. Turns out that Michael Hogben, Dr. Hogben, turned around at, at some point and said to Steve, he says, "No," he says, "rather than escalate this," he says, "I'm going to go by myself." Because Hogben was going to tell Fabrikant that he had to stay away from the CUFA offices on the Loyola campus because he was harassing the staff, which was his modus operandi ... So on that particular day ... we didn't know where Steve was. And when we picked up the phones, the phone lines had been cut for Concordia. So there was no phoning in or out of the university—obviously because they didn't want Fabrikant using the phone system and we were still on

---

**DONNA WHITTAKER** is a Concordia University alumna and long-time staff member who has worked at the university since 1982. She is currently Assistant to the Chair and Graduate Program Director in the Department of History. This interview took place at University Communications Services Studio on October 14, 2022.

traditional landlines. So, the whole system was just shut, obviously Bell must've just cut the lines ... so we stood there watching, and saw, I saw injured people coming out of the Hall Building, and Linda and I just stood there with our arms around each other [*gets choked up*], there was—sorry [*crying*].

It was just so tragic, and, finally security came and said, "Okay, uh, you have to step away from the windows. Because we don't know where he is, and we're afraid he'll start shooting. So please step away from the windows." And then within about twenty minutes later they came back and they said, "Okay, we want you to leave, but you'll have to go out through the back doors." Like so, onto Bishop, "Because you can't come out the front doors because everything locked off." So we said, "Okay, fine." So we went, we left. And then the horror played out on the news, and you saw how bad it was, and that there were four faculty members that were killed ...

The days that followed were tragic, I remember, because it was August, all the senior administration were away on vacation. I mean, everyone's away on vacation in August, right? And, the only one that was on campus was Chuck Bertrand ... He was the senior administrator that was available on campus. And he had the tragic responsibility of going in and identifying the bodies. And, I'll never forget; he called us in and we all went to the alumni room in the Hall Building, the H-110, which is large. And, I mean, it was standing room only, it was packed full of everybody, and, and ... Chuck sat on the stage and he cried [*gets choked up*]. Broke my heart [*crying*]. I just walked up to him afterwards and I just looked at him and we just looked at each other and he walked over and he hugged me, because there was nothing to say.

# THE SCHOOL OF GRADUATE STUDIES: 50+ YEARS OF CULTIVATING A GRADUATE AND RESEARCH CULTURE

Joanne Beaudoin

**HISTORICALLY,** Concordia's School of Graduate Studies has provided academic leadership and administrative guidance in fulfillment of Concordia University's commitment to deliver high-quality education and training to graduate students and postdoctoral fellows, in the university's eventual aim to become a top comprehensive university. In Canada, universities are typically, and more recently, categorized as "comprehensive" when they meet the criteria of having a significant amount of research activity and a wide range of undergraduate, graduate, and professional programs.[1] Research activity thrives with a solid foundation of graduate students, postdoctoral fellows, and active faculty researchers. However, before Concordia could achieve this status, several important steps had to be taken. The first step happened even before Concordia University's founding, when the idea of developing a graduate presence had begun to germinate at Sir George Williams University (SGWU), one of Concordia's two founding institutions. This chapter details some of the key decisions and actions that contributed to shaping the School of Graduate Studies as it looked by 2023 and reflects on some of the challenges encountered along the way.

## Cementing a Foundation

Graduate programs at Concordia predate both the university itself and the School of Graduate Studies. In fact, the earliest references to graduate programs date back to growing discussions within Sir George in the early 1960s. At that time, faculty had an interest in creating undergraduate honours programs, which simultaneously led to an

---

Eight years after joining Concordia, JOANNE BEAUDOIN became the administrative director of the School of Graduate Studies in 1998, a role that would take her into retirement in 2021. She worked with a dedicated team of professionals and five deans. This front-row perspective and archival research was combined with personal recollections shared by over twenty individuals and former School of Graduate Studies personnel, who participated in roundtable conversations for this chapter.

interest in offering graduate degrees as well. The impetus stemmed from faculty conversations around what could be done for particularly gifted undergraduate students.

According to D.B. Clarke, it was in 1962 that the Planning Committee of the Board of Governors approved a recommendation to introduce honours programs, with the following caveat:

> The committee has supported the introduction of Honours degree programs at the undergraduate level as developed by the Faculty and approved by the Faculty Council. The committee has recorded that this University should give primary attention to undergraduate instruction and that whatever is done must be compatible with our parallel Evening University programme. Having said this, the Committee would encourage and support developments that would provide research opportunities for faculty members and a modest but appropriate graduate studies programme as expansion proceeds. It is recognized that it is extremely difficult to offer a satisfactory undergraduate programme without provision for research and graduate work.[2]

Clarke also argued that the introduction of honours programs was primarily designed to help future SGWU graduates who wanted to pursue graduate studies at SGWU (or elsewhere for that matter). He added that an additional aim in creating honours programs was to help SGWU recruit faculty members who had interests in developing subject matter expertise in their students, by encouraging research in areas of specialization as required in such programs.

Within that context, the University Academic Planning Committee of SGWU established the Board of Graduate Studies (BGS) in 1963 and approved its first graduate degrees in 1964—namely, master's degrees in art education and in education. The board was responsible for reviewing and approving new graduate program proposals (which included ensuring the department had the faculty and other resources necessary to deliver quality programs), reviewing application and admissions standards and procedures, assistantships and fellowships, program time limits, and other related subjects of importance to graduate studies.[3]

However, in 1961, just two years before SGWU established a board of graduate studies, the Quebec government had begun a detailed reform of the entire provincial education system by launching the Royal Commission of Inquiry on Education in the Province of Quebec, which became known simply as the Parent Commission, named after the commission's chairperson, Alphonse-Marie Parent. By the end of their three years of work, the commission had made over five hundred recommendations in three reports, many of which led to significant changes in Quebec's education system. Some of the reforms included the eventual creation of CEGEPs

14.1 The School of Graduate Studies' former location on Mackay Street. The school is now housed in the administrative offices located in the GM Building.

(pre-university college and vocational schools), establishing a provincial loans and bursary program, the creation of the Université du Québec network, and the creation of a Ministry of Education, to name a few.[4] The introduction of CEGEPs and loans and bursaries led to larger than ever student enrolment in undergraduate programs, which would be an eventual boon for institutions with graduate programs. However, another of the report's recommendations was to limit the charters of Sir George, Bishop's University (known as the University of Bishops' College until its name change in 1958), and the Université de Sherbrooke. That particular recommendation was very concerning to SGWU since it had already begun to introduce graduate programs in a methodical manner. It therefore came as a relief when the Committee of Quebec Universities came out in support of the plans that the three targeted universities had for their own futures, and the newly established Ministry of Education indicated that it was not their intent to follow each and every recommendation of the Parent Commission to the letter. With that assurance in mind, Sir George proceeded as planned, but in a more conservative manner.[5]

THE SCHOOL OF GRADUATE STUDIES 157

According to Clarke, the BGS's early days included "a considerable amount of infighting between departments with the Board, unfortunately, caught in the middle," a theme that would prove to be recurring. The tensions stemmed from questions around jurisdictional concerns, with faculties and departments asserting their sovereignty over program regulations and delivery, and the BGS trying to fulfill the responsibilities of its mandate and establish institution-wide common standards and practices. An indication of the strife was the 1969 call to review the board's effectiveness, the first of several more reviews to follow over the years.[6]

The conservative approach to rolling out graduate programs, as well as jurisdictional tensions, were characteristic of how the early post-merger decades were to unfold, and that was the environment in which Stanley French, who chaired the BGS at the time, was appointed as the dean of graduate studies, a leadership position he successfully maintained throughout the first ten-plus years post-merger (1971–1986).[7] As is to be expected during any transition period, those early years were marked by questions around the new university's mission and identity, while the jurisdictional issues raised at SGWU remained mostly unresolved. The distinct missions of the two founding institutions did not include extensive research, and, by extension, the need for competitive graduate programs and active student recruitment was not a priority in the early post-merger years. Although SGWU had been heading in that direction, the culture there had not yet been firmly entrenched, nor was it widely accepted by the faculties that the Graduate Division (which formally became the Division of Graduate Studies in 1981–82) should play an important regulatory role in graduate studies in general at Concordia University.

Despite any ambivalent attitudes towards the place of graduate studies, however, the pendulum had already begun to swing by the time of the merger. By 1975 there were close to three thousand students enrolled in thirty-nine programs, including nine doctoral programs. Significantly, by the time of the merger, SGWU ranked eleventh in graduate enrolment in Canada, and more importantly, fifth in part-time graduate enrolment. Part-time enrolment in graduate programs would become a defining characteristic of Concordia's graduate student body in the decades that followed, creating non-traditional opportunities for many.[8]

An advantage of being a "new" university is that the typical constraints around tradition have not become entrenched. This circumstance allowed for novel program development, such as the creation of the Special Individualized Program (known initially as SIP, and then as the Individualized Program [INDI] from fall 2012). The SIP/INDI program allowed students at both the master's and PhD levels the opportunity to design their own research goals in areas not covered by existing graduate programs and to explore topics outside the normal boundaries of research and creation.[9] The program was rather unique at the time with only a few universities offering something similar, and ongoing internal surveys indicate that it remains one of the very few such programs in the 2023 Canadian graduate education market. In addition to affording students the opportunity to create their own inter- or trans-disciplinary program, the SIP/INDI program also allowed academic departments to "incubate" potential future programs by testing student interest as well as the department's research capacity to sustain a graduate program of its own. At Concordia's fiftieth anniversary marker, over 160 students have graduated with SIP or INDI degrees, and the program continues to fulfill a niche need.[10]

In the mid-1980s Dr. Fred Szabo began his tenure as dean of graduate studies (1986–1991) and immediately embarked on a campaign to encourage the academic departments and administrators to share his vision to make Concordia an institution recognized for excellence in graduate education, and to move past the jurisdictional squabbling that had carried forward since the establishment of the BGS some twenty years prior. It was Dean Szabo's vision that the Division of Graduate Studies could and should be instrumental in providing academic and administrative leadership to all graduate program faculty, staff, and students. Graduate programs were typically housed within an academic department, under the umbrella of a distinct faculty, each with their own long-established cultures. The faculties understandably treasured their independence in determining for themselves what programs and degrees to offer, how to design their own curriculum, and establishing their own admission standards and practices. As a relatively new player in the graduate landscape, Concordia had begun the detailed process of establishing how graduate programs should be governed, and that included a certain level of centralized coordination and quality assurance, a concept that had significant opposition, dating back to the early days of the creation of the BGS. Undeterred, Dr. Szabo persevered with his mandate, working collaboratively and creatively to persuade detractors that there was a place for an institutionally coordinated approach to graduate program delivery.

In the late 1990s, the Division of Graduate Studies became the School of Graduate Studies, and the BGS was changed to Council of the School of Graduate Studies. The two changes were significant because they gave the School of Graduate Studies a governance structure more closely aligned with that of the faculties, a move that the school hoped would garner it more influence. That restructuring was one of the recommendations arising from the Review of the Division of Graduate Studies,[11] which was brought to a vote at the university's Senate meeting of November 1991, where the motion passed, but with 25 percent (6 of 24) members abstaining; it was clear that almost twenty years after the merger, there was still work to be done to convince the faculties that a school of graduate studies would be a positive and necessary contributor to Concordia's academic goals.[12] Also in the 1990s, Dr. Martin Kusy (Dean of Graduate Studies, 1992–1997) and the decanal team drafted and implemented two important documents: the *Graduate Program Standards* and the *Guidelines for Supervisors and Graduate Students*, both of which were approved by the Council of the School of Graduate Studies and the University Senate in 1992–93. The approval of the *Standards* and *Guidelines* was noteworthy because it demonstrated that at last the institution was beginning to appreciate that across-the-board standards and practices were better for Concordia than ad hoc departmental approaches to program delivery and supervision.

## Integrating with Research Administration

Two decades after Concordia's founding, and nearly a decade after the formal establishment of the School of Graduate Studies and its own council, the role of the dean of graduate studies was revised to include the oversight of the Office of Research Services, and Claude Bédard was appointed as the first dean of graduate studies and research (1997–2002). The title and role change were pivotal indicators of a change in the university's culture; there was a keen interest in linking the two portfolios to emphasize the relationship between robust graduate programming and meaningful research.[13] During the 1990s the university's research funding picture had been consistently hovering around the $17 million mark, and that figure needed to increase if the university planned to be nationally and internationally competitive.[14] The university's administration was poised to position Concordia in such a way as to benefit from newly announced national and provincial research infrastructure programs known as the Canada Foundation for Innovation (CFI, 1997) and Canada Research Chairs program (1999).[15] To apply to these new programs, institutions were required to draft institutional research plans outlining their priorities. Tasked with that undertaking, Dr. Bédard was instrumental in leading Concordia's faculty deans to collaborate with their colleagues and the dean of graduate studies and research to map out comprehensive plans for research development, and by extension, graduate program growth. By the late 1990s, even though graduate enrolment had surpassed five thousand students, the vast majority were still enrolled in course-based programs that did not have a research component. Concordia was graduating an average of sixty doctoral students per year by the late '90s, which represented a small percentage of the total number of graduate students on campus, and not enough to take the university to the next level in terms of research.[16]

One of the ongoing challenges in the drive to improve Concordia's standing in the national comprehensive university picture was the inadequate level of graduate fellowship funding, which in 1997 was hovering under $1 million, the lowest level of graduate fellowship funding among all Canadian comprehensive universities. Concordia's founding cultures were still entrenched by the late 1990s, prioritizing need-based funding as opposed to merit-based criteria alone, a key distinguishing feature in a highly competitive graduate student recruitment landscape. There was

160  BUILDING THE INSTITUTION

also a need for the administration to educate Concordia's donors and its Board of Governors to the overall benefits of a robust graduate fellowship endowment, which would go a long way to recruiting and retaining the best students, and, in turn, enhance the university's research reputation. The turn of the millennium marked the beginning of that cultural shift.

With the university's newly accepted Strategic Research Plan, impressive success rates in CFI infrastructure funding in the program's first five years, and a slow but gradual increase in thesis-based program enrolments, the Board of Governors decided in 2003 the timing was right to create a position tasked with graduate studies, and research promotion and administration at the vice-president level. The title and role of the dean of graduate studies and research, after a brief stint of six years, reverted to focusing on graduate studies, while the new position of vice-president of research and graduate studies was established. The link between the two portfolios had been formalized at the highest level, clearly recognizing the importance of graduate studies and research in Concordia's future.

Elizabeth Saccà became Concordia's fifth dean of graduate studies in 2002, and she was the first woman to hold the position. Dr. Saccà's tenure began during a period of significant change and renewed turmoil, as fiscal austerity had become entrenched in Concordia's operations, demands for services had increased, and the faculties were once again simultaneously demanding more autonomy in graduate program administration and legislation, while calling for either a reduction or elimination of the School of Graduate Studies and its role in establishing and maintaining standards and practices for graduate programs and regulations across the university. In the early 2000s the school was unable to move forward with much of Dean Saccà's academic and administrative vision. In an oddly timed decision, the position of dean of graduate studies was eliminated at the end of Dr. Saccà's tenure in 2007, shortly after the appointment of Louise Dandurand as the university's first vice-president of research and graduate studies. The tensions that had existed since before the merger were still significant enough that forward momentum was a constant struggle for the school, and the elimination of the dean's position created more uncertainty around the school's future.

At the time of the new vice-president's arrival in 2006, the School of Graduate Studies had been operating in some iteration for just over forty years. While it had become widely accepted that there was need for various centralized services as provided by the school,[17] it was still not a unanimous view. In addition, there were different opinions regarding the school's role in areas such as defining admission standards, recruitment, administering internal fellowship competitions, reviewing and approving curriculum changes and/or new program proposals, for example.

Within the first year of her vice-president mandate, Dr. Dandurand initiated a Review Committee of the School of Graduate Studies to formally determine the school's role within the newly established sector that she headed, and hopefully satisfy the remaining detractors. The university-wide committee examined each element of the school's mandate, its relationship with multiple academic and administrative units, and the role of its council.[18] The result was an affirmation of the school's mandate, notably widened to include a formalized structure for postdoctoral fellows, and a call to begin a search for a new dean. This period also marked the formal Senate approval of the Policy on Postdoctoral Fellows, another indication that Concordia was moving forward with an expanded research agenda.

In 2010 Graham Carr was appointed as the school's sixth dean of graduate studies. With a champion at the vice-president level and a clear mandate to move the School of Graduate Studies ahead with both its traditional role and new initiatives, Dr. Carr began his term with a focus on securing competitive funding for all graduate students, providing academic departments with flexibility and advance notice on the amount of fellowship funding they would have available, and enhancing graduate-level recruitment activities and initiatives.[19] In addition, resources were provided to launch what became GradProSkills, a program that would offer complimentary skills and professional development to all graduate students and postdoctoral fellows (one of Dean Saccà's top priorities during her tenure), at no cost to the registrants, making Concordia's graduates and researchers more job- and world-ready than ever before.

## Reaching Out and Up

In 2015, under Concordia's President Alan Shepard's leadership, the university adopted its *Strategic Directions* plan, which included "Double our research" as one of its nine key strategies. The *Strategic Directions Game Plan* included budgets dedicated to advancing the plan's goals, and the School of Graduate Studies would play a part in helping the university meet its targets. With the budgetary and leadership provided via the *Strategic Directions* plan, Dr. Paula Wood-Adams (Dean of Graduate Studies, 2011–2020) created and implemented initiatives that enhanced and promoted student and postdoctoral research, recognized and rewarded excellence in graduate student supervision, provided skills training for students and postdoctoral fellows, and promoted interdisciplinary studies; she was also instrumental in advocating for and securing increased fellowship funding for the recruitment of top doctoral students. On the purely academic side, the school adopted a more active role in curriculum reform and development, as well as undertaking a review of its own (then) SIP program, which had recently been redesigned and rebranded as the more aptly named INDI program.

Throughout each stage of the school's evolution, one constant had always been the goal of fostering a sense of community with the many individuals and units within the university as well as with the external organizations that were integral to the school's and graduate students' success. Every graduate program has a dedicated academic program director, typically with extensive experience in graduate teaching, research, and supervision, and virtually all have administrative staff and/or advisors who are in constant contact with their students. Over the years, the school had maintained a close rapport with these key individuals, via formal structures such as the Assembly of Graduate Program Directors, or less formal gatherings such as orientations, topical workshops, and training sessions with newly appointed academic and administrative staff. Those structures helped and continue to help the school stay grounded and aware of any issues or systemic problems as they arise, enabling the School of Graduate Studies to be more responsive to changing realities at the program level.

By the time of Concordia's fifty-year anniversary, the graduate community is vast. Inasmuch as the digital world enabled real-time communication and action, maintaining meaningful professional relationships with the internal and external communities continued to cement Concordia's graduate presence on the local, national, and international stage. By participating in prestigious partnerships such as the ALGANT consortium and in a multitude of cotutelle agreements, for example, Concordia has been steadily growing its international graduate and research profile.[20] Additionally, leadership roles on bodies such as the Canadian Association for Graduate Studies, the Canadian Association of Postdoctoral Administrators, and the Northeastern Association of Graduate Schools position Concordia as an important contributor to graduate education on a global scale. The school's academic and administrative staff have for years been invited to present at provincial, federal, and international conferences on a number of topics, another indication that Concordia's voice on graduate matters is widely valued and respected.[21]

### What Lies Ahead?

In the 2021–22 academic year, there were 113 graduate programs offered, over 2,000 graduating students, and close to 9,000 graduate students and 250 postdoctoral fellows who chose Concordia as the place to further their goals and dreams.[22] Over its first 50 years, Concordia has been home to Vanier scholars, Trudeau scholars, Banting postdoctoral fellows, Fulbright scholars, hundreds of provincial and federal granting agency recipients, fellowship recipients from private and para-public donors, as well as full- and part-time graduate students who made daily sacrifices to further their education. A diverse range of valedictorians spoke to the pride they had in Concordia and its communities, and large cohorts of graduating students completed their graduate degrees and went on to contribute in a myriad of ways all around the world.

The growing interest in degrees that cross over disciplines or combine disciplinary approaches are challenges for the future, as most universities are traditionally structured along disciplinary lines within established academic Departments. Equity, diversity, and inclusion is another principle that must take root within academia, for society to benefit from perspectives and values that have been silenced for too long. The School of Graduate Studies can be a leader in moving these changes forward. With its team of experts in graduate studies, and access to research on significant shifts and trends in graduate education around the world, the school is uniquely placed to ensure that Concordia is at the vanguard in graduate education for generations to come.[23]

In tracing the tremendous growth and development in graduate studies and research at Concordia in its first fifty years, there is no doubt that it has arrived as a significant presence within the Canadian and global context. When asked what the future held for the School of Graduate Studies at Concordia, Dr. Faye Diamantoudi, dean of graduate studies, opined on how the School of Graduate Studies would continue to guide the faculties in adjusting to what a graduate education should provide to students in a rapidly evolving environment.[24] In addition to advanced disciplinary knowledge, graduate students of the future must be equipped with professional skills adaptable to a host of markets, with the evolving reality that up to 80 percent of alumnae with graduate degrees do not go on to academic careers. The 2020 pandemic was also a stark reminder that change could come without warning, making adaptability a critical component of success. Challenges are an impetus to discovery and growth, and for Concordia to be a trailblazer in the graduate and research community, it must continue to push forward and plan ahead, as it did in the 1960s when a group of academics in an aspiring university decided it was time to begin to offer a small number of graduate degrees to its students.

## NOTES

1   The "comprehensive" categorization applies in the Canadian context and does not include institutions with medical and law schools.

2   Douglass Burns Clarke, *Decades of Decisions: Sir George Williams University, 1952–53 to 1972–73* (Montreal: n.p., 1977), 152.

3   The board was headed by successive chairs until it established a search committee in 1971 to find its first dean of graduate studies. For more on this, see Clarke, *Decades of Decisions*, 154–55.

4   For more on the Parent Commission, see Serge Dupuis, "Royal Commission of Inquiry on Education in the Province of Quebec (Parent Commission)," *Canadian Encyclopedia*, June 18, 2020, https://www.thecanadianencyclopedia.ca/en/article/royal-commission-of-inquiry-on-education-in-the-province-of-quebec-parent-commission.

5   Clarke, *Decades of Decisions*, 154.

6   Clarke, *Decades of Decisions*, 156.

7   The first chairman of the board (1963–1967) was Dr. S. Madras, Dean of the Faculty of Science. In 1967 the Office of the Dean of Graduate Studies was created, and Professor Martin Deming Lewis became acting dean in 1967; he was appointed dean in 1969 and resigned in that fall. Given his very short tenure, Dr. Lewis's "official" term of a few months failed to be counted as

time progressed, and Dr. Stanley French became known as the "first dean of graduate studies." Dr. French became acting dean in January 1970 and formally became the dean in 1971. For more on this, see Clarke, *Decades of Decisions*, 155.

8 This information is drawn from a November 1982 Graduate Studies Office internal report, *The Evolution of Graduate Studies, 1965–1982.*

9 Although the Humanities PhD at the time allowed for some leeway for students to create their own version of a humanities degree, SIP was different because it was not restricted to the humanities, and it did not compete with the humanities program for prospective students.

10 These statistics are derived from Concordia University's Spectrum Research Repository database, accessed May 28, 2023, https://spectrum.library.concordia.ca/.

11 This information is drawn from an October 1990 Graduate Studies office internal report, *Review of the Division of Graduate Studies.*

12 Concordia University Senate, Minutes of meeting of November 1, 1991, https://archive.org/details/us-91-5/mode/2up.

13 Outgoing dean Claude Bédard drafted and submitted a retrospective analysis and report upon completion of his five-year term, titled *Graduate Studies and Research at Concordia University: 63 Months of Achievements and Challenges, June 1997 to August 2002, Bilan and Epilogue.* Bédard submitted the report to Jack Lightstone, then provost and vice-rector, research.

14 By 2022 the research funding picture had improved dramatically, as reported in the printed version of *Concordia President's Report 2023: Making a Difference in Our World*, which states that the university had received $75.8 million in research income in the previous year. The *President's Report* is available online at https://www.concordia.ca/content/dam/concordia/publications-reports/docs/Presidents-Report-EN.pdf.

15 The CFI is a grant program that funds large-scale research infrastructure projects at Canadian universities, colleges, research hospitals, and non-profit research institutions. Since its inception, Concordia has received close to $40 million from the CFI, with additional funds being contributed by the Quebec government, typically via the Ministère de l'Enseignement supérieur. The Canada Research Chair program formulaically allocates and invests over $300 million per year to universities for use in attracting and retaining world-class faculty researchers.

16 Bédard, *Graduate Studies and Research at Concordia University.*

17 The lesser controversial responsibilities under the school's purview included managing the (then) Special Individualized Program; publishing the *Graduate Calendar*; establishing specific institution-wide standards and regulations; administering the thesis publication and defence processes; administering the academic code of conduct for graduate students; and some elements of graduate student performance monitoring, to name a few.

18 The committee's findings were summarized in an internal document titled *Report of the Review Committee of the School of Graduate Studies* (Office of Vice-President, Research and Graduate Studies, December 18, 2007).

19 See *Concordia Journal* 5, no. 13 (April 1, 2010): 9.

20 The ALGANT consortium was established in 2004, and in 2023 its website lists nine participating "research and educational establishments." The consortium "offers a two-year world-class integrated master course and a joint doctorate program in pure mathematics, with a strong emphasis on algebra, geometry, and number theory. Both programs have received the Erasmus Mundus label." More information about the participating institutions can be found at https://algant.eu/index.php. A "cotutelle" refers to an agreement on joint supervision between two universities at the doctoral level, and it allows the students to get a double/joint PhD degree delivered and recognized by both institutions.

21 Recent presentations include "Future Directions for Engaged Graduate Scholarship and Professional Development" and "Designing Graduate Experiences with Intention: Centering Access and Inclusion" at Northeastern Association of Graduate Schools, Portsmouth, 2023;

"An Outcome-Based Proposal for the Future of the PhD: We're All in This Together" at Northeastern Association of Graduate Schools, New Orleans, 2021; "The Implications of 'Big Data' for Graduate Education," at Strategic Leaders Global Summit on Graduate Education, Singapore, 2015; "Interdisciplinary Graduate Programs: Opportunities and Challenges," at Council of Graduate Schools, San Diego, 2013.

22  Statistics obtained from the School of Graduate Studies, January 27, 2023. The exact numbers are as follow: 2,117 graduate students graduated; 237 postdoctoral fellows under contract; 8,933 registered graduate students; 113 graduate programs listed in the *Graduate Calendar*.

23  Faye Diamantoudi in conversation with Joanne Beaudoin, Montreal, Quebec, January 24, 2023.

24  Faye Diamantoudi was interim dean of graduate studies from 2020 to 2023, and formally appointed to a five-year term in February 2023.

**François Houde**
*Four Horsemen* (detail), 1989
Industrial glass boxes, metal (6.5 metres)
Stairwell, Vanier Library Building, Loyola campus

Marie-France Brière
*Figures en lisière* (detail), 2011
African black granite, Georgian white marble and stainless steel (6.1 metres high)
Exterior, Centre for Structural and Functional Genomics, Loyola campus

# 15 | RESEARCH AT CONCORDIA

Jean-Philippe Warren, Julien Larregue, and Vincent Larivière

## Changes in the Focus of Social Sciences and Humanities Research, 2000–2021

*Julien Larregue and Jean-Philippe Warren*

**SINCE 2000 CONCORDIA UNIVERSITY** has strongly consolidated its fields of research. It has expanded in many areas, taking advantage of the recruitment of new professors and the influx of students from across Canada and abroad. The domains of the social sciences and humanities have experienced increases in research funding as well as research applications, and are the focus of analysis here. It is not our intention to map the entirety of this production, whose dynamism is equalled only by its diversity. We will simply provide an overview of the changes in social sciences and humanities research, as they can be understood from an analysis of grant applications (both successful and unsuccessful) submitted to the Social Sciences and Humanities Research Council (SSHRC).[1]

It is clear that not all social sciences and humanities research goes through SSHRC and that the submission of an application to SSHRC is not in itself a guarantee of excellence. However, following the evolution of the vocabulary used in SSHRC grant applications may help better understand some of the trends in research at Concordia over the past twenty years.

### Three Main Lexical Clusters

Evidently, the multivocal, transdisciplinary, and transversal nature of the research conducted at Concordia implies that many works escape any simple categorization based on watertight themes. Nevertheless, by using a lexicometric analysis (through Alceste with Iramuteq softwares) of the summaries of the English and French keywords

---

JEAN-PHILIPPE WARREN is Associate Professor in the Department of Sociology and Anthropology, Concordia University. He is also a fellow of the Royal Society of Canada and co-director of the Democracy and Pluralism research axis of the Centre for Interdisciplinary Research on Diversity and Democracy.

JULIEN LARREGUE is Assistant Professor of sociology at Université Laval and a member of the Centre interuniversitaire de recherche sur la science et la technologie. His award-winning book on contemporary biocriminology, *Héréditaire L'éternel retour des théories biologiques du crime* (2020) is forthcoming (2024) in English with Stanford University Press.

of the projects submitted to SSHRC, it is possible to identify certain major lexical clusters, with all the precautions that this kind of exercise requires. Among the 5,429 projects analyzed, 5,200 (95.8%) could be classified in one of the three main lexical universes projected in the factorial correspondence analysis (Figure 15.1).

The first domain (in green) agglomerates social and political themes. It revolves around the issue of governance. The concepts associated with it are those of identity, nationalism, public policy, law, and minorities. The focus of the projects on Quebec and Canada seems to be more accentuated within this first domain.

The second set of words (in blue) brings together interventionist and pragmatic themes. It revolves around the issue of risk management. The concepts associated with it are those of development, behaviour, competence, regulation, and organization.

**15.1 Correspondence factor analysis of keywords for SSHRC projects**

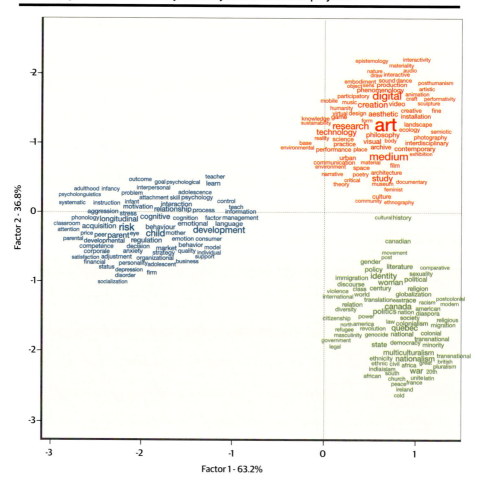

170  BUILDING THE INSTITUTION

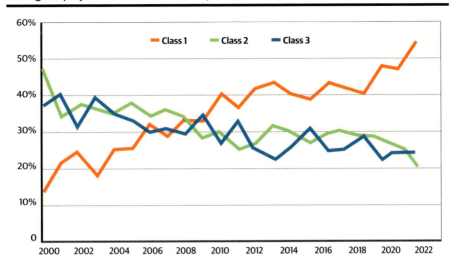

15.2 Temporal evolution of the respective place occupied by the lexicometric clusters among the projects submitted to SSHRC, 2000–2021

The third lexical universe (in red) intertwines artistic and historical themes. It revolves around the issue of narrative. The concepts associated with it are those of medium, aesthetics, creation, translation, and communication.

## A Certain Evolution

Over the past twenty years, the relative importance of each lexicometric cluster among SSHRC project submissions has changed significantly (Figure 15.2). While the second and third lexical clusters have become relatively less popular, the first lexical cluster has been the object of increasing interest in SSHRC grant applications (successful and unsuccessful). Indeed, the first lexical cluster, which represented less than 15 percent of applications in 2000, now accounts for more than half of them.

This development reflects, on the one hand, the growth of certain research sectors, including digital archives, gaming, and cultural studies. Concordia has become one of the most dynamic places for research on decolonization, feminism, queer theory, and anti-racism, among others areas. Such a development reflects, on the other hand, the "cultural turn" of the social sciences and humanities, a turn that can be observed throughout North American universities. It is symptomatic, in this respect, that, for the whole period, students are more likely than professors to be found in the third lexical cluster (42.6% versus 30%). These figures seem to confirm that the new generations of researchers are more involved in projects that are more related to critical theory and discourse analysis.

In conclusion, it bears repeating that research at Concordia does not necessarily involve applying for a SSHRC grant. Obviously, the brief lexicometric analysis presented here does not exhaust the richness of the projects carried out by Concordia's researchers. It does, however, provide a window onto some of the trends in research over the past twenty years.

What we can observe is that three main fields of interest structure the research projects: some are more oriented towards governance, others more towards risk management, and others more towards narrative. This last field of interest is the one that has recently attracted the largest proportion of researchers.

Together, these developments demonstrate not only the great dynamism of research at Concordia, but also its ability to adapt to the changing challenges of the contemporary world.

**NOTE**

1   Although the majority of SSHRC submissions originate from the Faculty of Arts and Science, researchers in the John Molson School of Business, the Faculty of Fine Arts, and the Gina Cody School of Engineering and Computer Science are far from absent from the pool of applicants.

# 50 YEARS OF RESEARCH

Vincent Larivière and Jean-Philippe Warren

The past fifty years have witnessed a prodigious expansion of research at Concordia University. This expansion has taken many forms and followed a myriad of avenues. The dynamism of research at Concordia is matched only by its remarkable diversity. The publication of articles is only one of the variables that allow us to grasp the development of academic research. Nevertheless, such a variable is now considered representative enough to offer a good overview of general trends in most fields of research. In the present text, we have used data from the Web of Science to construct a number of tables that show not only the progression of research at Concordia, but also its growing involvement in international networks.

VINCENT LARIVIÈRE is Full Professor of information science at the École de bibliothéconomie et des sciences de l'information, l'Université de Montréal. He is scientific director of *Érudit* journal, associate scientific director of the Observatoire des sciences et des technologies, vice-rector of strategic planning and communications, and the first UNESCO Chair in Open Science.

## Growth in Research

As Figure 15.3 shows, Concordia researchers are publishing more and more articles each year. Between 1980 and 2020, the number of articles published increased by a factor of almost eight, while over the same period, the number of faculty members of the Concordia University Faculty Association less than doubled (from approximately 600 to 1,000). While the proportion of articles authored by Concordia researchers in Canada as a whole stagnated, if not declined, from 1980 to 2000, it jumped significantly between 2000 and 2021, from less than 1 percent to 1.8 percent (Figure 15.3). This increase is all the more impressive when we take into account Quebec's low demographic growth compared to other Canadian provinces.

Figure 15.4 shows disciplines by number of articles published as a proportion of the Canadian total. While virtually all disciplines have improved their ratio between 1980 and 2021, it is interesting to note that the greatest progress has been made in the arts and humanities. Clinical medicine and health also performed well, even though Concordia University has no faculty of medicine or department of pharmacology.

## Research Networks

Fifty years ago, university research was much more solitary than it is today. Large research teams are now a reality in most disciplines. It is only natural, therefore, to see a proliferation of collaborative articles. An analysis of collaboration with Canadian colleagues (Figure 15.5) reveals that the main partners of Concordia University researchers are from Quebec.

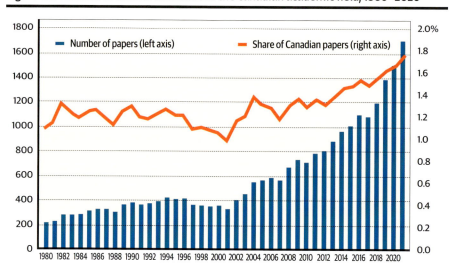

Figure 15.3 Number of articles and share in the Canadian academic field, 1980–2020

### 15.4 Disciplines in which Concordia publishes the most articles, 1980–2000 and 2001–2021

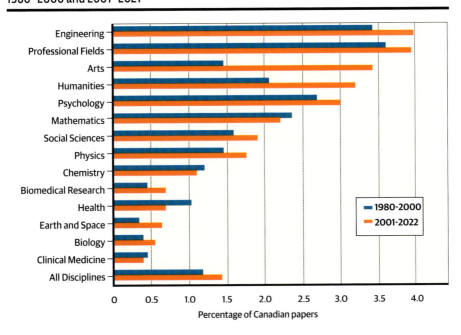

### 15.5 Top 20 institutional affiliations of Concordia University researchers' Canadian collaborators, 2001–2021

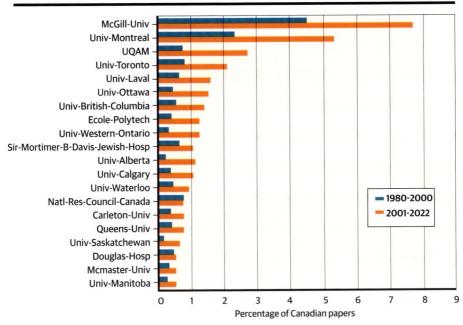

**Figure 15.6 Percentage of articles written in international collaboration, 1980–2021**

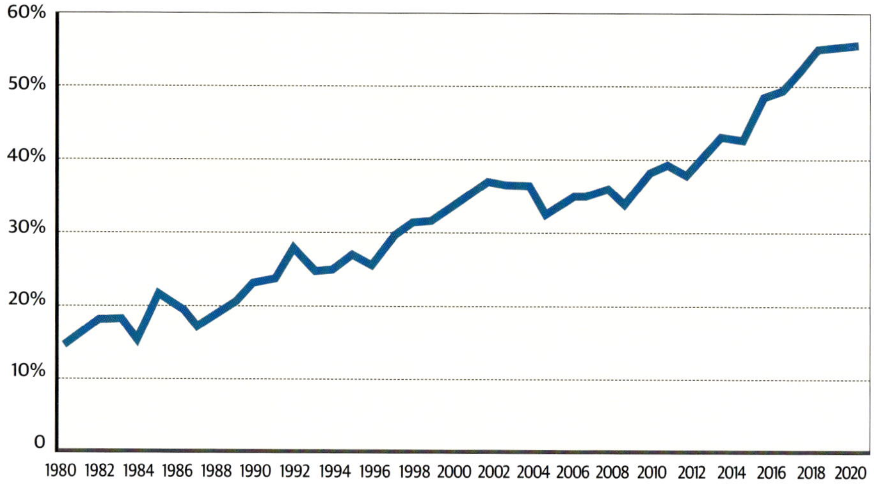

McGill University stands out. On average, from 2000 to 2020, nearly 8 percent of articles published by Concordia researchers were co-authored with McGill colleagues. Sir Mortimer B. Davis Jewish General Hospital, affiliated with McGill University, ranks tenth on the list. The Université de Montréal and Université du Québec à Montréal (UQAM) come second and third, respectively, having experienced a significant rapprochement with Concordia University over the past twenty years. Greater interaction between the French- and English-speaking research communities, encouraged in particular by the adoption of English as the lingua franca of science, probably partly explains this trend. Geographically close, the Université Laval, the University of Ottawa, and Polytechnique Montréal rank fifth, sixth, and eighth, respectively. The University of Toronto and the University of British Columbia, Canada's two largest institutions of higher learning in terms of research, rank fourth and seventh, respectively. Although still not very popular, collaborations between Concordia and establishments situated in the western provinces are clearly increasing.

## International Networks

In 1980 research at Concordia was hardly international. As Figure 15.6 shows, the percentage of articles co-authored with researchers from other countries was low (around 15%). Since then, this percentage has risen steadily. Today, more than half of articles published by Concordia researchers are co-authored with international colleagues.

An analysis of the institutional affiliations of Concordia University researchers' collaborators (Figure 15.7) reveals that, over the past two decades, two Chinese institutions have dominated international collaborations. The Chinese Academy of Sciences is the world's largest research organization, with one hundred institutes and sixty-nine thousand full-time employees. Nanjing University, one of China's most

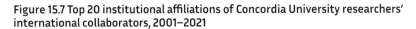

Figure 15.7 Top 20 institutional affiliations of Concordia University researchers' international collaborators, 2001–2021

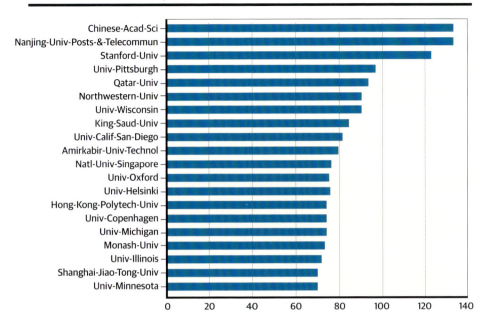

prestigious higher education institutions, follows in second place. Other Chinese institutions appear on the list, reflecting the fact that China now produces almost a quarter of all articles published worldwide. American universities, including Stanford and Northwestern, are obviously present in Figure 15.7. The University of Pittsburgh, a public university known for its large research teams, comes fourth. Oxford University in England and Monash University in Australia reflect both the prestige of these institutions and Concordia's integration into Commonwealth networks. The list also includes King Saud University, Saudi Arabia's largest university, and Amirkabir University of Technology in Tehran.

## Conclusion

Over the past fifty years, the development of research at Concordia, as measured solely by the number of articles published, has followed an impressive upward curve. The establishment of a vast network of collaborations in Canada and abroad is a clear sign of this rapid progress. From Australia to China, and from the United States to Iran, Concordia researchers have countless exchanges with colleagues around the world. The fields explored are extremely diverse: in anthropology as in engineering, in the arts as in computer science, the expertise of Concordia researchers is increasingly recognized and in demand. Quantity does not equal quality, of course, but there is no denying that the dynamism of its researchers has enabled Concordia to rank among the top research establishments in Canada and beyond.

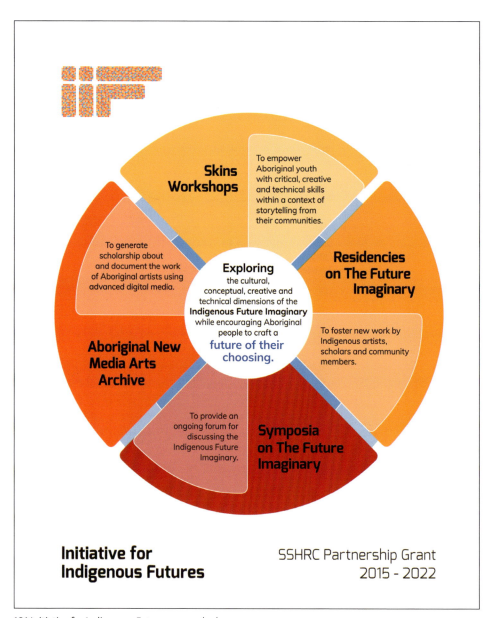

16.1 Initiative for Indigenous Futures research plan.

# BUILDING ABORIGINAL TERRITORIES IN CYBERSPACE (ABTEC)

Jason Edward Lewis and Skawennati

> So, Owisokon, at the very beginning ... of the Skins process ... she was asking these questions: What is this project, what are you going to do, what are you going to be teaching them? Finally, she says, "And what do yous want anyway? Why are yous doing this?" And because it was Owisokon, who I have known for many years, I felt free enough to say, "Well, we want to change the world."
> —Skawennati

## Beginnings

In a sense, Aboriginal Territories in Cyberspace (AbTeC) traces its origins to May 1999 when Jason and Skawennati met at the Sync or Stream Streaming Media Symposium, hosted by the Banff New Media Institute, in Banff, Alberta. This first meeting initiated a two-decade-long dialogue on Indigenous people and digital media, fueled by Jason's research into new forms of digital media in Silicon Valley and Skawennati's development of the virtual art gallery CyberPowWow. CyberPowWow's "main goals [were] to overcome stereotypes about Aboriginal people; to help shape the World Wide Web; and to generate critical discourse—both in person and online—about First Nations art, technology, and community."[1] It showcased Indigenous people, challenging the predominantly white, male norms already established in the digital world, and clarified their intention to have Indigenous people participate fully in shaping the future of digital and networked media.

---

JASON EDWARD LEWIS is a digital media theorist, poet, and software designer. He founded Obx Laboratory for Experimental Media and co-directs Abundant Intelligences, the Indigenous Futures Research Centre, and Aboriginal Territories in Cyberspace. Lewis is the University Research Chair in Computational Media and the Indigenous Future Imaginary and Professor of computation arts at Concordia University.

SKAWENNATI is a visual artist whose practice questions our relationships with technology and highlights Indigenous people in the future. Her machinima, still images, sculpture, and textiles have been presented and collected internationally. A Kanien'kehá:ka (Mohawk) of Kahnawà:ke residing in Montreal, she co-directs Aboriginal Territories in Cyberspace.

## Manifesto

In our 2004 manifesto "Aboriginal Territories in Cyberspace," we emphasized that Indigenous people were eager to engage with new technologies, particularly if they improved our ability to communicate with one another over the vast distances of Turtle Island and helped us better tell our stories. We realized the need to critique the Silicon Valley rhetoric that described cyberspace as a blank slate, upon which anybody anywhere could inscribe their desires. As descendants of generations of peoples who were continually assaulted by Western technology, we understood that a system developed as a military tool was not "blank" and was slowly being harnessed for capitalist exploitation.

AbTeC started with three goals:

1. The creation of original artwork that addresses the future of Indigenous people in North America.
2. Educating Indigenous youth in digital media production (including video games) in a way that emphasized the integration of Indigenous stories and storytelling techniques into the process.
3. Developing a trajectory whereby young Indigenous people can move from new media consumption to media production to technology development and bring that production and development activity back to their communities.

## From Manifesto to Practice

Getting this vision funded, however, was initially challenging. The major government funders had not yet developed funding envelopes that were supportive of Indigenous research methodologies, and were just establishing funding opportunities for research-creation. A project that combined both was a tough sell, until, in 2004, the Social Sciences and Humanities Research Council (SSHRC) established an experimental Aboriginal Research Network grant. We assembled a majority-Indigenous research network of collaborators to explore the three goals, and wrote a proposal. And we were successful! We received $400,000 from SSHRC—and immediately ran into an almost terminal challenge.

It had taken us several years of conversations with different organizations in Skawennati's home community, Kahnawà:ke, to find a community partner who wanted to collaborate. Indigenous community stories had rarely been told in interactive media and there was much justifiable suspicion. When we told community members we thought video games might be a fruitful medium for telling some of the old stories, we were met with a barrage of questions: Which stories? Who would be telling them? Who would see them? How would they be distributed? Would somebody owning the game then think they owned the story? Of particular concern was that the youth would make "Grand Theft Rez," turning the stories into blood-soaked shoot 'em ups whose only point was to simulate murder and mayhem. Several potential partners never quite believed this approach could be done in a culturally generative and safe way, and, after initially expressing interest, decided to pass on collaborating with us to produce the workshops. When we did finally find a partner to join us on the grant application, we were elated. We got the money and their board of directors got cold feet. They withdrew their collaboration, forcing us go looking again. We eventually found another collaborator in Owisokon Lahache, an arts and culture teacher at the Kahnawake Survival School, the local high school.

We based AbTeC out of Jason's Concordia research-creation studio, Obx Labs. We assembled our team of artists, scholars, activists, and technologists. We prototyped designs for an Indigenous-grounded video game workshop, and Skawennati began exploring machinima (machine + cinema = movie-making in virtual environments). The former became the Skins Workshops on Aboriginal Storytelling in Digital Media, and the latter eventually resulted in *TimeTraveller™*, a nine-part machinima series.

The seed for the Skins Workshops was planted in a conversation between Skawennati and the feminist game designer Celia Pearce. Skawennati and Pearce attended the Skinning Our Tools: Designing for Context and Culture Symposium, also at the Banff New Media Institute. Their conversation revolved around strategies to actively promote the creation of improved and diverse representations of Indigenous characters in digital media. Skins began by incorporating Indigenous stories and storytelling into video games, and later into other digital media. Our project aimed to empower First Nations youth as media creators, fostering experimentation with digital tools for preserving culture, advancing languages, and self-determined images amidst pervasive stereotypical portrayals of Indigenous Peoples. The hope was to empower them to have greater control over their destinies in the evolving landscapes of cyberspace.

Created by Skawennati, *TimeTraveller™* tells the story of Hunter, a young Mohawk man in the twenty-second century, who is lost and disconnected from his ancestors in a high-tech society. Hunter utilizes an emerging virtual immersion technology called "TimeTraveller™" to experience historical events significant to First Nations People. In so doing, Hunter gains insights on how to integrate his heritage with his hyper-modern life and construct a personally meaningful vision of the future. Filmed in the multiuser virtual world of Second Life, Skawennati's machinima series emerged from her frustration with the near absence of Indigenous people from the future imaginary of popular science fiction. This absence was indicative of the tendency for popular media to portray Indigenous cultures primarily as historical entities, often neglecting their contemporary presence and agency in the world.

16.2 Skawennati, *Face-Off*, 2010, machinimagraph from TimeTraveller™

16.3 Jason Edward Lewis (concept), Kari Noe (illustration), *Quartet*, 2019. From the Abundant Intelligences project.

Both Skins and *TimeTraveller*™ led us to focus AbTeC more and more on Indigenous futurisms. In our work with Indigenous youth, we realized they had challenges in imagining futures based in their communities' traditions. We realized that their future, too, had been colonized by the West. We were motivated by how *TimeTraveller*™ illustrated the transformative potential of envisioning futures rooted in specific Indigenous communities, which inspired us to actively promote storytelling, intellectual discourse, and community dialogue that embraced a similar approach. We were also aware of the work that Anishinaabe literary scholar Grace Dillon had been doing to develop the concept and necessity of Indigenous futurism, shedding light on both historical and contemporary Indigenous science fiction practices. In 2008 we built AbTeC Island in Second Life to serve as our headquarters in cyberspace. AbTeC Island served multiple purposes: the location where Skawennati filmed the machinima productions; an environment where we could teach 3D modelling in the Skins Workshops; and, eventually, a virtual exhibition space called AbTeC Gallery. This gallery has featured forty-five Indigenous artists from Canada and around the world in six exhibitions.

## The Initiative for Indigenous Futures

In 2013 Jason gave a TEDxMontreal talk on the future imaginary. Building on our experiences with our projects envisioning tangible Indigenous futures, he proposed an initial definition: "A 'future imaginary' is a vision of the future that is shared by a group of people and used to motivate change in the present. Future imaginaries provide groups with shared vocabularies for envisioning the future and strategies for getting to the future they desire. Such imaginaries … create a field of 'future facts,' a fully realized reality that exists somewhere down the timeline, waiting for us to catch up to it."[2] This definition guided AbTeC's next big effort, the Initiative for Indigenous Futures (IIF), which partnered universities and community organizations to support artists, academics, youth, and Elders to imagine our communities in the future. IIF expanded AbTeC's range of activity to include the following initiatives:

- Residencies and commissions: hosting Indigenous artists, scholars, community activists, policy planners, etc., to spend concentrated time envisioning the future of Indigenous communities in Canada. We coupled these with commissioning original artwork from Indigenous artists to create visual manifestations of future imaginaries;
- Indigenous Digital Art Archive: a database of information on and documentation of work by international Indigenous digital media artists; Future Imaginary Lecture, Interview, and Symposia Series: establishing a series of public presentations and dialogues through which the conversation about Indigenous futures could take hold and thrive.

Like all AbTeC projects, IIF was a research-creation effort that combined scholarly investigation, creative production, and community engagement, bringing the academy, the studio, the community, and industry together to find common ground. From 2014 to 2023 we partnered with Indigenous communities across North America and beyond, including with people from the Kanien'kehá:ka, Kānaka Maoli, Cree, Lakota, Anishinaabe, Diné, Métis, Inuit, S'Klallam, Mi'kmaq, Dogrib, Gwhich'in, and Māori nations.

## Abundant Intelligences

IIF spawned a new research direction exploring Indigenous approaches to artificial intelligence (AI). In 2018 Jason led the writing of "Making Kin with the Machines," an award-winning essay that advocates for broadening AI research to incorporate Indigenous epistemologies.[3] The essay directly led to the Indigenous Protocol and AI Workshops in 2019, and the resulting position paper (2020), comprising two dozen original insights on the development of "Indigenous AI," was edited by Jason.[4] These three items—the essay, workshops, and position paper—established Indigenous AI as a field of rich scholarly, artistic, and technological activity and, resulted in the largest project grant in Concordia history to fund a research program called Abundant Intelligences from 2023 to 2029. Working with a team of Indigenous knowledge holders, scholars, AI scientists, and artists, Abundant Intelligences imagines how to conceptualize and design AI based on Indigenous Knowledge systems. The approach, rooted in Indigenous epistemologies, provides robust conceptual frameworks for developing technology that can integrate into existing lifeways. The goal is to advance methods that recognize the abundant multiplicity of ways of being intelligent in the world, and to improve AI to better serve Indigenous communities and others.

## Outcomes

Our combined research-creation outcomes have been multiple over the last twenty years.[5] We've supported and trained over 200 undergraduate students, graduate students, and postdocs, with a near majority of them Indigenous. We have secured $30 million in funding. We have held 59 Skins Workshops with more than 600 participants over 184 days of instruction in Montreal, Kahnawà:ke, Val D'Or, Waterloo, Vancouver, Maple Ridge, Regina, Yellowknife, Honolulu, and other locations. We've hosted 10 residencies and held 3 symposia, and conducted public lecture series with over 30 speakers and interviews. We have created over 800 research products and 367 knowledge mobilization events, including presentations at academic, art, and cultural events; we've given interviews with print, radio, television, and web media; we have published in peer-reviewed and edited journals and book collections as well as in textbooks for secondary and post-secondary education; we have presented exhibitions and artistic performances; published video games, machinimas, and other forms of digital media.

## Only at Concordia

We recognize how AbTeC's growth was nourished by Concordia. The department in which Jason teaches, Design and Computation Arts, trains students across a wide range of critical and technical making practices, and we have been able to recruit artists, designers, programmers, and critical cultural thinkers from within this single department. The remarkable multidisciplinary capabilities of Design and Computation Arts students has allowed us to make creative, critical, cultural, and technological contributions. We have also benefitted from the overall richness of Concordia's student body, as we have been joined by research assistants from a range of disciplines, including computer science, studio arts, art history, English, sociology and anthropology, and communication studies.

In the early years, the Hexagram Institute for Research-Creation in the Fine Arts, and in the later years, the Milieux Institute for Arts, Culture, and Technology, housed us and provided extensive facilities for working across all manner of digital media. The Faculty of Fine Arts, and Concordia in general, played a key role in securing recognition for research-creation within provincial and federal academic funding agencies.

As described above, AbTeC's key research outcomes are as likely to be creative works as scholarly publications. Artworks serve as boundary objects that are effective at reaching into not only the Indigenous community but also academic and policy circles, in ways that academic analysis and writing so often fail. Artworks are tangible points in cultural discussions, ones with which Elders and youth, aunties and uncles, beaders and video gamers can readily engage. Even in academic and policy circles, our creative works vividly depict the lived experiences of contemporary Indigenous people, emphasizing the need for a culturally grounded foundation in these often narrowly focused discussions. Having an administrative apparatus at Concordia that understood and supported this approach has been invaluable.

The Office of Research played a crucial role in supporting the entire AbTeC trajectory, provided funding and helped us collaborate with peers to enhance our funding applications. The Office of Research also learned how to better provide effective support for faculty who want to work in deep engagement with Indigenous communities, evolving policy and expectations to reflect the different realities found on the ground in those communities and continually making it easier to be true community collaborators. It takes a village to keep a research program like AbTeC going for twenty years. Concordia faculty, administrators, and students all contributed to an abundant ecosystem in which we have been able to flourish, and for this we say, *niawenkó:wa* and *mahalo nui loa*.

## NOTES

1   Jason Lewis and Skawennati Tricia Fragnito, "Aboriginal Territories in Cyberspace," *Cultural Survival Quarterly* 29, no. 2 (2005): 30.

2   Jason Lewis, "The Future Imaginary," TEDxMontreal, Société des Arts Technologiques, Montreal, September 14, 2013.

3   Jason E. Lewis. N. Arista, A., Pechawis, and S. Kite, "Making Kin with the Machines," *Journal of Design and Science* (2018), https://doi.org/10.21428/bfafd97b.

4   Jason Edward Lewis, ed., "Indigenous Protocol and Artificial Intelligence Position Paper," Indigenous Protocol and Artificial Intelligence Working Group and the Canadian Institute for Advanced Research, Honolulu, Hawai'i, February 2020, www.indigenous-ai.net/position-paper.

5   Our research and creation outcomes can be viewed at our project websites: http://www.abtec.org/, http://www.indigenousfutures.net/, and http://www.indigenous-ai.net/.

**Effets Publics – Rose-Marie Goulet, Alain Paiement, Randy Saharuni, Guy Bellavance**

*Untitled* (detail), 1992

Multi-media installation (varied dimensions)
Atrium, J.W. McConnell Building
and Webster Library, SGW campus

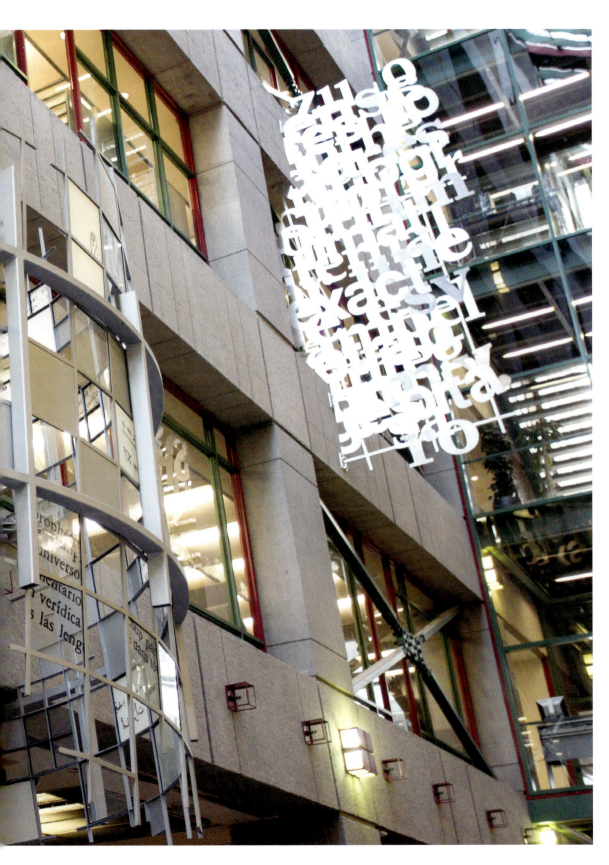

17.1 A student in the late 1960s is shown here using an analogue card catalogue system, which in 1992 was replaced with the CLUES online catalogue system.

# THE TRANSFORMATION OF CONCORDIA LIBRARY

## William M. Curran

**LIBRARIES HAVE BEEN** fundamentally transformed as a result of unprecedented changes in how information is acquired, stored, and retrieved in a way that few could have imagined thirty-five years ago at the onset of the World Wide Web.[1] This chapter provides an overview of Concordia's library as it evolved since the founding of the university in 1974, a merger of two academic institutions, two traditions, two philosophies, two campuses, two staffing units, and several union contracts. It highlights the profound changes, not only of the physical library buildings, procedures, and access policies but also of the variety of library services and their delivery, which have been designed to keep pace with the needs and demands of users of academic libraries over time.

The twenty-first-century library has had to mirror the changes in how students, scholars, and researchers work and has evolved in step with new academic methodologies.[2] The academic library has become a hub for a new generation of faculty and students that supports experimentation and innovation in processes that embrace research across many communities and disciplines. To do that, academic libraries developed a matrix of new services identified to serve information needs in a fast-changing digital world. This required a fundamental change from what libraries did traditionally (i.e., collect and circulate books) to focus on what users really needed, when they needed it, and where they were to find it. The dawn of digital publications shifted the collection growth out of a predominantly physical space into a virtual one, and thus created a different paradigm of library space design, such as the learning/study environment. Information technology had a significant impact on the learning-centred paradigm, abetting an intentional, autonomous learning pattern for users.[3] Concordia University Library, as other academic libraries, had to transform into a different environment for that to happen.

---

WILLIAM M. CURRAN, MEd, MLS, is Adjunct Professor, School of Information Studies, University of Ottawa. He was director of libraries at Concordia University from 1998 to 2008 and university librarian at Bishop's University from 1989 to 1998. He served as president of L'Association pour l'avancement des sciences et des techniques de la documentation (ASTED) (1995–96) and chair of the Sous-comité des bibliothèques, Conférence des recteurs et principaux des universités du Québec (2001–02).

17.2 As an urban university Concordia's Sir George campus is embedded into Montreal's dynamic cityscape. A view of the McConnell Library Building being built in November 1988 shows the integrative relationship between city and university.

In the early days of the founding institutions, Sir George Williams University (SGWU) and Loyola College, academic libraries operated along similar lines and offered, more or less, the same services. As long as books and periodicals were purchased, placed appropriately on shelves, and quiet spaces provided, academic libraries followed a similar routine. Faculty and students had the same expectations of college and university libraries. As for the library's general collection, the content of Sir George Williams's collection was substantial in the fields of business and commerce whereas Loyola's was strong in the fields of arts, science, humanities, and social sciences, while both institutions offered degrees in commerce and engineering. The content would reflect the curricula. Loyola had founded its popular Communication Studies Department about ten years before the merger. SGWU had been offering evening and part-time courses for many years, whereas the majority of courses at Loyola, until the mid-1960s, were offered in the daytime.

As was the case in most universities in North America, the enrolment of baby boomers in the mid-1960s as well as the growing presence of international students in the late 1970s and early 1980s resulted in the need for additional space for classrooms, dormitories and residences, athletic facilities, and libraries and other study spaces. Concordia University was no exception. At the time of the merger, both

17.3 A gift from the Simpson's department store to the Loyola Student Association, this replica of Michelangelo's Statue of David became a fixture of the Loyola campus. Installed on a pedestal in 1966 at Vanier Library, the statue would later be toppled by vandals in 1987.

Concordia University, Montreal  Vol. 13 No. 9 November 3, 1988

# Construction starts on downtown library complex

## Everyone is invited to the ground-breaking

by Ken Whittingham

It's finally happening.

Nearly 20 years after the idea was first proposed, construction is about to start on Concordia's downtown library complex.

Faculty, students, alumni and staff will join government and University officials on the site tomorrow morning at 11:30 a.m. to mark the official sod-turning for the $40-million complex.

The entire University community is welcome to attend. Afterwards, everyone will be invited to cross the street to the lobby of the Henry F. Hall Building to join in a toast to Concordia.

Tenders for phase one of the six-storey, 20,975-square-meter library complex were issued October 7, 1988. The winning bid was awarded to the construction firm of Hervé Pomerleau Inc.

The company's previous projects include Le Windsor (the renovated Windsor Hotel building on Peel Street) and L'édifice La Laurentienne, the 25-storey office tower on the corner of Peel Street and René Lévesque Boulevard.

Concordia's library was designed by the architectural consortium of Werleman & Guy Blouin & Associés.

During the coming months the contractor will shore up portions of the foundations and inner walls of the 76-year-old Royal George Apartment Building, erect fencing around the perimeter of the library site — bordered by de Maisonneuve Boulevard, Mackay Street, Bishop Street, and the laneway between de Maisonneuve and Ste-Catherine Street — remove existing mechanical and electrical services on the huge lot, and demolish all but the façade and first bay of the Royal George building.

### Integrate façade

The east side of the new library complex, on Bishop Street, will integrate the front section of the Royal George, including the structure's 76-year-old glazed terra-cotta façade.

Months of study, including government analyses, concluded that maintaining the Royal George in its entirety would add $5 million to the overall cost of the project; maintaining the façade alone will cost $1.5 to $2 million.

Once the Royal George is readied, excavation will begin on the rest of the site.

Phase Two of the project, the construction of the new building, will begin in late spring. Total construction time is 28 to 36 months.

Concordia's downtown library facilities are currently spread over 11 floors in four separate buildings. All 11,000 square metres of existing downtown library space will be incorporated into the new building, along with additional study space for graduate and undergraduate students and badly-needed seminar rooms, conference rooms and faculty offices.

*See EVERYONE page 2*

17.4 A rendering of the final proposal for Concordia's new library pavilion (LB) on the Sir George Williams campus, integrating the façade and front part of the former Royal George Apartments, as imagined in 1988.

the SGWU and the Loyola libraries were short of space and in need of expansion. Concordia soon enjoyed a reputation for excellence in business, communication studies, fine arts, and psychology, offering full-time and part-time programs as enrolments increased, which resulted in overcrowding in the libraries on the Loyola campus as well as on the downtown campus. By 1985 it became clear that both of Concordia's libraries needed additional space and an overhaul of operations to avoid costly duplication, as can happen when separate entities are merged. In 1989 an expansion and renovation of the George Vanier Library building was carried out.

However, the congestion on the downtown campus—in the Norris Library as well as in the Science and Engineering Library in the Hall Building—urgently needed to be addressed. While the renovation of the Vanier Library could be completed within the parameters of the Loyola campus, renovations on the downtown campus presented a very different set of challenges. Between 1967 and 1976 the city of Montreal had hosted Expo 67 as well as the Olympics Games. The downtown area of the city was booming, but Concordia, as an urban downtown institution, did not have a campus per se, nor did the university own many properties onto which it could expand or erect new buildings.

Thus, it was not only Concordia's library that needed space, but the downtown campus needed to find additional quarters for a number of departments. Accordingly, after a very long wait, thanks to major donations from the R. Howard Webster Foundation and the McConnell Foundation, a $65 million edifice was proposed directly across from the Hall Building.[4] This proposal, however, included the demolition of the Royal George Apartments bought by Concordia in 1979. As with many plans, delays were inevitable. A controversy arose over the preservation of the front of the Royal George building, which had a white glazed terracotta façade (classified as a historical monument). An agreement was reached to restore and integrate the façade into the new library building, as were special rooms set apart by an atrium on each floor thus incorporating the "Royal George" identity. The new building was built right to the sidewalk with an outdoor portico and an indoor atrium, squeezing as much space from the structure as possible but providing no exterior green space. Nonetheless, the large atrium surrounded by massive windows provided natural light making the new library an inviting place for users.

In 1992 the new McConnell Building was opened and became known as the "Library Building." The library was initially expected to occupy the second through fifth floors, which were reinforced to provide support for bookshelves, but other needs for space were identified by the university, and the library was not at first provided space on the fifth floor. The new library housed the collections of the Norris Library and Science and Engineering Library (moved from the Hall Building) as well as the library's Technical Services unit and book storage, which had been housed in rented spaces in the Shuchat Building. Thus, for the first time, services, collections, and staff were working together from one facility on the downtown campus. That same year, the library purchased its new automated library information system (INNOPAC), a top-of-the-line model whereby users could access information of shelf locations of the content of the collection (via the CLUES online catalogue system) through sixty-five computers spread across both libraries, replacing the manual card catalogues forever. The new system also featured modules for purchasing materials designed to increase efficiency in procedures.

Notwithstanding the new building, several factors external to the library were affecting the library's space needs and the provision of new services for users. Enrolment on both campuses as Concordia's reputation for excellence spread and as programs and faculties merged. Graduate studies, and diploma and certificate programs were attracting significant numbers of students. When the Webster Library opened in 1992, Concordia had a population of approximately 26,000 students.[5] Within 12 years, that number would increase to 30,905 with 160 programs in 4 faculties.[6] Concordia was now one of Canada's largest and fastest growing urban universities. Space shortages soon became a critical issue on both campuses.

Most profound of all the changes in the information world during this time was the advent of the (then relatively new) internet, which radically transformed how research was conducted and how information was stored and retrieved, online and in print. Changes brought about by the internet, in turn, had a direct impact on research, teaching delivery, and the kinds of assignments required of college and university students. It was said that there was, at this time, an explosion of information available to scholars worldwide, not necessarily because there was an increase in the quantity of information but because of the ease with which information was becoming readily available.[7]

In the library, not surprisingly, there were severe shortages of seating space, seminar rooms, quiet study space, and group study space.[8] These space issues created another major problem for the library: noise. Students in management need to discuss case studies, identify issues, propose solutions, for example, and undergraduate and graduate students need to discuss assignments, and prepare and rehearse group presentations. The congestion in Webster was particularly problematic. Students were not being deliberately noisy but because there were so few seminar rooms, carrels and tables were placed in very close proximity without partitions. When a group would gather at a table and a discussion began, another group would sit at a neighbouring table and voices were raised. In desperation some smaller groups could be seen in group discussions sitting in stairwells. The situation also became a problem for those students who simply needed quiet places to study and to write papers and dissertations. Especially around the noon hour between 11 a.m. and 2 p.m., it was not uncommon

17.5 The inauguration of the McConnell Building in 1992 was an auspicious occasion that signalled a revamping of Concordia's downtown campus.

to see students come into the library, walk through the third and fourth floors seeking, without success, a place to sit and in frustration, head back out. All Concordia students have a right to their library, regardless of whether they are part-time or full-time, whether they are discussing cases, preparing reports/class presentations, or studying quietly. Every learning function belongs in the academic library, be it solitary or in groups.

A pilot project was initiated to offer students better access to their library by providing longer opening hours. During exam periods, the libraries remained open for twenty-four hours a day. Its enormous success was applauded and eventually the policy of twenty-four-hour access was instituted for the entire fall and winter terms. Some departments offered courses on both campuses and requested that pertinent collections be available for students at both libraries. To better serve their students, some faculties offered courses exclusively on the downtown campus regardless of where the library collections happened to be, which created accessibility problems as the library could not afford to duplicate collections. This scenario was not unique for Concordia Library; indeed, between 1986 and 1998, costs of scholarly journals rose 207 percent and monograph costs rose by 45 percent, and 85 percent of the library's purchases were through foreign publishers. Between 1990 and 1999 the combined Canadian Association of Research Libraries purchasing power diminished by 42 percent.[9] Consortia agreements such as the Canadian Research Knowledge Network created economies of scale in subscribing to online journals and publications. As no single academic library could provide exhaustive collections, interlibrary loan policies among academic libraries were instituted by Conférence des recteurs et principaux des universités du Québec and Canadian Association of Research Libraries to aid scholars in accessing materials. (Conférence des recteurs et principaux des universités du Québec was disbanded in 2014 and replaced by the Bureau de coopération interuniversitaire.)

In 2002 approximately 15 percent of the library's periodical collection was available only in electronic format while another 25 percent had an electronic component. It was predicted that within five years, 90 percent of periodicals in the fields of science, medicine, and engineering would be exclusively in electronic format.[10] It did not take five years for that prediction to come true. Some periodicals were still only available in print, but this changed quickly. For the libraries, the need to provide access to information available in different formats required a different budget operation for computer and copying equipment. At that time, many students did not own portable computers, tablets, or smartphones. Access to online journals purchased by the libraries required appropriate equipment and workstations on site—in sufficient numbers to address the needs of an ever-growing number of library users. There was a need for graphic workstations and colour printers in each library. Workstations

17.6 The Webster Library Transformation Project was a three-year project that began in January 2015. University Librarian Guylaine Beaudry, who oversaw the project, is seen here with President Alan Shepard and Provost Benoit-Antoine Bacon, reading entries in a guest book written by patrons who visited the newly added spaces in the fall.

usage increased 69 percent between 1998–99 and 2000–01.[11] The Electronic Reserves service was initiated in 2004 to provide access for users to articles and readings on their computer screens at home or elsewhere.

A fully staffed Systems Unit was established within the library to help address these changes. A systems librarian was appointed at the level of assistant director, reflecting the importance of the position in the organigram. The technical staff of the Systems Unit required different levels of competencies and training. Computer technicians were needed in the library to ensure that the workstations remained fully functional as these were in use twenty-four hours per day during the term.

Each year, the number of workstations increased in the library. New services such as loans of tablets and laptops, along with automated check-out and renewals, became the norm. In 2003 Concordia's virtual interactive reference service was launched. And the library's 2003–2004 report cites that interlibrary loans of books rose 26 percent. With the complexity and the multidisciplinary nature of scholarly research, it was essential to establish information literacy, training for library users to access and assess the value of digitized materials, to use the wireless networking within the library, to be familiar with the online data-based archives and ejournals as well as other publications. This training formed part of a pedagogical mandate for the librarians. With the internet at everyone's fingertips, university students needed to acquire the learning and critical thinking skills needed to access, evaluate, and use information effectively across all disciplines. The opening of David and Lillian M. Stewart Orientation Room in Webster Library provided twenty-eight hands-on computers offering an array of information literacy programs.

While academic libraries everywhere were experiencing similar changes in services at this time, the critical lack of physical space remained the main problem at Concordia's Webster Library. A number of external factors to the library eventually contributed the solution to the library's crying need for additional space. The opening of the Richard J. Renaud Building and the move of the science departments and laboratories to the Loyola campus (2003), the opening of the Engineering and Computer Science Visual Arts Building (2005), and the Molson Building (2009), all provided space onto which the university could expand its operations. As a result, the fifth floor of the McConnell Building became available for the library's expansion. The Grey Nuns Chapel also became available and was converted into an additional library study space (2014).

The library embarked on a long-awaited plan taking into account its responsibility to explore and develop new ways to support learning, teaching, and research and to provide services in line with changing needs. The modern academic library is composed of physical and virtual spaces that provide resources and services to the Concordia community engaged in diverse learning, teaching, and research activities. Silent spaces must be available for reading, writing, and study but collaborative spaces must also be available for peer-to-peer learning, group work, seminars, and workshops. Spaces for experimentation and discovery using new technologies more than ever must also be available to enhance learning and teaching. The extensive process of transforming Concordia libraries for the emerging digital age had begun. In 2009 to comply with Tri-Council's policy on open access, Spectrum, Concordia's institutional repository, was established to preserve a digitized compendium of research, theses, and special collections belonging to the university. The purpose is to ensure not only storage of theses, research articles, and research findings but also open access and to increase the visibility of faculty research and the university's overall research output. Concordia University Press was launched in 2016. Created within the Library, it is a non-profit, open-access publisher focusing on new scholarship in the humanities, social sciences, and fine arts.

The harmonization of the two libraries had also involved combining the two special collections. The contents of each distinct unit reflected the institutions' traditions and culture. Sir George, for example, had an extensive archival collection, which included the papers of Canadian poet Irving Layton as well as

# BiblioFile
### The Libraries' Newsletter for Faculty

http://library.concordia.ca

Fall 2003

## In This Issue...

**Chat online with a librarian**
New service designed to help you while you search . . . . . . . . . . . . 1

**Enhanced keyword searching in CLUES**
New options allow you to improve search precision . . . . . . . . . . . 2

**Donors help Libraries in many ways**
Special collections and services benefit from generosity . . . . . . . . . . 2

**While you were out**
Following up on the science move . . 3

**Literature Online (LION)**
New database for the Literatures in English . . . . . . . . . . . . . . . 3

**Investext Plus: a real plus!**
Impressive business database added to our collection . . . . . . . . . . . 3

**New York Times**
Searchable archive on ProQuest Historical Newspapers . . . . . . . . . 4

**Libraries welcome new librarians** . . 4

*BiblioFile* is a newsletter for faculty meant to complement the news relating to the Libraries found on our website (**http://library.concordia.ca**)

The newsletter is prepared by the Publications Committee of the Libraries. Comments and feedback may be directed to Patrick Labelle (LB-209; ext. 7685; patrick.labelle@concordia.ca).

## Chat online with a librarian

Online library assistance is going live this semester with a new service that utilizes advanced computer communication technologies to facilitate library research. Students and faculty can now chat with a Concordia librarian, from 2 p.m. to 5 p.m. on weekdays, without having to break away from their online work.

Designed to respond directly to people while they are searching the library catalogue and databases, or when they need more information about the Libraries, this online chat service complements our existing in-person, telephone, and e-mail reference services. It also has the potential to broaden the scope of web-based information seeking by offering the opportunity for exchange and guidance in the online environment.

Since unfamiliarity with online resources such as library catalogues and databases is an acknowledged barrier to research, a service that permits librarians to intervene, in real time, while a search is in progress, could help people overcome such barriers. This vision has spurred an increasing number of academic libraries to experiment with live electronic reference.

To access Concordia's Ask A Librarian live, you must first download and install a small plug-in from the Libraries' website (**http://library.concordia.ca/services/helpcentral.html**). A chat button then appears in the upper right corner of your Internet browser (Netscape or Internet Explorer) when you are linked to certain parts of the Libraries' website. By clicking on this chat button, you initiate a call for assistance that is answered by a Concordia reference librarian.

In addition to chat, the librarian can escort you through an online search. In a process known as 'application sharing', the librarian links up with your computer screen to demonstrate search techniques or navigate to useful resources. This virtual reference technology can transform a simple chat exchange into a genuine instructional encounter during which you see exactly how the librarian applies various search strategies. Your consultation with a librarian happens when you most need it, rather than before or after your online search takes place. After the call, a transcript of the chat session, showing the hyperlinked addresses of websites that were visited, arrives by e-mail, making it easy to revisit them.

Developed by a working group of Concordia librarians, the online chat service is a pilot project whose goals include evaluating both the demand for, and the usability of, live electronic reference in our libraries. Powered by *Question Point*, software introduced by OCLC and used in over 100 academic and research libraries including the Library of Congress, the service is

---

17.7 An issue of *Bibliofile* from Fall 2003, the *Libraries' Newsletter for Faculty*. This newsletter was published by the Concordia University Libraries to keep faculty and staff informed of developments in library science, circulation and research methods, as well as collections.

those of others who had taught there, whereas Loyola had important records of Thomas D'Arcy McGee.

## New Spaces and Technology

In September 2017 the last phase of the Webster Library transformation was completed. The notable accomplishments included an increase of 27 percent of space allocation as the library expanded to the fifth floor of the McConnell Building, appropriately accommodating the needs of a student population now reaching over 46,000. The library transformation was celebrated in a number of different architectural publications, attesting to its success. It provided 21 kilometres of books, 3,300 study seats, 22 types of study space, dissertation writers' rooms, as well as an unsurpassed quality of other features, including inviting, well-aired, lighting; an array of equipment; a diversity of seating of spaces, chairs, glass partitions. A technology sandbox offers facilities for digital exploration, including 3D printing, 3D modelling, virtual reality, Arduino 101, Linux, analogue synthesizers, and a visualization studio featuring the interactive artwork, Proteus.[12]

As of 2022–23, Concordia Library holds 2,351,352 titles in its collection, and in that academic year, loaned 27,315 laptop tablets, and offered over 312 workshops on information resources and sandbox technology.[13] The library proudly offers its users the Webster Library, the Vanier Library, and the Grey Nuns Reading Room. This transformation resulted in Concordia's Library now being an enviable flagship and model for other academic libraries. In a vision statement, Concordia justly defines its library as an "intellectually inspiring and engaging environment, which provides collections and services fundamental to academic success, to creation, to the advancement of knowledge, and to lifelong learning. Concordia Library is committed to serving society, supporting discovery and the freedom of speech and intellectual inquiry."[14] Concordia's Library is now a masterpiece, accomplished through the expertise and perseverance of two of my successors and their respective teams, Mr. Gerald Beasley, and Dr. Guylaine Beaudry. I salute and congratulate them. Transformations of this magnitude do not occur overnight. The effort required to invest in its library paid handsomely for Concordia University. From the cramped, stuffed, quarters of yesteryear's academic library, the modern academic library has morphed into a bright, active learning laboratory where seamless access to collections in print and digital formats is virtually assured. Plans are currently underway to effect a similar renovation in the Vanier Library on our Loyola campus.

**NOTES**

1   Scott Bennett, "Libraries and Learning: A History of Paradigm Change," *portal: Libraries & the Academy* 9, no. 2 (April 2009): 181–97, https://doi.org/10.1353/pla.0.0049.

2   See the essays in Council on Library and Information Resources, *No Brief Candle: Reconceiving Research Libraries for the 21st Century* (Washington, DC: CLIR, 2008), https://www.clir.org/pubs/reports/pub142/.

3   See Michael Wescott Loder, "Libraries with a Future: How Are Academic Library Usage and Green Demands Changing Building Designs?" *College & Research Libraries* 71 (April 2010): 348–60; and Geoffrey T. Freeman, "The Library as Place: Changes in Learning Patterns, Collections, Technology, and Use," in *Library as Place: Rethinking Roles, Rethinking Space*, e d. K. Smith (Washington, DC: Council on Library and Information Resources, 2005), 1–10, https://www.clir.org/pubs/reports/pub129/freeman/.

4   Ken Whittingham, "The Shape of Things to Come: New Downtown Library Interior is Startling, Dramatic and Functional," *Concordia's Thursday Report* 16, no. 2 (February 20, 1992): 2. This special issue of *Concordia's Thursday Report* featured numerous articles detailing various aspects of the new library complex.

5   The *1991–92 Concordia Annual Report* (p. 2) specifies, 22,496 undergrads and 3,439 graduate students for a total of 25,935 students.

6   *Concordia Annual Report, 2003–2004*, 9, https://archive.org/details/concordia-presidents-report-2003-04-english/. Of the total 30,905 students, 25,987 were undergraduates and 4,918 were graduate students.

7   David Lewis, "A Strategy for Academic Libraries in the First Quarter of the 21st Century," *College & Research Libraries* 68 (May 2007): 418–34; Sarah M. Pritchard, "Deconstructing the Library: Reconceptualising Collections, Spaces and Services," *Journal of Library Administration* 48, no. 2 (February 2008): 219–33, https://doi.org/10.1080/01930820802231492.

8   H. Lea Wells and Jordan M. Scepanski, "Programming New Learning Spaces: The Changing Nature of Academic Library Buildings," in *Technological Convergence and Social Networks in Information Management*, ed. S. Kurbanoğlu et al. (Berlin: Springer, 2010), https://doi.org/10.1007/978-3-642-16032-5_8.

9   *Concordia Libraries Annual Report 2001–02*, 6, https://archive.org/details/librairies-annual-report-2001-2002.

10  *Concordia Libraries Annual Report 2001–02*, 6.

11  *Concordia Libraries Annual Report 2001–02*, 5.

12  For details of the transformation, see James Roach, "3 Years, 4 Phases, and 113% More Study Seats," *Concordia News*, September 18, 2017, https://www.concordia.ca/cunews/main/stories/2017/09/18/webster-library-transformation-4-phases-113-per-cent-more-study-seats.html; and "Concordia Delivers Webster Library's Cutting-Edge Digital Transformation," *Concordia University Magazine*, Spring 2018, 3.

13  For the most recent numbers, see Concordia Library's "Annual Reports & Fast Facts," https://library.concordia.ca/about/statistics/.

14  Concordia University Library, *Inspiring Success: Concordia University Library Strategic Plan, 2016/21*, 2, https://library.concordia.ca/about/plan/strategic-plan.pdf.

17.8 Presentation of Books in the Futurology Section of the Vanier Library. *From left to right*: Dr. J. McGraw (Philosophy Professor at Loyola), Harrington E. Manville (Director, United States Information Service), and Joseph Princz (Librarian).

# ORAL HISTORIES: Research and the City

## LYNN HUGHES, THE GENESIS OF HEXAGRAM

Fine Arts was in the, the garage on Crescent Street, Crescent and René Lévesque, which is now called the VA Building. It's an old garage. The VA, it was really the leftover art school, I guess. It was sort of in transition from being an art school to becoming really part of a university. So, it was officially part of a university faculty, but was physically separate, and I think psycho-socially separate. It was still very much an art school mentality that didn't, in my view, take advantage of the fact that it was in the university, and didn't influence the university in any way. And that's the big thing that's changed now ... I think I'm an interdisciplinary person anyway, as you can see, and so for me, it was incredibly important and exciting that in a university you have immediate access to all of these amazing other disciplines. It's still not something that everybody knows how to take advantage of. It depends on what your path has been and who you are, I guess. But it's very, very important, and that really started to happen, I guess, for the university when we moved into the new building. It would have been happening on all kinds of different levels.

---

**LYNN HUGHES** is Professor Emerita in the Department of Studio Arts at Concordia University. She is Honorary Concordia University Research Chair in Interaction Design and Games Innovation. This interview took place at the Centre for Oral History and Digital Storytelling on December 16, 2022.

**HENRY HABIB** is Distinguished Professor Emeritus at Concordia University who founded the Department of Political Science at Loyola College in 1961. He also served on the Board of Governors since 1971. This interview took place at the Centre for Oral History and Digital Storytelling on December 15, 2022.

**MAÏR VERTHUY** is a Distinguished Professor Emerita at Concordia University who was the co-founder and first principal of the Simone de Beauvoir Institute. She has been inducted into both the Order of Canada and the Ordre national du Québec. This interview took place at University Communications Services Studio on November 7, 2022.

**LORNA ROTH** is Distinguished Professor Emerita in the Department of Communication Studies at Concordia University. A former graduate of Sir George Williams University who went on to complete her PhD at Concordia, she began her teaching career at the university in 1979. This interview took place at University Communications Services Studio on December 9, 2022, and on Zoom on December 10, 2022.

For me it happened, and I think for many people around me when we did the Hexagram Institute ... It's now called Research and Creation in Art and Technology. So that was in 2000, or '99 ... Barbara Lane was associate dean for research and asked me, the dean asked her, to write a CFI grant, a Canada Foundation of Innovation grant, for next generation technology for the faculty. I mean, it was at a point where it was clear that the art schools needed to have a major upgrade in technology, and it was very expensive. You couldn't just go out and buy a couple of cameras; it was all kinds of things coming down, you know, that were going to be much more major than that. UQAM was in the same situation. I guess both schools asked the government to give them money to buy new technology in a big way. And the government, in my understanding, the Quebec government basically said this is the shotgun marriage: if you get together, we'll seriously consider giving you serious money for technology, but you have to do it together.

That's the genesis of Hexagram. It started off as a very practical thing that way. But the wonderful thing was that we were forced to do it with UQAM. So, I don't know if Barbara asked me to do it, probably partly because I spoke French ... Anyway, what happened was that I wrote the CFI grant with Louise Poissant from UQAM, who's now the head of the FRQSC. And, well, she's a wonderful, wonderful person. The two of us really got on well together. I think it was a pleasure to write it together. But what it meant from, I guess both ends, but certainly from my end, was that I had to conceive of a structure. I think we called them research axes, so they were like research clusters for the future, sort of looking ahead twenty years. It required me to imagine something, which was really interesting to do, and it required me to get other people to imagine it [*laughs*]. Because I had to, I had to group people together, and say, okay in the next fifteen years, what do you think is coming, and how would you describe the research around it? Even using those words, *research*, was a new thing in fine arts ... And so, I got various submissions from people. To a large extent I rewrote them or wrote them so they fit together better. But I absolutely needed people to give me seeds or baby plants so that I could develop something around that.

But the other very important part of that was just the getting together. I vividly remember the first time we had a meeting together with the people at UQAM in a big, huge conference room in UQAM. Very, very big table. And we basically sent out an invitation to both sides saying anybody who's interested in working digitally, who already does or thinks they're interested in the future somehow, even if you're not sure how, come on down. And so, we got this table with all these people around from both sides, and it was really interesting to meet the people from UQAM, but it was also really interesting to meet people from Concordia. I mean up until that time I didn't know people in design, they didn't know me, at all ... That was really an incredible thing. That's been a very long journey because ... when the money came in that was the first time the Canada Foundation for Innovation had ever given money to something that wasn't basically hard science or engineering, or medicine ...

I think we did a good job of writing it and we did lots of good things. It was very important that the Quebec government backed this ask … It coincided with the new [Engineering, Computer Science and Visual Arts Integrated Complex (EV)] building, that also helped. Most of the infrastructure came to us. Subsequently, a little bit went to UQAM … Hexagram was the top two floors of the fine arts side … Hexagram at Concordia was sort of like an equipment depot. That's understating it, but I mean, many people used it as an equipment depot …. It took people really a long time to think of it as being more than that …. It certainly came in with Milieux, that the idea was that borrowing equipment was incidental. In fact, most of that equipment is now gone, not all of it, there's some specialized equipment like interactive textiles equipment and various particular kind of high-end things that are still attached to Milieux. But most of the equipment, fancy new cameras which are no longer fancy … Because equipment is just equipment [*small laugh*]. And what was important about Hexagram, I mean it was important to get new equipment, but what was important was that aspect of people working together and sometimes working across disciplines … It coincided with the notion in Quebec of research-creation. That's not a coincidence: both of those things were reinforcing each other.

## HENRY HABIB, "AN ARRANGED MARRIAGE, NOT A LOVE MARRIAGE"

At Loyola we were eight or nine professors, and at Sir George maybe nine. So, we became eighteen, nineteen. And now I think it's thirty or forty right now. It grew, but in 1974 to '78, there were eighteen of them. And different, you had to balance between them and try to not annoy this one and then, it took a lot of work. Especially in the first years, because some were … not comfortable with their colleagues from the other institution and, it was … an arranged marriage. It was an arranged marriage, not a love marriage. It was an arranged marriage. And, and arranged marriages succeed, and we have succeeded, I think.

Since Concordia was created, we've had excellent people. We've had excellent rectors and excellent deans. You were dealing with the history people. Chuck Bertrand was in history. He was one of the best deans that we had. A dynamic man and all that, and I enjoyed working with him very much. Unfortunately, he passed away a few years ago. And he became even interim rector at one point. Chuck Bertrand, he was quite a dynamic person in the institution. I have great respect for him and Dr. [Frederick] Lowy, he presided over the institution for more than ten years. And, I worked with him very closely, too, because he asked me, apart from my duties as a professor, to be an advisor to, to the rector. And, Dr. Lowy, I travelled with him to Britain and France, and then we travelled to Lebanon, and we established a Concordia chapter. There were three hundred students in that Concordia chapter. They came from the whole region of the Middle East. And then from Lebanon, we went to Jordan, and from Jordan we went to Israel. So, it was an interesting situation.

## MAÏR VERTHUY, BETHUNE UNIVERSITY

I was absolutely horrified at the idea that this joint institute that we were creating with Loyola was a decision of the Quebec government and not a voluntary decision on the part of either Loyola or Sir George Williams. It was imposed upon us for a variety of historical reasons ... I thought it was a ridiculous name. If you looked it up in the phone book—because there were phone books then [*chuckle*] —you have Concordia Trade Union, Concordia Travel Agency and things like that, and then at the end of it, Concordia University. So, I thought it really put us in our place as far as being serious was concerned. There was a group of us that wanted to call it Bethune University, for a variety of reasons. One is, Bethune is a very Canadian name and I doubt if there's a city in Canada that doesn't have a Bethune Street. But also because Norman Bethune was a Canadian hero, he was a *great* man. He died in the service of helping others. China supported him ... So, we fought very hard to get the university called Bethune University because it was Canadian and because it was that of a great man. But the church won out. Loyola had more backing from the, the church which is, was in itself, of course, naturally a powerful organization. And so it ended up being called Concordia. And the irony in this situation is that shortly afterwards, this place outside Concordia was called Bethune and the Chinese erected a statue there in memory of the hero. So, it would have been a perfect commitment had people known that in advance. But they didn't, and so we have Concordia University here and Bethune there [*laughter*].

## LORNA ROTH, PARTICIPANT OBSERVATION

[In the late sixties, after completing my third year of Sir George Williams's BA degree, I decided to become a schoolteacher and shifted to McGill's one-year senior Elementary School program. In that way, while teaching all day, I could return to Sir George and finish my fourth year at night. During this final year, my focus was on sociology courses. It was here that I met Taylor Buckner.] I don't know if you knew him. He was a really interesting guy. He was a fresh PhD [who came up] to Montreal from Oakland, California. His thesis was on the problems [of violence] in Oakland where he had joined the police force and studied it from a participant observation point of view and written his work from that perspective ... He was into difference; he was into living on the edge. And that's when I started thinking about how important it is to be on the edge of things [how innovations take place at these edges], and how important it is to study marginality for this reason. Which I've done my whole life.

... All my stuff, if you look at all my [academic research], it's all about non-normative ... ways of looking at the world ... I think it was his first year here that I studied with him. What year was it? I think was '71. Something like that ... His course was on urban lifestyles, on a Friday night in Montreal. And it was a brilliant course.

Well, I'll tell you about it, because it's part of a lost history. He divided the class into teams. [His idea was for each of us to find a place somewhere in the region of a metro station and go there every Friday night to do an analysis of its sub-culture for the whole year.] There was a leader of the team. Each leader of a team of three or four or five [students]—it depended on how large the group was [or] who was interested in doing that work – the leader of the team would be part of the administration of the course. We would meet at [Professor Buckner's] house every week at night or sometimes every two weeks, depending on what the project would be that he wanted us to do. There were probably about ten of us or maybe twelve .... We'd have drinks; we'd have food. And we would talk about the project for the next week. And what we did is, each one of us, with our teams, we would meet our team at a metro station, at a different metro station. And in those days, there were mostly metro stations like from Atwater east. There weren't many that crossed over [north/south]. It was like the beginning of the metro. So we would meet them at a station, and we would give them their assignment for that [evening,] and they would go out and do their assignment ... [Group leaders also did the assignments.] And they were all ... [about] participant observations, or interviewing. Qualitative methodologies. And it was amazing. And then they would come back at the end; we would meet at the end of the evening, at the metro station. They would give us—you know, tell us what they did and what was going on, whatever. And then we would tell the administrative group the next week how it went, etc. So, it was very democratic, and very, very interesting. Really fascinating. But we had to find a place—and it was marginal places he wanted us to go to—we had to find a place somewhere in the metro station region, and go there every Friday night for the [duration of the class.] The courses lasted [two semesters] in those days.

... We had a guy in our class who was in the RCMP. And we were always very suspicious—I hope he doesn't listen to this [*both laugh*] ... We were always very suspicious [of him], you know, is he going to report or—why is he here? You know [*laughs*] ... But he was very cooperative and very nice, and we liked each other; we became friends. Because we were in the same area. I was a leader and he was in the group, but he often came with me. I guess he was maybe worried. I was a young, hot girl, you know [*laughs*]. And it was like St. Laurent Boulevard [St. Laurent metro group], you know, with the prostitutes and other things going on. We would go from place to place together and evaluate whether this would be a good [site] to do a study ... [At] first I thought I would do a study of a tattoo parlour ... St. Laurent had the last tattoo parlour ... [for] the sailors ... [who] would come [from] Old Montreal, at the bottom of Boulevard Saint Laurent ... Tattoos saying "Skunky " or "Mother" or, you know, women with big breasts wearing shoes that were like [transparent] plastic ... that didn't have covers on top, just the [stiletto] heels [*laughs*]. And their feet would sit in the heel, and they had nothing to keep the heels on their feet. Those were in the tattoo images. They were called flashcards and they were all over the walls. [Take your pick!]

I went there quite seriously thinking that I would study [the process], and I learned a lot. I mean, these big, hunky guys would come in; [husky] guys on motorcycles, and you thought that they were going to be really strong and powerful and they weren't going to cry or anything. [Surprisingly] they'd start crying ... [as soon as the tattoo needles pricked their skin. And then there were opposite unexpected reactions from] skinny people who would arrive at the seat where the work would be done and they [wouldn't even] blink an eye [the brave ones.] They were probably in deep pain, but they didn't [show] anything ... But then I realized, if I was going to do participant observation, I would have to get a tattoo. That was well before women got tattoos, in the early '70s or late '60s ... So anyways, that didn't work.

Then I wanted to go to a prostitution bar, but I figured I'd have to be a prostitute [to fulfill the course requirements] ... At each place I went, I studied it and I'd [think], "Oh, that's interesting ..." Interesting in a way that I would never, as a nice Jewish girl from Snowdon, would never go into one of these places. You know, "You ... went *there*?!" ... [*Laughs*] Anyways, I ended up going into a pool hall, on the corner of Saint Catherine – between St-Alexandre and Bleury ... It was called the Windsor Pool Hall and Billiards, or the Windsor Pool Hall and Bowling Alley. It [took up] a whole block.

And it was like—if you saw any of the films in the early days with Jackie Gleason ... like *The Hustler* [1961] ... the pool hall [reminded me of that, it had a very similar look and feeling]. Like the dark room with green lights shining on the table with the balls and everything. Everybody standing around; very quiet because they're making bets. They were really hustling there. Making bets, and the tension, you could cut it with a knife. But anyways, I walked in there and I thought ... it was kind of cold; it was the end of October or something; it was really cold. So all the poor people who were homeless, they're all sitting around the edges, because it was warm and they stayed there until they got booted out because the pool hall closed; it wasn't open all night. I walked in and I felt the tension, and I [immediately] realized this is where I'm going to do it. Not a single woman there ... I must have had such guts; I can't believe it [even to walk in and look around]. Gilles had gone a long time ago ... He didn't want to go in there ... I walked all the way across the pool hall and they were all [staring] at me, you know? "Who the hell is she?" And I got to a place where there was a seat available and I sat down. Am I allowed to use swear words or anything?

*Piyusha Chatterjee: It's up to you. We won't edit.*

You won't edit? Well—

*PC: Unless you want to.*

So I sat down there, and this guy was sitting next to me. He eventually became my best witness, like my best interviewee. [After he closely looked at me up and down, his first words were] "Who the fuck do you think you are, coming into our territory? Get the hell out!" I said, "No fucking way. I can be here just like you can. It's public space." [He walked away slowly.] [*Draws in a deep breath and then bursts into laughter!*] And you know … I ended up going back every single Friday night for a year. He became my best informant …

[Currently, when we] do any [academic] research, we have to fill out ethics forms—we have to apply to the Ethics [Committee in the Research Department which often takes months to give us feedback and permissions to go ahead with our project]. "You have to do this, that, and the other" to adjust [to their guidelines]. We didn't have such things in those days. No ethical forms. And no necessity to tell people what you were actually doing.

# Community Activations

SOCIAL CHANGE 1970-1971

The Native Peoples of Canada: Proposed Syllabus

I.  Historical Background:

Sept. 21  Introduction -- Gail Valaskakis, Loyola College
Sept. 28  Indians before European Contact -- Ernest Benedict, North American
          Indian Travelling College
Oct. 5    Indian and European Contact: Champlain judged by his Indian
          Policy -- Bruce Trigger, McGill University
Oct. 19   Legal History of Indian-White Relations in Canada -- Douglas
          Saunders, University of Windsor
Oct. 26   Analysis of the Reserve System -- Michael Mitchell, National Film Board

II.  Psychology and Culture:

Nov. 2    Patterns and Consequences of Communal Life -- Jerry Cambill,
          White Roots of Peace
Nov. 9    Life Style: Attitudes & Thought Patterns -- Tom Porter, Iroquois
          Longhouse
Nov. 16   Language & Culture: Relationship and Implications -- Jerry McNulty,
          Laval University
Nov. 23   Art, Music, and Oral Traditions -- Gail Valaskakis, Loyola College
Nov. 30   Traditional Indian Education & Implications -- Velma Bourque,
          Caughnawaga

III.  Sociology:

Dec. 7    Indians and the Family -- Willie Dunn, National Film Board
Jan. 4    Indians & Political Organization -- Frank Howard, M.P., Ottawa
Jan. 11   Indians & their Economic Systems & Implications -- Harold Cardinal,
          Alberta Indian Association
Jan. 18   Education and its Psychological Impact on Native North American Youth --
          Peter Sindell, McGill University
Jan. 25   Urbanization -- Maria Arguelles-Canive, Loyola College

IV.  Myth and Religion:

Feb. 1    Historic Native Religions & Philosophy -- Peter Diome, Caughnawaga
Feb. 8    Eskimo Religion & Philosophy -- Elija Menarik, CBC Northern Service
Feb. 15   Myth of Indians in Non-Indian Art & Religion -- Ron Wareham, Loyola College
Feb. 22   Relationship between Indian Art & Religion -- Charles Paris, Loyola College
Mar. 1    Religious Schools & Reserves -- Bill Akin, Loyola College

V.  The Contemporary Situation:

Mar. 8    Native Peoples & the Health, Welfare & Legal Situation, Boyce
          Richardson, Montreal Star
Mar. 15   Hawthorne Report -- H.B. Hawthorne, University of British Columbia
Mar. 22   White Paper -- Jean Chetien, Minister of Indian Affairs, Ottawa
Mar. 29   A proposal for Red Power
          (a) Economic & Cultural -- Tony Antoine, Alberta Native Brotherhood
Apr. 5    (b) Politics & Direct Action -- Andy Nicholas, New Brunswick Indian Assoc.


* * * * * * *


19.1 Social Change 1970–71, The Native Peoples of Canada, proposed syllabus, Loyola College.

# EARLY INDIGENOUS PROGRAMMING AND PEDAGOGIES, 1970–1990

Colby Gaudet

**IN THE FALL SEMESTER** of 1970, Loyola College offered a new course called Native Peoples of Canada. Organized by Gail Guthrie Valaskakis of Loyola's Department of Communication Arts, it was a collaboration of "Montreal area universities and colleges, and the McGill Inter-tribal Council."[1] This initiative explored the potential for establishing a "Native North American Studies Program." The course at Loyola was the experimental first run, asking how Indigenous peoples "will be able to control their own lives and future."[2] It became a success and was offered throughout the 1970s, bridging the institutional merger that brought together Loyola College and Sir George Williams University. Native Peoples of Canada anchored the campus in critical social and civil rights discourse, making early Concordia a site of activism, decolonial thought, and pedagogical experimentation—all areas identified by historians as characterizing student, youth, and public cultures of the late 1960s and early 1970s in Montreal and Toronto.[3]

Loyola's Department of Communication Arts was established in 1965 by the Jesuit priest John E. O'Brien. It was the first academic program of its kind in Canada, and it aimed "to develop in students a scholarly and creative approach to mass media."[4] In 1966 the program was being led by six male instructors, three of whom were Jesuit priests, including O'Brien. The following year Gail Guthrie Valaskakis, a tribal member of the Lake Superior Chippewa Indians in Wisconsin, was hired to the new department. She had recently completed graduate studies at Cornell University.[5]

As Loyola was a Roman Catholic college, the launch of Communication Arts was an official response to the recent message of Vatican II that "social communications" were to be used "in the service of morality, truth, charity, and the common good."[6] Pursuing this message further, in 1967 O'Brien oversaw the design of Expo

---

COLBY GAUDET holds a PhD from Concordia's Department of Religions and Cultures. An interdisciplinary researcher, he studies histories of religion, empire, and colonialism. In 2021 Colby was the lead investigator for the research project Exploring Concordia's Colonial Past: An Examination of the University's Past and Present Relationships with Indigenous Peoples.

67's Christian Pavilion where some of the innovative insights of communications theory were on public display.[7] During this time Loyola also absorbed the ideas of Catholic liberation theology promulgated from the Global South. Reflecting this influence, by the late 1960s many lectures were listed in campus papers under the headings "Third World Studies" and "Social Change." This climate provided a productive ground in 1970 for an interdisciplinary course at Loyola examining the social concerns and systemic injustices experienced by Indigenous peoples in Canada.

A forerunner of the Native Peoples course was a "'Teach-In' on the position of Indians in Canada today." It took place at Loyola in March 1970 and included "guests from reservations at St. Regis [Akwesásne], Cornwall & Caughnawaga [Kahnawà:ke]."[8] Films from the National Film Board's (NFB) Challenge for Change program were also screened. It is likely this screening included the recent NFB short film *You Are on Indian Land* (1969). Made by NFB's Indian Film Crew (IFC), it depicted the December 1968 blockade by Kanienkehá:ka of Akwesásne of the international bridge between Ontario and New York. In the wake of this and other events, the Loyola course's social and political relevance was the key to its success.

Several well-known Indigenous speakers engaged Montreal campuses in 1970–71. Vine Deloria Jr., author of the popular *Custer Died for Your Sins: An Indian Manifesto* (1969), spoke at McGill during an "Indian teach-in" in February 1970. Deloria delivered a talk called "Indian Values and World Views."[9] Métis activist Howard Adams from Saskatchewan was a visiting lecturer at Sir George Williams University in the summer of 1970. Adams stressed the urgency of Métis peoples taking "control of our own communities" that have been "controlled by a White power structure."[10] Henry Jack of the Native Youth Movement spoke at Loyola in March 1971. He presented "A Proposal for Red Power: Economic and Cultural Aspects."[11] Jack was the founder of the Native Alliance of Red Power, "a decidedly youth-oriented New Left Vancouver body with connections to west coast Maoist and Trotskyist political organizations."[12] Jack also spoke at a Montreal Black Power rally acknowledging in his speech the potential solidarity between Black and Indigenous communities.[13]

Building on these examples, the new Loyola course was brought to life by a network of activists, organizers, professors, and government officials. A "proposed syllabus" (Figure 19.1) featured a collaborative, yet vigorous schedule composed entirely of guest speakers. The fall semester of 1970 saw four speakers (all men) from the Haudenosaunee Six Nations. First were Ernest Benedict and Michael Mitchell of Akwésasne, both involved in the 1968 blockade on Cornwall Island. Benedict was a respected Elder and helped establish and operate the North American Indian Travelling College, an Indigenous-organized educational initiative. Mitchell and another Loyola guest speaker, Willie Dunn, a Mi'kmaw musician, were members of NFB's IFC.[14]

Two other Haudenosaunee speakers that semester were representatives of important traditional institutions. Jerry Gambill spoke on "Patterns and Consequences of Communal Life." He was a member of White Roots of Peace, a collective of traditionalists who "lectured on the teachings of the Great Peacemaker and the Great Law of Peace that serves as the foundation for the Haudenosaunee Confederacy."[15] Gambill was also an editor of *Akwesasne Notes*, a newspaper created to support the cause at the Cornwall border crossing. He was close friends with and one-time San Francisco roommate of Richard Oakes, the Mohawk activist who led the occupation of Alcatraz Island in November 1969.[16] Additionally, Tom Porter of the Iroquois Longhouse spoke at Loyola on "Lifestyle: Attitudes and Thought Patterns." Porter was featured in the NFB film *These Are My People…* (1969) about the history of the Longhouse. Like *You Are on Indian Land*, it was produced by the IFC for the Challenge for Change program. Described as "dialogue films," the IFC projects "represented and participated in a much larger political and cultural shift in the relationship between Native peoples and Canada … The utopian hope emanating from the Board at the time was that filmed communication could spur dynamic social change."[17] The IFC was engaged in spreading this spirit of change via screenings and talks at Loyola.

At the start of 1971 Cree activist Harold Cardinal, then leader of the Alberta Indian Association, was a guest speaker on the subject "Indians and Their Economic Systems and Implications." Cardinal was well known for his influential book *The Unjust Society* (1969), a critical response to the assimilative governmental policies proposed in the Trudeau administration's White Paper. Velma Bourque and Gail Guthrie Valaskakis were the only Indigenous women speakers in the first year of the course. Bourque spoke on "Traditional Indian Education and Implications." Valaskakis engaged the group on Indigenous "Art, Music, and Oral Traditions." Bourque, a Mohawk of Kahnawà:ke and a student at Loyola, later received the Evening Students' Association Medal in October 1972, acknowledging her for "play[ing] a major role in starting Loyola's Native Peoples of Canada course."[18]

Among the course's non-Indigenous speakers was Bruce Trigger, a McGill professor and specialist in Huron-Wendat history. H.B. Hawthorn, an anthropologist from the University of British Columbia, discussed his governmental report, "A Survey of the Contemporary Indians of Canada." Otherwise known as "The Hawthorn Report" (1966–67), it established a context for the Canadian public's understanding of Indigenous issues. The Loyola campus paper *The Happening* suggests a scheduled talk by Jean Chrétien, then minister of the Department of Indian Affairs and Northern Development, never took place. The date originally assigned to Chrétien on the syllabus was later replaced in the campus paper with the listing "guest speaker to be announced."[19] Several Loyola professors spoke on historical, religious, and sociological topics. Notable issues critically tackled by non-Indigenous speakers included "Education and Its Psychological Impact on Native North American Youth," "Religious Schools & Reserves," and "Urbanization."[20]

The Native Peoples course was renewed for a second year at Loyola and was well represented in campus publications. In September 1971, a front-page feature announced, "new courses, [a] new degree and diploma programs [were being] offered." Among these new courses was Native Peoples, which would "concentrate on two aspects of the crisis of the indigenous people of Canada[:] Lands and Treaties[,] and Education."[21] The language of "crisis" emphasized the critical approach of the course. The focus on treaties and education, coupled with the terminology of "indigenous people" makes the course stand out for its time. The course also addressed the James Bay Cree's resistance to Hydro Quebec developments. From 1974 to 1977, lawyers for the Grand Council of the Crees spoke about the ongoing James Bay settlement in Northern Quebec.[22]

Benedict, Mitchell, and Porter returned annually to Loyola and Concordia throughout the 1970s. In a recorded lecture from 1974, Mitchell described to students the Haudenosaunee worldview including Turtle Island, the Great Tree of Peace, and the ways of traditional Longhouse governance.[23] Other invited Indigenous speakers included Ray Fadden of the Six Nations Indian Museum in New York, activist and poet Duke Redbird, Wilfred Pelletier of Toronto's Rochdale College, Inuit broadcaster Elijah Menarik of CBC Northern Services, Anishinaabe artist Robert Houle, Andrew Delisle and Max Gros-Louis of the Indians of Quebec Association, and Jim Sinclair of the Non-Status Indian and Métis Society of Saskatchewan.[24] Valaskakis continued to take an active part in the course, each year presenting a lecture on communications and Indigenous art.

By 1974 board members of the new Manitou College in La Macaza were regular speakers in the course; these included George Miller, Velma Bourque, and Blair Stonechild.[25] Bourque later prepared a report on the "Amerindianization" of Quebec's education for Indigenous students.[26] Other speakers included Arthur Manuel of the Native Youth Movement, Mohawk artist Mark Montour, and Arnold Goodleaf of the Confederation of Indians of Quebec.[27] By 1979–80 the course was absorbed into the Department of History, where it remained until its last appearance in the 1985–86 undergraduate calendar.[28] The course existed for fifteen years.

In addition to Native Peoples of Canada, Concordia's Simone de Beauvoir Institute began including Indigenous women speakers in their programming by the late 1970s. A panel of Indigenous women was organized in 1976 for a women's studies advanced seminar. It featured Mary Two-Axe Earley from the Native Women's

Association of Canada, alongside representatives of the Montreal Native Friendship Centre and Quebec Native Women.[29] Two-Axe Earley spoke at Concordia again several times, including an event in 1981 organized by the Simone de Beauvoir Institute at which the Mohawk activist "addresse[d] the state of Indian rights (or lack thereof) for native women in Canada."[30] Maria Campbell, Métis author of the autobiography *Halfbreed* (1973), participated in a women's studies conference in 1980. She spoke "on the status of Indian and Métis women."[31]

The Sir George Williams campus also hosted fundraising events for Indigenous causes that were not tied to academic courses. In April 1973 several events took place in the Hall Building as part of "James Bay week" organized by the Save James Bay Fund, an initiative "to raise money to help finance the Indian and Inuit court battle against the James Bay [hydroelectric] project." Indigenous musical and spoken-word performances on campus included those by Gordon Tootoosis, Sarain Stump, Alanis Obomsawin, Tom Jackson, and Duke Redbird. Free discussion panels with a number of these individuals took place over several days at the Karma Coffee House located nearby on Crescent Street. Traditionalist musical ensembles included "the Dog Rib Indians and Eskimo Drum Dancers." A lineup of non-Indigenous performers also supported the James Bay fundraising events, including several well-known folksingers such as Joni Mitchell and "not Peter, Paul & Mary but just Peter Yarrow."[32]

Indigenous-themed events declined at Concordia during the 1980s. One of the last events centring Indigenous issues was the Inuit Studies Conference organized by Valaskakis in 1984. Hosted in the Hall Building, the conference included speakers and attendees from the Inuit Broadcasting Corporation, Inuit Tapirisat of Canada, the Nunavut Land Claims Project, and the Inuit Women's Association. An exhibition of photographs and video art accompanied the conference.[33]

There were minimal references to any matters pertaining to Indigenous students, events, or programs in the weekly Concordia papers between 1985 and 1990. In the fall semester of 1990 that abruptly changed with responses to the Kanehsatà:ke Resistance, otherwise known as the Oka Crisis. Several initiatives were organized on campus to address the well-being of Indigenous students in the aftermath of this traumatic event. By October 1992 a report on Indigenous education at Concordia called "A Circle of Learning: The Path to Justice and Hope" was released. The report recognized the legacies of harm done by colonialism and missionization, and it named the "cultural genocide" of the Indian residential school system. It analyzed resources and initiatives then available for Indigenous students in Montreal and at Concordia, and made recommendations for the future.[34]

## NOTES

1 Native Peoples of Canada syllabus, Indian Studies—Social Change, 1970–71, HA07148, Concordia University, Records Management and Archives. All other campus publications and calendars were retrieved from the Records Management and Archives digital collections, Internet Archive, https://archive.org/details/rma-concordia-publications?tab=collection.

2 *Loyola Evening Division and Summer School Calendar, 1970–71*, 39.

3 Funké Aladejebi, *Schooling the System: A History of Black Women Teachers* (Montreal and Kingston: McGill-Queen's University Press, 2021); Bruce Douville, *The Uncomfortable Pew: Christianity and the New Left in Toronto* (Montreal and Kingston: McGill-Queen's University Press, 2021); Scott Rutherford, *Canada's Other Red Scare: Indigenous Protest and Colonial Encounters during the Global Sixties* (Montreal and Kingston: McGill-Queen's Press, 2020); Sean Mills, *The Empire Within: Postcolonial Thought and Political Activism in Sixties Montreal* (Montreal and Kingston: McGill-Queen's University Press, 2010); Gary Miedema, *For Canada's Sake: Public Religion, Centennial Celebrations, and the Re-making of Canada in the 1960s* (Montreal and Kingston: McGill-Queen's University Press, 2005).

4 *Loyola Alumnus* 10, no. 2 (Fall 1966): 10.

5 *Loyola President's Report*, 1966–67, 9; Gail Guthrie Valaskakis, "The Chippewa and the Other: Living the Heritage of Lac du Flambeau," *Cultural Studies* 2, no. 3 (1988): 267–93; Jo-Ann Archibald, "Creating an Indigenous Intellectual Movement at Canadian Universities: The Stories of Five First Nations Female Academics," in *Restoring the Balance: First Nations Women, Community, and Culture*, ed. Gail Guthrie Valaskakis, Eric Guimond, and Madeleine Dion Stout (Winnipeg: University of Manitoba Press, 2009), 125–48.

6 Richard John Neuhaus, "The Decree on the Instruments of Social Communication, *Inter Mirifica*," in *Vatican II: Renewal within Tradition*, ed. Matthew L. Lamb and Matthew Levering (Oxford: Oxford University Press, 2008), 354; John D. O'Brien, "The Ministry of Communications in the Jesuit Province of English Canada, 1842–2013," in *Builders of a Nation: Jesuits in English Canada, 1842–2013* (Toronto: Novalis, 2015), 215–18.

7 *Loyola President's Report*, 1966–67, 10; Miedema, *For Canada's Sake*, 168.

8 *The Happening*, March 1–15, 1970.

9 Suzanne Morton, "Indigenous McGill" (Montreal: McGill University, 2019), 13–14, https://www.mcgill.ca/indigenous/files/indigenous/indigenous_mcgill_october_2019_0.pdf.

10 "Métis Adams: These Are Desperate People!" *Sir George Williams University Issues & Events*, September 15, 1970, 3–5.

11 *The Happening,* March 16–31, 1971.

12 Bryan D. Palmer, "'Indians of All Tribes': The Birth of Red Power," in *Debating Dissent: Canada and the Sixties*, ed. Lara Campbell, Dominique Clément, and Gregory S. Kealey (Toronto: University of Toronto Press, 2012), 205.

13 Mills, *Empire Within*, 113.

14 Michelle Stewart, "The Indian Film Crews of Challenge for Change: Representation and the State," *Canadian Journal of Film Studies* 16, no. 2 (Fall 2007): 61–65; Noel Starblanket, "A Voice for Canadian Indians: An Indian Film Crew," in *Challenge for Change: Activist Documentary at the National Film Board of Canada*, ed. Thomas Waugh, Michael Brendan Baker, and Ezra Winton (Montreal and Kingston: McGill-Queen's University Press, 2010), 38–40; Miranda J. Brady, "Media Activism in the Red Power Movement," in *Race and Media: Critical Approaches*, ed. Lori Kido Lopez (New York: New York University Press, 2020), 230–40.

15 Kent Blansett, *A Journey to Freedom: Richard Oakes, Alcatraz, and the Red Power Movement* (New Haven, CT: Yale University Press, 2020), 112; Paul A.W. Wallace, *White Roots of Peace: The Iroquois Book of Life* (Santa Fe, NM: Clear Light Publishers, 1998).

16 Blansett, *Journey to Freedom*, 113.

17 Stewart, "Indian Film Crews," 49.

18    *The Happening*, October 24, 1972.

19    *The Happening*, March 16–31, 1971.

20    Native Peoples of Canada syllabus, Indian Studies—Social Change, 1970–71.

21    *The Happening*, September 15, 1971.

22    *The Happening*, January 28, 1974; *FYI*, November 4, 1976; *Thursday Report*, November 3, 1977.

23    Michael Mitchell, "Indian Government: 1950 to the Present," recorded lecture, Native Peoples of Canada, filmed 1974, Concordia University, https://youtu.be/2KlkwwFmvEM. See also, Tom Porter, "The Traditional Way," recorded lecture, Native Peoples of Canada, filmed 1974, Concordia University, https://youtu.be/Lphi-LnU7wc.

24    *The Happening*, March 6, 1973, November 12, 1973, November 26, 1973, January 28, 1974, and March 11, 1974.

25    *Transcript*, November 15–21, 1974; *FYI*, February 27, 1975.

26    Velma Bourque, "Amerindianization Quebec: Report, 1972–1977" (Department of Indian Affairs and Northern Development Quebec, 1977); Blair Stonechild, *The New Buffalo: The Struggle for Aboriginal Post-Secondary Education in Canada* (Winnipeg: University of Manitoba Press, 2006).

27    *FYI*, March 18, 1976; *Thursday Report*, December 8, 1977, and March 2, 1978.

28    *Concordia Undergraduate Calendar, 1979–80*, 212. Native Peoples of Canada had always been cross-listed in the History Department, first at Loyola, and later at Concordia; see *Loyola College Calendar, 1971–72*, 167, 172.

29    *FYI*, November 25, 1976.

30    *Thursday Report*, September 24, 1981. Also, *Thursday Report*, February 23, 1978, October 22, 1981, March 15, 1984, and March 22, 1984.

31    *Thursday Report*, May 29, 1980.

32    "James Bay: Musical Waves," *Sir George Williams University Issues & Events*, March 30, 1973.

33    "Conference to Highlight Concerns of Inuit," *Thursday Report*, November 8, 1984, 5.

34    "A Circle of Learning: The Path to Justice and Hope," *Concordia's Thursday Report* supplement, October 22, 1992; "Shows of Support for Native Peoples in the Mohawk Crisis Are Increasing," *Concordia's Thursday Report*, September 27, 1990, 4; André Perrella, "Centre for Mature Students Hosts Panel for Native Concerns," *Concordia's Thursday Report*, September 27, 1990, 4; John Timmins, "Fine Arts Expresses Support for Mohawks during Crisis," *Concordia's Thursday Report*, September 20, 1990, 5.

**Nicolas Baier and Cabinet Braun-Braën**
*Untitled,* 2003

3M on glass (22 x 25 metres)
East Façade, Engineering, Computer Science and
Visual Arts Integrated Complex, SGW campus

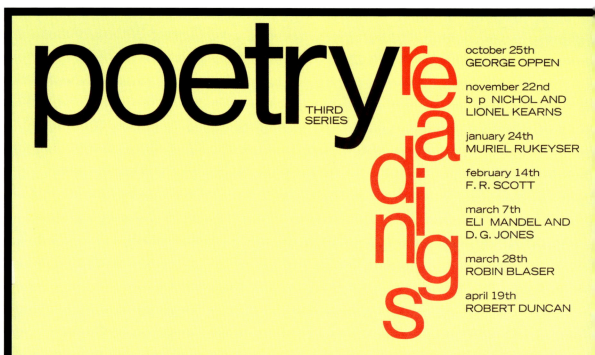

20.1 Poster designed by Robert Reid for all readings in the Third Series (October 25, 1968–April 19, 1969) of the Sir George Williams University Poetry Series.

# THE POETRY SERIES AT SIR GEORGE WILLIAMS UNIVERSITY

Jason Camlot

**BETWEEN** 1966 and 1975 faculty members of Sir George Williams University (SGWU) hosted a poetry reading series that was conceived as an ongoing encounter between local poets and a diverse range of writers from across the United States and Canada.[1] An article in the SGWU publication *Post-Grad* in 1967 described it as "a series of controversial poetry readings" that attracted hundreds "of dedicated students, staff and guests—often practicing poetry themselves" plus poetry lovers and "curiosity seekers."[2] One of the benefits noted was the "opportunity to hear several new poets who write specifically for live reading rather than for the printed page," and the "effect" of the series is described as that "of a group of people sitting together in deep discussion."[3] Sponsored by "The Poetry Committee" of the Faculty of Arts, the SGWU Department of English, and the Canada Council,[4] and organized primarily by English Department professors, these readings brought more than sixty poets from across North America to read at SGWU and helped situate the university as a site for the audition, discussion, and practice of new writing in Canada.[5]

Known simply as The Poetry Series, audio recordings of these readings were made using mobile reel-to-reel tape machines. The SGWU Instructional Media Office was undergoing a process of substantial renewal in 1966. Room H-110 and other classrooms in the recently completed Hall Building, where many of the series readings took place, were fully equipped for recording and monitoring, and the university's newly established recording services were available "for the recording of tapes 'on location.'"[6] In retrospect, one feature that makes the SGWU Poetry Series stand out from other series of this period is the quality of its audio documentation. With the original reel-to-reel tapes now digitized, the recordings of these events can be listened to online.[7]

The Poetry Series recordings document an important transitional moment in the history of English-language writing in Quebec that brought and introduced many

---

**JASON CAMLOT** is Professor of English and Research Chair in Literature and Sound Studies at Concordia University. His recent books are *Phonopoetics* (2019), *Vlarf* (2021), and the co-edited collections *Collection Thinking* (2023), *Unpacking the Personal Library* (2022), and *CanLit Across Media* (2019). He directs the SpokenWeb research partnership.

American writers and local poets such as Irving Layton, D.G. Jones, Michael Gnarowski, Henry Beissel, and Richard Sommer (the latter two would later teach creative writing workshops at Concordia) to the Montreal poetry community.[8] The series also brought in major Canadian poets from outside Quebec such as Al Purdy, bill bissett, Frank Davey, Earle Birney, and Margaret Atwood, and influential American poets like Allen Ginsberg and Robert Creeley. In The Poetry Series recordings we hear a local poetry community interacting with and literally performing itself alongside contemporary national and international poetic philosophies and practices. Through the series, the university became an important site for an extracurricular sounding of the local, national, and international state of poetry.

The geographical distinctions between local (Montreal), national (Canadian), and international (mainly American), and the aesthetic distinctions defining a diverse range of poetic forms and practices audible in the series, suggest different senses of authorial purview, poetic purpose, reach, and imagined poetry communities in relation to each other. Attempts to define what "Canadian" literature is, and to account for its status in relation to the rest of the world—topics of great debate during this period—represent another important frame for these public performances. Organizing committee member and English Department professor Howard Fink remarked that Canadian and American poets were selected and sometimes paired up so they could be heard and considered in relation to each other, in part because it was felt that "the only way Canadian literature was going to be properly responded to, understood and evaluated was if comparisons were made with American" literature.[9] The reading series also documents competing versions of literary modernism, pronouncing themselves from the podium and challenging Montreal students, faculty, poets, and the wider community to reconsider the position that English Montreal writing held in relation to the future of Canadian and North American literature.

In one of the first recorded readings of The Poetry Series (a reading held in November 1966 featuring Canadian poets Phyllis Webb and Gwendolyn MacEwen), organizing committee member Roy Kiyooka explained the initial rationale of the series program: "Now perhaps some of you are wondering what these readings are all about and how the choices are made … In short, this is our attempt to sound just that diversity that so much characterizes the North American Poetry scene."[10] It is interesting to frame an encounter with American and Canadian poets considering the growing significance to scholars and poets in the 1960s interested in identifying the distinctive elements of "Canadian" (as compared to American) literature. By the late '60s it had become important to ask whether Canadian literature was a viable cultural category and whether "America" (i.e., the United States of America) was a creatively beneficial friend or culturally dominating foe. Scholars of both Canadian and Québécois literature were theorizing the nature of their own cultural and linguistic colonization (by the US and their European forebears), and the possibility of a literary practice that could represent the locus of resistance to such cultural domination.[11] Fink, a native Montrealer, felt that both Canadian *and* American literature were underrepresented in the curricula of Canadian literature departments and hoped to explore comparisons and connections between the two. George Bowering, who arrived at SGWU in 1967, was the keen student of Americanist Warren Tallman at the University of British Columbia (UBC), a member of the West Coast Tish group that saw the great potential of applying the methods of new American writers like Charles Olson and Jack Spicer to an exploration of the Canadian experience. American influence was not at odds with the development of Canadian literature, in Bowering's opinion. The period during which he was active in curating The Poetry Series highlighted numerous experimental American, West Coast Tish, and Toronto New Wave Canada poets.[12]

This openness to multiple forms of poetry from within and beyond Canada's borders went against the grain of certain critics of the period who were concerned with the American colonization of Canadian culture. For example, poet and academic Robin Mathews, who launched an effort to ensure that the majority of Canadian university faculty positions went to Canadian citizens rather than foreign nationals, described the poetic experiments of the Tish poets as representative of a "U.S. invasion and colonization of a part of the poetic culture of Canada."[13]

The binary that informed Mathews's association of American imperialism and poetics can be heard in local debates about the meaning and value of particular readings in The Poetry Series, as articulated in editorials and letters published in the SGWU student newspaper, *The Georgian*. For example, following the appearance of San Francisco–based poet Gary Snyder in November 1971, one letter to the editor wrote to "protest this genre of fake poetry which seems to derive from W.C. Williams' dictum 'no ideas but in things' which we believe is anti-poetry and anti-life,"[14] while another, in the next issue, attributed such an attack to "inexcusable ignorance" and praised Snyder's reading as "a welcome relief from the insufferable dullness and second rate poetry produced by certain Montreal poets" including "Irving Layton and Leonard Cohen."[15] Such print sources reveal how controversial and important the reading series was as a staging ground for the young, aspiring poets in the city.

In the audio documentation of The Poetry Series readings, we can hear in performance a range of approaches to reading poetry out loud that represented differing models of poetics, the poet, oral performance, artistic community, and the nature of the poetry event itself. The Poetry Series was constructed from the beginning to highlight contrasting modes of poetry and poetics, with very different kinds of poets sometimes paired up in a single reading so that the difference between them would be clear.[16] With Bowering's arrival in Montreal in 1967 to fill a poet-in-residence post left vacant by Irving Layton's departure, the series took on a deliberate avant-garde turn. One of Bowering's goals as a new member of The Poetry Series organizing committee was to bring the lessons he and his peers had learned from exposure to certain late American modernists while in Vancouver in the 1960s and their subsequent experience in channeling "the American influence into a Modernism of their own devising" further east than it had yet travelled.[17] Bowering's curating of the series was aesthetically, pedagogically, and polemically focused. He even referred to the information notices he typed, mimeographed, and disseminated to inform people about the readings as "propaganda sheets."[18] In addition to bringing avant-garde Canadian poets to Montreal, Bowering initiated invitations to several influential Americans, as well. In his introduction to Ted Berrigan (December 4, 1970), the first of several New York School poets Bowering booked, he refers to the newly defined program as a "kind of avant-garde series."[19] As a result of this new explicitness in defining the direction for the series, the students, faculty, and poets in the audience were exposed to performances of long poems, open forms, and other poetic alternatives to the short lyric modes that continued to dominate Montreal poetry through the 1960s. Now you had David Ball reading his long piece "The Boring Poem" in its entirety, George Oppen reading nearly his whole *On Being Numerous* without intermission, and Allen Ginsberg chanting Hare Krishna for thirty minutes prior to an hour-long performance of his musical adaptations (voice and harmonium) of Blake's songs. The younger poets who were in attendance at the readings—some Bowering's students and future Montreal poets and poetry organizers, such as Artie Gold and Endre Farkas—were being shown not only that poetry could be different from Montreal-based modernist precedents, but that these alternative models were available to them for the purpose of local emulation and extrapolation. Key lessons learned by witnessing and hearing such readings included how the poet could function as an emblematic vehicle of the creative process and how the poetry reading could function as a force of collective, poetic participation.

Where the first phase of The Poetry Series provided exposure to variety, this second phase was framed as a sign of potential transition for English-language poetry in Quebec towards a new kind of Canadian avant-garde—one that embraced American open-field poetics but, at the same time, made something distinctly local of it. Bowering brought with him from Vancouver Olson's idea that you should "dig where you are at the moment and know more than anyone else does" and attempted to use his influence on the programming of The Poetry Series to illustrate how this might be done.[20] In the end, however, Montreal was not amenable to digging for him and he left Montreal and returned to the West Coast to teach at Simon Fraser University in 1971.

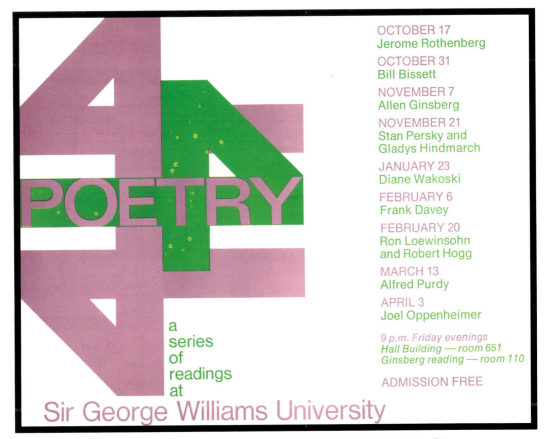

20.2 Poster designed by Robert Reid for all readings in the Fourth Series (October 19, 1969–April 3, 1970) of the Sir George Williams University Poetry Series.

Following Bowering's departure, the programming of The Poetry Series became less obviously focused on the staging of a specifically Canadian avant-garde and its significant American precedents, and featured fewer poets, overall, due to a decrease in funding from the Canada Council. Organized poetry readings had now become ubiquitous across the country and money to support them had to be spread thinner to support them all.[21] The complexity of The Poetry Series is partly a result of the fact that the series was very well funded up until the early 1970s, which allowed the organizers to showcase a diverse range of poets. The series folded in 1975.

The precedent set by The Poetry Series as an occasion to stage poetic philosophies and community allegiances influenced numerous Montreal reading series that followed. One of the first organized responses to The Poetry Series was a reading tour of the local colleges (CEGEPs) by ten young Montreal poets; in his editor's note in the anthology published to accompany the readings, Michael Harris commented on the recent practice of the colleges and universities "to bring into the city poets from elsewhere in Canada and America." This college tour, and "the establishment of the series of readings at Véhicule Art on St. Catherine Street" in 1972, were designed, instead, to provide a regular platform for *local* voices.[22]

The emergence of the Véhicule Art series and a plethora of literary journals and presses that followed underscores the influence The Poetry Series had on local writers. Endre Farkas and Ken Norris have written that Bowering's "most important contribution to the new generation of Montreal poets was the institution of a series of readings at SGWU which exposed them to the diverse experimentation that was taking place across Canada and the US … This would result in numerous local readings and the establishment of a number of little magazines and small presses."[23] Out of the early Véhicule Art readings emerged a loosely defined collective known as the Véhicule Poets. The readings, performances, magazine, and chapbook productions of the Véhicule Poets (from the mid-1970s on) represented the most explicit continuation of the lessons learned from the process- and community-oriented avant-garde models Kiyooka, Hoffman, Fink, and especially Bowering had brought to the SGWU series. As Bowering wrote of being a young creative writer in Montreal in the early '70s, "young poets looking for poetry were not given much of a chance to find it outside the living legends," namely, Layton and Cohen. The SGWU Poetry Series gave such poets somewhere to look and the Véhicule Poets looked with the greatest intent at that moment.[24]

While The Poetry Series was not part of the English department's course curriculum, it can be understood as an important extracurricular impetus that would eventually lead to the development of one of the first university bachelor's degree creative writing programs in Canada. A few creative writing courses had already been offered as part of the curriculum of SGWU's Department of English since the mid-1960s (at a time when public speaking was still part of the English curriculum). The 1964–65 *Sir George Williams Calendar* lists two "full" creative writing courses, one in poetry and another in prose, designed to offer "advice and critical reading of their work to advanced students with a special interest and ability in written expression."[25] When The Poetry Series was running, creative writing courses were offered by writers-in-residence such as Layton, Atwood, and Bowering. And then, English faculty members who had been hired to teach academic courses but also had creative practices, such as poets Henry Beissel (a medievalist) and Gary Geddes (an expert in the work of Joseph Conrad), represented support on the ground for the institution-alization of creative writing as a program. The first MA thesis in creative writing, poetry, was completed by John McAuley in 1974, just before the merger of SGWU

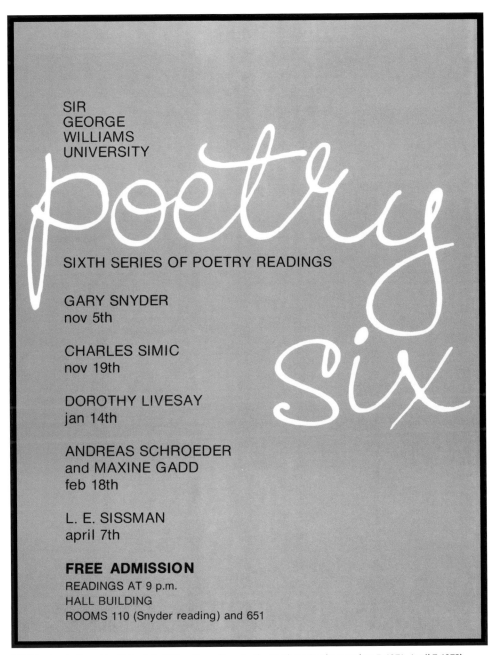

20.3 Poster designed by Robert Reid for all readings in the Sixth Series (November 5, 1971–April 7, 1972) of the Sir George Williams University Poetry Series.

with Loyola. The next two were Concordia University theses by Andre (later Endre) Farkas and Michael Harris in 1976 and 1978, respectively.[26] All three of these students would have been regular attendees of the Sir George Williams Poetry Series readings, and McAuley and Farkas were students of Bowering and active members of the Véhicule Art group that was inspired by their experience of The Poetry Series to start up its own reading series at Véhicule Art. A thirty-credit minor in creative writing first appeared in the Concordia calendar in 1977–78.[27] The BA major in creative writing appears in the calendar for the first time in 1983–84. There is sparse documentation available in the university archives to prove a direct causal connection between the effects of The Poetry Series and the establishment of creative writing programs at Concordia soon after the series ended, but the documentation we do have leaves little doubt that this reading series, which brought contemporary literature as a tangible and living experience to the university, created the context from which to imagine the conversion of a programmed reading series into a university program.

### NOTES

1   A longer version of the research in this chapter was first published as "The Sound of Canadian Modernisms: The Sir George Williams University Poetry Series, 1966–1974," *Journal of Canadian Studies / Revue d'études canadiennes* 46, no. 3 (Fall 2012): 28–59.

2   "Poetry Readings," *Post-Grad*, Spring 1967, 13, 18.

3   "Poetry Readings," 19.

4   "Poetry Readings," 13.

5   Howard Fink, Stanton Hoffman, and Roy Kiyooka initiated and organized the series from 1966 to 1970 along with George Bowering (1967–71), and consulting support from senior English faculty member Wynne Francis. Other members who served on the committee periodically included English professor Richard Sommer and writer-in-residence Margaret Atwood. Fink notes that one model for such a series came from his experience as a McGill student in the 1950s of a poetry series organized by Louis Dudek. Another model Fink mentions would have come from Kiyooka's involvement in readings organized by Warren Tallman and others at UBC in the early 1960s. Howard Fink, interview with author, November 2, 2012.

6   Harvey Oberfeld, "Audio-Visual Facilities Best in Country," *The Georgian*, October 14, 1966, S-4.

7   "SGW Poetry Reading Series," SpokenWeb Montreal, https://montreal.spokenweb.ca/sgw-poetry-readings/.

8   American poets included Robert Creeley, Michael McClure, Charles Reznikoff, Ted Berrigan, David Bromige, Robert Duncan, Allen Ginsberg, Kenneth Koch, Jackson Mac Low, and Jerome Rothenberg.

9   Fink, interview.

10  Phyllis Webb, Poetry Reading, recorded November 18, 1966, I006-11-130, English Department fonds, Concordia Records Management and Archives (hereafter RMA).

11  Among the important Québécois events of the 1960s and '70s was a series of public readings called Poèmes et Chansons, organized to raise funds for the legal defence of founding Front de libération du Québec (FLQ) members Pierre Vallières and Charles Gagnon. This series led into the organization of La Nuit de La Poésie held at Théâtre du Gesu in Montreal (March 27, 1970), which featured twenty-three Québécois poets representing several generations and billed as the largest poetry event ever to take place in Quebec. This significant event, documented in Claude

Labrecque and Jean-Pierre Masse's film documentary *La Nuit de la poésie 27 mars 1970* (Office national du film du Canada / National Film Board of Canada, 1970), show the poets' awareness and interest in the techniques of the Beat and Black arts movements and reveal a very different sense of the connection between poetics and national identity than that heard in the SGWU Poetry Series. See also Jeffrey Cormier, *The Canadianization Movement: Emergence, Survival, and Success* (Toronto: University of Toronto Press, 2004), 1–39.

12  George Bowering, interview with author, October 12, 2012, mp3 recording, author's collection.

13  Robin Mathews, Preface to *Poetry and the Colonized Mind: Tish*, ed. Keith Richardson (Ottawa: Mosaic Press, 1976), 7.

14  Avi Boxer, Bryan McCarthy, and Graham Seal, "Re: Reverand Richard J. Sommer [letter]," *The Georgian*, November 12, 1971, 4.

15  Stephen Morrissey, "Inexcusable Ignorance [letter]," *The Georgian*, November 26, 1971, n.p.

16  Fink, interview.

17  Warren Tallman, "Wonder Merchants: Modernist Poetry in Vancouver During the1960s," *boundary 2* 3, no. 1 (1974): 66–67.

18  Gladys Hindmarch, Poetry Reading, recorded November 21, 1969, 1086-11-020, English Department fonds, RMA.

19  Ted Berrigan, Poetry Reading, recorded December 4, 1970, I086-11-13, English Department fonds, RMA.

20  Bowering, interview.

21  Fink, interview.

22  Michael Harris, "A Note about This Collection," in *Poetry Readings: 10 Montreal Poets in the CEGEPS*, ed. Michael Harris (Lasalle, QC: Delta Canada, 1975), n.p. CEGEP is the acronym used for Collège d'enseignement général et professionnel.

23  Andre Farkas and Ken Norris, "'Introduction' to *Montreal: Poetry of the Seventies* (1978)," in *Language Acts: Anglo-Québec Poetry, 1976 to the Twenty-First Century*, ed. Jason Camlot and Todd Swift (Montreal: Véhicule Press, 2007), 44. Andre Farkas later changed the spelling of his name to Endre.

24  George Bowering, "On Not Teaching the Vehicle Poets," in *Vehicle Days: An Unorthodox History of Montreal's Vehicle Poets*, ed. Ken Norris (Montreal: NuAge Editions, 1993), 115.

25  *Sir George Williams University, Arts, Science, Commerce, Engineering Academic Calendar, 1965–66*, 156.

26  "Concordia University M.A. Poetry Theses, 1974–2006," in *Language Acts Anglo-Québec Poetry, 1976 to the Twenty-First Century*, ed. Jason Camlot and Todd Swift (Montreal: Véhicule Press, 2007), 382.

27  *Concordia University Undergraduate Calendar, 1977–78*.

Department of History presents

# *CRIME*
# PROTEST &
# PUNISHMENT

## IN 19th CENTURY BRITAIN

# GEORGE RUDÉ

FOREMOST AUTHORITY ON
EUROPEAN CROWDS AND
MOB VIOLENCE

WED., NOV. 8    10:30-11:30am    VKC 152

21.1 This undated lecture poster was one of many such talks that the public intellectual Rudé gave at university campuses in Canada and elsewhere in the 1970s and 1980s.

# HISTORY FROM BELOW: GEORGE RUDÉ AND MONTREAL AS A RADICAL CROSSROADS

Brandon Webb and Matthew Penney

**MID-MORNING** in Concordia's Hall Building—the core of the downtown campus. Students spill into the corridors, chatting and meeting old friends or new ones, rushing to their next class or climbing the stairs as a broken escalator waits to be fixed. These everyday interactions of student life provide a backdrop to some of the most important and explosive moments in the university's history. Starting with this mixing of people with different backgrounds and experiences can also help bring us to the "who?" and "why?" of student protests, interventions, and activism.[1] Many of the same students seen going to classes on a non-descript day may have taken part in the Black Lives Matter protests in summer 2020 or were among the half a million who marched in Montreal during the global climate strike in 2019. The same people but in different crowds.[2]

Crowds can shape our everyday or they can make history. Sometimes they do both. George Rudé, a professor in the Department of History, first at Sir George Williams University (SGWU) and then at Concordia between 1970 and 1987, was described by historian A.J.P. Taylor as "put[ting] mind back into history" in a way that "restored the dignity" of ordinary people left out of its dominant narratives.[3] A renowned researcher, teacher, and public intellectual, Rudé was the historian of the crowd.[4]

Until Rudé, crowds were given short shrift by historians. In historical sources they appear as fearsome, unruly—a symbol of the "shock" of the modern city and the feeling that something had been lost amid bustling anonymity. The crowd has often been conceived as the target of moral invective, mixing feelings of fear and fascination. In popular literature, crowds have typically been described with suspicion. Edgar Allan Poe left us an archetypal image of the modern crowd by describing the spectre

---

**BRANDON WEBB** completed his PhD in history at Concordia in 2022 and has published on film and print history, as well as the cultural Cold War. A Kluge Fellow at the Library of Congress, his current book project is a labour and cultural history of American political cartooning.

**MATTHEW PENNEY** is Associate Professor in the Department of History at Concordia. He is a specialist in modern Japanese history and has an interest in critical social thought globally.

of crime and disorder hidden within it. In Poe's rendering, the crowd is painted as a jostling, faceless mass into which suspicious figures disappear at will, while reappearing with subversive or violent intent.[5] Police and security forces still view crowds this way. From this perspective, every protestor is a potential provocateur, and the crowds they belong to are corralled and controlled to halt their relentless, disconcerting momentum. Rudé wrote to cut through these prejudices and use the concept of the crowd to highlight agency in history. Historical change, which is regularly viewed through the lens of a battlefield or seen taking place behind the scenes at the courts of kings, also comes from new ways of seeing and acting that emerge from collectivities, even, or perhaps *especially* from fluid or momentary ones.

In contrast to the then dominant French Annales school of historiography, which tended towards the *longue durée*, Rudé took a more granular approach to both periods and people. Drawing largely from police and prison records deposited in the Archives Nationales and the Paris Préfecture de Police, Rudé painted a portrait of everyday life from 1787 to 1795 to show that the world-shaking events of the French Revolution were not simply a rupture guided by political elites. Whereas some historians described elements of the *sans-culottes* with such dismissive terms as "*la canaille*" and "*la derniere plebe*," Rudé instead ascribed to the crowd a revolutionary agency borne of hardship and active political engagement. Eschewing both contempt and romanticism, Rudé argued forcefully that the popular classes of the past could not be treated as a "disembodied abstraction and the personification of good or evil."[6] As he explained, "the popular elements composing the *sans-culottes*—the peasants, craftsmen, journeymen, and labourers—have begun to appear as social groups with their own distinctive identity, interests, and aspirations, whose actions and attitudes no longer be treated as mere echoes or reflections of the ideas, speeches, and decrees of the journalists, lawyers, orators, and politicians established in the capital."[7] Such a description, attentive to the struggles of people who were often written out of history, exemplified what a "history from below" approach looked like.

This chapter connects Rudé's insights into the crowd with events that have significantly shaped Concordia's history from the late 1960s to the present. In so doing, we ask, What can Rudé's work tell us about the social movements that students have led throughout the years? And how have the crowds formed in moments of student dissent shaped our perceptions of protest?

### Political Exile

Historian Harvey Kaye described Rudé as "one of the truly great social historians, joining together the most critical European historical traditions, the British Marxist, and the French revolutionary."[8] Yet in the tense climate of the early Cold War, such sympathies raised anti-communists' suspicions. In the 1950s Rudé, who joined the Communist

21.2 A portrait of George Rudé during his years at Sir George Williams University/Concordia. Following his retirement, the Department of History renamed its main seminar room the George Rudé Seminar Room.

Party of Great Britain following a trip to the Soviet Union in the 1930s, lost out on career opportunities because of his political beliefs. Loosely affiliated with the renowned group of British Marxist historians who pioneered innovative ways of writing history from below,[9] his peers and mentors included E.P. Thompson, author of *The Making of the English Working Class*, and Eric Hobsbawm, who collaborated with Rudé on *Captain Swing*, an important study of the "Swing" revolts by agricultural laborers that shook England in the 1830s.[10]

Despite this noteworthy pedigree, Rudé was shut out of the postwar British academy and forced to find work elsewhere. In 1959 he took up a teaching post at the University of Adelaide, located in the hometown of his wife, Doreen, who aided Rudé's research efforts. Throughout this period, Rudé avoided overt political activity, but nonetheless was subject to security checks prior to and after securing his faculty appointment at Adelaide. His impact, however, could not be so easily suppressed, as evidenced by a biannual George Rudé Seminar that was inaugurated at the University of Melbourne in 1978 and which continues in Australia to this day.

With Rudé's prospects for career advancement limited, the Rudés relocated to North America in 1970.[11] The growing reputation of SGWU's History Department in the late 1960s, along with Montreal's closer proximity to his native England and archives in France, made the city an attractive landing spot. Reflecting on Rudé's career, *Concordia Journal* editor Barbara Black depicted his story as "a poignant one" that, despite significant hurdles, resulted in "groundbreaking" scholarship. History professor Carolyn Fick, whose own pathbreaking research on the Haitian Revolution was partly inspired by Rudé, described her colleague and mentor as "put[ting] names and faces on the 'crowd,' up until then commonly called the mob or the rabble by more traditional historians."[12] Rudé also lent critical support to labour struggles at the university during his years at SGWU/Concordia. In 1971 he co-authored a report that *The Georgian* student newspaper described as encouraging stronger ties between striking library workers and faculty members.[13] Whether contesting contemporary structures or top-down historical narratives about the past, Rudé's politics and ideas linked up with many of the actions of student activists who have struggled for change either in the classroom or outside it.

## Montreal as Radical Crossroads

Rudé came to Montreal during a momentous moment in the city's history as well as the history of student politics more broadly. The rebellious "spirit" of May 1968 stretched far beyond Paris and Prague as students in North America protested the Vietnam War and racial discrimination across a range of institutions. At McGill University, the Black Writers Congress, which a number of politically active Sir George students from the Black diaspora helped organize, featured radical luminaries such as C.L.R. James and Walter Rodney. These events centred the city as a hub of 1960s counterculture within Canada. A year later, SGWU made headlines after a group of Black students from the West Indies, who saw their complaints of racist discriminatory treatment from a white biology professor go unheeded, protested the administration's meek response. What followed became one of the most infamous episodes in the history of Canadian higher education. The language sometimes used to describe this event—"the Computer Centre riot"—displaces the intentions of the occupation that made use of one of the few tools available to students to have their voices heard.[14]

Over the years other student groups at Concordia have drawn similar lessons about the power of crowds to reveal injustice. In January 1982 the *Thursday Report* reported on what appeared to be a spontaneous clash in the Hall Building as members of the Iranian student community—then the largest Iranian student population in Canada at the time—confronted a group of pro-Khomeini supporters who had allegedly been bussed into campus to show support for Iran's new regime.[15] *The Link* followed up with a series of reports that exemplified Rudé's approach to unpacking the complex ways crowds are formed. *Link* reporter Philip Authier, who would later become a journalist for the *Montreal Gazette*, wrote that many of the Iranian students who confronted the pro-Khomeini supporters had recently experienced difficulties renewing their passports with the Iranian consulate in Ottawa. Other Iranian students reported not having funds disbursed while some, in an echo of Cold War–era surveillance, expressed fears that they would be barred from returning to Iran due to their opposition to the regime. In this instance, the university responded by helping set up an emergency fund for the impacted students.[16]

Twenty years later a different institutional response emerged as the Hall Building was once again the site of controversy. In 2002 a new generation of student activists, weened on the global outlook of a local anti-free trade movement, protested then former Israeli Prime Minister Benjamin Netanyahu's campus visit. Invited by the Jewish student group Hillel, the ensuing anti-Netanyahu "riots" made international news.[17] The 2004 documentary film *Discordia* captured the frenzy of that's day events, as well as the subsequent suspension of pro-Palestinian student activists who were then active in a radicalized Concordia Student Union (CSU). Less known was a 2003 CSU report that documented the hostility and discrimination that Palestinian student groups and Muslim students had reported facing following the terrorist attacks of 9/11. In a historical parallel to the circulation of political pamphlets in the revolutionary era of the late eighteenth century, the CSU report described how postering and tabling on campus had become a point of contention among student groups and the administration.

The CSU's report embodied a history-from-below ethos that complicated the sensational media headlines that lazily tried to portray student protesters as potential "terrorists." The report also centred a question that Rudé often asked in his lectures: "What is a protester?" In his lecture notes, Rudé scribbled that there were two predominant ways of looking at this question: "to some all protest [is] a Crime; to others all Crime=Protest."[18] The media images of shattered glass and throngs of riot police may have proved to many observers that the anti-Netanyahu protest was a criminal act. But this observation failed to register the contextual factors that led to these events. If, as Rudé argued, violence is "an elastic term," understanding why protests happen require us to investigate the structures aligned against crowds.[19] As Zev Tiefenbach, one of the students suspended by the university for his involvement in the protest, later recalled, "bringing people together into collective institutions and *building* these collective institutions is what makes social movements sustainable."[20]

Tiefenbach's reflections show why universities are public spaces where crowds and ideas converge to form new collectivities. In notes for a guest lecture at Queen's

University in 1976, Rudé expressed this idea when he wrote that his goal was "to present collective protest (of which violence [is] a part) as a socio-historical phenomenon" that varied across time and place.[21] Montreal has been one such place where the meanings attached to crowds has been contested. The historians, student journalists, and activists who seek to understand the "faces in the crowd" today, either through research or activism, practice something that was at the centre of Rudé's historical imagination: the collective action of the crowd has power to shape the course of events.

## Conclusion

In Rudé's writings the crowd is never one thing. A surge of moving bodies cannot be reduced to an undifferentiated mass of people thrown together by random events. For Rudé the crowd was composed of real individuals whose motivations diverged and converged with those around them—a collectivity in motion. While recent scholarship has complicated some of Rudé's reflections by drawing attention to how violence within crowds can stymie their aims and intentions, the continued salience of Rudé's work is that crowds manifest through individual expressions across collective frameworks. Seen this way, crowds form in and through contradictions, much like institutions. Both represent the limits handed down to them from the past. But whereas institutions are slow to change, crowds point towards the possibilities of transformations with explosive potential but whose future has no guarantee.

The calls for justice in 1969, 1982, 2002, and beyond can still be heard today. Outrage proliferates across crowds, which form and reform, giving those demands a possible trajectory beyond the moment they are first articulated. The crowd can help us to understand these lines of engagement that Concordia students have laid down time and again, just as the history of these struggles can cast Rudé's work in a new light at present.

### NOTES

1    This chapter draws on George Rudé's published writings as well as unpublished notes that are part of his personal archive that he deposited at Concordia University Records Management and Archives (hereafter RMA). Nancy Marrelli helped secure the George Rudé fonds, but sadly Rudé passed before he could provide information on his files. Concordia's archivists have digitized many of these files which can be accessed on Internet Archives: https://archive.org/search?query=creator%3A%22George+Rud%C3%A9%22.

2    Without the mixing of people of different social classes and backgrounds in the crowds of the everyday, the crowd in time of crisis—the revolutionary crowd of the French Revolution in Rudé's work and the crowds in protest of our own time—could not materialize. See Andrew Charlesworth, "George Rudé and the Anatomy of the Crowd," *Labour History Review* 55, no. 3 (Winter 1990): 28–32.

3    Quoted in "George Rudé, 1910–1993—Marxist Historian: Memorial Tributes," *Socialist History Society Occasional Papers Series*, no. 2 (1993).

4    George Rudé, *The Crowd in the French Revolution* (Oxford: Oxford University Press, 1967, first published in 1959 by Clarendon Press). Rudé followed his popular book with a broader survey of crowds in history. Also see George Rudé, *The Crowd in History: A Study of Popular Disturbances in France and England, 1730–1848* (New York: Wiley & Sons, 1964).

5    Edgar Allan Poe, "The Man of the Crowd," in *The Complete Stories* (New York: Alfred A. Knopf, 1992), 442–50. First published in 1840 by the literary journal *Atkinson's Casket*.

6    For a discussion of previous approaches, see Introduction to Rudé, *The Crowd in the French Revolution,* 2–4.

7    Rudé, *The Crowd in the French Revolution*, 5.

8    Harvey Kaye's contribution to the "George Rudé, 1910–1993—Marxist Historian: Memorial Tributes," *Socialist History Society Occasional Papers Series*, no. 2 (1993): 11.

9    For more on Rudé's relation to this influential school of historical writing, see Harvey J. Kaye, "George Rudé, All History Must Be Studied Afresh," in *The Education of Desire: Marxists and the Writing of History* (New York: Routledge, 1992), 31–64.

10   Eric Hobsbawm and George Rudé, *Captain Swing* (New York: Verso, 2014, first published by Lawrence & Wishart in 1969).

11   For more on Rudé's struggles obtaining faculty appointments outside the UK, see Doug Munro's conference paper, "The Politics of George Rudé's Appointment to the University of Adelaide," presented at the 19th George Rudé Seminar held at Deakin University, July 11, 2014. Also see Doug Munro, "The Strange Career of George Rudé—Marxist Historian," *Journal of Historical Biography* 16 (Autumn 2014): 118–69.

12   Barbara Black, "Political Rebel, Fine Scholar: George Rudé," *Concordia Journal*, February 22, 2007, http://cjournal.concordia.ca/journalarchives/2006-07/feb_22/008725.shtml.

13   This report formed the basis of a strike motion put forward by History Professor Frank Chalk that called for faculty support for the striking library workers. This motion was defeated by a faculty vote. See George Huculak, "SGWAUT: No Strike!" *The Georgian* 25, no. 23 (November 26, 1971).

14   For more on the 1969 events and its legacies, see Désirée Rochat and Annick Maugile-Flavien's insightful contribution to this volume, "These Halls of Ours: Black Student Presence and Black Montreal Youth History."

15   "Iranians Clash," *Thursday Report* 5, no. 14 (January 14, 1982).

16   Philip Authier, "Iranian Students Clash in Campus Riot," *The Link*, January 8, 1982.

17   For more on how the CSU authors described the history of student struggles at the university, see *Concordia Student Union Report on Racism and Discrimination: An Investigation into Racial Discrimination against Muslim and Arab Students at Concordia University*, May 2003, P0263 Concordia Student Union fonds, RMA.

18   "Convicts" lecture notes, April 6, 1978, P009 George Rudé fonds, RMA, https://archive.org/details/convicts-1978/page/n3/mode/1up.

19   "Popular Violence in Historical Perspective" lecture notes, November 3, 1976, P009 George Rudé fonds, RMA, https://archive.org/details/popular-violence-in-historical-perspective-1976_. These notes were in preparation for a talk set to take place at Queen's University (Kingston, ON).

20   Interview with Zev Tiefenbach, February 13, 2023, 01:39:34, Concordia at 50 Oral History Collection, I0007-09-0047, RMA. Selections from this interview are quoted elsewhere in this volume.

21   See page 2 of Rudé's "Popular Violence in Historical Perspective" lecture notes.

## VISUAL STORY

# The 1969 Sir George Williams University Student Protest against Racism: A Curator's View

Christiana Abraham

22.1 Bird's eye view from the Henry Hall Building showing iconic computer cards and other debris tossed from windows during the computer centre occupation, 1969.

The 1969 Sir George Williams University student protest has been described as a watershed event in the history of the university, and one of Canada's most significant student actions against racism. From January 29 to February 11, 1969, students occupied the ninth-floor computer centre and the seventh-floor faculty lounge of the Henry Hall Building in protest against racial discrimination at the institution. The sit-in was spurred by what students have described as inaction on the part of the university to a complaint nine months earlier (in April 1968), by six Black and Caribbean students from the biology department against a professor they believed was deliberately failing them because they were Black.[1] The two-week dissenting action ended when police stormed the sit-in in the early morning of February 11, and arrested ninety-seven protestors while a suspicious fire was set to the building.[2]

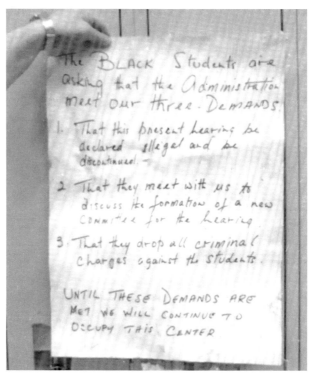

22.2 List of student demands posted outside the sit-in. The handwritten demands in black and white outline their position on the hearings and critical negotiations that were taking place, 1969.

The fiftieth anniversary of this protest (in 2019) provided an opportunity to revisit this important history through an archival exhibition of the protest. As part of a two-week program of commemorative events organized by the research collective Protest and Pedagogy, I curated an exhibition titled *Protests and Pedagogy: Representations, Memories and Meanings*.[3]

Held at Concordia University's 4[TH] Space, the exhibit sought to introduce this history to a generation of students, staff, faculty, and community members, many of whom were not familiar with this event.[4] Sourced from Concordia University's Records Management and Archives, and collections from Montreal's Black community, the exhibition featured more than 250 artifacts comprising images, documents, newspapers, interactive digital components, and audio-visual archives that brought together a unique collection of visual and documented histories of the protest.[5]

My interest in revisiting this protest was to interpret its meanings, lessons, and legacies in the contemporary moment. What do these compelling visual accounts and documents teach us about this protest so many years later? While

22.3 Police arrest students in the aftermath of the protests and occupation, February 11, 1969.

conducting this archival work, I found glaring gaps in this history in the formal archives, particularly from the perspective of the Black community. In addition, the event had been represented in the mainstream media through clichéd frames such as a "radical riot."

Presented through grassroots, decolonizing approaches, the resulting exhibition focused on untold stories, and views of the protest. The exhibition's framing offered rare insights that combined community memory and histories from members of Montreal's Black and Caribbean community with archival artifacts resulting in an expanded community archive of the event.

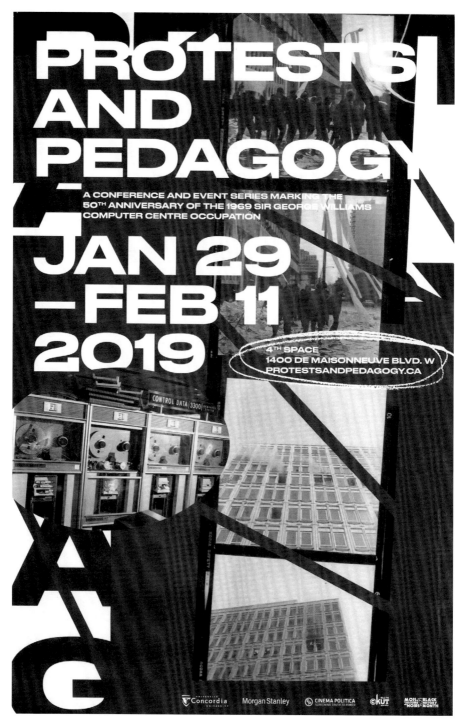

22.4 Poster for Protests and Pedagogy conference and event series marking the 50th anniversary of the 1969 SGW Computer Centre Occupation, at 4TH Space, 2019.

22.5 *Protests and Pedagogy* exhibition at 4^TH Space.

22.6 Installation view of pop-up exhibition, *Protests and Pedagogy* with computer cards in foreground at Media Gallery, Communication Studies and Journalism Building, Loyola, February 2019.

Some of the highlights included black-and-white images that traced the affair's chronology through lesser-known aspects of this protest, including the students who were arrested. Some of the novel views highlighted stories of the women who participated in the protest as student leaders, victims of police violence and subsequently jailed.

A focus on the student press drew attention to the importance of student publications during the occupation. These presses provided detailed accounts of the day-to-day unfolding of the protests and remain a hidden archive about the affair. Student newspaper *The Georgian*, for example, carried regular detailed bulletins about the negotiations with university administration.

Attention to the visual cultural history of this event offers poignant details of the often overlooked but enriched value of these archival materials. Among some of the narratives that they paint are pictures of the wider role of this protest in Canadian civil rights and Black power movements in the postcolonial context of the 1960s. They also visually represent and thereby accentuate the significance of student activism in pointing out injustice and driving change at the university.

**NOTES**

1   The students who made the complaint were Rodney John, Terrence Ballantyne, Douglas Mossop, Wendel Goodin, Kennedy Fredrick, and Allan Brown.

2   The arrests were followed by lengthy court trials resulting in fines and deportations of some of the foreign students. Three student leaders eventually handed fines and prison sentences included Roosevelt Douglas, Anne Cools, and Brenda Dash. For more retrospective accounts of the incident and aftermath, see *The Fire That Time: Transnational Black Radicalism and the Sir George Williams Occupation*, ed. Ronald Cummings and Nalini Mohabir (Montreal: Black Rose Books, 2021).

3   Collaborators of this exhibition included Nalini Mohabir and Kaie Kellough.

4   For a more detailed analysis of this exhibition, see Christiana Abraham, "Critical Curating as Decolonial Practice: Protests and Pedagogy: Representations, Memories and Meanings— Anatomy of an Exhibition," *TOPIA: Canadian Journal of Cultural Studies*, no. 44 (March 2022): 67–93, https://www.muse.jhu.edu/article/854453.

5   A large number of these images were commissioned by the university for insurance purposes in the aftermath of the fire.

CHRISTIANA ABRAHAM is Assistant Professor in Communication Studies at Concordia University. A scholar and independent curator, her scholarship is interested in the destabilization and re-visualization of visualities in anti-racist and decolonial pedagogies. Her teaching and research are in critical race pedagogies, media studies, visualities, and gender; de/post-coloniality and Global South media.

# THESE HALLS OF OURS: BLACK STUDENT PRESENCE AND BLACK MONTREAL YOUTH HISTORY

Annick Maugile Flavien and Désirée Rochat

**WITH OUR CHAPTER**, we explore the social and spatial geographies and activism of Black youth and students in and around the expansive halls of Concordia University's history, from its founding institutions to now. For Concordia, a university that has so deeply weaved itself in the geography of the city, these "halls" span streets and neighbourhoods, cultures and languages, privilege and marginalization. We also pay particular attention to the roles that Montreal Black youth and students have played in bringing knowledge and change to the institution, while recognizing the roles the university and its space played in/for student organizing. In this not-quite-linear continuum, we understand Black student presence and activism throughout Concordia through the metaphor of waves, where undercurrents are always at work before, beyond, and after more visible peaks and where the sea floor also influences how the waves peak. These waves are read in conversation with Black youth movements, social actions, and collective organizing in Montreal.

Based on archival research, institutional document analysis, and experiential knowledge, we highlight the ways Black students have forged a variety of spaces for themselves as forms of political activism over time, on campus and beyond. Our chapter's theoretical framework brings together theories from Black geographies,

---

**ANNICK MAUGILE FLAVIEN** is a three-time graduate of Concordia University, where she spent over a decade participating in anti-racism initiatives and founded Concordia's Black Perspectives Office. She is currently a PhD student in community health at Concordia, researching family/kin caregiving as a determinant of overall Black community health.

**DÉSIRÉE ROCHAT** is a community educator and transdisciplinary scholar with a PhD in educational studies from McGill University. Guided by an integrative approach connecting historical research, community archival preservation and education, her work documents, preserves, theorizes, and transmits (hi)stories of Black communities' activism. Rochat is currently a Fonds de recherche du Québec—Société et culture postdoctoral fellow at the Centre for Oral History and Digital Storytelling at Concordia University.

social learning, social movement studies, and storytelling. Through storytelling, we make sense of and tell this history of Concordia in recognition that in the historically top-down anti-Black framework of Canadian universities, the bulk of Black presence did not proliferate in the university's administrative structure or classrooms but rather in the subversive use of its halls and open spaces.

## Personal and Historical Groundings

In Black storytelling there's a beautiful heritage of retelling stories, and the angle from which the story is retold is as valuable as the story itself, as characters and space begin to reveal themselves and deepen our understanding of where this retelling belongs in relation to others. These stories could potentially stand on their own, but it is in understanding their connections and interdependence that we truly engage with their strength—a network of theories and values that grow and propagate as they continue to be heard and told as part of a common root that is not easily mapped but easily felt and recognized by its patrons. Such a rich history filled with impactful figures and transformative events could be told from many different viewpoints, so we'll begin by positioning ourselves as storytellers to better frame our lens and recognize the multitude of Black voices that own a piece of this story.

We, Désirée Rochat and Annick Maugile Flavien, respectively Haitian Swiss and Haitian, with family histories of community activism, met as a community youth workers, and crossed paths again in our professional careers at Concordia, after having both completed academic degrees at the university. For Désirée, the documentation, preservation, and transmission of Black thoughts and histories became core to her community education and organizing practice, leading her to pursue graduate studies. These experiences laid the ground for her research work in which the university sometimes became a complex ally. Most recently, as the Concordia Library researcher-in-residence for the 2021–22 academic year, Désirée was able to delve deeper into the content of various Black community-related archival fonds held at Special Collections, as well as reflect on the meaning and tensions of having these fonds preserved at Concordia University. For Annick, the legacy of her parents' political and community work and her own personal and community experiences of Blackness in Montreal led to a search for and claim to Black belonging in the city, which she fostered through mapping, connecting, and creating space for Black social presence with and within institutions. As the founder of Concordia's Black Perspectives Initiatives and then Black Perspectives Office, and a three-time graduate of Concordia University, all through which she worked at Concordia as a student employee, she had the opportunity to bring twelve years of searching for, hearing, and witnessing Black stories into the fibre of how she approached transformative institutional work.

We often see the word *waves* used to describe social thought, movements, and change. This visual of an external force of friction and pressure causing a cyclical rise, peak, break, and fall across the sea level is easily recognizable and adequately demonstrates the cyclical nature of social activism. What isn't as discussed is that the shape and speed of rise, peak, break, and fall of a wave is highly dependent on the shape of the undercurrent and the sea floor under the wave. In social terms, the foundational shape and strength of every wave is the community under the movement, the groundwork that comes before the peak and continues when the water is calm again. In looking at a timeline of Black presence at Concordia, and around the world, the wave peaks and breaks are most easily found and highlighted in a way that essentializes movements often without contextualizing the forces of friction and rarely addressing the continuous community groundwork that shaped the wave. In this telling of the waves of Black presence at Concordia, we explore three change-making waves that propelled and anchored Black presence at the university: the rise of Black presence in Canadian universities, the rise of Black community establishment in Montreal, and the rise in cross-community connections through youth culture. Through the broad retelling of these generational waves, we centre community groundwork as the structure through which this presence can be understood, in recognition of its unique value and local specificity.

## A Rise of Black Presence in Canadian Universities, 1950–1969

Choosing where to begin a story is a delicate task that can easily misconstrue who does or doesn't belong in the history. We start our telling in 1950 with a strong acknowledgement of the centuries of documented Black presence in Montreal prior to this point and a curiosity for the untold stories from that time that have yet to be uncovered, while also pinpointing that the 1950s is a moment of shift in the social makeup of Black presence in Montreal and a shift in student recruitment for the founding schools of Concordia, Sir George Williams University (SGWU), and Loyola College, where Loyola was an unchartered university, while Sir George Williams became a chartered university in 1948.[1] Academically, the 1950s was a convoluted time where legislated racial segregation in schools still existed in Ontario and Nova Scotia, and informal racial segregation was rampant across the provinces, yet the need for labour led to immigration policies that targeted Black Caribbean women first as domestics and later as nurses in the 1950s and 1960s, which led to a stronger Black presence in Montreal.[2] This presence led to an even greater influx of Black international students when, in 1962, Canada ended legislated racial discrimination in its immigration policies and moved towards a point system in 1967 that allowed more student migration and a reunification for many families, laying the ground for a wider, more diverse community. This opening toward international students without parallel efforts toward encouraging recruitment of local Black students created an enduring dynamic where international Black students had more academic mobility in Montreal universities than locally born and/or raised Black students. In the Concordia archives, this rise of international Black student presence is represented by a dominance of the Black Caribbean student voice that shapes the Black culture at SGWU. The Loyola College archives, on the other hand, as an unchartered university that would have recruited less of an international student body, remains silent on Black presence, which speaks to the difference in environments prior to the merger that formed Concordia University. At SGWU the formalization of Black student connections started as early as 1953 with the founding of the West Indian Society.[3] Throughout the 1960s, with the rise of Black and Caribbean political conversations on a global and local level, the Black students of SGWU invested in interuniversity and local community connections through active participation in organizing or in attending various conferences such as the Montreal Congress of Black Writers at McGill in 1968.[4] In 1969 the West Indian Society widened its scope and became the Caribbean Students Union, while the Black Student Association was founded, and the first informal Black studies program was initiated.[5]

These decades of connections fostered a strong community of Black and non-Black activists across the Montreal universities and community organizations who stood against different forms of anti-Black racism. It was this community of thinkers and change-makers that organized the peaceful occupation of the SGWU Computer Centre in January 1969 to denounce the treatment and grading of Black students by a SGWU professor and the mishandling of these race-based student complaints by the administration. In unclear circumstances, after many days of negotiation and peaceful protest, the occupation took a tragic turn when a fire broke out in the Computer Centre and the riot police were called to handle the situation.[6] This event had dramatic life-changing impacts on the students who were arrested, particularly the Black Caribbean students who were impacted by the racial discrimination of the legal system as well as the precarity of their immigration status. One of the most recognized archival video clips of this tragic event was taken from Mackay Street where we see students throwing the computer printing paper from the windows of the ninth floor of the Hall Building in an effort to subdue the fire as onlookers watch the scene and bystanders chant racial slurs against the Black students in the burning space.[7] This archive reminds us that this protest belongs not only to SGWU's history but also to the racialized history of Montreal, Quebec, Canada, and beyond. This dramatic peak in the wave of Black intellectual activism significantly impacted and involved local Black communities, which, in conjunction with global rise of Black activism, likely offered a local catalyst towards the formalization of the community efforts they had been preparing over the last decades.

252   COMMUNITY ACTIVATIONS

## A Rise in Black Community Establishment in Montreal, 1970–1999

The 1970s and '80s witnessed a significant surge in the institutionalization of Black organizations in Montreal and a diversification of the immigrating Black communities across class, education, and nationalities, which gave rise to many new Black community organizations and allowed older Black organizations to increase their membership.[8] This community growth was strongly felt in the francophone universities due to the rise in francophone African and Haitian immigration. At Concordia, the Caribbean Black culture dominance of the 1960s and early '70s began to shift towards a diversification of Black cultural identity. African students and their student groups became another important cultural influence in the university.[9] Through the hosting of their social events and gatherings on campus, the students practiced a form of cultural activism that embedded their presence at the university by utilizing the space to express their identities. In the words of the Black Students Union (est. 1969), which considered itself to represent all the Black students' organizations at the Sir George Williams campus, "In the past we have been responsible for organizing many on-campus activities with the aim to further developing our social, cultural, political and educational aspirations … The time has come, however, when we feel that it is vitally important that we 'reach out' beyond the confines of our campus and engage the Black Community in meaningful dialogues. As a result we are endeavouring to organize a three day cultural program from Thursday, November 20 to Saturday, November 22, 1975."[10]

This desire to express Black cultural identity in public space was also felt throughout the city with the advent of festivals such as Carifesta, established in 1974, which literally brought Black culture to the streets of Montreal.[11] In many ways, the streets of the city became an extension of the halls of the university for these students, where they got to engage with a diversity of Black identities, celebrate Blackness, practice and theorize their knowledges of Blackness, and fight against anti-Black racism. This rich environment of thought and collaboration produced a fury of Black intellectual, political, and cultural production, where students and community groups proliferated and disseminated a number of radio shows, magazines, newspapers, music, arts, programs, events, and shows, which were physically documented and preserved in ways that did not extend into subsequent generations.

In reaction to this uptake of public space by Black community organizations, Black student voices, and the increase of Black population in Montreal, however, the city was not silent and there was a stark increase in Black surveillance, police brutality, systemic racism, and public anti-Black sentiment.[12] Public acts of anti-Black racism such as the police attack on Black youth on Rue Bélanger in 1979, and the anti-Black treatment of Black workers such as nurses and taxi drivers became more and more flagrant and stimulated a surge of mobilization in Black communities.[13] In the mid-1970s, the names of Black student groups and associations were included in lists of

Black organizations in the city. Their inclusion in these lists demonstrates that they were understood by Black community members as part of community life and institutions.[14] Being more established and connected at this point allowed for Black organizations' transformative work to greatly advance some of the change that we continue to benefit from today.[15] These cross-city collaborations again echoed into the walls of the university as the Black students attempted to formalize their coalitions across Montreal universities and colleges and organized events together.[16] These attempts are documented in publications such as the short-lived newsletter *Black Student Voice*, the organ of the Black Students Union.[17] By the 1990s these student groups and activists were calling for deeper integration within the institution, and a call for a Black studies program was revitalized as the student groups worked towards embedding themselves within the physical and administrative space of Concordia.[18]

## A Rise in Cross-Community Connections through Youth Culture, 2000–2020s

Though solidarity, allyship, and activism between Black and non-Black communities had been present for many generations, the 2000s marked a shift in public discourse that moved away from a one-dimensional perspective on discrimination towards a more multifaceted and intersectional understanding that had been introduced by scholars such as Kimberley Crenshaw in 1989. This change in discourse, coupled with the rise of underground socially active hip hop culture in Montreal, had a profound power of unification in social activism and significantly raised the political awareness of youth and students in the city. As in the 1970s, Black and non-Black students were leveraging the space of the university to enact their cultural activism and foster collective thought. One prime example was the student-run Hip Hop Symposium, which students used as a "forum designed to talk about the deeper questions affecting the community" and a tool to "legitimise the culture at Concordia University by giving people a space to talk about the often-controversial side of Hip Hop."[19] This legitimization of Black knowledges and practices was amplified as Black and non-Black scholars pushed for universities to expand their view and understanding of research and academics. Practices such as oral history and research-creation became accepted within universities, which changed Black community access to university and demanded a reform of the ethics of university-led community research. These changes allowed for Black research, knowledge, and stories to break from their extracurricular confinement and grow further with the curricular activities of the university, though this curricular activity was still largely led by non-Black scholars. Again, the call for a Black studies program was made public again in 2016 by students through the Black Studies Collective. Like the generations before, in addition to their petitions for Black studies program, the Black students contributed immensely to the proliferation of Black knowledges at the university, bringing in Black scholars and speakers who could fill in the void they were denouncing. This organizing also greatly benefitted non-Black students as their interest and investment in Black culture and Black knowledges continued to grow. Though this uptake varied on a spectrum between reverence and appropriation, it allowed for a common social justice vocabulary, which created a global opening to address anti-Black racism head on.

In 2020 the flagrant disparities of the COVID-19 pandemic, the murder of George Floyd, and decades of activism against anti-Black racism culminated into a unique moment where activist vernacular became valid, acceptable, and necessary. Though this opening was short lived, it created many opportunities for activists and communities who were ready to put in place their transformative work, and it activated institutions that have been unwilling to budge for generations to participate in and initiate internal transformative work. Internally and externally, universities were called to examine and uproot their systemic racism. At Concordia, over seven thousand students, staff, alumni, and faculty petitioned for active planning against anti-Black systemic racism, and the university committed to and fulfilled the creation of the President's Task Force on Anti-Black Racism, the formalization of the Black Perspectives Initiative within the Office of the Provost and Vice-President, Academic (the Black Perspectives Office), the creation of the NouLa Black Student Centre run by the university, and made a formal apology to the students involved in the Computer Centre Occupation of 1969.[20] As we write this chapter, much of the transformative work remains to be done with the university's cooperation and support, but there is no doubt that without the drive of the generations of Black students at Concordia, none of this would have been possible.

## Making Space/Taking up Place

Though the approaches, aims, and strategies of Black students who organized at Concordia varied over time, the undercurrent of their activism was consistently driven by the need to create space centred around Black lives in such an institution. Within this political organizing framework, space emerged as a prerequisite to be able to take one's rightful place; this entailed creating community spaces, spaces of care, and intellectual spaces while also pushing to take up institutional space. These four overlapping types of spaces can be used to better understand and draw the connections between the work of Black students fifty years ago to that of the students who now walk through Concordia's halls. Though we highlight these types of spaces, we are cognizant of the fact that there remain spaces within the university where Black community members continue to be absent.[21]

### Creating Community Spaces

One of the responses from students to feeling alienated from the university has led them to create Black community spaces inside and outside the institution, as well as spaces that brought Montreal's Black community members to the institution.

As their presence was (and remains) often minimal in numbers in the classroom, the various student groups, associations, and unions opened opportunities for students to be together in the university. These associations also mirrored the changes in student demographics. At first, groups were mostly initiated by international students (from the Caribbean in the 1950s and '60s and from the African continent in the 1980s), whereas, since the 1990s, local students have been important forces of campus organizing. In more recent years, Black alumni have also created their own association, testament to the connections some of them forged to each other during their studies.[22] The need for community space has also translated over time in coalitional work between students, faculty, and staff.

Cultural activism had always been a strategic way to create both a sense of collective identity and a way to bring Black community members inside the university walls. For instance, in the 1970s and '80s, multiple cultural and artistic events co-organized by students and community groups were held at SGWU and then Concordia. The connections forged between students and community groups also translated in students being involved in community organizations. Many Concordia students are pictured in activities at the Negro Community Center (NCC), in its journal *Afro-Can* in the late 1980s,[23] while various articles also recount events held at Concordia.[24] But as all community spaces, those forged by Black students for themselves, and in alliance with other Black community members inside and outside Concordia, were also not devoid of tension, illustrating the diversity of Black experiences, realities, histories, and visions. There were, for example, intergenerational tensions during the 1969 SGWU protests, and diverging opinions about the role of students in community and political organizing.[25]

*Forging Spaces of Care*

While Black students' care and support came in great part from community institutions and members outside Concordia at first, in recent years, students have increasingly organized spaces of care for themselves inside the university. The first goals of these spaces were mainly to address mental and physical health, as well as overall well-being in a way that recognized the particular, collective needs of Black students. Black Mental Wellness Week initiated by the Black Perspectives Initiatives, as well as projects developed in partnerships with organizations such as Black Mental Health Connections, exemplify how spaces of care for Black students are becoming institutionalized, for instance through the creation of a NouLa Black Student Centre. Some of the spaces of care have also been centred around the transmission of intergenerational stories. Through activities with the Black Alumni Network and Council or closed discussions with invited speakers, the opportunities for people to share and hear others' stories relating to the experiences and presence of Black community members in academia have opened collective spaces to reckon with the intimate experiences of racism in such institutions and the toll these experiences have on mental and physical health.

### Activating Intellectual Spaces

In the late 1960s Black students across North America became increasingly vocal about their need to engage with scholarship by Black scholars and about Black communities and societies that could counter what they received and often deemed negative in their formal class material. In the United States, African American students' activism was instrumental in the development of the first Black studies program in 1967 and the establishment of the discipline across the country. In 1968 at SGWU, the Black Student Association, with the support of some faculty lecturers, were also vocal about this need, and created intellectual spaces outside of classrooms with the goal of eventually having this material enter their formal curriculum. In January 1969 they initiated the first informal Black studies programs, with a series of invited guest speakers. This intellectual space brought students to engage with a range of topics from jazz to history to economy and political science. Over time, students and faculty—sometimes separately and sometimes in alliance—continued to organize a variety of activities to engage with Black studies scholarship whether through guest speakers, conferences, forums, or symposiums.[26] Students also undertook different communication strategies to disseminate and translate scholarship and reach other students through mediums like radio shows and podcasts, creating a discursive intellectual space on air. Many of them also used their graduate studies to bring in Black stories within their academic work, creating a space that was anchored in and built from their communities' knowledge. Though there has not yet been a formal Black studies program, various Black professors initiated courses, such as the "first university-accredited course on Black Women's Studies" at a Canadian university developed and taught by Dr. Esmeralda Thornhill at the Simone de Beauvoir Institute in 1983, and the Black Montreal course on the "major themes, issues, and debates in Montreal's Black history from its origins until today," developed and taught by Dr. Dorothy Williams.[27] In 2022, building on more than fifty years of demands for a formal Black intellectual space and the creation of a Black studies program, the *President's Task Force on Anti-Black Racism Final Report* once again echoed this recommendation,[28] and in 2023, through the initiative of the Black-led feminist organization Harambec, Dr. Thornhill's work was honoured with the creation of the annual Dr. Esmeralda Thornhill Black Feminist Speaker Series.

### Taking up Institutional Space

Finally, students have also worked to take space within the structure of the institution, demanding, in some instances, the opportunity to work more directly with administrative units. These demands demonstrate the quest to address the structural transformation of the university. These student efforts led to the institutionalization of initiatives by Black students and alumni in various cases such as the Black Community Initiative in 1997.[29] In the 2020 petition mentioned earlier, some of the demands also related to the gain of institutional space through the transformation of Black Perspectives Initiatives into the Black Perspectives Office, a more formal and long-term unit. The creation of institutional space remains an ongoing endeavour as Black students, faculty, and staff work with allies across the university. This work often continues through the daily, sometimes invisible labour of many.

## Conclusion

Though the idea of waves of movements and activism could imply that there is a rest period in between peaks of waves, the reality is that there are no beginnings, ends, or rest points. Undercurrents are always present through the fluctuations and peaks of different heights and strengths. As international efforts to tackle racism lose some of the momentum of 2020, questions remain as to how anti-Black racism will continue to be confronted within academic institutions in the long run. At Concordia, the implementation of the *President's Task Force on Anti-Black Racism Final Report* recommendations is allowing for conversations and actions to transform the space of the university. Many questions remain to be addressed to ensure the accountability and responsibility of the university towards Black students, faculty, and the wider community. Transformative work ultimately demands changing the very fabric of the institution, not just being integrated in it.

Understanding that the undercurrent of more than fifty years of student organizing and activism is what allowed for the wave of 2020 to gain strength like never before, it is imperative that we be realistic about the real time frame of the work needed to continue this transformative structural work and that we acknowledge the crucial role that Black students have played over time. Transformation is never fast, nor is it linear; much like waves in the oceans, its shape and pace move through the impulse of internal and external forces. As we enter this next generation of transformative Black activism, we honour the legacy of the past, present, and future of Black students' contributions to this enduring work.

NOTES

1    "Merger of Loyola College and Sir George Williams University," n.d., Concordia University, Records Managements and Archives (hereafter RMA), accessed November 3, 2023, https://www.concordia.ca/offices/archives/stories/merger.html; "Sir George Williams University History," n.d., RMA, accessed November 3, 2023, https://www.concordia.ca/offices/archives/stories/sgw.html.

2    Agnes Calliste, "Women of 'Exceptional Merit': Immigration of Caribbean Nurses to Canada," *Canadian Journal of Women and the Law*, no. 6 (1993): 85; Dorothy W. Williams, *The Road to Now: A History of Blacks in Montreal* (Montreal: Véhicule Press, 1998).

3   President's Task Force on Anti-Black Racism, *President's Task Force on Anti-Black Racism Final Report* (Concordia University, 2022), 40, https://www.concordia.ca/provost/initiatives/task-force-anti-black-racism/reports.html.

4   David Austin, *Fear of a Black Nation: Race, Sex, and Security in Sixties Montreal* (Toronto: Between the Lines, 2013); Paul C. Hébert, "'A Microcosm of the General Struggle': Black Thought and Activism in Montreal, 1960–1969" (PhD diss., McGill University, 2015).

5   President's Task Force on Anti-Black Racism, *Anti-Black Racism Final Report*, 40.

6   P. Kiven Tunteng, "Racism and the Montreal Computer Incident of 1969," *Race* 14, no. 3 (1973): 229–40, https://doi.org/10.1177/030639687301400301; Michael O. West, "History vs. Historical Memory Rosie Douglas, Black Power on Campus, and the Canadian Color Conceit." *Palimpsest* 6, no. 2 (2017): 178–224, https://doi.org/10.1353/pal.2017.0012.

7   Archival footage and sources documenting the events can be seen in the documentary the *Ninth Floor*, directed by Mina (National Film Board, 2015) and in the collections: "1969 Sir George Williams University Protest," n.d., Concordia University, accessed November 3, 2023, https://www.concordia.ca/about/history/1969-student-protest.html ; and "Computer Centre Protest," RMA, https://www.concordia.ca/offices/archives/stories/computer-centre-incident.html.

8   Organizations founded between 1970 and 1975 include La Maison d'Haïti, the Quebec Board of Black Educators, the Bureau de la communauté chrétienne haïtienne de Montréal, the Black Studies Centre, the Black Community Central Administration of Quebec, the Côte des Neiges Black Community Association, the Notre-Dame- de-Grâce Black Community Association.

9   In 1980 an event at McGill University, sponsored by the Alliance of Africans in Quebec and the McGill African Students Association brought together African student groups from various universities and CEGEPs in Montreal, including the Concordia University African Students Society. See "African Students Association Celebrate African Week," program pamphlet, F035-022-10, F035—Black Studies Centre fonds, Concordia University Library, Special Collections (hereafter CULSC).

10  Letter from Charles A. Thompson, president of the Black Students Union to the Black Studies Centre, November 7, 1975, F035-022-22, Black Studies Centre fonds, CULSC.

11  During that period many Black community events, including cultural and art events, were hosted at SGWU, such as Carifiesta shows or the *Negro Folklore and Art Exhibit* part of the Quebec Black Week Festival in June 1974. "Carifiesta Jump Up Dance," poster, F032-001-07, F032—Leon Llewellyn fonds, CULSC; "Quebec Black Week Festival," poster, F035-010, F035 Black Studies Centre fonds, CULSC.

12  Austin, *Fear of a Black Nation*; and Robyn Maynard, *Policing Black Lives: State Violence in Canada from Slavery to the Present* (Halifax: Fernwood Publishing, 2017).

13  Rutland, "Profiling the Future: The Long Struggle against Police Racial Profiling in Montreal," *American Review of Canadian Studies* 50, no. 3 (2020): 270–92, https://doi.org/10.1080/02722011.2020.1831139. Sean Mills, *A Place in the Sun: Haiti, Haitians, and the Remaking of Quebec* (Montreal and Kingston: McGill-Queen's University Press, 2016); Alain Saint-Victor, "De l'exil à la communauté: Une histoire de l'immigration haïtienne à Montréal 1960–1990" (MA thesis, UQAM, 2018).

14  "Black Organizations of Montreal," F035-022-14, F035—Black Studies Centre fonds, CULSC.

15  The creation of the ombuds offices at SGWU and Loyola College was a direct response to the SGWU affair of 1969.Tom Peacock, "'People Need an Opportunity to Tell Their Story': Ombuds Office Celebrates 35 Years of Promoting Fairness at Concordia," *Concordia University News*, December 3, 2014, https://www.concordia.ca/cunews/main/stories/2014/12/03/people-need-an-opportunity-to-tell-their-story.html.

16  Students across universities collaborated for events such as the symposium Focus on Liberation, held March 27–30, 1974, at Dawson College, sponsored by the Black students associations of Dawson College, SGWU, and McGill University. "Leading Home: Focus on Education and Liberation," conference pamphlet, F032-002, Leon Llewellyn fonds, CULSC.

17    *Black Student Voice* 1, no. 1 (March 1973), F013-008-58, F013 NCC/Charles Este Cultural Centre fonds, CULSC.

18    Colin Dennis, "Fighting for Black Studies," *The Link*, March 1992, 5; Colin Dennis, "Concordia Black Studies Far from Being Programmed," *The Link*, February 18, 1992, 7; Brady Leddy, "Lots of Talk, Little Action to Begin Black Studies Courses at Concordia," *The Link*, February 5, 1993, 3.

19    Alejandro Sepulveda, "Life Stories of a Montreal Hip Hop Group: Culture, Community and Critical Pedagogy" (PhD diss., McGill University, 2016), 197.

20    "Concordia Statement on Black Lives," accessed November 3, 2023, https://docs.google.com/forms/d/e/1FAIpQLSdgicx76FZ2mY72WyPrOIAPLvQGTvVt6dlPxQ3 R-asebCo-ug/viewform; Marcus Bankuti, "Faculty among Thousands Calling for Action on Anti-Black Racism at Concordia,," *The Link*, June 16, 2020, https://thelinknewspaper.ca/article/faculty-among-thousands-calling-for-action-on-anti-black-racism-at-concordia. See also NouLa Black Student Centre, https://www.concordia.ca/students/noula.html.

21    President's Task Force on Anti-Black Racism, *Anti-Black Racism Final Report*, 59–60.

22    "Black Alumni Network and Council," Alumni Networks, Concordia University, n.d., accessed November 3, 2023, https://www.concordia.ca/alumni-friends/alumni-network.html.

23    The centerfold of the *Afro-Can* publication of March 1984 showcases some Concordia students teaching at the NCC Garvey Institute, while the one for April 1984 shows a photo of Mark Odle, a Concordia student, volunteering at the NCC. "The Negro Community Centre Is Education," *Afro-Can* 4, no. 3 (March 1984): 10–11; "Young Volunteers at NCC," *Afro-Can* 4, no. 4 (April 1984): 11.

24    Derek Knights, "Caribbean Talent Abounds at Concordia," *Afro-Can* 4, no. 3 (March 1984): 3; Anthony Hall, "Concordia Caribbean Student Union Cultural Week," *Afro-Can* 4, no. 12 (December 1984): 16.

25    "Black Students on Campus," *Black Action Party*, October 1972, F013-HA4171-003, F013 NCC/Charles Este Cultural Centre fonds, CULSC.

26    In March 2019 the conference Living Black Studies: Reimagining Black Canadian Studies was held at Concordia, organized by coalitions of students, faculty, and community members.

27    Howard Bokser, "Concordia's Simone de Beauvoir Institute Honours Trailblazing Black Educator and Human Rights Advocate Esmeralda Thornhill," *Concordia News*, November 13, 2023, https://www.concordia.ca/news/stories/2023/11/13/concordia-s-simone-de-beauvoir-institute-honours-trailblazing-black-educator-and-human-rights-advocate-esmeralda-thornhill .html; "Dr. Dorothy Williams to Teach Black Montreal at LCDS," notice, Concordia University News, July 8, 2019, https://www.concordia.ca/cunews/artsci/loyola-college/2019/07/08/dr—dorothy-williams-to-teach-black-montreal-at-lcds.html. In 1969–70 James H. Whitelaw, SGWU'S curriculum coordinator, and Concordia's associate vice-rector inquired into the possible development of a Black studies program at the university. "Ethnic Groups and the University," January 1970, I0038 Academic Planning Office fonds, RMA.

28    President's Task Force on Anti-Black Racism, *Anti-Black Racism Final Report*, 67.

29    For more about the creation of the Black Community Initiative, see Dave McKenzie's chapter in this collection.

# "WE COULD WRITE HISTORY": TELLING STORIES OF THE FIRST GENERAL UNLIMITED STUDENT STRIKE

Nadia Hausfather and Anna Sheftel

**IN 2012 QUEBEC** witnessed the longest, largest general unlimited student strike of its history.[1] Hundreds of thousands of students across the province, including Concordia students, voted to strike indefinitely to halt the government's proposed university tuition increases. They stopped attending classes and filled streets with direct and creative actions and demonstrations.[2] While Quebec has a long tradition of student strikes, the 2012 strike was the first of its kind at Concordia—yet little has been published about the Concordia experience.[3]

In this chapter, we focus on the strike at Concordia through the stories of students who mobilized for or participated in it. As oral historians we understand that no story is ever complete: the strike at Concordia encompassed multitudes of experiences. We draw from recent life history interviews with fifteen Concordia participants spanning a range of programs, carried out as part of a research project exploring the legacies of the strike across Quebec.[4] We asked about memories of the strike and the significance of these experiences ten years later. Our own positionalities informed the process: Nadia was a student organizer at Concordia before, during, and after the strike; Anna was a professor at a university in Ontario who participated in solidarity with the students.

---

**NADIA HAUSFATHER** is a postdoctoral intern at the Université du Québec à Montréal (UQAM), exploring the (emotional) experiences of professors and teachers during Quebec's general unlimited student strikes. She completed her PhD thesis in humanities at Concordia in 2017 about the experiences of student participants in those strikes, for which she was awarded the Award for Excellence in Oral History by the Centre for Oral History and Digital Storytelling in 2018.

**ANNA SHEFTEL** is Principal and Associate Professor in the School of Community and Public Affairs at Concordia University. She is an oral historian of genocide, immigration, and activism. She has published extensively on oral history practice and ethics, most notably *Oral History Off the Record: Toward an Ethnography of Practice* (2013), co-edited with Stacey Zembrzycki, which won the Oral History Association's 2014 Book Award, and "Talking and Not Talking about Violence: Challenges in Interviewing Survivors of Atrocity as Whole People," which won the Oral History Association's 2019 Article Award.

## Step by Step: The Groundwork of Concordia's Students and Structures

The enormity of the 2012 strike stunned Quebec society, but it did not come out of nowhere. Students across Quebec started organizing when Premier Jean Charest's Liberal government announced tuition hikes in 2010.[5] Mobilization for the strike at Concordia similarly grew from organizing that had been happening on campus, in some cases for decades.

"Raymond" arrived at Concordia in 2000. For the first time in his life, he began to thrive academically, motivated by his increasing understanding of the problems of capitalism. Raymond was "really inspired" because "There were a lot of groups forming [on-campus] like the People's Potato and anti-globalization movements ... so all these things I was reading about, I could actually see people taking action." He joined the Concordia Student Union's (CSU) judicial board "as an entry point to politics." By the summer of 2009 Raymond was an experienced elected representative of Concordia's Graduate Students' Association (GSA). Upon learning that Concordia's Board of Governors would increase international tuition by up to 50 percent for certain programs, Raymond and Nadia, a GSA councillor at the time, founded Montreal Students Against Tuition Increases and organized a demonstration to stop the increase.[6] Montreal Students Against Tuition Increase continued organizing events about student struggles, collaborating with provincial student associations and campus groups such as Quebec Public Interest Research Group (QPIRG) Concordia. Montreal Students Against Tuition Increases then changed its name to Free Education Montreal (FEM).

Meanwhile, Rushdia was a master's student who had been elected as the geography graduate student representative in 2009, and was creating a formal student association in her department. On April 1, 2010, she joined the biggest protest she had ever attended in Canada, against the provincial government's announcement of increased public service user fees, including tuition.[7] She thought, "if we can get this many people together, we can do big things." She met FEM members at that protest, thereafter joined FEM, and was elected as a GSA councillor. Advocating for accessible education came naturally to Rushdia, as in India she had personally "struggled a lot for education" for herself and her siblings, at one point having stopped her studies to raise money for her younger sister to have quality education. Now, joining FEM members at meetings of the Association pour une solidarité syndicale étudiante (ASSÉ), she was impressed to learn about the possibility of a student strike, which she hadn't expected would happen in Quebec.

FEM "was at the forefront of mobilizing for the student strikes at Concordia," recalls Raymond. The key moment was the announcement of the tuition hike because "all of the mobilization that we were doing internally became now an external issue, where it's not just Concordia anymore, there's a huge threat that's coming externally."

Given the pressing context, FEM continued organizing with campus groups, inviting students to join workshops and demonstrations—such as the Quebec province-wide one in December 2010 against tuition hikes, which, recalls Rushdia, extensively mobilized Concordia students.[8]

Alex was one of them. Her interest in the tuition campaign came partly from personal experience. Growing up in Edmonton in "a very low-income household" meant that "getting to university and even going, it was hard to go through university and … to have to work pretty much full-time." At Concordia, she was active with the People's Campus Coalition, which she recalls as "working at this intersection of social, environmental food justice." She had been involved with the Concordia greenhouse and Tap Thirst, as well as People's Potato, "a very radicalizing place for me to work" because they "saw the intersections between access to food and other kinds of political rights" alongside economic justice.[9]

Mobilization at Concordia against tuition increases continued from 2010 into 2011.[10] For Alex and others, Valentine's Day 2011 stood out when recalling the months preceding the strike—because of the Wintry Hot Accessible Love-In for Education (WHALE). Initiated by FEM and sparked by a petition for the CSU to have a general assembly, the WHALE "was an important step," according to Rushdia, because the CSU and the GSA held simultaneous general assemblies that voted to oppose provincial tuition hikes.[11] After the assemblies, as per her plan with other students, Alex screamed, "Let's go for a march!" Students walked "around campus and through the buildings" holding a banner that stated "Fight for Your Right to Education." It "was the entire width of the road!" remembers Alex. "I felt like the WHALE was really important in showing people that it is *possible* to do those things at Concordia," she adds, "and *that*, I think, went to shape people's confidence in the strike."[12]

From there on, recalls Raymond, "all of it started to snowball … The activists no longer contained this. It was bigger than anybody really had planned." The Concordia Mobilization Squad ("Mob Squad") was formed. It was open to anyone, included CSU representatives, and worked and overlapped with the aforementioned groups. Together they built the momentum for November 10, 2011. That day, Concordia students joined the province-wide one-day strike and demonstration— the final ultimatum to the provincial government before the general unlimited strike.[13]

Many activists at Concordia continued organizing with Mob Squad for the strike, independently from the GSA and the CSU. At Mob Squad meetings, members decided "who's contacting each department for a general assembly," recalls Rushdia, to help departmental student associations take the lead and to encourage "democratic deliberations and decision making about collectively taking the ultimate step": the strike.[14]

## Person by Person, Vote by Vote: The Strike as a Transformative Moment

Around this time, Gabriel joined Mob Squad. Having dedicated most of his energy growing up to playing soccer, he had become interested in student politics at Dawson College but had been reluctant to join because he didn't know anyone. When he started his undergraduate degree at Concordia's School of Community and Public Affairs (SCPA), classmates invited him to a Mob Squad meeting at the GSA House, and this time he didn't hesitate. He soon became an organizer of the SCPA Student Association (SCPASA) strike.

In many students' recollections, it took just one or two friendly students who understood Quebec's student movement to encourage them to get involved. Simon, in the Department of History, had moved between Canada and the United States before arriving at Concordia. Despite caring about politics, he had never felt comfortable taking action. What changed his perspective were a couple of francophone friends he made, through the Graduate History Students' Association, who believed a strike could change things. Simon soon became an organizer of the History Graduate Student Association strike.

As strikes rolled out province-wide from February to March 2012, Concordia student associations voted in general assemblies on whether they would join. Andrea was a visual arts major and sexuality studies minor on the executive of the Women's Studies Student Association (WSSA) at the Simone de Beauvoir Institute (SdBI).

24.1 Students discuss and debate during the general assembly of the Geography Undergraduate Student Society on February 29, 2012, before voting to strike.

24.2 Students vote to strike during the general assembly of the Fine Arts Student Alliance in the Concordia Student Union lounge on March 1, 2012.

Raised in a conservative religious community, a fine arts course in her first year transformed her political thinking, leading her to the SdBI. She remembers the strike vote: "It was in the Hall H-110 room, it was in that big auditorium … when we actually voted to adopt it, the motion passed unanimously … The CSU president at the time had been there just to watch, and I remember her saying, 'You just made history! You're the first anglophone university department to vote on a student strike mandate.' So we were all like … whoa … It felt important and monumental."[15] Rushdia remembers, "At some point there was a general assembly happening in the CSU lounge, and in the People's Potato space, and before that there was the GUSS [Geography Undergraduate Student Society] general assembly that happened in the classroom. It was just amazing! And then people were literally coming to the [mobilization] table, asking 'How can I have my general assembly?'"[16]

Rushdia would explain to them, "It's okay if you don't have an association! You can write a petition, you know? And if you get so many students to sign, you can have a general assembly!" She remembers with glee the "great leap for Concordia students to experience direct democracy" and build democratic cultures: "This collective power was building" and "everybody owned it." Per Andrea and Gabriel, their respective associations—WSSA and SCPASA—mobilized quickly. Alex recalls that at GUSS assemblies, students had long, "generative" discussions, which helped some change their minds to support the strike. Others had more conflictual or tense experiences in their assemblies.[17]

24.3 Members of the Women's Studies Student Association picket their queer theory class, on March 22, 2012.

Because a general unlimited strike was a tactic new to Concordia students, they debated what it meant to strike. For students like Gabriel and Rushdia who were exposed to Quebec's student strike history, it was clear that voting to strike meant blocking your classes.[18] So at the GSA, which voted an unlimited strike mandate in regular assemblies for six months, and the CSU, which voted for a one-week strike, some questioned whether it was worth it to have a strike that didn't block Concordia buildings and thus was mostly symbolic, because some classes continued. Aude, a master's student in history, recalls another complication: history undergraduate students were not striking, but many master's-level courses were cross-coded with undergraduate ones. How to implement the graduate strike mandate while respecting the undergraduates? Simon also remembers a lack of consensus among the graduate students about what striking entailed: "There was a group of us who stood outside the classes in the History Department … and we would kind of sit outside of the elevators, with banners and stuff. Half the people who voted to go on strike kept going to class … It was like they all read it as this was a symbolic thing that we voted for, but not something we actually do." Furthermore, some students didn't show up to vote and ignored their association's democratic process and strike mandate.

Other departments, such as the SCPA, SdBI, and Department of Geography, Planning and Environment saw students picketing classes more effectively. Gabriel and Andrea remember their respective SCPA and SdBI pickets as relatively easy because of faculty and student support and the ability to focus picketing mostly on one building. It was not so easy in geography, where Alex recounts students "shut down" classes for eight weeks, by disrupting, blocking, or chaining doors. Some professors and students were supportive of the strike, whereas others were hostile. Alex remembers the experience as "scary, because [students] tried to physically fight us, and [some] professors were provoking students to fight us, it was tense. But the feeling of organizing, it was great." For Gabriel, too, the strike was a time of learning, whether at general assemblies, at marches, or in cafés in between strike actions: "You're taking learning that normally happens over a decade in an organizer or activist's life, and you're cramming it into six months … Every day, twenty-four hours a day you're just, like, living and breathing activism and organizing and social justice and how it works." Indeed, Concordia students and professors recall being educated and mobilized by undergraduate and graduate students—often mentioning presentations given by "Beth," a FEM member and GSA executive. Simon recalls, "To me the thing that kind of changed things the most was the work that the *undergrads* mostly … had done to block De Maisonneuve [Boulevard] and make … impromptu assemblies to make decisions about whether they would give lanes to the cops … so that was really exciting to watch and to see it function!"

24.4 On March 15, 2012, the first day of Concordia Student Union's one-week strike, students gather with drums and banners outside the Hall Building.

Concordia students occupied the boulevard in front of the Hall Building with creative and educational activities during CSU's one-week strike, coinciding with the province-wide protest on March 22, 2012.[19] These events stand out in students' memories as interrelated and unusually sunny, warm, and exciting. Aude remembers "arriving on De Maisonneuve, which was closed [to traffic] and we were making protest signs and banners in front of Concordia … We arrived to the [larger] march from Concordia … It is March 22 when I saw the magnitude of the movement."

Indeed, as the strike gained momentum, Concordia students joined and actively participated in the provincial student strike coalition (Coalition large de l'Association pour une solidarité syndicale étudiante [CLASSE]) decision-making,[20] as well as in the daily, nightly, and monthly demonstrations that brought out tens and sometimes hundreds of thousands.[21] For many, the marches signalled a moment of possibility. Of the nightly ones, Andrea remembers, "That break in routine and habit made me feel like just because things have always been a certain way, doesn't mean they can't be different. That, I feel, was the most important lesson."

Memories of the strike are not entirely positive. In this chapter we do not broach the province's and university's sometimes harsh responses, because the focus is on students.[22] For many student organizers—especially women and queer and racialized folks—the strike was the coming to fruition of hard work and long-held convictions about what was possible, including at Concordia; but it was simultaneously exhausting, disappointing, and at times traumatic. Some burned out and avoided Concordia afterwards. There was a partial victory in the September 2012 ousting of the Liberal government and the cancellation of the tuition increase, even though tuition would be indexed. Yet some students had allowed themselves to dream bigger—free education, a more just society—and had endured months of violence and stress. Alex recounts, "The strike ending and ending in a way that wasn't really a win, it was really impactful on me, and part of it was that suddenly … all of that feeling, that space, that sense of place, it was just gone." It was "frustrating … and sad," adds Alex, because at Concordia "the strike just ended. And then we were writing our final exams. And it was kind of like, what was all of that for? … Everything was back to normal so quickly … which is a super confusing feeling."[23]

For some, the experience was transformative. Simon was elected as a GSA councillor in the summer of 2012 and continued what the strike started: mobilizing for general assemblies and helping departmental student associations improve their democratic structures. The strike allowed Simon and Gabriel to build lifelong friendships with like-minded people. It cemented Gabriel's views about the power of "general assemblies and democratic decision-making structures rooted within accountability structures" to build mass movements. Gabriel soon after joined other 2012 activists who had formed the Concordia Food Coalition,[24] to be elected as the incoming CSU executive team. He feels that lessons learned from the strike allowed their CSU to better support departmental student associations, including when the latter voted to strike in 2015. They also transformed the Hall Building's previously for-profit café and bar into student-run, non-profit solidarity cooperatives (Reggie's bar, Hive Café), expanded the free lunch at Loyola campus, founded the CSU daycare, and created a housing cooperative for students—infrastructures Gabriel is proud to say are alive to this day.

The strike impacted student organizing at Concordia, and the lives of students who participated in it, even ten years later. Gabriel works for a faculty union and considers himself a labour organizer for life:

> I got to experience that moment … as an eighteen-year-old, you know? … Such a formative year, where you're kind of deciding who you *are* and everything, and then you experience that and then it just like *clarifies* all that … like I understand what my role is in this world … part of this long historical trajectory of people fighting for change, and for me the sense of identity comes from that, you know? … You actually did it, and you stopped the tuition increase … Had I not done the thing that I did, multiplied by the thousands other versions of me doing the same thing, on a bunch of different campuses and universities, like the tuition would just be double right now in Quebec … It was like, it's not hopeless, like we could create change in the world, and the history is not yet written, you know, like we could write history.

Simon now feels "okay to care about things openly"; during his PhD on neighbourhood activism at the University of Toronto, he participated in student and labour campaigns. Alex became a public interest lawyer. Rushdia works on youth empowerment as a teacher, organizes for anti-colonial, anti-racist, and migrant justice struggles, and is doing her PhD about power dynamics in social movement organizations. Andrea works in higher education and is now more "critical of the university as an institution," as the strike forced her to "grapple with the reality that a place I dearly loved … could also be rife with problems and entangled in unjust systems like capitalism." She organizes around labour issues on campus. The strike was a key moment in all these students' lives, an important reminder that learning at Concordia extends beyond the classroom. Engaging in student-led discussions, practising direct democracy every week for months, standing arms linked in front of classrooms and in the streets, seeing themselves as agents of social change and hope—these experiences were central to this generation of students at Concordia. Their legacies will affect student organizing on campus, and the world beyond, for decades to come.

## NOTES

1   The authors would like to acknowledge Rushdia Mehreen for feedback, edits, and documentation provided for this chapter, including her archives: Rushdia Mehreen, "List of Concordia Student Associations on Strike (2012)," *Voilà*, August 9, 2023, http://rushdia.virtualstack.com/category/concordia-mobilization/. Many thanks also to all who generously provided interviews and photographs.

2   The logic behind general unlimited student strikes is that stopping classes indefinitely threatens the government: if a cohort of students across the province doesn't graduate on time, the government would have to spend money to prolong the semester, the next cohort of students would be delayed, and the labour market would be depleted of graduates/workers. Furthermore, students have more time to engage in protest actions; see CLASSE, "Qu'est-ce qu'une GCI?," accessed August 30, 2023, https://bloquonslahausse.asse-solidarite.qc.ca/verslagreve/quest-ce-quune-greve-generale-illimitee/index.html. For information about the diversity and creativity of actions, see Jennifer Spiegel, "*Rêve Général Illimité?* The Role of Creative Protest in Transforming the Dynamics of Space and Time during the 2012 Quebec Student Strike," *Antipode* 47, no. 3 (2015): 770–91, https://doi.org/10.1111/anti.12133. For more about Quebec's student strike history, see Arnaud Theurillat-Cloutier, *Printemps de force: Une histoire engagée du mouvement étudiant au Québec (1958–2013)* (Montréal: LuxÉditeur, 2017).

3   Nadia's work is among the limited literature specific to the strike at Concordia. See Nadia Hausfather, "Feeling the Structures of Québec's 2012 Student Strike at Concordia University: The Place of Emotions, Emotional Styles, and Emotional Reflexivity," *Emotion, Space and Society* 40 (2021): 1–8, https://doi.org/10.1016/j.emospa.2021.100809; "Ghosts in Our Corridors: Emotional Experiences of Participants in Québec's General Unlimited Student Strike Campaigns (2005–2012)" (PhD diss., Concordia University, 2017). For another academic piece documenting a Concordia student's experience, see Natasha Blanchet-Cohen et al., "'*Du carré rouge aux casseroles*': A Context for Youth-Adult Partnership in the Québec Student Movement," *International Journal of Child, Youth and Family Studies* 4, no. 3.1 (2006): 444–63, https://doi.org/10.18357/ijcyfs43.1201312624. Zines and other independent publications have mentioned/documented Concordia's strike; see, e.g., Alex Matak, *What Kind of Allies Are These? Reflections on Power and Politics within the 2012 Student Strike at Concordia University* (independently printed zine); and Laura Ellyn et al., *En Grève: A Graphic Account of the Montréal Student Strike* (Victoria: FriesenPress, 2014).

4   Some participants preferred pseudonyms (e.g., Raymond, Beth). We were helped by research assistants Romy Shoam and Karl Ponthieux in indexing and identifying themes in the interviews.

5   See, for example, Hugo Bonin, "'It's a Student Strike but a People's Struggle': Class in the 2012 Quebec's 'Maple Spring,'" *Working USA: The Journal of Labor & Society* 19, no. 3 (2016): 341–57, https://doi.org/10.1111/wusa.12246.

6   The Board of Governors passed the motion nonetheless. Its effects and that demonstration are documented in Free Education Montreal, "Concordia University's International Students Protest against Un-warned Tuition Hike," YouTube, accessed August 30, 2023, https://www.youtube.com/watch?v=vADsdSqmRCc. Raymond explains he had led a legal battle to disaffiliate the GSA/CSU from the Canadian Federation of Students, which granted the GSA access to funds that could be redirected to these forms of student activism.

7   See Lisa-Marie Gervais, "La contestation prend son envol," *Le Devoir*, April 2, 2010, https://www.ledevoir.com/politique/quebec/286260/la-contestation-prend-son-envol.

8   About the demonstration and Concordia's busload of attendees, see Sarah Deshaies, "To Quebec City We Go!" *The Concordian*, November 30, 2010. Examples of 2010 FEM activities included a public debate about education funding with the Concordia president and a week of protests against Concordia's new graduate tuition fee payment structure. See Free Education Montreal, "Concordia University Students' Anti-Celebration – Angry Week – Introduction," YouTube, accessed August 15, 2023, https://www.youtube.com/watch?v=d_54TX6etqE.

9    For more information about some of the student groups mentioned in this chapter, see "Concordia Student-Run Food Groups Research Project," accessed August 15, 2023, http://concordiafoodgroups.ca/.

10   For example, in January 2011, FEM co-organized a panel; see QPIRG Concordia, "Panel: The Real History of Concordia," January 10, 2011, http://www.qpirgconcordia.org/2011/01/panel-the-real-history-of-concordia-from-the-computer-center-riots-to-corporatization/.

11   The petition that sparked WHALE was written and launched by Concordia student Matthew Brett in fall 2010 (see https://www.ipetitions.com/petition/studentmovement). Rushdia explains one reason the WHALE was important was to lower CSU's quorum to be able to fit their general assemblies into the largest room on campus. See also Evan LePage, "Petition Calls on CSU to Become More Involved in Tuition Fight, Organize General Assembly," *The Concordian,* November 30, 2010. For visuals, numbers, and the diversity of the WHALE actions, see Simon Liem, "1,200 Turn Out against Tuition Increases," *The Link,* February 15, 2011, https://thelinknewspaper.ca/article/1200-turn-out-against-tuition-increases; Evan Lepage, "897 Students Make WHALE Motions Binding," *The Concordian,* February 15, 2011, https://theconcordian.com/2011/02/897-students-make-whale-motions-binding/; Laura Beeston, "All You Need Is WHALE: Students Stage 'Flash Love-in' for Accessible Education," *The Link,* February 8, 2011, https://thelinknewspaper.ca/article/all-you-need-is-whale); and Free Education Montreal/CUTV, "Concordia 'Flash Love In' for WHALE on Valentine's Day!" YouTube, accessed August 30, 2023, https://www.youtube.com/watch?v=Vwnyri6XYCY.

12   These quotes appear in Hausfather, "Ghosts in Our Corridors," 226.

13   Both the GSA and the Arts and Science Federation of Associations—the largest undergraduate faculty student association at Concordia—had held assemblies on November 3, 2011, voting for a one-day strike on November 10 against tuition increase. "Systematic class announcements, proper flyering, and consistent tabling on the Hall building Mez[zanine], having posters everywhere," and consistent mobilization since WHALE, throughout summer and fall, contributed to high participation from Concordia, recalls Rushdia (e.g., see FEM members' November 10 announcement, https://www.youtube.com/watch?v=ZEQATqTdb8E, accessed August 5, 2023).

14   These quotes appear in Hausfather, "Ghosts in Our Corridors," 132. Rushdia explains that FEM members influenced Mob Squad's direction, forming a large part of its strike committee, in part because they had knowledge/experience from attending ASSÉ/CLASSE events and had produced an English-language booklet about student strikes in Quebec. For information about the Mob Squad's complex relationship to the CSU and the GSA, see "Fighting Fees in 2012," *The Concordian*, December 6, 2011, http://theconcordian.com/2011/12/fighting-fees-in-2012/. About Quebec student movement's direct democracy model, see Rushdia Mehreen and Ryan Thomson, "Affinities and Barricades: A Comparative Analysis of Student Organizing in Quebec and the USA," *Student Politics and Protest: International Perspectives*, ed. Rachel Brooks (London: Routledge Press, 2016), 63–80.

15   Fifty out of a total of two hundred WSSA members were present at this unanimous vote: "Almost 6,000 ConU Students Reported to be on Strike," *The Concordian*, March 6, 2012, https://theconcordian.com/2012/03/over-6000-conu-students-reported-to-be-on-strike/. SdBI was supportive of the students: Simone de Beauvoir Institute, "A Word from the Principal," *eSimone* 3, no. 2 (May 2012): 1. Many were unaware that the Geography, Planning and Environment Graduate Students Association (GeoGrads) was in fact the first Concordia student association to vote, two weeks earlier, for an unlimited strike mandate—upon the condition that fifty thousand other students have a strike mandate across the province, including three Concordia associations, including the Geography Undergraduate Student Society (GUSS), followed by a paper ballot vote. See GeoGrads, *GeoGrads Minutes*, February 16, 2012, https://geograds.wordpress.com/documents/.

16   This quote and those from Rushdia in the next paragraph appear in Hausfather, "Ghosts in Our Corridors,"132–36.

17    A few hours after WSSA's strike vote on February 29, twenty-two SCPASA members voted in favour of the strike, with two against and four abstentions, according to *The Concordian*, "Almost 6,000." At the same time, thirty-five of thirty-eight students voted yes at the GUSS assembly: see GUSS, "GUSS GA Minutes February 29, 2012," *geographyonstrike*, https://geographyonstrike.wordpress.com/ga-minutes/. For a list and timeline of student associations at Concordia that voted, see Mehreen, "List of Concordia Student Associations on Strike (2012)"; Laura Beeston, "Grassroot General Assemblies," *The Link*, February 28, 2012, https://thelinknewspaper.ca/article/grassroot-general-assemblies; and Julian Ward, "Upcoming Demonstrations and General Assemblies: It's Going to Be One Hell of a Week," *The Link*, March 12, 2012, https://thelinknewspaper.ca/article/upcoming-demonstrations-and-general-assemblies.

18    For example, geography graduate students voted to block classes "in a non-confrontational manner" (GeoGrads, "GeoGrads Minutes," April 17, 2012, https://geograds.wordpress.com/documents/). Gabriel says he held "hard" pickets (intended to block, disrupt, or shut down classes another way)—as opposed to "soft" pickets (intended to inform and allowing students to choose whether to go to class)—to ensure that his association's democratic strike decision was respected, so students who did not attend class were not unfairly penalized for missing class time, and to ensure the strike's effectiveness.

19    This was the day when the peak number of students were on strike across the province (more than 300,000 out of 450,000). See Theurillat-Cloutier, *Printemps de force*.

20    CLASSE is an enlarged coalition of ASSÉ, formed to organize the 2012 student strike. For the list of Concordia associations that voted to join, see "Les membres de la CLASSE," accessed August 30, 2023, https://bloquonslahausse.asse-solidarite.qc.ca/laclasse/membres/index.html. For examples of CLASSE-related motions, see GUSS, "The Strike Mandate," *geographyonstrike*, April 2012, https://geographyonstrike.wordpress.com/the-strike-mandate/; and GUSS, "Motion for CLASSE Congress from Students of Colour Montreal," *geographyonstrike*, https://geographyonstrike.wordpress.com/ga-minutes/.

21    Many students were quick to cite the Concordia University TV (CUTV), who, before the era of livestreaming, created a mobile camera set-up that allowed them to broadcast live every night, which became central to the strike experience across Quebec. For more about CUTV's role and innovation, see Elise Thorburn, "Social Reproduction in the Live Stream," *triple C* 15, no. 2 (2017): 423–40, https://doi.org/10.31269/triplec.v15i2.774.

22    About Concordia's institutional response, see Rushdia Mehreen, "Mobilization at Concordia – A Retrospect," accessed August 5, 2023, https://rushdia.virtualstack.com/mobilization-at-concordia-a-retrospect/; and Hausfather, "Feeling the Structures."

23    This paragraph's quote appears in Hausfather, "Ghosts in Our Corridors," 346, which describes in more detail the ups and downs of participants' experiences, including female, racialized, and queer students.

24    See n9 above.

# **ORAL HISTORIES:** Student Activism

### ZEV TIEFENBACH, FOUNDING OF PEOPLE'S POTATO

Part of my politics had moved towards food politics. I was *really*, really interested in food politics; I was really interested in what we ate, how we ate, and social justice as it related to food systems. That was really important to me. In Victoria, one of the main organizing bodies that I had worked with was called Food Not Bombs, and that's an anarchist organization that believes in the distribution of free food.

And so, I was looking for organizations that had food politics, and I was immediately introduced to Le Frigo Vert. I went in there; I visited; I got to know the people who worked there. By the time I became a student in September 1997, I had a work-study job at Le Frigo Vert as the education coordinator. I kind of landed at Concordia exactly in the milieu that I would be most excited about. I was studying photography and creative writing, and working at Le Frigo Vert as the education coordinator, so I was giving workshops, organizing conferences, all on food politics and things like that. And it wasn't *just* food politics. We talk more about the history ... it was really also about food distribution and the mechanics of food production. How to do really simple things to eat really healthy and—and have a good diet? ...

At Frigo Vert, especially at the time, there was a strong feminist component. A big thing that Le Frigo Vert was involved with was the distribution of menstrual products and having open and safe conversations about women's health ... We had a strong relationship with El Corazon, and this kind of movement in Montreal of promoting and working with women's health, which was *part* of the package of what Le Frigo Vert was. So, I had that job in 1997 through 'til ... something like August 1998.

*Piyusha Chatterjee: How did People's Potato come about? What inspired you to think about this organization, or this initiative?*

In the history, I think it's *very* important to think about Concordia and the CSU at the time. The CSU, Concordia Student Union, was becoming increasingly radical.

---

ZEV TIEFENBACH was a student activist in the late 1990s and early 2000s. He co-founded the People's Potato and helped organize other student-led initiatives. He completed his undergraduate degree in 2021. This interview took place on Zoom on February 13, 2023.

GENEVA GUÉRIN is a Concordia alumnus and former student activist who graduated in 2003. In the early 2000s she organized a fundraising campaign that provided seed money for the Sustainable Concordia Project. This interview took place on Zoom on December 7, 2022.

Um. And, becoming increasingly active, in terms of anti-capitalist, empowered politics. And I think it's also important to mention that there was also a *very*, very strong Palestinian solidarity movement at Concordia at this time as well, which was *very* much interconnected with what the CSU was doing. And so, the actual, mechanical genesis of the People's Potato came about in September, August 1999. The CSU was organizing a huge conference and I think it was called Activism in the Age of Neoliberalism. And I think the main organizer of this conference was Tom Keefer; he was the VP of communications in the CSU. The president of the CSU at the time was Rob Green. These are people who were, and are, *deeply, deeply* committed to radical politics in a myriad of forms. I should also mention that the CSU at that time had a researcher on staff, named Dave Bernans – also a very, very radical, professional, rigorous academic who did huge amounts of research on the corporatization of the university systems, and the relationship between corporations and the university and our public institutions. So, these people are all *very* instrumental and *very*, very supportive of radical politics in general.

So, August 1999, the new CSU executive is in place; they're organizing this big conference at the Loyola campus. And I run into Rob Green and probably Tom Keefer on the street, and they said, "*Oh*, Zev, nice to see you! We have a job we want you to do." Oh, okay, sure; I'm always up for a job. And I think I'll just mention as a – as a preface that, since I arrived in Montreal, I was very involved in food, and QPIRG – the Quebec Public Interest Research Group. QPIRG and Le Frigo Vert shared the same building, and there was a lot of interrelationships between those two organizations ... When they would go off into the country to meet and have their visioning and so on, I would be the cook that would serve everybody their food. I was known locally as a food service provider of ethical and high quality, generally vegetarian, mostly vegan food. I was known as a cook, so Rob and Tom approached me and said, "Hey, we're having this huge conference; can you cater it?" I said, "Sure, let's look at that." But it was a big conference, and so they wanted something like five hundred meals a day, or something in that order of magnitude. I said, "Okay. Sure, I can—I can work on that." And I put together a team of people. Some of the principals of that team were my cousin, Janice Tiefenbach. There was someone who kind of was already involved, and they said, "Oh, here, work with Zev," and her name was Marguerite Bromley. An excellent friend of mine who I collaborated with in all kinds of ways was Michael Barkey, and he had been a volunteer of mine when I was education coordinator at Le Frigo Vert. And there was another woman named Jennifer Raso ... And I hired them, effectively, to help me cater this huge, huge conference. And I think, at the end of the conference, after working together in this *really* intensive way, making this *wonderful*, wonderful food, and just working our butts off and having such a fun time, we kind of said, "Hey, why wouldn't we do this every day?" You know, and we, as part of this conference, purchased these huge, huge pots, and we had all this equipment that we purchased to do this job, and we thought, "Yeah, let's—

let's do that." We started to talk to the CSU, and we ... we were talking to the Engineering Student Association, ESA, and we were talking to the Commerce Student Association, and we're like, "Hey, let's put together a little bit of a plan." And it was actually the Commerce Student Association that said, "Look, we'll give you money; we'll help fund this. But you need to write a business plan. We're tired of flaky activist people saying, 'Oh, we need to save the world,' but can't write a business plan. So if you write a business plan ...'"

## GENEVA GUERIN, "THAT IS WHY SUSTAINABLE CONCORDIA IS STILL AROUND TODAY"

But when Netanyahu came, it's really what cemented adversarial dynamics between the CSU executive at that point and the administration. And I was working with the admin on a different project with a different strategy, and so that was seen as being threatening. So, I was asked to leave. And it ended up being very serendipitous because we left, but because so many people around the university in high places were very motivated to continue doing this, we ended up fundraising the same budget through discretional funding from chairs of departments or the different VPs and we just kind of cobbled together ... I think it was $25,000. But on top of that, the university give us an office, we were given office space, we were given a bunch of resources. And because we couldn't pay this army of researchers, which is what the original $50,000 budget was, we had to come up with a different strategy, and that strategy ended up being "go talk to all the professors and see if they're open to allowing their students to do, in lieu of XYZ term paper, if they could do the research on this particular indicator, and that be their term paper." And so, we ended up putting together a team of over a hundred student researchers that way to research all of these different socioeconomic ecological indicators. And, honestly, that is why Sustainable Concordia is still around today and as big as it has become. Because I think we were successful in that first year in engaging a lot of people and giving a lot of people space and agency to participate and to influence the outcome and to be part of the process and to design the process. I think it's one of the most successful things I've ever participated in, actually, 'cause it was so large scale, it was so new and then the impact of it was actually pretty enormous. Maybe a drop in the bucket compared to what needs to happen [*chuckle*] in the world ... It's what I felt like I could do the most efficiently at that time. Of course, today, *sustainability* is a bit of a dirty word, it got very co-opted by oil [*chuckle*] and different sustainability ratings where the top six are oil producers, so, there's a backlash against a lot of sustainability language as well.

**Adad Hannah**
*Leap,* 2011
Glass (230 square metres)
Façade, PERFORM Centre,
Loyola campus

26.1 Esther Savouré, Tayla Shair, Gabrielle Sénécal, and Mady Brown celebrate the 2022 RSEQ XC Championships in Rawdon, QC.

# BREAKING THE TAPE: TRACK AND FIELD, CROSS-COUNTRY RUNNING

John Lofranco and Gavin Taylor

**EVERY CROSS-COUNTRY RUNNER** knows the moment of anticipation: down in a crouch, silently still, bare shoulders brushing against another's, eyes fixed on the trail ahead—the tension not released until a gunshot rings out in the crisp autumn air, setting a herd of bodies galloping into motion. In this moment, the athlete experiences the bare elements of the sport, combining the solitude of individual competition and the camaraderie of a team with a common purpose. Generations of runners have lined up at the starting line in a Concordia singlet, although the story of cross-country running and track and field has not followed a straight and narrow path. Unlike major varsity sports such as hockey and football, track and field has rarely appeared in news headlines, has struggled to receive funding for decades, and lacks any dedicated on-campus facilities at Concordia. It has occupied a tenuous place at the university, effectively abandoned for over a decade in the 1980s, and scraping by thanks to the do-it-yourself ethos of coaches and athletes since then. Yet it has persisted, and like other minor sports such as rugby, wrestling, curling, baseball, and skiing, it remains a fixture of the life of the institution. Its story tells something significant about where Concordia has come from, and where it is going.

To understand the evolution of this program in the five decades since Concordia's founding, it helps to place it in the context of the explosive expansion of student recreation and athletics at universities in the 1960s. During this period, Loyola College's athletics program grew from four to forty different sports. Sir George Williams University also had an active athletics program; in the 1962–63 academic year, hundreds of students competed in thirty-seven different sports at the

---

JOHN LOFRANCO has taught in Concordia University's Department of English and coached the Stingers Cross-Country and Track and Field teams since 2003, with five years off as the club coach at McGill. He has represented Canada as both a coach and athlete, and coached athletes who have represented Canada internationally.

GAVIN TAYLOR is Senior Lecturer in the Department of History at Concordia University, where he has taught since 2004, specializing in the colonial history of North America. He was an assistant coach with the Concordia Cross-Country running team between 2005 and 2014.

intercollegiate, intramural, and recreational levels.[1] The athletics program, however, was hamstrung by a dearth of facilities: intercollegiate and intramural teams needed to shuttle back and forth to off-campus sites ranging from the YMCA, the HMCS Donnacona naval barracks, Lower Canada College, the Montreal Thistle Curling Club, the Lachute Golf Club, the Somerled tennis courts in Notre-Dame-de-Grâce (NDG), and Northmount High School.[2] The track-and-field program, which regularly attracted some thirty students for try-outs every year, faced similar challenges, being forced to train at Kent Park (now Parc Martin-Luther-King) in Côte-des-Neiges; while the cross-country team, or "harriers" as they were then known, did their workouts on Mount Royal.[3] In the winter, the squad would train three times a week on a metre-wide concrete track between the orange and grey sections of the Montreal Forum.[4]

The program was strong enough to produce stars such as middle-distance runner Bill Peel, who was Sir George Williams's athlete of the year in 1967–68, and has the distinction of being one of only three track-and-field athletes ever inducted into the Concordia Sports Hall of Fame. Leading the team to its first Ottawa–St. Lawrence Athletic Association conference championship in his freshman year in 1966, Peel went on to win the national cross-country championship in 1968 and was honoured the same year with the Colonel E. Gill trophy for the top athlete in the university.[5] The team was "small but good," according to Dr. Alvin Shrier, a sprinter, now professor in medicine at McGill. Concordia was competitive in sprinting and jumps, fielding a team that typically ranked with the Royal Military College among the top institutions in the conference in track and field and cross-country, winning back-to-back conference titles in 1966 and 1967.[6]

Following the merger with Loyola College, however, the track-and-field program slipped into obscurity, an unintentional casualty of the fusion of two distinctive institutions. While Sir George Williams had a long sporting tradition rooted in its affiliation with the YMCA, there was a greater emphasis on participation than competition.[7] Students were not required to pay a fee to support athletics, and coaches were often put in a position of having to make the best of limited facilities and budgets. Loyola, by contrast, had an athletics culture more oriented toward competitive varsity sports, which were deemed central to developing school spirit. George Short, an Olympic sprinter who was the director of athletics of Sir George Williams in the last three years before the merger, observed that Loyola "had a lot more finances to do things than we would have had," and was more aggressive in recruiting athletes from the United States.[8] This competitive approach had in fact earned the scorn of several francophone universities who sought to oust Loyola from the Quebec Universities Athletic Association, which had replaced the Ottawa–St. Lawrence Athletic Association after the 1970–71 season. In December 1972 the Université de Sherbrooke Vert et Or chose to forfeit a basketball game and pay a one-hundred-dollar fine rather

26.2 *Left to right*: Louis Marchand, team captain Jeremy Burg, Edgar Hudson-Aguilar, and Cedric Castello lead the Stingers off the line at the 2022 Capital XC Challenge in Ottawa, Ontario.

than play against a Loyola squad stocked with eleven American recruits. In the ensuing months, other francophone institutions joined the chorus, asking that Loyola be removed from the Quebec Universities Athletic Association unless it changed its recruiting practices. Loyola ultimately avoided expulsion as the Quebec Universities Athletic Association redrafted its rules for recruiting, but institutional differences in athletics remained a touchy issue during and after the merger with Sir George.

Among the sticking points was the relationship of the athletics program to academic programs in physical education at the university. Edmund Enos had founded the Department of Bio-Physical Education at Loyola, and was adamant that athletics be under the supervision of the head of the department. Enos's proposal prevailed, but there was grumbling about the tensions between the academic mission of the department and its role in promoting athletics and recreation.

The merger also strained the financial resources of athletics at Concordia, saddling the Department of Athletics with $36,654 in debt by 1975. Department administrators insisted that financial problems would not lead to cuts in programs, but by 1977—in the face of a general call for austerity at the university as a whole—it was clear that the department would have to set priorities with respect to funding.

"Some sports are more important than others," read an internal report in January 1977.[9] The university would have to prioritize funding on the basis of public support, number of spectators, and staff expertise; and some sports were thought to be better left to outside clubs. The lack of facilities—long a problem for Sir George and to lesser extent Loyola—was also identified as a matter of concern. The result was a two-tiered system in which varsity sports were given the lion's share of resources, while other teams were viewed as recreation and asked to do more with less.

Under these circumstances, a sport was likely to be dropped if it did not have sufficient support within or outside the university, leaving track and field and cross-country orphaned. By 1976 the track-and-field program was under the tutelage of Dale Munkittrick, a physical education specialist from the Eastern Townships who ran a track club at the Canadair facilities on the South Shore. Munkittrick seemed indifferent to the Concordia program, failing to communicate with the Department of Athletics and having the athletes run under club colours rather than as representatives of the university, which led to his dismissal by George Short in 1977.[10]

With no vocal advocate for the program in the department and the university facing a budget crunch, the track-and-field program received little support and depended on the initiative of coaches who were rooted in the club system and had a loose affiliation with Concordia, including the renowned Quebec coach François Pap, and Paul Charron, who took the helm of the team while a Concordia student in 1991, aligning it with his West Island Track Club.[11]

The challenges in developing a competitive team reflected a broader change in policy for the university. As director of athletics, Enos had placed an emphasis on varsity sports, bringing with him a sensibility he had developed at Loyola; winning teams in hockey, basketball, and football, he reasoned, would bring good publicity to Concordia and should consequently be supported. "He is a guy who would get things done, by hook or by crook," remembers Short. "You would say, 'You can't go through that wall, Ed; it's made of cement,' and he would go through that wall."[12] This approach rubbed some people the wrong way, and the discontent came to the surface in a 1985 report on athletics that was issued following extensive consultations with students and staff, along with research drawn from other universities. The committee report concluded that the Department of Athletics "has mostly defined its priorities, and allocated its physical, human and financial resources, in terms of service to the varsity athlete, and particularly the male varsity athlete. What is called for now," it continued, "is a realignment of priorities, and a consequent reallocation of resources. Hence the call for an emphasis on intramural and instructional programmes, particularly those with a fitness component which appeal to women, and the need for a wide selection of different types of activities to attract as many students as possible, including varsity athletics."[13]

The committee made three recommendations: a greater emphasis on fitness and recreational athletics; increased participation of women in the staffing of the department and its programs; and growth in the number of athletic programs, with a commensurate expansion of facilities, particularly on the downtown campus.[14] To some degree, the report would work to the advantage of minor sports such as cross-country running, but it was a mixed message. Varsity sports would not monopolize resources and attention to the degree that they did in the past, but other programs were more likely to be promoted as "recreation" than as competitive athletic fields. The university would give a green light to the creation of teams in various sports, but they were unlikely to receive the support necessary for the cultivation of competitive elite athletes in the areas of recruitment, facilities, training, and coaching.

The change in policy, and a changing of the guard when Bob Philip replaced Ed Enos as director of athletics in 1988, nonetheless opened up new opportunities. In 1983 the upper levels of administration in the department consisted entirely of men; the only woman in administration was Theresa Humes, who was responsible for women's intramurals. By 1994, though, most of the senior-level positions in the department were held by women, including Melanie Sanford as intercollegiate programs coordinator.[15] Sanford, along with Vladimir Pavlicik—a one-time track-and-field athlete who had assumed responsibility for intramurals in 1983 and eventually became the head of recreation at Concordia—recruited Suzan Ballmer to the position of cross-country and track-and-field coach in 1993. Ballmer had started competing in triathlons in 1986 while she was working on her master's in education at McGill University, and had organized the Furies Running Club, Montreal's first all-female running group. She had also started coaching an intramural triathlon club out of Victoria Gym, a converted elementary school gymnasium used by Concordia at the time, and seemed a good fit with the fledgling track program. Under Ballmer, the team had something of a revival; multiple athletes praised her for her encouraging coaching style.

Ballmer was one of two female coaches in track and field in the conference at the time—the other working at Bishop's—and she sometimes found herself at odds with the male-dominated establishment of the sport in Quebec. She remembers an athletics association meeting in Drummondville in which the McGill coach argued vehemently in favour of a policy that would benefit athletes, only to be voted down by the "old white men" sitting around the table. There was also discomfort over the easy fraternization between male coaches and female athletes, which had led to accusations of sexual harassment at Concordia and elsewhere. Ballmer's main goal, she said, was "creating a safe space for the athletes, especially the women athletes."[16]

When Ballmer left after the 1994–95 season, she was replaced as coach by Malcolm Balk, who had previously worked at McGill and was running a club team. He was offered the position by the new director of athletics and recreation, Harry

Zarins, who he knew from his time at McGill: "Besides the prestige and facilities, it was the salary that did it for me," he recalled with a note of sarcasm, remarking that he received $3,000 for coaching both women's and men's track and field and cross-country. "You had to love the sport to do it." Working on a shoestring budget, Balk piled runners into rented vans to bring them to meets, sometimes driving at night to return them to their homes on the West Island. The team continued to train on Mount Royal and at the Centre sportif Claude Robillard in Ahuntsic-Cartierville, where he encountered some talented sprinters and jumpers who he thought had potential to join the Concordia Stingers squad. Many of them hesitated because he was unable to promise them scholarships or better training facilities, but the team did include Lenroy Henry, a football standout and sprinter who won the Canadian Intercollegiate Athletic Union indoor championship in the sixty metre in 1996; as well as Headley Bent Jr., a middle-distance runner who finished a narrow second in the 1998 six-hundred metre Canadian Intercollegiate Athletic Union indoor championship. While Balk enjoyed working with the athletes, he had difficulty supporting a family with his modest salary and left the position in 2001.[17]

For the next two years, Concordia did not field a team at all; it was not until 2003 that John Lofranco (one of the authors of this chapter), who was teaching in Concordia's Department of English, decided to revive it. Lofranco had run cross-country both as an undergraduate at the University of Waterloo and a grad student at the University of New Brunswick, and was keen to provide Concordia students with an opportunity to enjoy competing in the same sport. Along with Leslie Gold, a former All-Canadian distance runner at McGill, he started organizing runs from the Victoria Gym, initially taking an all-comers approach to recruitment. The team also trained on Mount Royal, Kent Park, and a dirt track at Westmount High School, where they had to dodge bicycles, dogs, and the occasional stroller. The hope was that once he had built a critical mass of runners committed to training year round, Concordia would become a competitive team at the provincial and even the national level. Yet his plans were undercut by the lack of facilities and cross-country's status as a club rather than a varsity sport, which meant that runners did not have access to athletic therapy, nor was the team guaranteed pre-approved funding. To keep athletes in a competitive setting through the winter and summer, Lofranco decided to form his own club, Montreal Endurance, which would train at the Claude Robillard facilities during winter indoor track season as well as outdoors during the spring and summer. Within a few years, the Stingers were a rising force in cross-country, narrowly losing the men's provincial championship in 2010 with a team led by Ryan Noel-Hodge, Stéphane Colle, and Sofiane Guend.

The team also competed for the first time at the indoor track-and-field championships in 2005, with a small group of distance runners, and in 2007 with a small group of field event athletes led by Neil Martindale. Martindale was brought on by Lofranco to help develop the speed/power side of the team, but his enthusiasm was not welcomed by the department. Not having much knowledge of the university system, he showed up at Director of Recreation and Athletics Katie Sheahan's office with a cheque to cover league fees but was rebuffed. The department wouldn't take the money. Frustrated, Martindale only lasted one season. Concordia appeared on the indoor track circuit again in 2010, when Noel-Hodge finished with the second fastest 3000 metre time of 8:43.77, but was denied a silver medal because Concordia wasn't officially in the league.

After the 2013–14 season, Lofranco left the team to pursue coaching opportunities with McGill, frustrated with Concordia's continued lack of support of the team, and in particular of the Montreal Endurance group. Simon Driver, who had run cross-country for the Stingers as a graduate student, assumed the coaching position with the Concordia team for the next five years. Driver developed a two-stream club, combining a recreational club with a group of competitive runners who worked with the assistant coach, Michelle Ballentine, a middle-distance runner who had competed in the 2004 Olympics for Jamaica.[18] There was more support for the team through new Director of the Department of Recreation and Athletics John Bower III, who developed a plan for the so-called club teams to be able to achieve "varsity" status, if they met certain criteria. Bower also understood the importance of a link with a civil club and appreciated the collaboration at the time between Concordia's current coach, Driver, and former coach, Lofranco, at McGill. Bower left Concordia in 2017, but not long after his departure the university changed the designation of the "club" teams—namely, cross-country and track and field, men's rugby, wrestling, and baseball—to "Varsity 2," acknowledging that student athletes were competing against other schools, the same as the big-team sports.

The strained relationship between the team and administration reflected the mixed mission of athletics at the university. The sporting profile of Concordia drew from the distinctive traditions of Sir George Williams and Loyola: the former committed to athletics as recreation, often on a shoestring budget; and the latter more oriented toward competitive varsity sports. Over the past half century, the university has also developed its own distinctive sports profile, embodying the priorities of the institution and its students. The focus so far in the twenty-first century has been on building and modernizing facilities—particularly the construction of Le Gym on the Sir George Williams campus; and the PERFORM Centre and Stingers Dome at Loyola. While these projects created more space for training, recreational sports, and varsity teams, the university has not kept pace with institutions such as Université Laval, which used booster-club funding to become a sporting powerhouse in Quebec from the 1990s onward.[19]

TRACK AND FIELD, CROSS-COUNTRY RUNNING  285

Since returning to the team in 2018, Lofranco has sought to close this gap by placing a greater emphasis on fundraising. The track-and-field and cross-country programs raised over $30,000 from 2019 to 2022, more money than any other sports program other than men's and women's hockey and football. While the major programs were able to rely on big donors, the gifts to the cross-country team came disproportionately from alumni who could testify to the difference that the sport had made to their lives. Cross-country and track and field at Concordia will continue to survive in the same way it has for the last fifty years: through the passion of dedicated coaches and athletes.

**NOTES**

1   "Building Together: A Guide to the Sporting Tradition," *Concordia University Magazine*, November 1983, 19–20; *Annual Athletics Report, 1962–63*, I034.2/9530, Concordia University Department of Recreation and Athletics fonds, Concordia University, Records Management and Archives (hereafter RMA). Loyola also had a distinguished track-and-field tradition; for example, the College's Warren Joseph "Monty" Montabone represented Canada at the 1924 and 1928 Olympics, and set the national record in the 110-metre hurdles in 1927. See "Sports Hall of Fame Inductee: Warren Montabone," Concordia Stingers Official Website, accessed November 3, 2023, https://stingers.ca/hall_of_fame/inductee.php?id=99.

2   *Space Planning and Maintenance, 1957–1981*, Sir George Williams University Principal's Office, I010/4D, RMA.

3   *Annual Athletics Report, 1965–66*, I034.2/9530, Concordia University Department of Recreation and Athletics fonds, RMA.

4   "Track Team Preps for Centennial Event," *The Georgian*, February 21, 1967, 7.

5   "Sports Hall of Fame Inductee: Bill Peel," Concordia Stingers Official Website, accessed November 3, 2023, https://stingers.ca/hall_of_fame/inductee.php?id=145. "Monty" Montabone, a 1924 and 1928 Olympian (see n1), and Edward Cannon, who also played rugby in the 1920s, were the others.

6   Alvin Shirer, interview by John Lofranco, May 2023.

7   Paul Arsenault, "What Is Success?" in "Georgian Athletics, 1971–72," I034.2/9510, Concordia University Department of Athletics Fonds, RMA.

8   George Short, phone interview by Gavin Taylor, January 25, 2023. Mark Atchison, "Sherbrooke Snubs Loyola Cage Squad," *Montreal Star*, December 4, 1972; Memorandum to Magnus Flynn, Dean of Students, to Dr. J.W. O'Brien, Principal & Vice-Chancellor, December 6, 1972, I0147/11, Concordia University and Merger, RMA.

9   Meeting minutes, January 31, 1977, I034/511, Department of Recreation and Athletics fonds, Athletics Staff Meetings, 1975–1978, RMA.

10  Letter of George D. Short to Dale Munkittrick, January 26, 1977, I034/511, Department of Recreations and Athletics Fonds, Athletics Staff Meetings, RMA. Short had actually raced against Munkittrick when the two of them were younger.

11  Paul Charron, interview by John Lofranco, Montreal, January 2023; Jamie Knutson, interview by John Lofranco, Montreal, January 2023; Vladimir Pavlicik, interview by John Lofranco, Montreal, January 2023; Mike Hickey, "Training Has Become a Way of Life: Concordia Triathlete Swims, Bikes, and Runs for Hours a Day," *Concordia University Magazine*, December 1991, 19.

12  Short, interview.

13 Concordia Council on Student Life, *Concordia Council on Student Life Committee on the Role of Athletics, Final Report*, April 24, 1985, I034/511, Department of Recreation and Athletics fonds, Athletics Staff Meetings, 1979–1985, RMA.

14 Memorandum to Board of Governors, Concordia Council on Student Life Committee on the Role of Athletics, September 9, 1985, I034/511, Department of Recreation and Athletics fonds, Athletics Staff Meetings, 1979–1985, RMA.

15 Organization Charts, 1975–1985, I034/511, Department of Recreation and Athletics fonds, RMA.

16 Suzan Ballmer, phone interview by John Lofranco, January 2023; Laura Penno, interview by John Lofranco, January 2023. On the challenges faced by female athletes in distance running, see also Lauren Fleshman, *Good for a Girl: A Woman Running in a Man's World* (New York: Penguin, 2023).

17 Malcolm Balk, interview by John Lofranco, Montreal, January 2023; Patrick McDonagh, "Running Uphill," *Concordia University Magazine*, no. 19 (December 1996): 14–15. McDonagh stated in the article that Balk's salary was actually $2,000, even lower than he remembers. The salary is the same for the coach in 2023.

18 Simon Driver, interview by John Lofranco, January 2023; Chanel Jacques, "Stingers Cross-Country Preview: Team Looks to Run away from the Competition," *The Link*, September 1, 2014.

19 Justin Blanchard, "Varsity Blues: Concordia's Sports Clubs Can't Yet Earn Varsity Status. But That's Okay—They'll Wait," *The Link*, January 19, 2013, 17; Justin Blanchard, "Why Are the Stingers Struggling?: ConU's Sports Teams Are Having Trouble Finding Success. Here's How the Athletics Department Plans to Make Strides. Sort of," *The Link*, January 8, 2013, 16–17; Valentine Alibert, "Concordia's Lack of Sports: Students Create Opportunities for Themselves," *The Link*, February 7, 2023.

| 27 | VISUAL STORY

27.1 The men's football program at Concordia has a storied history. Celebrated coach Pat Sheahan led the 1998 squad to victory in the Dunsmuir Cup against rivals Laval Rouge. Here players Jason Casey (left) celebrates with brother Greg (centre) and teammate Dan Drummond (right).

# SPORTS AND ATHLETICS

27.2 In the early to mid-1990s Concordia's women rugby dominated their conference rivals. The team's 1994 championship was its fourth in a row. This action shot from 1997 shows Stingers players carrying on the program's winning traditions.

27.3 Team portrait of the Women's 1998 Hockey Championship team. The team's accomplishments led to it being inducted into the "team" category of the Concordia Stingers Hall of Fame.
Below: Champion Stingers celebrate their victory of the Canadian Interuniversity Athletic Union (CIAU) national title, *CU Magazine*, June 1998.

Opposite page:

27.4 The 1962–63 Loyola College's men basketball team was led by trailblazing coach, Jackson Winters. The team, which featured star player George Lengvari, beat its crosstown rival the Georgians, 49–48, in November, and would go on to play in the inaugural Canadian Intercollegiate Athletic Union tournament after winning its first ever Ottawa–St. Lawrence Athletic Conference championship. Winters coached the Warriors for three seasons and in 2022 was posthumously inducted into the Stingers Hall of Fame under the category of "Builder."

27.5 Stingers fans are not confined to rooting for their teams in Montreal. In 1998 fans travelled to Toronto's then Skydome where they cheered on the men's football team during the Vanier Cup.

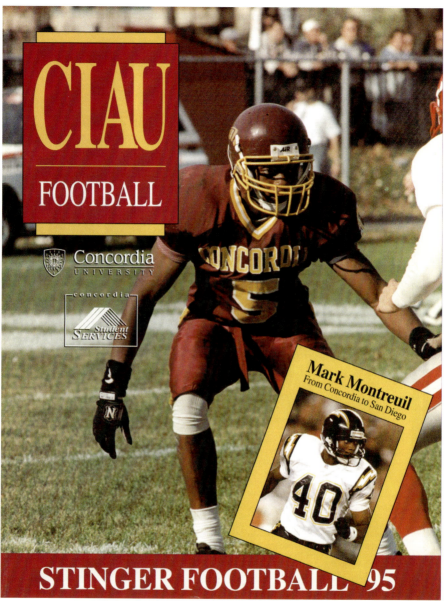

27.6 A 1995 issue of *CIAU Football* features Stingers football player Mark Montreuil. That year Montreuil was drafted 273rd overall in the NFL amateur draft. He would play three years for the NFL's San Diego Chargers.

27.7 The men's soccer team made history by winning Concordia's first national title on November 14, 1976. The winners of the CIAU national championship hoisted the Sam Davidson Memorial trophy after defeating the Dalhousie Tigers, 2–1. In 2003 the team was inducted into the Stingers Hall of Fame.

27.8 Following the merger, Concordia's men's hockey team experienced an era of dominance. Featuring the combined strength of two accomplished programs, the 1975–76 team accomplished an undefeated season, which carried over to the 1977 team shown here.

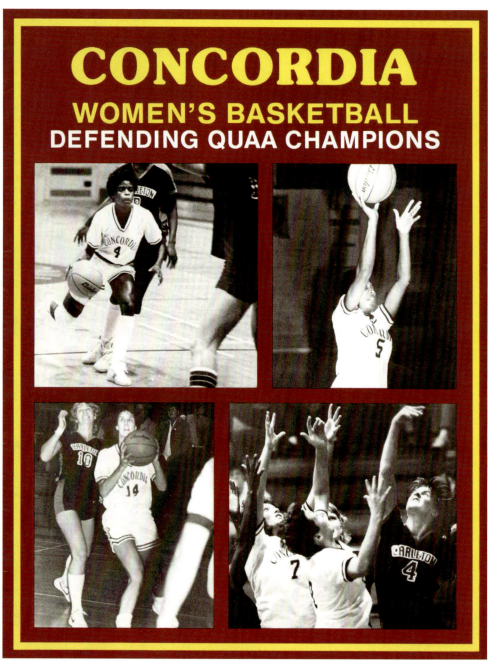

27.9 Concordia women's basketball yearbook, 1985–86. The Lady Stingers, as they were then called, were the Quebec University Athletic Association (QUAA) winners in 1984–85 and commenced the 1985–86 season as defending champions, led by associate coaches Poly Stevens and Sylvia Sweeney (a former Olympian who also starred on the legendary 1976–77 Stingers squad). Clockwise from top left: Debbie Grannum (#4), Maxine Clarke (#5), Domenica DiMarco (#7) and Sylvia Cesaratto (#14).

# ORAL HISTORIES: Athletics in Action

**PAUL CHESSER, "IT WAS THE COACH, IT WAS THE CITY, IT WAS THE UNIVERSITY"**

My name's Paul Chesser. I'm a two-time Concordia graduate, a former captain of the Concordia football team, [and] a former Concordia male athlete of the year. I'm inducted into the Concordia University Sports Hall of Fame, and in 2018 I returned to Concordia when I was appointed vice-president advancement … My wife and I were married in the Loyola Chapel. My wife also works at the university and she's a graduate as well. And, our twenty-one-year-old daughter is a student at John Molson. So, it's a family business.

*Piyusha Chatterjee: So, what made you choose Concordia at that time, '89?*

I guess there was a couple things. I was recruited to play football here at Concordia. I was recruited to play football at a number of Canadian universities, but … there was a coach here named Pat Sheahan who I really, really liked. I thought I would learn a lot and [he] has turned out to be a really important mentor in my life. Concordia, in 1989, was only fifteen years old. To be honest, I'd never heard of Concordia before Pat Sheahan came to North Bay and recruited me. You know, the opportunity to be at an urban university that had relatively small classes, play football, and live in a city like Montreal … that was an intriguing proposition. So, that's why: it was the coach, it was the city, it was the university, it just seemed to be the right fit for me.

---

**PAUL CHESSER** is Vice-President of University Advancement at Concordia University and an inductee in the Concordia Stingers' Sports Hall of Fame. In 1994 he was named Concordia Male Athlete of the Year. This interview took place at University Communications Services Studio on November 18, 2022.

# Viewpoints

29.1 Jazz legend Oscar Peterson shown in the rehearsal room of Victoria Hall in 1944.

# KEEPING TIME WITH OSCAR PETERSON: BETWEEN JAZZ ARCHIVES AND THE CONCERT HALL

Eric Fillion

**THE NIGHT** was cool, with a slight breeze, on Saturday, October 16, 1999, as people filled the Concordia Concert Hall to capacity. Inaugurated nearly a decade earlier, on December 15, 1989, the state-of-the-art venue was about to undergo a notable name change: to Oscar Peterson Concert Hall.[1] The Montreal-born superstar of the global jazz scene was present that evening, and he listened with emotion to the musical homage that Wray Downes's quartet had prepared for the occasion. Visibly touched, Peterson confided that, "in the swirl and radiance of the spotlight," he had failed to grasp the extent to which Montrealers esteemed him.[2] Conceived as a tribute, the renaming ceremony activated symbolic and aesthetic linkages that would soon make the Oscar Peterson Concert Hall a dynamic venue for forging new relationships to time, place, and community.

On weekdays, when the sun is up, we can hear echoes of Peterson's voice and music a few steps away, on the other side of the foyer in the adjacent Vanier Library. The Special Collections Reading Room welcomes scholars, artists, and community members seeking a window onto the past to think more deeply about the social and cultural politics of jazz culture. One can find traces of Peterson in the papers of his contemporaries Johnny Holmes and Herb Johnson, to name but two of the fonds acquired around the publication of John Gilmore's *Swinging in Paradise* in 1988.[3] The combined jazz-related holdings of Special Collections and Records Management and Archives (RMA) span several metres of textual records, hundreds of recordings and photographs, posters, and a wide range of artifacts. This corpus constitutes a unique repository in Canada, placing Concordia University at the heart of the story of jazz in North America.[4] Not only did this material make it possible to write pioneering

---

**ERIC FILLION** teaches at Queen's University. He has written on the history of Canada's cultural diplomacy (*Distant Stage*, 2022) and Quebec free jazz (*JAZZ LIBRE et la révolution québécoise*, 2019), and recently co-edited *Statesman of the Piano* (2023), which examines the incredible career of one of Oscar Peterson's early teachers.

Black artists back into the history of Montreal's musical life, but it also inspired (and continues to inspire) efforts to reimagine the city's cultural geographies.

In this chapter, I explore two meaning-making places: the Oscar Peterson Concert Hall and the reading room of Special Collections. In telling the story of Concordia's music-filled past and its connections to Peterson, I consider some of the ways in which jazz performance and jazz research can foster a greater understanding of Montreal's entangled histories and futures. From the establishment of a jazz society at Sir George Williams University (SGWU) to the acquisition of the bandleader Myron Sutton's personal papers and the pianist Oliver Jones's fundraising concert for Union United Church, Concordia's decades-long ties to jazz are not merely anecdotal.

*   *   *

Concordians developed an ear for jazz early on, thanks in part to the passion with which students at SGWU and Loyola College had championed the music. Established in 1956, the SGWU Jazz Society had as its mission "to further the knowledge and appreciation of jazz" while providing aspiring musicians with opportunities to play together.[5] It organized concerts, music workshops, and lectures, but also listening sessions that often doubled as demos of the latest hi-fi technology. It was at the time the "largest college jazz society" in Canada, according to *The Georgian*.[6] Students at Loyola College hopped on the bandwagon in 1963, establishing a similar group to "further the understanding and appreciation" of the music.[7] Jazz did not go silent in the aftermath of the 1974 merger. Concordia hosted Jazz Alive, a two-day festival that showcased local talent, both established and up-and-coming. The event was a success. It energized students and faculty, revealing their disposition to take jazz seriously.[8] By 1976 the university had assembled a jazz ensemble and launched a pioneering comprehensive bachelor of fine arts program that would soon include jazz studies as one of its concentration options—a first in Quebec.[9]

John Gilmore, whose research would form the backbone of Concordia's jazz-related holdings, was a student in that program. Born in 1951, he was older than others in his cohort, and therefore more attuned to jazz's broader significance as a sociocultural phenomenon. He was also mindful of the fact that there was no time to waste if he was to write a history of jazz in Montreal. Saxophonists Herb Johnson and Myron Sutton, for example, were both seventy-eight when Gilmore interviewed them in 1981. He had been a student of Andrew Homzy, a tuba player and bandleader, who was also a lecturer in music at the time. By the summer of 1984, Gilmore had conducted dozens of interviews with musicians, many of whom had preserved—often in less-than-optimal conditions—decades-old scrapbooks, photographs, recordings, and memorabilia. A conversation between Homzy (by then an assistant professor) and his former student resulted in a trip to Niagara Falls to meet and convince the now-widowed Mae Sutton of the "need to properly conserve and document what remains of our popular and jazz musical heritage."[10] The handwritten receipt they gave her stipulated that the donation of her late husband's materials was for "preservation, study, and research by those interested in Canadian culture in general and those interested in the development of jazz in Montreal."[11] A collecting area was born at Concordia.

Gilmore's initiative had another supporter at the university: Nancy Marrelli. As director of archives, she had in the past held on (for safekeeping) to some of the research files that the student-turned-historian was accumulating. Marrelli began acquiring and preserving documents on the history of jazz in Montreal at "the suggestion of John Gilmore ... with the collaboration of the music department."[12] The mid-to-late 1980s was a busy time in terms of acquisition. Beverley Thompson, writing for the *Niagara Falls Review*, reported that Sutton's materials were "the first in the just-established jazz collection at Montreal's Concordia University."[13] Other inaugural fonds and collections included those of Gilmore, bandleader John Holmes, and Alex Robertson, a textile worker and jazz enthusiast who "spent many years methodically scanning microfilms of old Montreal newspapers looking for articles and advertisements relating to jazz."[14] That Concordia was designated "the jazz repository for the city" in 1987 certainly helped call attention to the important work that was being done on the eve of the publication of Gilmore's *Swinging in Paradise* and its companion book, *Who's Who of Jazz in Montreal*.[15]

Disappointment must have swept over those committed to grow Concordia's jazz-related fonds when Library and Archives Canada announced in 1991 that it had accepted the first of several donations by Oscar Peterson.[16] Born in 1925 in Montreal's Saint-Antoine neighbourhood, Peterson learned to play the piano at a young age with the encouragement of his father, an amateur musician and porter for the Canadian Pacific Railway. Before long, the aspiring artist distinguished himself during performances at church and local community halls, eventually finding his way to the airwaves of the Canadian Broadcasting Corporation. His nascent recording career received a major boost following an unannounced performance at Carnegie Hall on September 18, 1949. Peterson's New York debut, as part of promoter Norman Granz's Jazz at the Philharmonic, made him an immediate star. He would establish a successful career in the United States and subsequently perform on countless international stages, from Brazil to Japan and the Soviet Union, where he wore the hat of jazz ambassador for Canada. Peterson had been living in a suburb of Toronto for more than three decades by the time he delivered his first boxes of materials to Library and Archives Canada.[17]

Yet Peterson's life in music, entangled as it was with that of other artists and jazz aficionados, was bound to also leave its imprint in many of the archival records held at Concordia. Photographs of the pianist, captured in the heat of the moment on concert stages or in the intimate settings of rehearsal spaces, are found in the John Holmes fonds and the Dorothy Harper collection. They make it possible to eavesdrop, so to speak, on sessions long past.[18] In an interview with Gilmore, Johnson described how a fifteen-year-old Peterson, the "only coloured" member of Holmes's big band, got his start at Victoria Hall.[19] Johnson, who worked with Louis Metcalf's International Band in the mid-to-late 1940s, also remembered fondly the many times that Peterson helped him "score charts" at the notorious Café St. Michel.[20] Another cassette tape opens with the famed pianist Oliver Jones, a student of Daisy Peterson Sweeney (Oscar's sister and a fine pianist herself), reminiscing about his music-filled youth in the same neighbourhood that the Petersons lived in.[21] There are textual records too. "I never met Oscar Peterson," jazz buff Jack Sadler confessed, before describing in detail his many serendipitous encounters with the "gentleman" pianist's music between 1941 and 1976.[22] His speech, preserved in the Peter K. Johnston fonds, follows the border-straddling, "superlative musician" beyond Montreal, underscoring how big of an impression he made on audiences.[23]

Whereas the fonds at Library and Archives Canada opens a window onto Peterson's exceptional career, the above documents and many others preserved at Concordia reveal the constellation of relationships as well as the ebbs and flows that shaped the pianist's life and legacy. Tom Hardie, in a 1995 issue of the *Jazz Vine*, explains that Concordia University Archives is "a place for jazz lovers."[24] But it is also more than that. Increasingly, it has become a destination for those seeking a much deeper understanding of Montreal's entangled histories and geographies of Blackness. The jazz-related fonds and collections preserved at RMA and at the Vanier Library's Special Collections offer a necessary counterpoint to the silences that often await those looking at state and institutional archives for insights into the histories of Black Canadians. These materials work against the process of invisibilization by making audible—even visible—a vital Black presence in Montreal. In fact, much insight can be gained by putting Concordia's jazz-related holdings in dialogue with documents found in other fonds with recent accruals: from the Black Theater Workshop fonds to the Negro Community Centre fonds, the Black Studies Centre fonds, and the Little Burgundy Oral History Project, among others. This broader archive compels us to do the urgent work of re-examining the shapes and contours of Montreal's cultural geographies, not just its jazzscape.

Although it inscribed Oscar Peterson's name on a prominent campus in the west end of Montreal, the renaming of the concert hall was evidently not an explicitly political or activist event. It did, however, make an important statement by calling attention to one of North America's jazz greats and the local community that nurtured his talent. Concordia had paid tribute to Peterson in the past: an honorary doctorate in 1979 and a Loyola medal in 1997 "for outstanding Canadian leadership and achievement."[25] Both initiatives left an archival trail at RMA, adding layers to the stories found in the fonds preserved at Special Collections. Staged as part of the university's twenty-fifth anniversary, the renaming ceremony was also an invitation to consider the interplay between music performance and music education in relation to Montreal's Black community and jazz heritage.

The process of renaming the concert hall was not without complications. The Faculty of Fine Arts wished to recognize Peterson for the support he had shown to the music department on various occasions in the past, but a dissenting voice argued that Maryvonne Kendergi, a survivor of the Armenian genocide with a successful career as a musicologist and as a cofounder of the Quebec Contemporary Music Society, deserved to be considered, especially since no building at Concordia bore the name of a woman.[26] The motion in favour of Oscar Peterson Concert Hall nonetheless passed unanimously during the June 17, 1998, Board of Governors meeting.[27] Time was of the essence, since efforts were under way to revitalize, or rather halt the "decline," of the Loyola campus.[28] The sum of $8 million went towards the expansion and revitalization of the Vanier Library. Included in this work was the common foyer that would connect Special Collections' jazz sanctuary to the Oscar Peterson Concert Hall. The renaming of the venue may not have been part of the redevelopment project, but it certainly aligned with the university's desire to bring "vitality" and "flow" to the Loyola campus.[29]

The new name of the concert hall "has a nice swing to it," remarked Len Dobbin from Montreal's *Mirror*.[30] *Le Devoir*'s Caroline Montpetit was equally enthused, noting that it was about time that Peterson be recognized in this way. A wide range of publications reported positively on the event, from the *Globe and Mail* to the prominent Chicago-based jazz and blues magazine *DownBeat*.[31] Concordia's media relations team did a stellar job. As for those who could not attend the ceremony, they could watch it live on the internet. Not a small feat in 1999.[32] Those tuning in heard the local composer Vic Vogel open the evening with a solo number on the piano. Wray Downes, one of Peterson's former protégés and a professor at Concordia, offered the other highlight of the evening accompanied by drummer Michel Lambert, bassist Dave Young, and guitarist Richard Ring. The quartet's performance was a moving musical homage to Peterson, who responded with deep heartfelt thanks: "This is a moment I will forever take with me."[33] Upon leaving the venue at the end of the evening, attendees lingered in front of the photographs and artifacts that adorned the walls of the hall's lobby. The archives had joined in, reaching across the campus and into the Oscar Peterson Concert Hall to mark the event.[34]

The venue would come to hold considerable importance for music and other performing arts students. It also offered a stage for celebrating the cultural contributions of Montreal's Black community and its relationship to the broader diaspora in

North America. In addition to hosting Black History Month events, the Oscar Peterson Concert Hall would feature several jazz revues in its programming, including Jeri Brown's *936 Laurel Place*, presented on December 7–8, 2000, to celebrate Black music from the 1930s to the 1970s (i.e., from Duke Ellington to Quincy Jones).[35] Nearly three years later to the day, Oliver Jones, soul singer Michelle Sweeney, and "Montreal's Queen of Jazz" Ranee Lee joined others into helping Little Burgundy's Charles H. Este Cultural Centre in its effort to establish a Black resource library and working spaces for local artists.[36] On November 19, 2015, Jones sat at the venue's piano once again in support of the neighbourhood where he and Peterson were born. Conceived as a tribute to his former friend, who had passed in 2007, the concert doubled as a fundraising event for Union United Church. It was a concert of music with an ear on the past and the future.[37]

*   *   *

The year 2025 will mark the one hundredth anniversary of Oscar Peterson's birth, and Montreal plans to have a downtown square named after him for the occasion. The announcement followed a passionate, albeit unsuccessful, campaign to have the Lionel-Groulx metro station rechristened after the virtuoso pianist.[38] Debates surrounding acts of commemoration underscore the extent to which public spaces are a "contested terrain."[39] Concordia's concert hall occupies a place of its own, because its establishment preceded, maybe even anticipated, some of the important conversations that have energized participants in the grassroot campaign to properly acknowledge Peterson's legacy in Montreal. It is also a venue where a broad range of people (artists and audiences; professors and students; as well as curators and community activists) engage each other around the experience of music. The concert hall's proximity to Vanier Library's Special Collections may be fortuitous, but it is no less crucial, especially as it invites—even if only symbolically—further reflections on the ways in which music fosters relationships to place and community. At this particular juncture, where jazz research and performance meet, opportunities to learn about and embrace Montreal's entangled histories present themselves. Listen, and follow the music.

## NOTES

1    "The Opening Inaugural Concert for the New Concordia Concert Hall," December 15, 1989, I002/5160G, HA4886, Concert Hall, Concordia University, Records Management and Archives (hereafter RMA). The venue officially opened to the public on January 27, 1990. See "Concordia's New Concert Hall Opens to the Public," press release, January 17, 1990, I002/9211A, HA4880, Concert Hall, RMA.

2    Cited in Anita Grace, "Concert Hall Celebrates Oscar Peterson," *Concordia's Thursday Report* 24, no. 4 (October 21, 1999): 1.

3    John Gilmore, *Swinging in Paradise: The Story of Jazz in Montreal* (Montreal: Véhicule Press, 1988).

4  Other notable jazz research centres include, Rutgers University's Institute of Jazz Studies, the Chicago Jazz Archive at the University of Chicago, the University of Idaho's International Jazz Collections, and Indiana University's Archives of African American Music and Culture, to name but four.

5  See "Jazz Society," in *This and Data: Student Handbook, 1961–62*, 25, Access Copies – SGW, vol. 30783, RMA.

6  Richard Comber, "Swing It Pop-Eight to the Bar ... Jazz Society Biggest Ever," *The Georgian*, December 3, 1957, 3.

7  See "Jazz Society," in *Loyola Handbook, 1963–64*, 60, Access Copies – Loyola, vol. 30368, RMA.

8  See J.T., "Rendez-vous pour jazzophiles," *Le Devoir*, April 17, 1975, 18; and Nighthawk, "Jazz Programs Planned for Concordia Students," *The Gazette*, August 30, 1975, 42.

9  J. Michael Kearns, "Thinking about Jazz Education in Canada: A Comparative Case Study of Collegiate Educators Regarding Pedagogy, Administration, and the Future of Jazz Education" (PhD diss., Indiana University, 2011), 270. Shortly after the merger, Concordia University offered a "Studio Music" specialization, which many understood as meaning jazz studies. That may explain why the Faculty of Fine Arts changed the specialization's name to "Jazz Studies" in 1983: "Minutes of the [University Senate] Meeting," May 27, 1983, I0171, RMA, https://archive.org/ details/us-83-8/; *Concordia University Undergraduate Calendar, 1976–77*, RMA, https://archive.org/details/concordia-calendar-76-77; and *Concordia University Undergraduate Calendar, 1977–78*, RMA, https://archive.org/details/concordia-calendar-77-78. Trained at McGill University, Steve Holt earned a bachelor of music, majoring in "Jazz performance," around the same time that the first cohort of students in "Studio Music" at Concordia graduated, but this was a "special program" arranged sometime in 1977 or 1978 to accommodate the pianist's interests and course of study: Maureen Peterson, "Meeting Inspires Dropout: Piano Player Finds the Key," *The Gazette*, February 17, 1979, 72.

10  Andrew Homzy to Mae Sutton, June 13, 1981, P004, 180, A-1.1-256, Concordia University Library Special Collections (hereafter CULSC).

11  Andrew Homzy, receipt for donation from Mae Sutton, July 19, 1984, P004, 180, A-1.1-256, CULSC.

12  Nancy Marrelli, *Stepping Out: The Golden Age of Montreal Night Clubs* (Montreal: Véhicule Press, 2004), 7.

13  Beverley Thompson, "City-Born Great Lives on in Jazz History Collection," *Niagara Falls Review*, August 10, 1984, 14.

14  *Jazz in the Concordia University Archives*, n.d., I002/9211F, HA4905, Music and Jazz Studies, RMA.

15  Simon Twiston Davies, "And All That Jazz: Archives Gets Treasure Trove of Jazz Memorabilia," *Thursday Report*, April 9, 1987, 6. See also John Gilmore, *Who's Who of Jazz in Montreal: Ragtime to 1970* (Montreal: Véhicule Press, 1989).

16  For details about the fonds and its accrual history, see "Oscar Peterson Fonds," Library and Archives Canada, n.d., accessed November 3, 2023, http://central.bac-lac.gc.ca/.redirect?app=fonandcol&id=211822&lang=eng.

17  For a detailed chronicle of Oscar Peterson's career, consult Gene Lees, *Oscar Peterson: The Will to Swing* (Toronto: Prospero Books, 2008).

18  See the photographs in P016, HA899, CULSC; and C024, HA6223, CULSC.

19  John Gilmore, interview with Herb Johnson, P004, 179, A-1.1-130, CULSC.

20  Gilmore, interview with Johnson.

21  John Gilmore, interview with Oliver Jones, P004, 179, A-1.1-134, CULSC.

22  Jack Sadler, "I Never Met Oscar Peterson," 1988, P199, HA6255, A1-4, CULSC.

23  Sadler, "I Never Met Oscar Peterson."

24  Tom Hardie, "Concordia University Archives: A Place for Jazz Lovers," *Jazz Vine* 3, no. 8 (September 1995): 5.

25 Howard Bokser, "Man of Note: Jazz Legend Oscar Peterson Receives the 1997 Loyola Medal," *Concordia University Magazine*, September 1997, 4. To read the full citation, "Oscar Peterson [English citation read by Rector Frederick Lowy]," I002/5160E, HA4863, Loyola Medal Ceremony, RMA. For the 1979 citation, see "Honorary Degree Citation – Oscar Peterson," June 1979, *Concordia University*, RMA, https://www.concordia.ca/offices/archives/honorary-degree-recipients/1979/06/oscar-peterson.html.

26 Arpi Hamalian to Frederick H. Lowy, February 26, 1998, I0052, HA6525, Concert Hall, RMA.

27 "Minutes of the Open Session of the Meeting of the Board of Governors," June 17, 1998, I0203, RMA, https://archive.org/details/bg-98-5/.

28 "Interim Report: Rector's Advisory Task Force on the Revitalization of the Loyola Campus," December 15, 1997, I002/9211A, HA4880, Revitalization of Loyola, RMA.

29 "Final Recommendations: Rector's Advisory Task Force on the Revitalization of the Loyola Campus," April 7, 1998, I002/9211A, HA4880, Revitalization of Loyola, RMA.

30 Len Dobbin, "Oscar Material: Concordia Concert Hall Rechristened," *Mirror*, October 14–21, 1999, 17.

31 See Caroline Montpetit, "En l'honneur d'Oscar Peterson: L'université Concordia dédie sa nouvelle salle au grand pianiste de jazz," *Le Devoir*, October 16, 1999, A-1; Martin Siberok, "Concordia Honours Peterson," *Globe and Mail*, October 17, 1999, D-7; and Jason Koransky, "Concert Hall Named after Peterson," *DownBeat*, September 29, 1999, I002/5160G, HA4887, Media Coverage, RMA.

32 Raw footage from the live broadcast was located and uploaded to YouTube during the course of the research for this chapter. See the following playlist: RMA, "Oscar Peterson Hall Inauguration," YouTube, August 16, 2022, https://youtube.com/playlist?list=PLuj-CkyQl2sIiFv DE_ahggo8oDwgkcVyv.

33 RMA, "Oscar Peterson Hall Inauguration."

34 Most of Concordia's jazz-related holdings were transferred from RMA to Special Collections in 2016.

35 Anna Bratulic, "Jeri Brown Puts Her Past into Her Students' Performance: Jazz Concert Explores Black Music from Ellington to Quincy Jones," *Concordia's Thursday Report*, December 7, 2000, 7.

36 "Who's Who of Montreal Jazz Takes Stage," *The Gazette*, November 3, 2003, 8.

37 Tom Peacock, "Don't Miss: Tonight's Oscar Peterson Tribute," *Concordia University News*, November 19, 2015, https://www.concordia.ca/cunews/main/stories/2015/11/19/oliver-jones-plays-oscar-peterson.html.

38 Marian Scott, "New Square on McGill College Ave. Will Honour Jazz Great Peterson," *The Gazette*, September 1, 2021, https://montrealgazette.com/news/local-news/mcgill-college-ave-to-be-named-after-oscar-peterson.

39 See Alan Gordon, *Making Public Pasts: The Contested Terrain of Montreal's Public Memories, 1891–1930* (Montreal and Kingston: McGill-Queen's University Press, 2001).

Kenneth Hensley Holmden
*Three Scenes of Nymphs in Canadian Landscapes* (detail), circa 1938
Oil on canvas (6.2 x 4.1 metres)
Auditorium 1.615, Engineering, Computer Science, and Visual Arts Integrated Complex, SGW campus

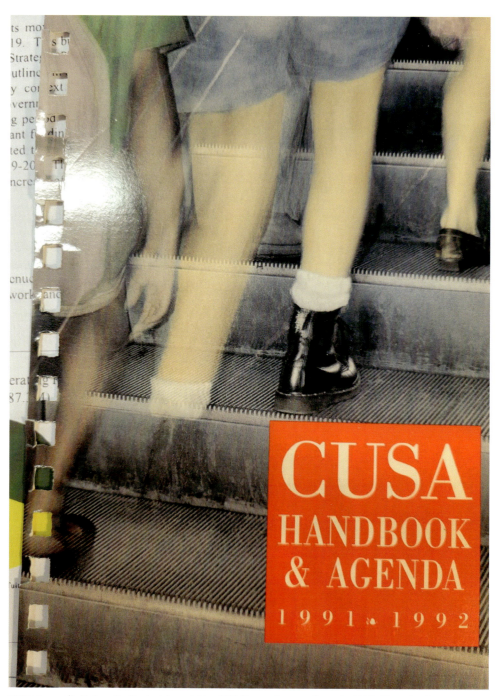

30.1 A Concordia University Student Association (CUSA) agenda cover from the 1991–92 academic year.

# REFLECTIONS ON STUDENT LIFE

Andrew Woodall

**STUDENT LIFE** is everything that happens outside the classrooms and laboratories and a central offering of any post-secondary institution, along with teaching, learning, and research. It is one of the primary ways that students become engaged with their university and feel part of something larger. It is where students find community and build agency.

At Concordia, it has always been led by students with support from various university offices and departments and, sometimes, despite them. Whether it is highlighting a particular issue on campus or in society, starting a group to meet an unforeseen need or organizing around a particular interest, Concordia students have used student life to increase the value of their university experience. Today, student life at Concordia is a rich tapestry of the full diversity of our university and our surrounding city and world. This diversity manifests itself in all its forms from cultural to philosophical to social interests. We have over 250 student groups that include accredited student associations, small interest-based clubs, and everything in between. They are involved with recreational, political, cultural, artistic, social, and environmental issues, among others. The work done under the guise of student life has also led to changes to Concordia's services such as advocating for gender-neutral washrooms or the founding of our Sexual Assault Resource Centre and the Centre for Creative Reuse.

The evolving reality of international students provides an example of how student life has changed over time. Originally, mostly undergraduate and few in numbers, Concordia's international student population has increased significantly in the past fifty years. Prior to the merger, both Loyola and Sir George Williams University had student-led associations for international students. In the late 1990s, a new organization was founded, the Concordia International Students Association, which acted primarily as a social network for undergraduate international students.

---

ANDREW WOODALL is a Montrealer who has worked in the voluntary and philanthropic sectors. He has been involved in starting student groups and non-profit organizations. He has also worked in Middle East peacebuilding and led a national merit scholarship program. He is currently Dean of Students at Concordia University.

30.2 Lhalyn Valencia (*centre*), co-president of the Filipino Organization of Concordia University Students, wins the Volunteer Award from the Dean of Students Office. The award was presented at the Concordia Council on Student Life Outstanding Contribution Awards ceremony, April 18, 2023.

Since then, the international student population has surged, and their needs have changed. This new crop of students comes with families and are generally less affluent. As such, mainstream student associations such as the Graduate Students' Association and Concordia Student Union and fee-levy groups like the People's Potato and Refugee Centre have stepped in to provide more fundamental assistance such as housing and food security.

In the next fifty years of student life at Concordia, we can expect the same social innovation that has led to the hundreds of existing groups as well as some expansion of existing activities and interests. One such area is around partnerships both with university departments and services and with external organizations. The challenges we face are such that student groups are increasingly collaborating with others, and Concordia service units are always looking for opportunities to complement our services with peer-led offerings. Nowhere is this more relevant than with experiential learning. Student life has always been one of the primary areas for co-curricular learning at Concordia. Whether it be building an electric race car or organizing a protest event, student life is fertile soil for learning. As Concordia strives to ensure all students have access to experiential learning opportunities, one can expect more formalized recognition of the learning happening in and around student groups throughout the university.

## ORAL HISTORIES: International Students

**ELIZABETH MOREY, "I ALWAYS KNEW WHAT WAS GOING ON IN THE WORLD"**

I saw an ad for international student advisor and I applied, and I got it. And it was one of the best jobs I ever had. I've had *many really* excellent jobs; that one—that one was really great ...

At that point there were two thousand international students at Concordia. Now there are—I checked it—there are over nine thousand. But it was just *me* and my secretary. So, every time there was a crisis around the world, students would be lined up at my door. I remember when there was a coup in Ghana, coming to school in the morning, and there was a lineup of students from Ghana at my door. So, I always knew what was going on in the world.

And we had a very big Iranian student population at the time. The students were all very anti-Khomeini and very actively anti-Khomeini. So, they were in trouble with their embassy. And so, the embassy took away their passports; when they went to renew their passports, the embassy took them away and cut off any money coming from their parents in Iran. We had this population of a few hundred, at least, Iranian students who had *no* income, *no* passports. So, we had to try and help them out. And the university agreed to put together an emergency fund they could apply to. And also, I worked with a lawyer who succeeded—I don't know how it happened back then—in getting them all special minister's permit to get their landed immigrant status right away, so they could work. So that was pretty special.

---

ELIZABETH MOREY has served in multiple administrative roles at Concordia University since the early 1980s. Prior to her retirement in 2011, she served as Dean of Students. This interview took place on Zoom on November 11, 2022.

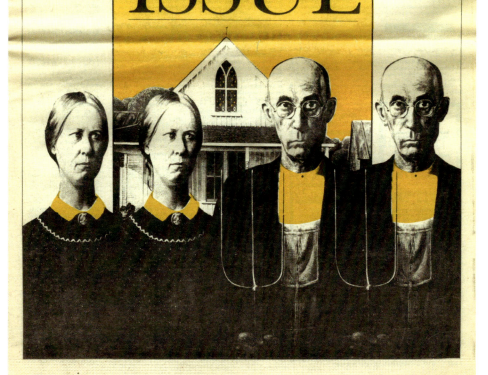

32.1 *The Link* was an early advocate for LGBTQ+ rights. In its famous "Gay Issue," from November 19, 1982, the student paper ran a series of reports highlighting contemporary and historical issues facing the LGBTQ+ community.

# CONCORDIA'S LEGACIES OF 2SLGBTQ+ STUDENT COMMUNITY BUILDING

Gregorio Pablo Rodríguez-Arbolay

**SINCE ITS FOUNDING** amid the feminism and gay liberation of 1970s Montreal, Concordia University has been site to a vibrant history of 2SLGBTQ+ student activism. With its establishment within what was then known as Montreal's west-end gay village, Concordia became entrenched within a longstanding legacy of queer space and organizing. From the gay strip club Apollo (where the John Molson School of Business now stands) to the infamous lesbian bar Chez Madame Arthur (the former home of the Simone de Beauvoir Institute), Concordia is built upon queer foundations.[1] Over its fifty-year history, Concordia's student-run organizations and media have been at the forefront of building our 2SLGBTQ+ community between the city and the university.

Lesbian and Gay Friends of Concordia (LGFC) was formed in 1978 through the collective efforts of students, staff, and faculty. It emerged out of a pre-AIDS political climate marked by the prior year's ground-breaking events. On October 21, 1977, police raided Le Mystique and Truxx, gay haunts located adjacent to the Sir George Williams campus. The next day, over two thousand people protested. Later that same year, gay activists (including Concordia students) lobbied the Parti Québécois to pass one of the world's first homonational legislations by including sexual orientation within the Quebec Charter of Human Rights and Freedoms.

From its inception, LGFC anticipated homophobia from staff, faculty, and students alike. Fortuitously, the LGFC found solidarity amongst allies at Concordia's student-run newspaper *The Link* (the result of a merger of Sir George Williams's and Loyola's pre-existing student periodicals). In 1982 *The Link* published its first special edition, "The Gay Issue," which was received with vandalism and threats against the writers.[2] Over the past forty years, *The Link* has remained committed to publishing special issues celebrating sexual and gender diversity.

---

Based between Tiohtià:ke and the Bronx, GREGORIO PABLO RODRÍGUEZ-ARBOLAY holds a PhD in cultural studies from Concordia University. His research and curation on queer of colour art and culture traces shifting visual rhetorics of race and sexuality in Quebec since the 1960s. He teaches humanities at John Abbott College.

32.2 Poster for an LGFC event, *Super-danse "Hollywood,"* where guests were invited to come dressed-up as their favourite celebrity, circa 1980s.

First formed as a mutual support group, LGFC quickly crystallized as a wide resource network for social events and political engagement. Concordia's gay and lesbian dance parties offered students a less commercial and more community-oriented milieu. Frequently hosted collaboratively, they united Concordia student organizations like LGFC, the Women's Collective, and Montréal's Group of Gays and Lesbians of Colour. Yet familiar tensions regarding political apathy and gender/racial parity plagued LGFC. In 1985 the Simone de Beauvoir Institute offered Canada's first lesbian studies course, galvanizing feminist students to form the Lesbian Studies Coalition of Concordia shortly after.

In 1990 LGFC disbanded and reformed under the more inclusive name, Concordia Queer Collective. Over the next thirty years, the group would rebrand as Concordia Out Collective, Concordia Queer Union, Concordia Sexual Diversity Alliance, and its present name, Queer Concordia.[3] Transgender Concordia, an offshoot club, was formed in 2013 to serve the needs of the trans and gender-nonconforming community.

Concordia students have been involved in momentous events that impacted the course of Quebec's history. From the activist takeover of the 1989 International AIDS

Conference to the 1990 Sex Garage police raid and the subsequent kiss-in at former Station 25 (corner of De Maisonneuve Boulevard and St. Mathieu Street). Without Linda Dawn Hammond's photographs of the events, there would be no visual record of the police's brutality.[4] In 1992 students and faculty organized La Ville en Rose, the first major Québécois LGBT conference. Pointedly, a small cohort of Concordia students protested the settler-colonial whiteness of the conference's commemoration of the 350th anniversary of French conquest.

Concordia has served as a hub for HIV/AIDS organizing since the mid-1980s, hosting an important range of scholars, scientists, activists, and artists. In 1993 the HIV/AIDS Project and Lecture Series was founded. The next year, its flagship course began, pairing students with internships at local AIDS service organizations—which continues to present day. The Project and Lectures Series cemented a longstanding connection to local communities, a model that has inspired subsequent civic partnerships at Concordia.

Over the past decade, Concordia 2SLGBTQ+ students have continued to foster networks between the university and diverse communities. Most notably, the Centre for Gender Advocacy recently co-spearheaded a campaign against transphobic articles within Quebec's Civil Code, resulting in a landmark legal victory for trans human rights. Concordia now celebrates this legacy of 2SLGBTQ+ student community building each fall term during Queer Homecoming.

**NOTES**

1   "The Queen Is Dead; Long Live the Queen!" *The Concordian*, September 29, 2009, https://theconcordian.com/2009/09/the-queen-is-dead-long-live-the-queen/.

2   "The Gender and Sexuality Issue," *The Link* 41, no. 1 (March 2021), https://thelinknewspaper.ca/back-issues/read/the-gender-and-sexuality-issue.

3   Jacques Prince, "Du placard à l'institution: l'histoire des Archives gaies du Québec (AGQ)," *Archivaria* 68 (Fall 2009): 295–309, https://archivaria.ca/index.php/archivaria/article/view/13241.

4   Jason B. Crawford and Karen Herland, "Sex Garage: Unspooling Narratives, Rethinking Collectivities," *Journal of Canadian Studies / Revue d'études canadiennes* 48, no. 1 (Winter 2014): 106–31, https://doi.org/10.3138/jcs.48.1.106.

33.1 Since its inception, Cinema Politica has hosted a diverse and wide range of activist-filmmakers. Seen here is Inuit filmmaker Alethea Arnaquq-Baril addressing an audience at a screening of her film, *Tunnit: Retracing the Lines of Inuit Tatoos*, February 8, 2016.

# CINEMA POLITICA:
# TWENTY YEARS OF SCREENING TRUTH TO POWER

## Svetla Turnin and Ezra Winton

**HEATED DEBATES**, revolutionary panels, firebrand speakers, snowstorms, ambulances, bomb threats, spiritual ceremonies, epic standing ovations, and so much more—it's been an action-packed two decades since Cinema Politica (CP) launched at Concordia in 2003.

As students in communication studies and political science we'd both seen *Manufacturing Consent: Noam Chomsky and the Media* (1992), which made us realize critical political films that question relationships of power have an immense transformative potential. We had no idea what we were throwing ourselves into when we started CP, and we'd never heard of a business plan either, but we had to try to create a space for engaged debate and movement building among students and wider communities. When our first screening of the commanding anti-war film *Come and See* (dir. Elem Klimov, 1960, Belarus) packed a classroom to standing room only, we knew we were onto something. We soon relocated to Sir George Williams University Alumni Auditorium (H-110), a seven-hundred-seater with one of the largest screens in the city, and Monday nights became Cinema Politica nights. Ever since, H-110 has been regularly full to the brim with students and non-students alike.

It didn't take long until CP organically grew into an international network of radical film screening chapters modelled after the Concordia series. By the end of the 2010s the semi-autonomous Cinema Politica Network boasted 110 chapters spanning four continents and dozens of countries. Unbeknownst to much of our Concordia audiences, CP "locals" sprouted up like rebellious weeds all over the world—at one

---

SVETLA TURNIN is the co-founder and executive director of Cinema Politica. She is also a film producer dedicated to supporting the work of underrepresented emerging artists, in particular women, queer, and trans filmmakers. Svetla's love for documentary has led her to consult and program for international festivals, markets, and film projects.

EZRA WINTON is a curator and educator from K'ó'moks territory. He is Assistant Professor at the American University in Bulgaria where he focuses on ethics, politics, and media. He recently co-edited *Indigenous Media Arts in Canada: Making, Caring Sharing* with Dana Claxton. Ezra is the co-founder and director of programming of Cinema Politica.

point we had a chapter on a tall ship, an itinerant local in Indonesia, and seven (!) *stadig* locals in Sweden alone. Our feisty student initiative had evolved into a rhizomatic non-profit organization that we ran out of Montreal. In later years CP launched a dedicated distribution arm and film streaming platform. Throughout, the Concordia screening series has been the insurgent jewel in the iconoclastic crown—still going strong to this day.

CP is a quintessential Concordia initiative. The campus has been home to a long history of social justice organizing, media activism, and progressive politics. From the Black-student-led anti-racism occupation of the Computer Centre in 1969, to the Netanyahu protests of 2002, to actions around queer and trans justice, Indigenous liberation, anti-fascist mobilization and accessible education, to combatting anti-Black racism and police brutality, to defunding and divesting Concordia's research and funding streams that support racial capitalism, war profiteering, and extraction colonialism, the campus has been a crucial nexus and forum for networks of radical politics and transformative justice. CP has been only one small part of this vibrant political campus life, and going into the Hall Building for weekly doses of political cinema and discussion has meant engaging in a transformative university space—a vital sign of community coming together, even on the most freezing of nights!

But being part of a vibrant and assertive activist community on campus did not always come easily. We remember the early days when the films we wanted to show were considered threatening to the status quo—with legal threats from Coca-Cola and Dominican Sugar farm dynasties—or uncomfortable for allies and funders in high places. We remember having to negotiate with the university whether to allow extra security guards (whom we considered threatening and oppressive to a progressive political space) at our events, just because some of our speakers were considered too radical, or the films too insurgent. We remember battling tooth and nail over the right to screen particularly prickly films, and we know this was all an indelible part of contributing to the campus and the community we (and our friends and accomplices) desired and needed—we knew these battles were worth every scratch.

We have heard from many former students that what they remember most vividly from their student days at Concordia was attending CP screenings. As co-founders, we have been awe-struck by the local and global impact of CP, and we remain grateful to all the crucial people who have kept this lefty initiative going over a period when many others have sadly folded (usually due to lack of funding, burnout, or both). The volunteers, staff, filmmakers, activists, and audiences' collective passion has ensured the wheels continue to whir, even when global pandemics, austerity economics, and neofascist governments have threatened to derail the whole project. Over the past twenty years we've had more than forty brilliant, kind, and dedicated student-workers who, along with well over two hundred volunteers and talented interns, helped make CP what it is today.

We have staged 530 screening events, brought scores of filmmakers and world-renowned luminaries such as Alanis Obomsawin, Steve James, Anand Patwardhan, Dolores Huerta, John Greyson, Maude Barlow, Winona LaDuke, Astra Taylor, Sylvia Federici, and a plethora of inspiring rising-star (at the time) filmmakers such as Nishtha Jain, Sabaah Folayan, Jason DaSilva, Henri Pardo, Ryan McMahon, Jorge Thielen Armand, Askold Kurov, Pavel Loparev, Mia Donovan, Karen Cho, and so many more. It is difficult to highlight specific screenings because there are so many that stand out like bright lights from the past, but a standing-room-only screening of Alethea Arnaquq-Baril's *Tunniit: Retracing the Lines of Inuit Tattoos* in 2016 is a particular high point. The director had not felt safe to show her film about the censorial colonial impact on Inuit facial tattoos publicly up until that point, four years after it was made, and so it was a huge honour that she decided to do so at CP. (You can watch the film on our streaming platform, and the stirring Q&A from that event [and many more] on CP's YouTube and Vimeo channels.) The audience showed their love for the film with an epic standing ovation, which preceded one of the most deeply rewarding and engaged discussions we've ever hosted.

A few more unforgettable highlights include The Yes Men driving through a deep, all-engulfing snowstorm all the way from New York, arriving just in time for a jam-packed auditorium of over seven hundred people eager to see their latest film; a lineup over several blocks long for the premiere of Naomi Klein and Avi Lewis's *This Changes Everything* with the directors in attendance; a defiant group of Wixarika land-protectors who presented *Huicholes: The Last Peyote Guardians* and performed a sacred ritual before the screening. These joyous and spirited moments are only a small part of Montreal's storied history of cultural politics, activism, and community building. We are honoured to be part of this history and know that documentary activism and movement building work continues to thrive at Concordia and many other campuses in Canada and beyond!

# VISUAL STORY: HISTORY OF STUDENT MEDIA

34.1 TV Sir George, created in 1969, was a forerunner to Concordia University Television, which now goes by the name, Community University Television (CUTV). CUTV, operating under the umbrella of the Concordia Student Broadcasting Corporation, is one of the oldest campus-run television stations in Canada.

34.2 Student operatives for the Loyola campus CIRL radio station circa 1980. CIRL came into existence on June 12, 1978 when the CRTC granted it a licence to operate as an AM station on carrier current, the first student radio station in Canada to be so licensed.

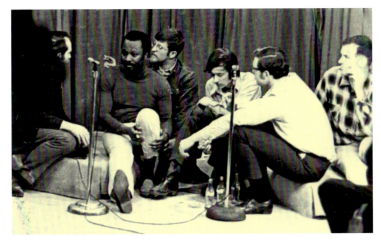

34.3 An event being filmed by TV Sir George volunteers in the early 1970s.

34.4 Poster of a collaboration between Radio Sir George (CRSG) and Concordia University Television (CUTV) for the Sound and Vision II dance party held Friday, April 13, 1984, the last day of classes in the 1983–84 academic year. CRSG would later merge with CFLI at Loyola in 1998, becoming CJLO, which continues to broadcast at 1690 AM and stream online at cjlo.com.

Out of over 1,500 Quebec students who protested in the provincial capital yesterday only 24 were from Concordia.

## ANEEQ strike
# Students protest financial aid

by Cindy Hoffman

QUEBEC CITY—Only a handful of Concordia students showed up at the provincial capital yesterday to protest against the unfairness of the loans and bursaries system.

L'association des etudiantes et etudiants de Quebec (ANEEQ) organized the one-day protest to call attention to the government's refusal to make public its reform proposals to the financial aid system.

In all, 1,500 students from across the province marched several blocks through icy roads and cold weather to the Quebec National Assembly.

Concordia was one of a few ANEEQ members which did not strike yesterday, but sent a student delegation instead. Twenty-eight CEGEPs and universities participated in the strike, including McGill which is not a member of ANEEQ.

"We decided not to strike, because lots of students would probably vote yes to a strike and then not show up at the protest, like they did last year", said CUSA co-president Robert Douglas.

He said that overall the protest was "a strong show of support and solidarity."

Yet, Douglas said he was disappointed by the poor turnout of Concordia students. Twenty students boarded the bus supplied by CUSA at a cost of $400. Another bus which had been chartered for the day had to be sent back because of the low attendance.

"Many students just don't care. Instead of protesting themselves they wait for other people to protest for them," said Douglas.

At the march, two students were carrying a large CUSA banner, while other Concordia students carried signs and chanted "Solidarité, solidarité" and "Education is a right; fight, fight for your rights."

"Election year is coming up soon," shouted one protester into a megaphone. "What happened to your promise to pour money into education, Ryan?."

The protester was referring to a 1986 Liberal election promise to increase financial aid by $24 million. Instead, education minister Claude Ryan cut $28 million from the financial aid system soon after the Liberals were elected.

Concordia TESL student Neil Dunn said he protested because he was afraid that without any pressure the government would eventually say it can't afford universal education.

The loans and bursaries given by the government are not enough for a student to get by without having to get a job, he said.

"This causes a financial problem which is a pain in the butt, a sick feeling in your stomach," said Dunn. "It distracts you and interferes with your studies."

CUSA external committee member Lisa Dowling was particularly concerned with the plight of part-time students, noting that Concordia has the highest percentage of part-timers in the province. Under the present system, part-time students are not eligible for financial aid.

"I know a lot of part-time students who really need the money," she said. "It's completely unfair that they are discriminated against."

Speakers at the rally directed comments toward Concordia and McGill, the only two anglophone schools at the protest.

"It is important to have solidarity between the francophone and anglophone universities," said Jean-Pierre Paquet as a few francophone students booed.

Addressing the gathering, a McGill student society representative said "it's not often that McGill and Concordia students get out on the streets and march like this."

**the Link**

Concordia University
Montreal, Quebec

Volume 8, Number 17
Friday, November 13, 1987

## Concordia talks tough again
# No Classes Tuesday

by Andy Riga

Reversing itself for the second time this week, the university has decided to cancel all classes and labs Tuesday as part of Concordia's "Day of Action."

At an emergency meeting yesterday morning, the university's board of governors unanimously voted that classes not be held November 17 so that students, faculty, and staff can protest Concordia's chronic underfunding problem.

In a memo distributed after the meeting, Rector Patric Kenniff said that "all classes and laboratories scheduled for the 17th of November are not to be held on that day."

The decision to cancel classes was unexpected because on Monday the executive committee of the board of governors had decided not to cancel classes. Instead, the administration would ask faculty to reschedule their classes.

Reaction to that decision was negative, and on Tuesday a planning committee decided that tougher action had to be taken. At an 8 a.m. meeting Thursday, Rector Patrick Kenniff was told by board members that a stronger message had to be sent out.

"A lot of people expressed to the Rector, and to the board of governors that there is no direction, and no strong voice from the top," said CUSA co-president Maxine Clarke. "So we asked that in a new memo (the rector) say something that will oblige people to listen."

According to the rector's executive assistant Catherine MacKenzie, the university is not changing its stance, because technically, the university is not saying it will close its doors.

Yesterday's decision also comes a day after the Rector received a letter from provincial education minister Claude Ryan. In it Ryan told Kenniff that changes will be made to the funding formula "soon," and that Concordia's requests were unrealistic.

"The differences between Concordia University and the government are much less serious than your campaign would have us believe," Ryan stated.

"In the next year or two, the government—with the help of the universities—will devise a more equitable funding formula to better reflect the realities of each university," the letter added. "It seems to me that it is in this common effort that we should be concentrating."

CUSA education vice president Randy Orr said he is disappointed with the timing but is happy the decision was made because it will allow students to participate without fear of losing a class.

"I think that its a little late. It's already Thursday - (the memo) only came out today," he said.

"They finally have decided that they want the largest number of people to participate and the only way to do that is to take a stronger stand," said Orr.

In a telephone interview yesterday, Ryan's aide, Luc Rheaume, said the university's actions will not have any effect on the minister's plans.

"Concordia got a chance to present its position when the minister met with them, their demonstrations won't influence Mr. Ryan's decision," he said.

"He has listened to Concordia and now we're waiting for the final decision on the distribution of the $40 million."

MacKenzie said the day of action will show Ryan the university wants a bigger share of the funds.

"The entire university community feels that the proposed allocation of the $40 million in extra money contains a rather cruel blow to Concordia's fortunes," she said. "We are going to be crippled."

Fifty busses will be leaving Concordia at 10:00 a.m. Tuesday headed for Quebec City, where a demonstration at the National Assembly is planned.

Meanwhile, demonstrations are also planned for Montreal. Picketers will march to Premier Robert Bourassa's office, Liberal Party headquarters, and the education ministry. Squads of Concordia people will also be on the streets and in some Metro stations asking for signatures on a petition demanding more equitable funding for Concordia.

### Day of Action

9:30 -- Pep rally outside Hall Building (Sir George) and Administration Building (Loyola)

10:00 -- Buses leave for Quebec City from Sir George and Loyola (FREE)

10:30 -- Phone blitz: nasty calls to Claude Ryan and Robert Bourassa

11:00 -- Flying Squads: armed with placards and banners, small groups will hit Montreal streets, marching and gathering names on a petition.

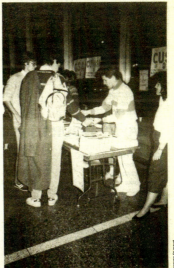

The smokescreen of confusion has cleared over this Tuesday's shutdown. All the CUSA preparation has not been in vain after all.

34.5 A cover of *The Link* from 1987 informs students how they can attend the upcoming "Day of Action" in Quebec. The protest was in response to chronic funding shortages that hobbled Concordia since the merger. Administration and students joined forces to petition the Quebec government for a more equitable funding formula.

# Ryan refuses to budge

**by Andy Riga**

QUEBEC CITY—As almost a thousand Concordia students protested outside the National Assembly yesterday, education minister Claude Ryan dashed the university's hopes of getting more funds this year.

More than 20 busses — considerably less than the 43 busloads originally scheduled—carried students, staff and faculty to the provincial capital to state Concordia's case for an increased share of the $40 million in additional funds Ryan set aside to alleviate university underfunding.

*The Link* accompanied a nine-member university delegation which was permitted inside the assembly building to meet Ryan and two of his aides.

Led by Rector Patrick Kenniff, the delegation presented the minister with ten sacks of letters from members of the university community, some of which Ryan read at the meeting.

But Ryan wasted no time in letting the delegation know their efforts were futile.

"I don't think there's any way I'm going to ask the government to change the distribution of (the $40 million in) funds," he said.

Kenniff was clearly disappointed and expressed his disillusion, saying to Ryan, "Since you've been minister, you've told me you recognize Concordia is in a bad position. Now, for the first time in a decade, there is more money for university education and Concordia isn't getting a fair share." He called on Ryan to change his mind and redistribute the $40 million.

Ryan was clearly angered at Kenniff's request, responding, "Don't tell me I have to change my recommendation. That's not debating in a civilized manner."

He said the university would have to wait until 1989 when the government revises its present university funding formula, which he has acknowledged penalises Concordia unfairly.

"We've always been patient," said Kenniff. "What you've told us today is we have to wait two more years. People are tired of hoping and waiting for you."

Student association co-president Robert Douglas responded angrily to Ryan's refusal to change his mind, telling the minister, "It's a sad day for post-secondary education. I have personally suffered the affects of underfunding and so have 20,000 other students. Library hours have been cut and almost every single aspect of education has been affected.

"The Liberal government has not kept its promise to fund properly and equitably all universities in Quebec," he added.

In an interview after the meeting, a discouraged Kenniff said of Ryan, "I feel he hasn't budged an inch. He hasn't even considered our proposal. The university has to understand it will now be a long struggle to change the government's mind."

He said he will now go over Ryan's head straight to Premier Robert Bourassa to make a last-ditch attempt.

When Douglas emerged outside to break the news to the Concordia protestors, a spontaneous chant of "Ryan is a weenie!" went up from the crowd. The chant changed to "Bullshit!" minutes later when Kenniff relayed Ryan's message that Concordia's request was unrealistic.

The mood was grim as the crowd learned the news.

"I's damn discouraging, said Audio Visual employee Jim Gregson, who described some of the ways underfunding affects the university. "No deodorants in the urinals, fruit flies in the urinals; these are just the little signs we see caused by cutbacks. I don't see why they think Concordia can get by with less money than any other institution.

Philosophy professor Christopher Gray tried to be optimistic about the usefulness of the protest.

"This demonstration might not get what we want now but it might help us keep what we already have and help us get more in the future."

Concordia deans laugh it up as they prepare to head for the Quebec city protest yesterday, but Claude Ryan had the last laugh when he refused to give Concordia more funds.

# the Link

# Protesters locked out

**by Aaron Derfel**

MONTREAL—More than 100 Concordia demonstrators descended yesterday on the Montreal Ministry of Education office to protest the Quebec government's unwillingness to give the university more money.

With classes cancelled for the day, the protesters boarded busses headed for the ministry office, where they vented their anger at education minister Claude Ryan, chanting, "Ryan's not fair, give us our share!"

Security guards quickly locked the doors at 600 Fullum St. just before noon, and would not let anyone in without checking their I.D. first.

The demonstrators continued shouting slogans and brandished signs until an official from the ministry came outside and talked to some of the protestors.

"I sympathize with Concordia," said the official who did not give his name. "You are underfunded...Concordia educates people from the wrong side of the tracks...I'm from the wrong side of the tracks myself...Ryan really does want to improve the education standard but unfortunately he inherited an un-coordinated staff from his predecessor and they're dragging their feet on the issue."

Hundreds of Concordia students, staff and faculty gathered at both campuses to participate in other forms of protest.

In front of the Hall building, protesters walked up and down the sidewalk and waved signs saying, "Concordia—penalised for 13 years of underfunding!"

As early as 8 a.m., students and faculty wrote slogans on picket signs and tagged protest buttons on their jackets. At Bishop's Court, the administration building, university deans arrived to pick up sacks of letters addressed to Ryan and Premier Robert Bourassa—in all over 10,000 letters.

Clutching a sack of letters, Rector Patrick Kenniff said he was encouraged to see students, staff and faculty all protesting.

"I think this is maybe a spectacular attempt to make the minister see the light, but we're very hopeful he will see the light," Kenniff told *the Link*.

"If the minister does not wish to respond to us, then we'll have to ask the Premier and his other cabinet collegues to respond at their level," he added.

Amid confetti flung in the air, a crowd of 600 chanted slogans for a group of TV reporters at the Hall building, and cheered as protestors boarded busses headed for the Quebec National Assembly.

Despite Kenniff's request that students sacrifice studying for a day in order to participate in the protest activities, many students used the day to catch up on a backload of academic assignments.

Engineering student David Train said he couldn't participate in the "day of action" because he had to work on projects and study for exams.

"As much as I like the idea of the protest, I just don't have the time," Train said as he studied with two other students in the Hall building.

"Some of our professors haven't even rescheduled labs. If they don't, how can we participate in the protest?" he asked.

A telephone blitz aimed at the MNAs representing the districts of Concordia's campuses was another protest activity.

Volunteers set up 32 telephones at both campuses, where students phoned Quebec City non-stop, but were answered by machines. Student volunteer Candice Bruno said she thought some phones were purposely taken off the hook.

Ryan met with Concordia's board of governors last month to discuss the effects of his temporary distribution plan on the university.

The governors told Ryan that his distribution of $3.7 million to Quebec universities to correct inequities in base funding is unjust for Concordia. Base funding is a fixed amount of money universities receive each year, and out of the $3.7 million sum, Concordia will receive $183,000.

Yesterday's protest was held to convince Ryan to give Concordia a fairer share of the base funding—at least an extra $500,000.

Vice rector finance Maurice Cohen claimed he didn't know how much the university spent on the 22 busses sent to Quebec City or on the full-page ads the university will place in Montreal dailies.

Cohen added, however, that Concordia has set up a special fund to pay for the protest actions which will be financed by contributions.

Although Concordia protesters got locked out of the Montreal Ministry of Education office yesterday, this little student seemed unperturbed.

34.6 *The Link* followed up its coverage of the "Day of Action" with more in-depth reportage. Its longstanding advocacy of issues impacting students continues to this day.

# ORAL HISTORIES: Student Perspectives

### PHILIP AUTHIER, ORIGINS OF *THE LINK*

I did my CEGEP at Champlain Saint-Lambert, where I worked for the student newspaper there called *The Bugle*, which was a great training ground, as was *The Link* later on. So, when I was at *The Bugle*, there was an organization, I think it still exists, called Canadian University Press, which was an association of all the student newspapers in Canada, and the editor of *The Georgian* at the time, a guy named John McKinnon, was interested in me coming to work for *The Georgian*—that was the last year of *The Georgian*, in fact. So, I came to Concordia.

*Piyusha Chatterjee: And what were your expectations coming to Concordia in '79?*

Well, in '79, obviously [it] was to get a BA and to get an education. But I also came because of *The Link*, which is the student paper. I was involved with the last year of *The Georgian*, which was '79, which was the university paper before the merger. And, so I caught the last year of *The Georgian* and the first years of *The Link*.

*PC: Okay, what was* The Georgian, *what was the shift between the two?*

... At the time Concordia was in full development but there were still two campuses: there was the Loyola campus and the Sir George campus. And there was an effort at the time to create a Concordia identity. So, I believe there was a certain amount of pressure to have one student newspaper as a uniting factor for Concordia ... My understanding is that there was a certain amount of pressure to merge the papers, to have one paper, which would reflect the Concordia identity.

*PC: So,* The Georgian *was the Sir George Williams paper?*

---

PHILIP AUTHIER is a Concordia University alumnus and former editor of *The Link* in the 1980s. He would go on to a successful journalism career, which included writing for the *Montreal Gazette*. This interview took place at the Centre for Oral History and Digital Storytelling on December 12, 2022.

GENEVA GUÉRIN is a Concordia alumnus and former student activist who graduated in 2003. In the early 2000s she organized a fundraising campaign that provided seed money for the Sustainable Concordia Project. This interview took place on Zoom on December 7, 2022.

Yes.

*PC: And what was the other one?*

*Loyola News* was the other, the paper at Loyola. You have to understand, both of these papers had long histories. They had a long existence. They were both very respected newspapers, student newspapers. And there's always been a culture of student journalism at Concordia, which was one of the other reasons that I wanted to come here—that it was considered a good place for student journalism. And, so, there was a certain pressure to create one paper and there was another implicit pressure there, both papers had ... staff shortages. So, there was actually an impetus inside the student journalism world to merge into one paper and combine resources. There were meetings between the two staffs. It was decided by a vote by the two staffs. There was actually a meeting of the people that were left on the two organizations at a CUP [Canadian University Press] conference in Edmonton. That was kind of like neutral ground for talking. You have to understand that both papers were very proud organizations ...

What we did is we tried to keep the best of both papers. And, for maybe the first years, we had offices on both campuses, and there was a very big effort to reflect both campuses, both Loyola and Sir George, and to cover those events ... It kind of worked out, because some reporters were taking more of their classes at Loyola and some of them were taking more here. So, it kind of worked out, we actually had a united staff, united staff covering both campuses ... You had a very small staff pulling themselves together and creating a new newspaper. So, it was a very difficult, it was a very difficult time. It was also very challenging because we were pooling resources, but we were also kind of new, we were not the veteran people ... so we pulled together. And then, we created the paper.

One of the strangest challenges was to find the name for the paper. A few names were kicked around ... But it's funny how you could get tripped up by something like that because it's complicated—a name of a newspaper is a complicated thing. Because, let's face it, all the good names are taken. You know, the *New York Times* ... [*laughter*]. So, we had a list and it was almost the last thing we did, we were almost near publication and we came up with the name *The Link* and there was a vote for it, and that, that became the name of the paper. And it's an excellent name because it was a little bit symbolic because we were connecting the two campuses, the two newspapers, the two institutions, and we were linking to our readers, which were the students that were helping to subsidize the paper.

## GENEVA GUÉRIN, ON 9/11

I played on teams my whole life and then when I moved to Montreal, the first thing I did was I called to find out if there's a soccer team at Concordia and when could I go for the tryout. And my year was really fun year because our coach was a Syrian, not any Syrian: Ammar Awad, who was the former captain of the Syrian national team and also played professionally in Europe, in Division One soccer. And you know, he has highlight reels of his goals, he was quite the thing. And actually, today he's the head of Abu Dhabi's entire football program, and he hired Maradona. Maradona's last job before he died was in that program [*chuckle*] ... He's a really big deal. And he was our coach. And it was hilarious because he didn't like questions, but I always have questions. And so he was always, like, "Geneva! Geneva!" [*laughter*] But we had this incredibly fun, wonderful relationship because I was political and I was constantly talking to him about Syria because he was a refugee. And that was the year September 11th happened. I remember going to soccer practice on September 11th and no one was saying a word and we were kicking around balls like zombies and, Ammar had nothing to say ...

I remember sitting in class, I was in my... mass propaganda class ... And we went out for the 10:15 break and someone said, "A plane just hit the World Trade Organization towers." And I was, like, in my head, confounded it with another World Trade Organization... the WTO, not the towers, but, the actual organization, and I was like, "Oh, cool." Totally ridiculous first reaction. And then the gravity of it all hit us, and then we went back into class and the teacher was immediately, like "What's going on? Let's just talk about this." And, and I think they let us go home early. And then, just watched television all day, alone like a zombie. Went to soccer practice. I remember the fluorescent lights and the dark pitch so well because it was that night and it was so weird. And then the next day we had this class where the professor was like, "This is the face of evil." And I was like, "It sounds like you've made a moral declaration about what evil is, I was wondering if you could just explain to us, please: what you think evil is" [*laughter*]. He was so troubled by my question that on my last assignment he wrote a whole page trying to explain why he said it and he was basically saying that he was guided by emotion in that moment. That was just crazy and to be in communication studies studying propaganda at the time was awesome because all of our teachers were, like, "Record everything. Record everything, the narrative is going to change so much as we get further away from what happened."

*Piyusha Chatterjee: How did it impact the campus? What was the student mood like then?*

I think it emboldened a lot of the Palestinian activists because there was a fear of an increase in anti-Muslim sentiment. I think it created a lot more active solidarity with Muslim students, so that that wouldn't happen. And I think that it ended up playing into this conflict between the Jewish Student Association and the Muslim students. And, ultimately, led to how big that demonstration was to stop Netanyahu from getting into the campus.

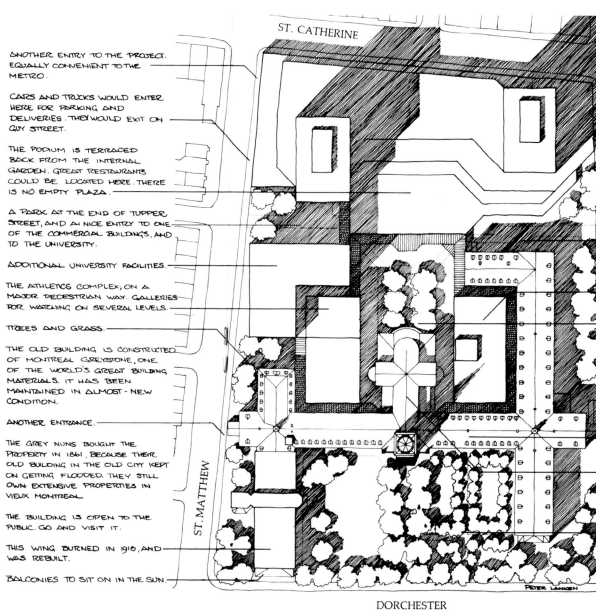

36.1 The 1975 proposal of Save Montreal for the Grey Nuns Residence.

# CONCORDIA UNIVERSITY AND THE LOSS OF HERITAGE AND HOUSING

## Eliot Perrin

THIS END OF THE SITE WOULD BE REDEVELOPED COMMERCIALLY; OFFICES, MOSTLY. THE RETAIL SHOPS MUST BE REPLACED: THAT IS WHAT STE-CATHERINE STREET IS ALL ABOUT. TOE BLAKE'S AND THE POOL ROOM SHOULD BE RELOCATED IN THE NEW BUILDING.

A MAJOR ENTRANCE TO THE PROJECT, AND TO THE UNIVERSITY, WOULD BE LOCATED HERE. ONLY ONE BLOCK FROM THE METRO, AND TWO FROM THE HALL BUILDING.

A PEDESTRIAN PATH, THROUGH GARDENS, COULD CROSS THE PROPERTY HERE.

THE LIBRARY WOULD BE LOCATED HERE. INVISIBLE FROM THE STREET. CONNECTED BY BRIDGES TO THE OLD BUILDING.

A GARDEN BEHIND THE CHAPEL, SURROUNDED WITH GLASS WALKWAYS.

THE MOTHER HOUSE OF THE GREY NUNS WAS DESIGNED IN 1869 BY VICTOR BOURGEAU, MONTREAL'S GREATEST ARCHITECT. HE ALSO DESIGNED THE HOTEL DIEU [1861], MARY QUEEN OF THE WORLD [1870], AND ST-JACQUES [1860], WHICH IS PRESENTLY BEING DEMOLISHED. THIS IS THE FIRST WING TO BE COMPLETED.

THE CHAPEL WASN'T STARTED UNTIL 1874, AND THE SPIRE WASN'T COMPLETED UNTIL 1890.

THIS COULD BE THE FIRST CAMPUS WITH TREES AND GRASS THAT SIR GEORGE HAS EVER HAD. THE OLD GARDENS COULD BE REPLANTED. UNIQUE IN MONTREAL.

THE CROSS ON THE CORNER MARKS THE SITE OF A DOUBLE MURDER IN 1752.

**THROUGHOUT THE 1960S**, Montreal experienced a construction boom, the result of Mayor Jean Drapeau's civic ambitions, as well as loose planning regulations that favoured redevelopment. Many, largely Victorian residences were demolished, replaced by either massive office and apartment complexes, or by parking lots to serve workers commuting in from the growing metropolitan suburbs. These commuters were further served thanks to the construction of Autoroutes 15 and 20, which necessitated the demolition of large swathes of Snowdon, what became known as Little Burgundy, and the city centre. Early opposition to the Autoroute 20's construction united wealthy Westmounters with working-class francophones in Hochelaga.[1] A local resident, architecture professor Joseph Baker, was inspired to rethink his approach to pedagogy, creating the Community Design Workshop at McGill University where students were taught the values of community activism via restoration programs of existing residences.[2] Meanwhile, plans to demolish the entirety of the Milton-Parc neighbourhood led to the formation of the Milton-Parc Citizens Committee in 1968, a group who would succeed in creating one of Canada's largest housing co-operatives just over a decade later.[3] A few years later, the demolition of the William Van Horne mansion in 1973 inspired the formation of the activist group Save Montreal. While Save Montreal is primarily known for saving some prominent landmarks, the retention of existing housing was one of the group's prerogatives.[4]

ELIOT PERRIN is a PhD candidate in history at Concordia University. He is also the archives coordinator for the Centre for Oral History and Digital Storytelling.

These groups represent only a handful of the myriad number of activist groups operating in Montreal from the 1960s through the 1980s. Community groups such as Save Montreal were rarely static and had overlapping memberships with other groups including both the Community Design Workshop and the Milton-Parc Citizens Committee. Unique to Save Montreal was the attention it paid to the city centre, highlighting the loss of the area's residential housing. Indeed, some of Save Montreal's first activism was protesting the loss of housing along Bishop Street, including the loss of apartments following Concordia's purchase and conversion of the Bishop Court Apartments into university offices in 1975.[5]

In 1982 Concordia announced its proposal to construct a new library building on an area bounded by De Maisonneuve Boulevard, Bishop Street, and Mackay Street. In order to do so, Concordia purchased the 1910-era Royal George Apartments, becoming a landlord to the tenants. Both Save Montreal and popular city councillor Nick Auf der Maur's party, the Municipal Action Group, advocated for the complete retention of the building. Claiming the downtown had already suffered from significant depopulation, the party argued that the destruction of affordable housing would only further exacerbate the city's housing crisis.[6]

Michael Fish, an architect and founding member of Save Montreal, was the clear leader in the attempts to force Concordia back to the drawing board. He drew up a proposal by which the university could build around the building, sparing the building and its units from the wrecking ball.[7] Royal George tenants proposed transforming the building into a housing co-operative via grants from the Canadian Housing and Mortgage Corporation. The university could even have access to the ground floor for office space and as an entrance point.[8]

University architects and officials dismissed the proposals, citing any changes would lead to cost overruns and the university's need for the space occupied by the Royal George site. Despite some legal wrangling with Montreal City Hall, Concordia was able to demolish the building in 1985, sparing only the building's terra cotta façade.[9]

Fifteen years later, Concordia was confronted again with opposition to the planned demolition of the York Theatre, a building it had acquired in 1998.[10] The 1938 theatre was the centerpiece of a structure that also contained upstairs apartments and commercial street fronts. Concordia argued it needed the site to build its new arts and engineering complex and that, given it already had multiple cinemas, had no need for another. Standing in opposition was Heritage Montreal, the national Historic Theatres Trust, local councillors such as Helen Fotopoulos.[11] Originally created as a funding branch of Save Montreal, Heritage Montreal eventually became the most well-known heritage advocacy group in the city. They met with university officials in an effort to champion the re-use of the building. Concordia grad and founding director of the Historic Theatres Trust Janet Mackinnon pointed out that no independent engineering report had been carried out and that Concordia was missing an opportunity to restore the functions of the building. Alongside the apartment housing that would be lost, the cinema was one of only three "streamline" art deco theaters in the country, the other two now nationally designated sites.[12] Nonetheless, with a demolition permit from the city, the building was demolished, with only a few token murals gracing an auditorium roughly where the York once stood.[13]

Montreal, like many North American cities, is currently in the midst of an affordability crisis as ever-larger amounts of income are dedicated to the cost of living. Since 2022, Concordia's Sir George Williams campus has become increasingly hemmed-in by condo construction, developments that only reinforce the economic divide faced both by Montreal residents and Concordia students. For the past sixty years, Montreal activists have confronted the barriers to accessible and affordable housing. Meanwhile, Concordia continues to grow as a university. As such, it will continue to be confronted with the spatial constraints faced by an urban campus. A retrospective of its history presents an opportunity to think about how the university interacted with past activism and what lessons can be gleaned to ensure that the Sir George Williams campus better integrates itself with both the city and its residents.

## NOTES

1. See Valérie Poirier, "'L'autoroute est-ouest, c'est le progrès!': Environnement et mobilisation citoyenne en opposition au projet d'autoroute est-ouest à Montréal en 1971," *Bulletin d'histoire politique* 23, no. 2 (hiver 2015): 66–91, https://doi.org/10.7202/1028884ar.

2. Joseph Baker, "An Experiment in Architecture," *Canadian Architect* (October 1973): 30–41.

3. See Claire Helman, *The Milton-Park Affair: Canada's Largest Citizen-Developer Confrontation* (Montreal: Véhicule Press, 1987).

4. See Eliot Perrin, "'Whose City Is It?': Save Montreal and the Fight for Democratic City Planning," *Urban History Review* 51, no. 1 (March 2023): 117–44, https://doi.org/10.3138/uhr-2021-0008.

5. Paul Dubuc, "Le sort des rues Bishop et Mackay," *Le Devoir*, May 22, 1975.

6. "Bishop Street Tenants Fight Demolition Plans," *The Gazette*, June 11, 1980.

7. Michael Fish, *Proposition à la Commission des biens culturels pour sauvegarder l'Édifice Royal George* (Montréal: Michael Fish, 1985).

8. Harvey Shepard, "Tenants Unite to Fight Threat of Demolition," *The Gazette*, February 16, 1982.

9. Daniel Kucharsky, "Landlord Rules out tenants' Co-op Idea," *The Gazette*, August 2, 1985.

10. "Mile-End Councillor Takes up Torch for York Theatre," *CBC News*, November 12, 2000, https://www.cbc.ca/news/canada/mile-end-councillor-takes-up-torch-for-york-theatre-1.238746

11. Matthew Hays, "Movie Palace Faces Last Curtain," *Globe and Mail*, November 5, 2000, https://www.theglobeandmail.com/arts/movie-palace-faces-last-curtain/article771391/

12. "York Theatre Has a History," *Concordia's Thursday Report*, accessed June 19, 2023, http://ctr.concordia.ca/archives/is280199/art16.html.

13. "York Demolished," *The Concordian*, September 5, 2001, https://theconcordian.com/2001/09/york-demolished/.

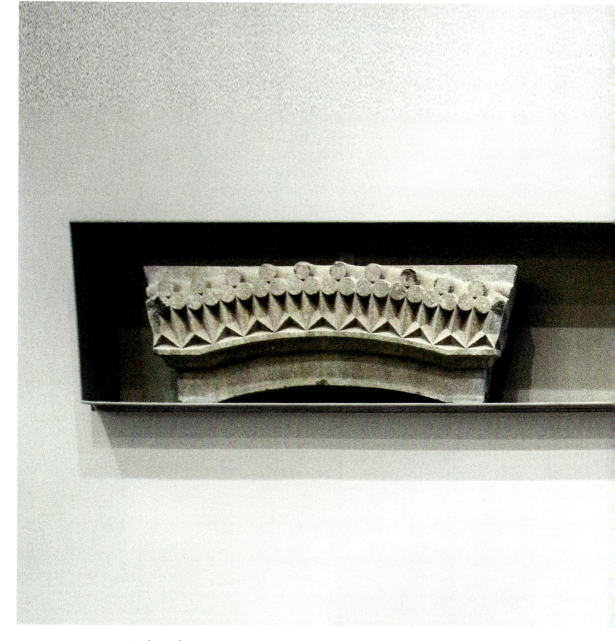

**Artist unknown**
***Lintels from the Thomas D'Arcy McGee House*** (dates unknown)
Montreal limestone (varied dimensions)
Abe and Harriet Gold Atrium, Engineering, Computer Science
and Visual Arts Integrated Complex, SGW campus

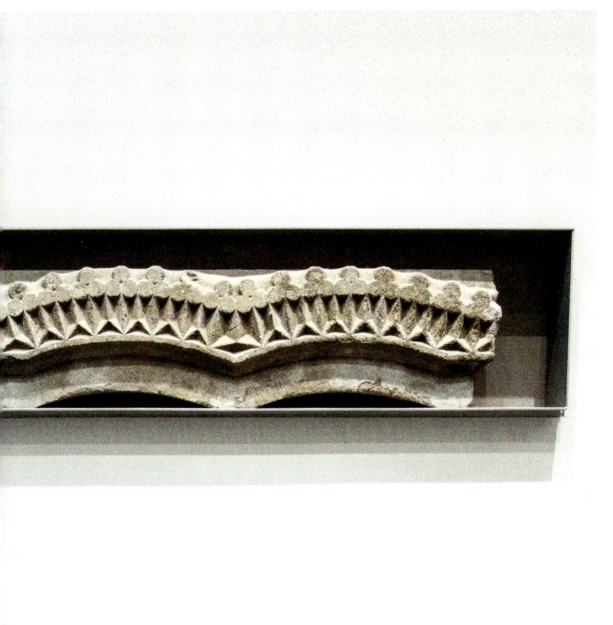

loyola campus, concordia university

# Centre for Continuing Education

First class mail

Something for Everyone

September /74

## CENTRE GROWS WITH NEW PROGRAMS

"The test and the use of man's education is that he finds pleasure in the exercise of his mind". Jacques Barzun, May 1958

by Lorraine Flaherty

Loyola's Centre for Continuing Education, designed to encourage Montrealers to return to academic study or acquire new practical, technical or recreational skills, was founded a year ago. The courses are non-credit and require no previous academic record or experience.

Besides academic programs, the 1974 fall and winter sessions offer contemporary study courses, craft courses, and practical courses. These range from lectures on Current Issues and the Reality of Death, to Batik, Painting, Basic Sewing and Career Planning.

*Five certificate programs* will be introduced this fall in Commercial Art, Journalism, French Conversation, Fashion (dress designing and pattern-making), and Business Management. These programs involve six or seven courses of 12 sessions each.

The Commercial Art program is made up of drawing and design courses with additional lectures on film, video, and typography. The certificate program in Journalism provides practical information for those interested in newspapers or a career in journalism, and offers courses in reporting, editorial and feature writing, and an examination of the role of the press in society.

Among the topical courses, *Current Issues* and *Moral Issues* are concerned with existing problems. Current Issues is a series of five independent lectures on subjects being discussed in Quebec, Canada and in the world. Experts will deal with several questions, among them confessional schools, are they outdated? and Montreal development, should it be free or controlled? Moral Issues looks at morality from two points of view - Is there a morality crisis? and Why? Discussions include the law and morality, morality in advertising, marriage and the family, and responsibility and conscience.

The Centre offers a three session course in career planning since choosing a career that will be challenging is a difficult task for many people regardless of age or working experience. The course is geared to all walks of life from university and high school graduates to housewives anxious to return to work.

Another practical course being repeated this year is *Effective Reading and Studying Methods*. Not a speed reading course, specialist Marvin Rafuse teaches reading and studying habits, skimming and scanning methods, and note and test-taking skills.

Among the craft courses offered are Batik, Jewelry-Making, Painting, Drawing from the Figure, Fashion Drawing and Photography. Batik, the ancient art of using dyes and wax to make designs on cloth is again being given by Judith Irany, well-known Montreal painter and batik maker. The Centre's jewelry-making course is open to beginners and advanced students and teaches how to use stones, metal and tools to create uniquely personal jewelry.

Except in certificate programs most courses run one term or 12 sessions. Fees depend on the number of sessions.

Registration is in progress for all 49 courses and can be done in person or by mail. The Centre is located at 7270 Sherbrooke St. W. For additional information call 482-0320, local 708.

**NEW THIS YEAR**

For the first time Loyola's Centre for Continuing Education is offering **CERTIFICATE PROGRAMS** to provide professional training in the following areas:
JOURNALISM, COMMERCIAL ART, FASHION, BUSINESS MANAGEMENT, and FRENCH CONVERSATION.

Students enroling in these programs must complete the required courses to receive a certificate. The courses may also be taken individually without registering in a specific certificate program. (For information see Course Descriptions pages 4 and 5.)

37.1 Centre for Continuing Education publication cover, Loyola College, September 1974.

# CONCORDIA CONTINUING EDUCATION: A HISTORY OF LIFELONG LEARNING

Kerry Fleming and Ursula Leonowicz

**BORN OF THE DESIRE** to encourage adult learners to acquire new practical, technical, or recreational skills as part of their personal and professional development, the Centre for Continuing Education (CCE, today known as Concordia Continuing Education) was established in the early 1970s as an advocate for lifelong learning. Committed to providing adults with skills development and knowledge acquisition, its core mission has been to serve adult learners in their professional development.

A first home to many newcomers seeking to upgrade their language skills in order to pursue their academic studies or find new jobs, CCE grew out of the evening courses offered at Sir George Williams (SGW). There, non-credited courses were offered in various departments until they were formalized in a single academic unit, in the summer of 1972.

During the 1972–73 academic year, CCE expanded its course offering at SGW and a year later, Loyola followed suit with its own Continuing Education Division. The two merged in 1974. Besides academic programs, the 1974 fall and winter sessions offered contemporary study courses, craft courses. and practical courses. These ranged from lectures on current issues and the reality of death to batik painting, basic sewing, and career planning. It provided an eclectic mix of learning opportunities for adult learners.

A full-time coordinator of music programs was appointed in August 1974 to develop the program, set up a concert series, and liaise with other Montreal musical organizations. Courses such as math, geography, accountancy, anthropology, applied social science, art, economics, education, English, French, interdisciplinary studies,

---

KERRY FLEMING has been a professional writer for over thirty years and a long-time contributor to CCE. His works include award-winning campaigns for leading brands, two books of poetry, a screenplay, magazine articles, rousing speeches, and a few tasty soup recipes.

URSULA LEONOWICZ is a regular contributor to *Concordia University Magazine*, *Globe and Mail*, *National Post*, and the *Montreal Gazette*. She writes for a variety of local magazines including *Diary of a Social Gal*.

management, mathematics, political science, psychology, religion, sociology, and Spanish, among many others, were available at this time.

Designed to meet the needs of learners—many of them newcomers—who wished to improve their proficiency in English for professional, social, and academic purposes, an expanded Intensive English Language Program was offered in the fall, winter, and summer terms of 1975, in conjunction with the Centre for Teaching of English as a Second Language. During the 1980s, new certificate programs in computers were being developed and language instruction became even more of a focus, even though the English Language Program had been an inherent part of CCE's offering since its inception. CCE offered summer, special, intensive, semi-intensive and evening English courses as well as French courses formulated for faculty and staff, business, regular, nurses, and translation purposes. The language courses prepared thousands of international, conditionally accepted students to pursue degrees at Concordia after the university imposed a new set of admissions policies on international students, requiring a minimum 550 TOEFL score.

In 1981–82, the applied arts section consisted of certificate programs in photography, fashion design and pattern making, apparel management, and textile design. Along the general interest courses offered were television production, studio and production techniques for radio, drawing, painting, museum education in Canadian galleries, bookbinding. and wine appreciation. There were also business certificate programs in investment, hospitality, tourism, business management, industrial security, journalism advertising, and public relations, among others.

Over the years, CCE has fostered a culture of lifelong learning by embodying empathy, inclusivity, and cultural sensitivity; staying attuned to the needs of learners, the business community, and society; caring for people and providing legitimate recognition for their personal and professional journeys and giving them opportunities to build upon their knowledge and skills. CCE has developed partnerships with organizations dedicated to integrating newcomers into the job market and created a skills certification program. In 2021 the certification of employability program was developed as a way of validating and certifying an individual's particular knowledge and skills in twelve competency areas identified as most sought after by employers. A validation of competencies service is also available to accurately measure the value of students' personal and professional accomplishments and build on them. In addition to developing training programs for specific communities, such as the Cree Nation in Mistissini, for example, or to empower women, as is the case with the certificate program it created in partnership with the Lise Watier Foundation, or in specific industries, such as the aerospace sector, all of CCE's training courses are online and available across Quebec and Canada.

37.2 A Centre for Continuing Education classroom, 2015.

CCE now serves some 3,500 students yearly with over 200 courses and workshops, as well as 40 certificate and diploma programs in everything from language studies to subjects such as cyber resiliency, data science, and artificial intelligence. A range of customized corporate training courses, particularly in technology sectors, but also in leadership, project management, and human relations, that are essential to professionals in search of lifelong learning in this day and age.

38.1 University of the Streets Café presents "How is Quebec changing?" at the Leonard and Bina Ellen Gallery on September 10, 2014, with Professor Sherry Simon, moderated by Jimmy Ung.

# THE ART OF CONVERSATION:
## 20 YEARS OF UNIVERSITY OF THE STREETS CAFÉ

Alexandra Pierre

**THE ATMOSPHERE** is hushed, yet lively. People arrive quietly for the University of the Streets Café conversation and are welcomed by a student or volunteer. They settle in, the regulars greeting each other from across the room as the evening begins. University of the Streets Café brings together Montreal community actors (engaged citizens, community organizers, artists, activists, etc.) and Concordians (faculty, staff, students) for public conversations on a wide range of topics. These events are free and bilingual. They last two hours, with the participation of twenty to forty people from diverse backgrounds and socioeconomic realities and take place in open, accessible community spaces such as community centres, museums, yoga studios, art galleries, bookstores, theaters, cultural centers and … cafés.

At the start of the evening, moderators, who include past and present Concordia staff and students, take the time to introduce the methodology of the public conversation model. Guests then introduce themselves and share their views on the evening's topic. Throughout the years, some of the questions discussed have included: How are racialized activists transforming environmental struggles? Can we succeed through failure? What does quality of life mean to seniors? Why do we eat what we eat? The themes cover everything from major political events to topics of general interest. The moderator then invites those present to discuss the evening's topic, drawing on their experiences, interests, expertise, and considering what they've just heard. Digressions are welcome if they fuel the reflections, but the moderator has the delicate task of framing the exchange while ensuring that the discussion can chart its own course. The moderator also ensures that the conversation keeps flowing, among other things by making sure the attention doesn't get too focused on the guests. Indeed, one of the particularities of University of the Streets Café is the role played by the guests: they get the ball rolling, but are not at the centre of the evening, nor are they considered

---

ALEXANDRA PIERRE works at the Office of Community Engagement after many years in community and women's groups. She is the first Black woman elected president of the Ligue des femmes. She is author of *Empreintes de résistance: Filiations et récits de femmes autochtones, noires et racisées* (2021).

38.2 University of the Streets Café presents "Density Interrupted: What Do Wild Spaces in the City Mean to Us?" at Arts Café on March 5, 2013, with Marke Ambard, Kendra Besanger, and Sara Finley (*standing*), moderated by Sasha Dyck.

the only ones with expertise. Once they've finished their short presentation, they become participants just like everyone else, making room for the experiences, perspectives, and ideas of others, as well as for the collective intelligence that fuels the event. Élise Ross-Nadié has been a regular moderator for the past few years, with six conversations to her credit. Élise considers each of the conversations in which she has taken part to be unique, always an opportunity to make discoveries and reflect collectively. She recalls a recent conversation on the history of marginalized communities at the Service à la Famille Chinoise du Grand Montréal: "As someone who comes from the Black community and is interested in its heritage, it was great to make connections with our stories and those of Montreal's Asian communities and to discuss with others the gentrification that is affecting the neighbourhoods inhabited by these different groups."[1]

The physical environment at University of the Streets Café is minimalist: chairs and small tables arranged in a café style, or sometimes in a circle, drinks and snacks, and that's it! No microphones, projected presentations, or recorders: technology and other gadgets often hinder concentration, discourage interventions and disturb the dynamic of the evening by preventing participants from truly engaging with what's being shared. This fluid yet structured methodology is one of the distinctive features of University of the Streets Café. This way of doing things, where great attention is paid to content, process, and logistics, has evolved over the years, due in part to the feedback received from participants and moderators.

Originally launched by the former Institute for Community Development in 2003 and coordinated by the Office of Community Engagement since 2013, Concordia has hosted more than four hundred of these public conversations over the past two decades. The University of the Streets Café discussions don't pretend to address all perspectives or solve the world's glaring problems in one evening, but they do contribute by offering a method and a space for rediscovering the art of public conversation. Participants can share ideas, draw unexpected links between critical issues, refine their thinking on subjects that matter to them, and be introduced to new perspectives by connecting with others. Ross-Nadié, for whom the University of the Streets Café is a unique way to connect with others, says, "University of the Streets Café is about taking the university out of the university. This idea of learning together by going to different places, going into communities, having horizontal functioning and exchanges ... it's wonderful!"[2]

**NOTES**

1    Élise Ross-Nadié, interview with Alexandra Pierre, November 28, 2023.

2    Ross-Nadié, interview.

# VISUAL STORY: 30 Things We Love about Concordia (2004)

# 30 Things We Love About Concordia

*On Concordia University's 30th anniversary, we look at what makes this institution special*

by Howard Bokser and Debbie Hum

September 1974: The Pierre Trudeau Liberals were basking in their recent Canadian election victory. Richard Nixon had resigned as U.S. president just weeks earlier. Jimmy Connors and Chris Evert were dominating the tennis world and social pages. Roman Polanski's *Chinatown* was in theatres and Andy Kim's *Rock Me Gently* on the airwaves.

And thousands of Montreal university students found themselves in a new home. The urban Sir George Williams University and the Jesuit Loyola College officially merged into Concordia University on August 24, 1974. Within two weeks, students were taking their first classes at the newly christened school on two campuses.

In the 30 years since, the 100,000-plus students who have passed through its doors certainly recognize Concordia's distinct character. Something — some *things* — make it like no other university in Canada.

In the following pages we look at 30 (or so) of those things — rather than focusing on the outstanding programs, research, professors and staff of the university, we highlight the extracurricular standouts of Concordia of the past 30 years. The list was compiled with the help of several Concordia staff, faculty, students and alumni, is in no specific order and is certainly not definitive. But hopefully it'll be a fun read.

## 1. Concordia memories

Within the following pages are some Concordia memories and observations from Concordia alumni and staff.

*"One Christmas someone decorated the little quad in the centre of Hingston Hall with a whole family of lit plastic snowmen and snowwomen. The industrious resident was so proud of his efforts that he told everyone he had done it. Meanwhile, a friend who also worked at Loyola and lived nearby told me that during the night someone had stolen her family of plastic snowmen right from her front yard! The resident was so busted. He apologized to my friend, of course, and did chores for her for the rest of the year."*
— Nancy Stewart, Faculty Personnel Coordinator, JMSB

*"Before the VA Building, the Faculty of Fine Arts used to be on the fifth floor of the Hall Building, a very close and intimate community. We all wore our art clothes — paint-splattered smocks — and were brought together by our common poverty and passion for creating art. We often had nude models for our life-drawing classes, and the engineering students were always very excited to come down and peek into the classroom windows. We put up wooden boards, but they still tried to worm a hole to look through."*
— Iris Biteen, BFA 77

## 2.

Concordians enjoy the 2001 Shuffle.

### Concordia Shuffle

One bonus of having two campuses 6.5 km apart is that it's the perfect distance for a nice stroll — especially if it's to raise money for student scholarships.

The annual Concordia Shuffle (**shuffle.concordia.ca**), begun in 1990, draws about 400 Concordia staff, faculty, students, alumni and friends each fall for a walkathon from the Sir George Williams Campus to the Loyola Campus and has raised nearly $600,000 for much-needed scholarships in its 14 years. Furthermore, it's an event that brings together all of the Concordia community for goodwill.

september 2004 issue    concordia university magazine

### Oscar Peterson Concert Hall

Born in Montreal's Little Burgundy district, for 20 years Oscar Peterson lived just a few blocks from Loyola. Although he's since moved to Toronto, Concordia honoured the jazz piano giant by naming its music venue the Oscar Peterson Concert Hall (*oscar.concordia.ca*) in 1999.

The 570-seat hall was built in 1990 and boasts a Japanese-style design that incorporates birch planks and a hardwood stage, excellent sight lines and ideal sound. That makes it one of the outstanding musical venues in Montreal's west end — and a fitting tribute to Oscar Peterson himself.

**Performers as varied as Oliver Jones and Roger McGuinn, former leader of the Byrds, have performed on the Oscar Peterson Concert Hall stage.**

### Student fashion

Bellbottoms are back in style . . . no, they're out . . . now they're back. Who can keep up? The only sure thing about fashion is that by the time you read about it in the newspaper, it's already yesterday's news. But the best way to see what's *really* in style is to visit campus. Or look back at the campus style of past years to see what was in vogue.

Concordia students have their own fashion sense, ever changing.

Students at Loyola, c. 1974, and current Concordia student Beth Cross.

### Office for Students with Disabilities

In 1980, there were only a handful of students with disabilities at Concordia when it established its Services for Disabled Students — now called the Office for Students with Disabilities (OSD) — making it one of the first universities in Canada to launch such an initiative. Today there are more than 500.

The OSD (*advocacy.concordia.ca/disabilities*) provides academic and support services for students with mobility, visual and hearing impairments, and with learning disabilities and health-related difficulties. Among the services are academic advising, volunteer reader services, classroom note takers, and oral and sign interpreters for the hearing impaired. Concordia's shuttle buses can accommodate wheelchairs, while accessibility to buildings and classrooms remains a priority.

So too does sensitizing the university community to the needs of students with certain challenges. The OSD's ultimate goal is to provide all students not just with access to facilities but with access to learning.

**Concordia human relations student Teri-Lee Walters.**

### Sir George Williams University legacy

According to *Maclean's Guide to Canadian Universities 2004*, 38 per cent of Concordia's 29,000 students are part-time — the largest proportion for any English Canadian university of its size, clearly one of the legacies of Sir George Williams University.

While that role is certainly not the only one bequeathed to Concordia by Sir George — others include an emphasis on teaching the "whole person" and an accent on teaching — undoubtedly one of Concordia's most striking features is its accessibility and flexibility. The university continues to attract people who wish to work by day and get a university education at night, mature students returning to complete their studies, immigrants or first-generation Canadians who might not otherwise have entrée to university, or young students who need to work their way through school. And for that they can thank the philosophy of SGW.

**Students at a nighttime Sir George business class, c. 1940s.**

*concordia university magazine*  **september 2004 issue**

## *Loyola College legacy*

Concordia's most obvious inheritance from Loyola is its campus: students, faculty and staff love the quiet, idyllic setting, classic architecture and green spaces.

But the real bequest of Loyola is more subtle. Jesuit education philosophy includes bringing morality into scholarship and stressing teaching. Concordia has long been known for small class sizes and a liberal approach to pedagogy. Its community mindedness, emphasis on athletics and alumni participation are all continuations of Loyola College's vision. The Jesuits taught their students to be men and women "for others," and the Concordia experience continues to impart that.

Loyola students enjoying the quad, c. 1970.

## *H-110: More than a classroom*

The Hall Building: It's old. Its facilities are inadequate and out of date. The escalators never work. Yet the Hall Building's ground floor, 700-seat H-110 has hosted a remarkable number of high-profile speakers, controversial events and great world cinema.

Luminaries who've spoken at H-110 over the past 30 years include the late novelist Mordecai Richler, feminist icon Germaine Greer, American consumer activist Ralph Nader and wrongly imprisoned American boxer Reuben "Hurricane" Carter. The room has also accommodated myriad open meetings on controversial or university issues for students, faculty and staff, plus countless class lectures and student gatherings.

From 1968 to 1998, the Conservatory of Cinematographic Art screened hundreds of world-class movies in H-110, including retrospectives on famed actors and directors, such as Jean-Luc Godard, who attended. And beginning in 2003 Montreal's FanTasia International Film Festival has been using H-110 as its venue. The tradition continues.

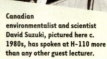

Canadian environmentalist and scientist David Suzuki, pictured here c. 1980s, has spoken at H-110 more than any other guest lecturer.

## *Hall Building highlights*

Who would've thought the Hall Building could actually be attractive? But recent renovations to two floors, the Arts and Science Learning Centre (*artsandscience.concordia.ca/aslc/*) on the fourth floor and the new mechanical engineering and computer science classrooms and labs on the eighth floor, have aroused admiring words along the lines of "It's nothing like the Hall Building!" The transformation has been gradual, and will continue in phases as other floors get renovated.

The surprisingly posh Arts and Science Learning Centre, on the fourth floor of the Hall Building, opened in 2001.

september 2004 issue   concordia university magazine

## 10 Convocation

After three or four years (or more) of some sweat and tears (hopefully no blood), you've finally earned that degree. So how do you celebrate? Convocate!

Even cynical souls have trouble scoffing at the emotional and inspirational (albeit a bit long) convocation ceremonies, students' final farewell to Concordia (until, that is, the alumni association and fundraisers come calling).

For Concordia's first dozen years, convocation was held at several locations on both campuses. Since June 1986, Place des Arts has been the elegant host (with the exception of 1999-2001, when its employees were on strike). Adding class to the events has been the long list of renowned honorary doctorates bestowed by the university, including those to Oscar Peterson (1979), Simone de Beauvoir (1986), Gratien Gélinas (1989), Louise Arbour (2001) and Seamus Heaney (2002). But on convocation day at Concordia, everyone is equal: everyone is a graduate.

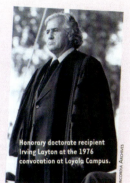

**Honorary doctorate recipient Irving Layton at the 1976 convocation at Loyola Campus.**

## 11 New buildings

The Concordia landscape has been changing dramatically over the past five years, with the opening of the Richard J. Renaud Science Complex at Loyola, the rising Integrated Engineering, Computer Science and Visual Arts Complex downtown, renovations underway at the Drummond Science and Hall buildings, and the new John Molson School of Business building to come.

This year, the $18-million acquisition of the majestic motherhouse of the Sisters of Charity of Montreal (commonly known as the Grey Nuns) is, says President Frederick Lowy, "the single most important acquisition Concordia has made since its creation." The addition of the new property, located just south of the Faubourg Ste. Catherine between Guy and St. Mathieu streets, will more than double the size of Concordia's Sir George campus and gain coveted green space for the Concordia community.

By the end of the decade, the university will hardly look the same as the one that we remember from the 20th century.

**The motherhouse of the Sisters of Charity of Montreal features great stretches of lawns canopied by old-growth trees, certain to be a hit with students.**

## 12 Art Matters

From controversial (phallic George W. Bush caricature by Allison Moore) to compelling (photography by Darren Ell of bullet-ridden homes on the Gaza Strip) to zany (the art of lies and mattress-jumping), the student-run Art Matters Festival (*artmatters.concordia.ca*) has taken Concordia and even some of Montreal by storm every March for the past four years.

Started in 2001 in celebration of the Faculty of Fine Arts' 25th anniversary, Art Matters was recognized as an outstanding student project with the Forces Avenir Award by the Quebec government. The two-week event showcases Concordia's student musicians, performers and artists at both on- and off-campus sites. Art, of course, is highly subjective, but the festival clearly comes out in good favour with Concordia students, who voted for the Art Matters fee levy last year, assuring its continuing presence in campus hallways and open spaces for years to come.

**Concordia's Art Matters has grown in size and stature since it began in 2001.**

## Shuttle buses

It began in 1976 as a 13-seat van that made seven return trips per day between the campuses. In the '80s, the Concordia community was served by yellow school buses; then came the wheelchair-accessible Big Reds in 1992. In March of this year, the university unveiled a new, eye-catching fleet. More importantly, the upgraded shuttle buses provide greater capacity and run on a percentage of biodiesel.

In all incarnations, the free shuttle service has been well used — during rush hours and peak periods, line-ups and complaints remain a tradition. But with 5,000 passengers and more than 100 trips between the campuses daily — 1 million passengers per year — the long-suffering but colourful bus drivers always keep their cool.

The first Shuttle bus, c. 1976, and the newer, flashier version.

## Women's hockey powerhouse

While their supremacy has waned in recent years, the women's hockey Stingers (*concordia.ca/stingers*) dominated Canadian university women's hockey through the '80s and '90s, winning the first two national championships in 1998 and '99 and many national and international tournaments. Through the years, the women's hockey team has been guided by coach extraordinaire Les Lawton, who's chalked up more than 500 career victories.

Concordia has trained some of the top elite women's hockey players, from Canadian Olympic gold medalist Thérèse Brisson, BSc 89, to Cammi Granato, attendee 97, Karyn Bye, DSA 95 — both 2002 Olympic silver medalists and 1998 gold medal winners with the U.S. women's hockey team — and scores of others.

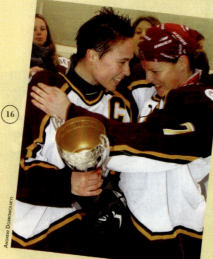

**Captain Lisa-Marie Breton and Marie-Claude Allard celebrate the Stingers' victory at the 2002 Theresa Humes Invitational Hockey Tournament at Loyola's Ed Meagher Arena.**

## Memories

*"I remember the life-changing trips to Japan and China in 1975 and 1976 that were part of Martin Singer's History of East Asia course, where we experienced the final phase of Mao's China, among other things. The groups were composed of undergraduate and graduate students, faculty members, physicians, lawyers, nurses, business people, scientists and housewives, ages 18 to 82."*

— **Edith Katz, BA 82, DIA 98, coordinator, marketing/communications, DIA/DSA**

ESL is a hot subject at Cont Ed, with an influx of students mainly from Asia and Latin America.

## Continuing Education

The Centre for Continuing Education (*concordia.ca/conted*) thrives as Montreal's premier destination for not-for-credit courses, for "lifelong learners" who wish to improve their skills and minds. Courses are aimed at providing professional skills in areas such as information technology, business and e-commerce, communications, public relations and human resources management. Cont Ed also specializes in instruction in English as a second language, which has grown exponentially in recent years thanks to an increased emphasis on recruiting international students.

Of the 9,000 students who enrol in Cont Ed each year, about 40 per cent already have Concordia experience, and many, including 15 to 20 per cent of the ESL students, become infected with enthusiasm for learning — and Concordia — and go on to sign up for the university's academic programs.

september 2004 issue   concordia university magazine

## Colleges

Concordia's five colleges are special and more personal environments for learning, with small classes and excellent faculty that attract the very best students from the Faculty of Arts and Science.

The **Liberal Arts College** provides a rich academic exploration of the development of Western civilization and culture through its core curriculum of the great books of Western civilization. The **School of Community and Public Affairs** is a place where academics and activism meet, offering a mix of academic and practical training that exposes students to a wide range of public issues. The **Science College** offers topnotch science students a broad-based scientific education focusing on both laboratory research and the role of science in history and contemporary society, with opportunities to interact with other scientists and explore cross-disciplinary activities.

The **Simone de Beauvoir Institute** has been a place where women's studies has matured into a field of rigorous academy, focusing on feminist perspectives and the evolving role of women in society. The **Loyola International College**, launched in 2001, offers an interdisciplinary program that explores issues of culture, international relations, religion and globalization. Until 2003, the Faculty of Arts and Science also housed **Lonergan College**, where faculty engaged in interdisciplinary dialogue about important thinkers and fundamental questions of value in culture, art, science and religion.

A School of Community and Public Affairs classroom, 1995.

Over the past two years the VA Building garden has blossomed into an attractive and functional meeting place.

## Visual Arts Building sculpture garden

You've seen it if you've passed by the corner of Crescent Street and René-Lévesque Boulevard over the past year: high in the sky, the guy on a pole, poised to take a step into empty air. Created by studio arts student Carrick Dennison, the work is a winning selection from the annual sculpture competition in the Faculty of Fine Arts, which each year installs two outdoor sculptures in the courtyard. This year, a backlog of works happily resulted in more sculptures than usual.

The annual sculpture competition has been a fixture since Fine Arts moved to the VA Building in 1979. Inside, the VAV Gallery continues to be the site of eclectic and forward-looking exhibitions of student works. Both spaces provide students with a very public display of their talents.

## Concordia mascots

Everyone loves Buzz the Bee, the Stingers' mascot. But some will recall the CUSA Bear, introduced by the Concordia University Students' Association in the fall of 1979 to boost school spirit. Soon afterwards, a group of Concordia students rescued the bear when McGill Engineering students kidnapped it. The big but cuddly bear quickly became a fun part of many student activities, distributing buttons, rallying cheers at sports events, dancing and joking with students and passersby. Around the same time, a bee mascot was introduced for the Concordia sports teams; in the first year after the merger, the Loyola Warriors and the Georgians remained separate teams and archrivals, but they were joined as a single set of varsity teams called the Concordians in 1975 and renamed the Stingers soon thereafter. The bee became a rallying presence at Stingers games and added some fun to other university events. The CUSA Bear quietly disappeared into hibernation after the last Winter Carnival in 1989. Apparently there wasn't enough honey in town for two mascots…

Today's mascot Buzz the Bee and the CUSA Bear (inset) in 1983.

Cinema professor Thomas Waugh and communications studies professor Chantal Nadeau organized the Sex on the Edge conference at Concordia, October 9-11, 1998.

## Queer Studies

This July, California governor Arnold Schwarzenegger hurled the ultimate insult at opposing Democrats by calling them "girlie boys." In other words, homophobia is alive and well in 2004.

That's old news to those in the GLBT2Q (gay, lesbian, bisexual, trans-gender, two-spirited queer) community. And that's why Concordia's minor in interdisciplinary studies in sexuality (*cinema.concordia.ca/sexuality*) — affectionately known as "queer studies" — remains vital.

The roots of the minor in sexuality go back to 1985, when the first lesbian studies curriculum was introduced at the Simone de Beauvoir Institute. 1989 saw the initial gay studies course on literature and film and in 1994 Concordia inaugurated HIV/AIDS: Cultural, Social and Scientific Aspects of the Pandemic. The 27-credit interdisciplinary minor, a joint effort of the Fine Arts and Arts and Science faculties that began in 1998, includes such courses as Queer Feminism; Sexuality, Identity and Politics; and Sexual Representation/Cinema, taught by queer studies driving force Thomas Waugh. As the long-awaited new major readies for its 2005 start-up, the current program head is sociology and anthropology professor Frances Shaver.

Aside from the courses' academic benefits, their presence sends a message to GLBT2Q students and, more importantly, the community at large, that at Concordia being a "girlie boy," "butch girl" or any other gay slur is not only all right, but cutting edge.

***Memories*** *"Some Loyola memories include Loyola Thé-Arts; Thursday and Friday night beer bashes in the Guadagni Lounge; Father Marc Gervais's Monday night movie classics at the F.C. Smith Auditorium, and winter carnivals in the '70s and '80s, with the fabulous snow sculptures in the quadrangle and the hilarious "dogsled" races at the football field. The 1984 Student Winter Carnival Beach and Pool Party moved at the last minute to the old Loyola Physical Plant Building, with students swimming and 'sunning' in a real pool in mid February."*
— *Jane Hackett, assistant to the Dean of Students*

Co-op students from different disciplines have worked at the Canadian Space Agency in Longueuil, Que., home of the Canadarm.

## Institute for Co-Operative Education

"Real Education for the Real World." Concordia's motto is never truer than for Concordia's co-op students (*co-op.concordia.ca*), who alternate academic semesters with program-relevant, paid workterms in the real world.

The Institute for Co-Operative Education started in 1990 and offers co-op programs in all four faculties, in fields as varied as actuarial mathematics, chemistry/biochemistry, accountancy, marketing, digital image/sound, building engineering and software systems. Employers have included Merck Frosst, Motorola, ViaRail and the Canadian Space Agency.

It's a win-win-win situation: students gain experience, networking opportunities and some pay; employers get quality employees and the knowledge that they're helping students; and Concordia, by acting as the conduit for this exchange, profits from the goodwill generated by the students and employers.

## Alumni involvement

From named scholarships and bursaries to representation on the board of governors, from the 23 Concordia University Alumni Association chapters to Homecoming, evidence of Concordia's alumni participation is everywhere. Loyola, Sir George and Concordia graduates have come together to consistently place the university in the top three in the *Maclean's* magazine rankings for alumni support among comprehensive universities.

Last year, more than 2,700 people participated in Homecoming 2003 — mostly alumni — and the CUAA keeps topping itself with new chapters, additional events, and more and more volunteers. Last year also saw 7,500 alumni donate nearly $6 million to Annual Giving Campaign programs, new records both. Concordia's 120,000 alumni continue to make their mark both out in the world and at their alma mater (*alumni.concordia.ca*).

Thomas Hecht and Owen Rowe look at their younger selves in the Sir George 1950 graduating class photo at Homecoming 2000.

september 2004 issue   concordia university magazine

## Diversity

Concordia, "the people's university," has always been a welcoming place for first- and second-generation Canadians, its evolving diversity over the years reflecting the new waves of immigration to Montreal. In fall 2003, the proportion of students who indicated English as their mother tongue was 55 per cent, French was 16 per cent, and other languages represented 29 per cent — including Armenian, Cree, Croatian, Farsi, Gujarti, Khmer, Korean, Punjabi, Serbian, Tagalog, Tamil and Urdu, to name just a few.

Diversity encompasses many dimensions beyond ethnicity, including different faiths, cultures, politics and lifestyles — and while this can bring about challenges, the whole experience at Concordia makes for important and rewarding life lessons in urban and global co-existence.

Concordia's multiculturalism is apparent to any visitor.

The Leonard & Bina Ellen Art Gallery permanent collection includes *Ici, la bas,* 1957, by Jean-Paul Riopelle.

## University Art Collection

From Emily Carr to Jean-Paul Riopelle and major artists in between, the Leonard & Bina Ellen Art Gallery (*ellengallery.concordia.ca*) houses outstanding works by renowned and emerging Canadian artists. The university collection began as six works in the early '60s; over the decades it has grown to more than 3,000 pieces that represent the scope of artistic periods, directions and styles in Canada. Outside of the gallery, public art on campus includes Walter Fuhrer's stainless sculpture *Transcendence*, at Loyola, and the hanging sculpture installed in the Hall Building lobby. The atrium of the Richard J. Renaud Science Complex is the new home for seven wooden sculptures by aboriginal artists from Africa, Papua New Guinea and British Columbia that were long in storage in the gallery vaults.

## John Molson MBA International Case Competition

Bring together 128 MBA students from 32 top business schools across the globe and 250 local business executives to serve as judges. Throw in a round-robin tournament consisting of five business cases. The result: the John Molson MBA International Case Competition (*mba-casecomp.com*), the oldest, largest and one of the most acclaimed MBA case competitions in the world.

The student-run contest has quickly grown from its humble beginnings in 1982 — when five Quebec and Ontario business school teams presented cases before a panel of professors — into an international event: the 2004 competition featured 15 teams from across Canada, 10 from the U.S., six from Europe and one from New Zealand. The competition provides a learning opportunity and networking boon for both the students and executives. And the 2004 competition was especially sweet: for the first time in the competition's 23 years, the home team finished in first place.

Concordia's winning case comp team at Montreal's Hilton Bonaventure Hotel, January 12, 2004.

concordia university magazine   september 2004 issue

## Student newspapers

Student newspapers are fascinating archives of campus goings-on and the issues that have been important at different times at Concordia, in Canada and around the world. Those who have served in the student press have generally taken their responsibilities at the vanguard of truth very seriously, whether it be radical, reactionary or simply kooky.

At Concordia, the expression of a diversity of views has been encouraged by the presence of at least two student papers on campus at a time — the *Loyola News*, *Georgian* and *Paper* in the early years and the *Link* and *Concordian* from the 1980s on, with the more recent addition of *Concordia Français*. The student journalists are a ragtag bunch, perhaps, but many are now major figures in the mainstream media, while others are making an imprint on the world stage in different ways. They all have one thing in common: at one time or another, they likely managed to irk the administration, which seems to be a rite of passage for student papers.

Some student paper headlines through the years.

Student and staff volunteers stuff 10,000 protest letters into bags for the Day of Action, November 1987.

## Student activism

The *Oxford Canadian Dictionary* defines "activism" as "vigorous action to further a cause." Under "student activism" it has a picture of Concordia — just kidding! But it certainly could.

Student activism is a trademark of Concordia, and while that doesn't always lead to campus peace (as we all know), its positive attributes include attracting — and producing — passionate, caring students who get more out of their education than textbook learning. Concordia has long nourished grassroots student causes and groups, such as QPIRG (Quebec Public Interest Research Group), the student-run health store Frigo Vert, and the "Greening of Mackay," a project that first emerged in 1971 and has been resuscitated several times in the past three decades.

Not all activism has been adversarial to the university administration: On November 17, 1987, Concordia rector Patrick Kenniff, student association co-president Maxine Clarke and 1,000 supporters armed with more than 10,000 letters boarded a bus to Quebec City for a "Day of Action" to protest government underfunding and tuition hikes. The Quebec government eventually amended its funding formula in Concordia's favour. The message: Activism can work.

## Student hangouts

On campus it may have been Reggie's — either location — or the Hive, the airport, the Guadagni Lounge or Java U. Off campus it could have been McKibbon's Pub, the Annex, Mr. Hot Dog or the other Java U. Maybe it was George's Souvlaki, the Seven Steps Bookshop, Brutopia or Van Horne Bagel.

No matter the place, hangouts play an important role in students' university experience. Whether hovering over coffee or a beer or two, in heated discussion, doing last-minute cramming or group projects, or just enjoying some free time, no matter where students congregate, they make it their home.

Students at the Guadagni Lounge, c. 1980s, in Loyola's Central Building, and at Reggie's original 7th floor Hall Building location c. 1980s.

september 2004 issue    concordia university magazine

## Engineers at play

Concordia's Annual Bridge Building Competition, in which student engineers from across North America and Europe compete to build the strongest bridge made entirely of wooden popsicle sticks, toothpicks, dental floss and white glue — and weighing no more than four kilograms — celebrated its 20th edition this year. Its origins date from the 1960s, from a suggestion by Sir George civil engineering professor Michael Troitsky to his bridge design students. Next year's competition will be renamed in honour of Professor Troitsky, who died this January.

Most importantly, all-nighters and shared successes and sorrows of the Bridge Building Competition, and other engineering student competitions including the Great Northern Concrete Toboggan Race, SAE Car-Building Competition and Engineering Games, bring students closer together.

**At the 2001 Bridge Building Competition, students watch their bridge sustain "the Crusher," a computer-controlled mechanism with a 10-ton capacity.**

## Institute in Management and Community Development

Concordia's Institute in Management and Community Development (*instdev.concordia.ca*) helps leaders of grass-roots community groups and non-profit organizations do their important work by teaching them to set strategies, raise funds, attract volunteers and manage operations.

Established in 1993 as part of the Centre for Continuing Education, the Institute offers the annual Summer Program, which draws hundreds of participants to Loyola each June for four days of training, as well as leadership development, fundraising and mentoring programs. Together with the Faculty of Arts and Science, the Institute offers a graduate diploma in community economic development. In 2003 the Institute also began the University of the Streets Café, bringing discussion groups to cafés, libraries and community centres.

**Engaged participants at the 2003 Summer Program.**

## Memories

*"My favourite view: overlooking the bustle in front of the Hall Building and de Maisonneuve from the third floor stairwell in the Webster Library. (I snapped some photos of the Benjamin Netanyahu riot from there.) I have fond memories of wandering out of Dennis Murphy's Propaganda class in the Bryan Building, my head swimming with ideas yet my notebook strangely blank — we spent all of our time talking instead of note taking."*

— **Luke Andrews, BA 00, senior website designer, Internal Relations & Communications**

## Annexes

Originally, Sir George bought the limestone Victorian houses on Mackay Street in 1968 to demolish them and replace them with an arts and library building. But, vetoed by the City of Montreal on the grounds that it would spoil the view from Sherbrooke Street, the annexes, including the red Scottish sandstones along Bishop Street, became home to small units, colleges and student associations. Although the houses present some problems (such as wheelchair access, balky plumbing and antiquated wiring), they add a distinct environment within Concordia.

**Concordia's Mackay Street annexes; in 1978 the doors were painted in bright (garish, to some) colours, but in 1999 they were repainted in Concordia maroon.**

concordia university magazine    **september 2004 issue**

# Snapshots

40.1 Tom Waugh (right), Distinguished Professor Emeritus of Film Studies and Interdisciplinary Studies in Sexuality, Cinema, with pioneering professor Robert Martin in 1989.

# QUEER AND SEXUALITY STUDIES: HOW CONCORDIA EMERGED AT THE FOREFRONT OF NEW AND VITAL DISCIPLINES

Matthew Hays

**WALKING INTO THE CLASSROOM**, it was as if we knew something groundbreaking was happening. It was September 1989, and about sixty of us gathered for a course called Representation and Sexual Orientation: Aspects of Gay Male Literature and Film, an interdisciplinary six-credit course created by two renowned queer scholars at Concordia, Robert Martin (English) and Thomas Waugh (Cinema). A "benign" fore title had been chosen for the course so as to avoid "outing" students; Martin and Waugh knew the registrar software would never include the last five incriminating words on transcripts: it was the 1980s, millions were dying of AIDS, and sodomy statutes were still in force throughout the United States.

Everything about the course was captivating. The curriculum spanned the usual suspects—Oscar Wilde, Virginia Woolf, Thomas Mann, and Jean Genet—to the contemporary moving image vanguard, including Rainer Fassbinder, Isaac Julien, and Marlon Riggs. If there was excitement and discovery going on in the classroom, not everyone was wild about the breakthrough. One tenured professor in the philosophy department wrote an open letter of complaint about the course. Meanwhile, the Simone de Beauvoir Institute offered a lesbian studies course at the same time as the "gay male" course. (In fact, in 1985, Professor Yvonne Klein attempted to teach a course titled Women's Sexuality—Lesbian Experience, but the name of the course had to be changed to Female Sexuality due to the controversy.) A full-fledged Lesbian and Gay Cinema course followed in 1992, taught by Waugh and Chantal Nadeau (Communication Studies) and remains part of the curriculum to this day.

These courses set the stage for what has become an extremely important part of Concordia's legacy as a progressive institution: its commitment to the expansion of ideas, curriculum, policies, and pedagogies around sexuality and sexual/gender

---

**MATTHEW HAYS** is an award-winning author with publications in the *Globe and Mail*, *Washington Post*, *New York Times*, *VICE*, *Guardian*, and *Cineaste*. He is the co-editor (with Tom Waugh) of the Queer Film Classics book series with McGill-Queen's University Press. He teaches media studies at Marianopolis College and Concordia University.

 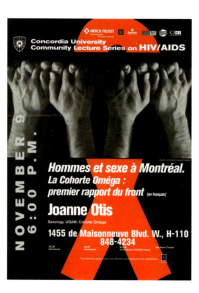 

40.2 Posters for the HIV/AIDS Lecture series organized by Thomas Waugh beginning in 1992. The series brought a wide range of international speakers to Concordia, including activists, artists, and scholars.

minority histories and communities. That original single course would eventually expand into the option for students to major or minor in sexuality studies for a bachelor's degree, scores of graduate students have tackled interdisciplinary queer research topics over the years, and experimental queer pedagogy has become a Concordia watchword. The cross-faculty minor in interdisciplinary studies in sexuality was officially launched in 1998, thanks to the benchwork of Profs. Waugh and Frances Shaver (Sociology), and the major arrived in the calendar in 2019, housed in the Simone de Beauvoir Institute. In 2002 Professor Trish Salah taught Advanced Studies in Queer Feminism and followed up in 2003 with Intro to Trans Studies, both through the Simone de Beauvoir Institute.

The interwoven emergence of queer and sexuality studies extended to breakthroughs in related interdisciplinary research. As an example, my own work and intellectual curiosity were in lock step with Concordia's evolution. My writing as a journalist often involved looking at art and/or politics through a queer lens or analytical bent. When I was struggling to finish my MA in media studies at Concordia in the 1990s, it was my straight-but-never-narrow professor, the late, brilliant Dennis Murphy who insisted that my idea of cross-referencing multiple interviews with queer filmmakers was both a perfect thesis project and publishable book. He was right on both fronts, as he served as my advisor, shepherding me through my degree and showing up at my book launch to say, "I told you so." The book, *The View from Here: Conversations with Gay and Lesbian Filmmakers* (Arsenal Pulp Press) won a 2008 Lambda Literary Award (which are the American queer book awards).

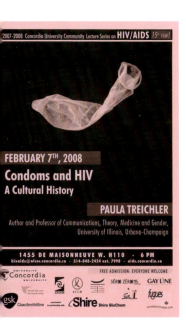
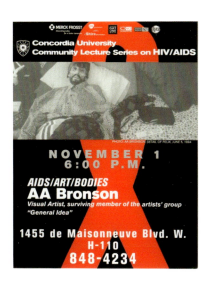

By this point, Waugh had become my mentor and friend, and his suggestion of a Queer Film Classics book series—in which a single author could write an entire monograph on a single queer movie—was also born at Concordia in 2008. After nineteen volumes at Arsenal Pulp Press and critical notice everywhere from *Cineaste* to the *New York Times*, the series now continues at McGill-Queen's University Press, with book number twenty-five launched in 2023 (*À tout prendre et Il était une fois dans l'Est*, by Concordia graduate Julie Vaillancourt, the first book in French), with no end date in sight.

Waugh also developed and oversaw the HIV/AIDS Lecture Series at Concordia three years after the literature and cinema course. Rightly predicting that the media might grow bored of the HIV epidemic, Waugh fought to keep those impacted by the virus in the public consciousness by setting up the series, which brought internationally prominent speakers to Concordia to discuss the scientific, ethical, artistic, and political implications of the health crisis, lasting for over twenty-five years. Speakers included a whole spectrum of experts from Luc Montagnier, French Nobel laureate who first identified the HIV retrovirus, to fierce Greek American vocalist Diamanda Galás, who became an AIDS activist upon the death of her brother. The series soon added a full-year interdisciplinary course to Concordia offerings, HIV/AIDS: Cultural, Social and Scientific Aspects of the Pandemic—still offered as a core course in the sexuality major in 2023, thirty years later. Thus, a huge part of Concordia's history has been about acknowledging the depth of human sexual experience, boldly going where no one has gone before while making things perfectly queer.

41.1 *Tracing Asian Canadian Art Histories and Aesthetic Alliances* vitrine in-progress during research residency at Artexte Documentation Centre, Montreal, March 14, 2015.

# THE STORY OF ETHNOCULTURAL ART HISTORIES RESEARCH (EAHR)

Alice Ming Wai Jim

**INCREASINGLY** universities in Canada are motioning to recognize the significant role and valuable insights of equity-seeking student groups in the history of activist movements and the ongoing project of decolonizing academia. These events have galvanized unprecedented anti-racism and anti-oppression activism on campuses across the country with more racialized students and faculty writing and speaking openly about their intersectional experiences navigating the elitist white spaces of the Canadian university system. How and why the Ethnocultural Art Histories Research Group (EAHR) came into existence in 2011 and continues to operate over twelve years out of Concordia University's Department of Art History is one of these micro stories that remains to be told. Raising awareness of the contribution of Black, Indigenous, and People of Colour (BIPOC) artists, curators, and researchers, EAHR has had a significant impact on the representation, experience, and well-being of visible minority fine arts students and faculty as well as

---

**ALICE MING WAI JIM** is a contemporary art historian and curator of Chinese descent born in Tiohtiá:ke (Montreal). She was appointed the Concordia University Research Chair in Ethnocultural Art Histories from 2017 to 2022. She is currently Concordia University Research Chair in Critical Curatorial Studies and Decolonizing Art Institutions.

early career scholars and practitioners of colour within both the institution and the larger context of the Montreal art world.

Since the mid-2000s the discipline of art history, and the encyclopedic museum as intellectual projects circumscribed by specific values and methods, have been widely critiqued as rooted in the European imaginary. Hence despite troves of evidentiary artifacts, the presence and experiences of artists of colour have been underrepresented and erased from art historical accounts from pyramids to Picasso and beyond. While Concordia's art history program is widely recognized as one of the most progressive programs in the country, it was not immune to cultural lag. The idea for EAHR came to me in response to students pursuing studies on racialized artists asking me about what to do during the gap years when I was not teaching "race" courses. At the time, I was the first full-time tenure track visible minority faculty in the department, hired in 2006 at the same time as the first Indigenous faculty member, Algonquin-Michif artist and art historian Dr. Sherry Farrell Racette. EAHR's mandate was to facilitate opportunities for exchange and creation, and to critically engage with issues of ethnic and cultural representation within the arts in Canada and beyond. Its objectives were to provide evidence of the need for the university to increase cultural diversity in faculty representation and curriculum, and to find administrative support for anti-racism initiatives within the faculty, which included anti-oppression workshops for both students and faculty. Unlike the two pre-existing fee-levy groups, the Art History Graduate Students Association, and the *Concordia Undergraduate Journal of Art History*, EAHR does not receive fee levies as its volunteer members are not student-elected through the referendum process, and in 2011, it was the only other student group in the department. As EAHR's first faculty advisor, I would and continue to train and mentor members through the various stages of projects planned for each year as well as help leverage funding as a faculty researcher through partnerships and my own grants.

The objectives for a research group crystallized quickly and the opportunity to initiate EAHR as a pilot project arose by tethering exhibition pedagogy and a curatorial project assignment to my undergraduate course Race, Citizenship, and Art in Canada, which I was teaching for the third time listed under the generic academic calendar title "Ethnocultural Art Histories." After inspiring conversations with students of colour Adrienne Johnson (BA, art history, presently a doctoral candidate at McGill) and Sally Sui Ling Lee (MFA, studio), who both became EAHR's first co-coordinators, the volunteer-based, extracurricular, student-driven research group was launched, providing a platform from which to organize DIY culturally diverse programming otherwise not on offer by the university.

Pedagogically speaking, EAHR was designed as a research community rather than as an advocacy or lobby group, although these were not mutually exclusive,

41.2 Planning meeting for the NYU Global Asia/Pacific Art Exchange (GAX) 2019 event Asian Indigenous Relationalities in Contemporary Art, June 2019, at the Gail and Stephen A. Jarislowsky Institute for Studies in Canadian Art, Concordia University. *Left to right*: Hanss Lujan Torres, Chiara Montpetit, Austin Henderson, Laurence Charlebois, Alexandra Nordstrom, the two Concordia University Student Research Awardees Renata Critton-Papp and Autumn Cadorette, Samantha Merritt, Mikhel Proulx, and Alice Ming Wai Jim.

bringing together students with similar interests to develop projects, undertake joint activities, share knowledge, and hone skills required to execute this research program. As much as possible, each coordinator position (in the areas of finance, events, projects, public relations) is occupied by two members—one graduate student and one undergraduate student—who provide and foster peer learning and support, collaboration, and open communication, as well as facilitate planned succession. Students within EAHR gain vital professional skills such as grant writing, curating, problem solving, and working within the university system, as well as beyond in artist-run centres and other arts and cultural organizations.

EAHR's activities over the years have included over a hundred research and knowledge-dissemination activities including multiple annual conferences and panels, over fifty public lectures, annual exhibitions, performances, screenings, catalogue publications, and Ottawa field trips to the National Gallery of Canada, Korean

Cultural Centre, and Canada Council Art Bank. EAHR has also built research residencies with Concordia Library and Montreal's Artexte art documentation centre where the first five years of EAHR's activities are archived and digitally accessible to the general public. The scope of coverage has ranged from racialized diasporic visible minority art histories alongside Indigenous directions and Black perspectives to that considered "non-Western," presented according to issues-based or thematic lines of investigation. For example, weathering the double pandemic of COVID-19 and woke racism, EAHR@10 organized an Instagram exhibition supporting twenty BIPOC artists for twenty weeks in the summer of 2020.

One of EAHR's key objectives is to increase the documentation of BIPOC cultural production. Thus, great attention has been paid to archiving EAHR's activities in terms of properly documenting processes and outcomes for future research. It is well known that student organizing contributes to protest movements and activism on numerous social issues. Yet historically, there has frequently been little to no documentation to be found on these activities. Imperative to the EAHR initiative was to ensure that students document their research activities. The turnaround of students is high, given the project-based nature of the annual program and that students graduate regularly. On average, core members stay active for two to three semesters. To pass on institutional knowledge, student members are trained to practice peer-to-peer knowledge exchange even before offboarding.

The story of EAHR demonstrates how ethnocultural art histories research is social justice work and how this work is also a significant part of Concordia's history of struggle and growth towards institutional transformation. The past few years have seen purported changes in major museums and universities, including Concordia, that has built up a critical mass of Indigenous and racialized visible minority faculty through strategic hires. We now have a generation of students who have gone through their degrees with EAHR experiences that have equipped them in some way to stay resilient and in solidarity against the slow burn of crises such as structural oppression, climate change, or both at the same time, and, also, imagine sustainable, survivable ethno-climate futures.

# THE HISTORY OF THE OTSENHÁKTA STUDENT CENTRE

Portia Lafond

**IN THE WAKE OF THE 1990** Oka Crisis between the Kanien'kehá:ka of Kanehsatà:ke and the Canadian military, Indigenous students met regularly at a coffee shop near the Hall Building. It was here where they discussed the importance of establishing a student-staffed Indigenous centre at Concordia. These student-led discussions were paralleled by institutional initiatives happening elsewhere in the university. A year later, the Native Research Project of Concordia University submitted a report to the Office of the Rector that contained thirty-nine recommendations outlining how the university could better address the educational needs of Indigenous students. The report examined the services, facilities, and programs then accessible to the university's First Nations, Inuit, and Métis student population. In 1992 the Office of the Rector responded to these findings by authorizing the formation of the Concordia Council on First Nations Education, which in turn recommended the creation of a First Nations Education Office. These efforts signalled an important step in the university recognizing that Indigenous students' studies "should encompass a holistic approach which is consistent with traditional First Nations education."[1]

As a result of Indigenous students' advocacy and organizing, the Native Student Centre finally opened its doors on September 8, 1992.[2] Initially, the centre was located in cramped quarters at 2110 Mackay Street. Within this small space, roughly thirty to sixty Indigenous students dropped by the centre per year. The centre emphasized traditional teaching practices and counselling services with the goal of reinforcing Indigenous cultural values and beliefs. Additionally, the centre offered resources such as academic advising and tutoring, as well as providing computer facilities and a student lounge. An arts and crafts component was included in the centre's programming, which gave a platform to Indigenous artists and speakers.[3]

To help connect students, the centre published *Arrowhead News*, a monthly newsletter that featured student articles on upcoming events, academic scholarships

---

**PORTIA LAFOND** is a Concordia graduate and former staff assistant at the Otsenhákta Student Centre.

42.1 In 1995 Manon Tremblay was appointed director of the Centre for Native Education. As described in her oral history interview excerpted earlier in this volume, Tremblay led the centre for fifteen years, where she attended to a host of needs that directly impacted Indigenous students. (The full transcript of this interview can be accessed at Records Management and Archives.)

at Concordia, as well as lighter fare such as recipes and jokes. In 2000 *Arrowhead News* became a four-page format that continued to publish on crucial Indigenous history and current events. Additionally, the centre included a kitchen equipped with a fridge, microwave, oven, coffee maker, kettle, toaster, dishes, and utensils. The centre also kept food on hand for disadvantaged students, which more financially secure students contributed to by way of donation.[4]

Due to space issues, the centre moved multiple times in the years ahead, before settling in its current location in the Hall Building. In the early 2000s the centre adopted the name the Aboriginal Student Resource Centre. In 2021 a naming competition was held to rename the centre. Indigenous students voted to rename it the Otsenhákta Student Centre (OSC).[5] In the Kanien'kéha language, the word *otsenhákta* means "near the fire"—a place that provides warmth and safety, where counsel is given, and ideas are shared between equals. To decolonize the university, students thought it was essential to adopt this name.

On September 16, 2022, the OSC, hosted its first Powwow, which was open to the wider university community. The event was meant to celebrate First Nations, Inuit,

42.2 A beading workshop hosted by the Centre for Native Education in February 1997. In addition to workshops, the centre has hosted other participatory activities such as dancing, performances, and singing, all of which aim to connect Indigenous students with traditional cultural practices. The centre was renamed the Otsenhákta Student Centre in 2021 and an annual Powwow was inaugurated in 2022.

and Métis students and mark the thirtieth anniversary of the OSC. Attendees gathered to watch singing and dancing. These performances showcased Indigenous knowledge and cultures. The Powwow also supported Indigenous entrepreneurs by showcasing handmade crafts and natural products. This was a momentous day in Concordia and OSC history as it contributed to efforts to decolonize the university.

The centre remains a welcoming space for all registered Indigenous students. It offers a warm, safe place with various resources for students travelling outside their community to attend Concordia, and provides academic resources and hosts cultural events such beading and moccasin making. The OSC also hosts social events such as skating and bowling, while remaining committed to ensuring Indigenous students feel safe and get the support they need to succeed in a colonial setting. Its weekly electronic newsletter, whose content is produced by student staff, remains a hit. This digital successor to *Arrowhead News* keeps Indigenous students informed and includes popular sections such as students' pets. This is a fun way to reach and engage other Indigenous students in a digital format. The OSC also provides an Indigenous graduation ceremony, in which Indigenous students can celebrate their accomplishments with other Indigenous students and staff. It is a beautiful event that aims to share Indigenous pride.

The future of the OSC is bright. Currently, there are plans to hire more cultural staff to further help make the university more culturally safe. The OSC hopes to see a potential First Peoples house, similar to those found in other Canadian campuses, providing additional space for Indigenous students to live and access resources. The OSC has come a long way since the 1990s, changing multiple names and locations, while grappling with changing resources. Throughout it all, the centre has served Concordia's diverse First Nations, Inuit, and Métis communities all the while striving towards a decolonized future for the university's diverse Indigenous student population.

NOTES

1  Internal Memorandum: First Nations Education, September 24, 1992, 2–6, I0057, Concordia University, Records Management and Archives (hereafter RMA). Gail Valaskakis, who chaired the Concordia Council on First Nations Education, circulated this internal memorandum with the Office of the Rector, the vice-rectors, and faculty deans. Included in this memorandum was a background summary of the Native Research Project at Concordia and other related initiatives aimed at extending Indigenous education at the university.

2  In 1994 the centre was renamed the Centre for Native Education.

3  Manon Tremblay, "Welcome to Our History – Activity Report for the Centre for Native Education," April 1997, P0169, Advocacy and Support Services fonds, RMA.

4  Information in this paragraph comes from *Centre for Native Education Annual Report, 2000–2001*, I0169 Advocacy and Support Services fonds, RMA.

5  Christian Duran, "Concordia's Aboriginal Student Resource Centre Gets a Meaningful New Name," Concordia News, January 25, 2021, https://www.concordia.ca/news/stories/2021/01/25/concordias-aboriginal-student-resource-centre-gets-a-meaningful-new-name.html.

**Anthony Howe**
*Di-Octo II* (detail), 2017

Stainless steel, fabricated by Show Canada (7.62 metres high)
Exterior, Henry F. Hall Building, SGW campus

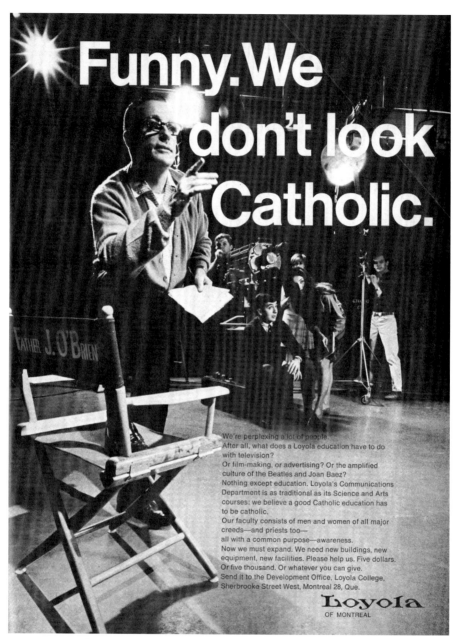

43.1 The above advertisement in *Time Magazine* illustrates the changes that Loyola underwent in the 1960s. In a sign of the times, the college's promotional material in these years emphasized de-confessionalism and a shift towards a more secular liberal arts education.

# A SHORT HISTORY OF THEOLOGICAL STUDIES AND ITS NON-CONFESSIONAL PEDAGOGY

Gabriel A. Desjardins

**THE DEPARTMENT OF THEOLOGICAL STUDIES** is distinct for its non-confessional approach to the discipline, as compared with programs that focus on a particular Christian denomination, be it Catholic, Orthodox, or the many forms of Protestantism. Concordia's non-confessional approach allows students to explore their faith (or lack thereof) without doctrinal or creedal pressure, providing them with the means to experience diverse perspectives and to question their own views.

I experienced this non-confessional approach firsthand while studying theology at Concordia. I was what could be labelled a "fundamentalist," a religious person who believed in a strict, literal form of this tradition and of the Bible. Attending a non-confessional department of theology enabled me to question my fundamentalist upbringing. It presented me with a broad range of theological, spiritual, and religious perspectives, which in effect allowed me to broaden my own view of the world. The Department of Theological Studies had a profound impact on the trajectory of my life, and in turn I was curious about the trajectory of this department. I wanted to know how a department with roots at Loyola College, a Jesuit institution, had developed into a place where no overriding doctrine dictates its curriculum, and where a past fundamentalist like me could have the course of their life altered.

After delving into Concordia's archives, I was surprised to learn that Theological Studies has wrestled with openness and ecumenism since its inception in the 1960s. Loyola College itself began fostering an ecumenical identity in the years leading up to the 1974 merger with Sir George Williams University (SGWU). However, the Department of Theological Studies struggled in the post-merger context, with SGWU bringing its own Department of Religion to the newly founded Concordia University. As a result, the Department of Theological Studies rallied behind the Catholic identity of Loyola in an attempt to remain relevant, yet as the years progressed it returned to the ecumenism it fostered prior to the merger; and it is this return to openness that

---

**GABRIEL A. DESJARDINS** is a graduate of the Department of Theological Studies at Concordia University. His research explores evangelical fundamentalism and methods for promoting dialogue. He has published with the *Journal of the School of Religious Studies McGill University*, *Studia Universitatis Babeș-Bolyai Theologia Reformata Transylvanica*, and *Word in the World*.

has made the department into a place where students can learn the discipline in a non-confessional manner, and as such where they can interact with diverse perspectives and cultures, which, as was my experience, can have the effect of broadening their own perspectives. In this brief chapter, I demonstrate key elements of this transformation.

## The Ecumenism of Loyola College

The story of the Department of Theological Studies begins with Loyola College, which itself stretches as far back as 1848 with the founding of St. Mary's College by the Jesuits of Montreal.[1] The Jesuits are generally known for being ecumenical. However, like many places of higher learning at the time, Loyola College aimed to provide a Christian education that would permeate its curriculum, even though a distinct department of theology was not created until the 1960s. It was in the same period that the department was created and within the context of Catholic education that Loyola fostered a disposition of openness and ecumenism, particularly through the presidency of Reverend Patrick G. Malone, often referred to as "Father President."

Malone's presidency lasted fifteen years (1959–1974), during which he "transformed the college into one of the most progressive Catholic campuses in North America."[2] His efforts impacted the Department of Theology, which taught compulsory courses in Catholic theology to all students. Twelve credits were required by each student and much of the focus was on the Catholic tradition. Towards the end of the 1960s, compulsory Catholic theology was becoming increasingly irrelevant as more and more students from diverse theological and faith backgrounds joined the college.[3]

## The Dechene Affair, 1967

By the late 1960s, the Department of Theology was employing "non-Jesuit" professors,[4] one of whom was Arthur (Art) Dechene. He was known for approaching theology with a critical lens, which created tension among some faculty members in the department.[5] This professor was also embroiled in controversy during the 1966–67 academic year, where a letter was sent by college administration insinuating that Loyola would not renew Dechene's teaching contract for the upcoming academic year (1967–68) since he did not have a doctorate. Dechene believed that the administration made this decision due to his unconventional way of teaching theology, and as such he felt it an affront to his academic freedom. Students agreed with Dechene and saw the administration's decision as demonstrating the need for student representation on college governance. They argued that the vast majority of faculty at Loyola did not have a doctorate and that the same was true of faculty in the Department of Theology.[6]

This controversy resulted in a student rally that occurred on the steps of the Loyola Chapel in January 1967, where students were told to stop attending theology classes until the issue was resolved.[7] Encouraged by students from campuses throughout Canada who also began seeking and obtaining representation on faculty councils, boards of governors, and other such committees, the student rally at Loyola College successfully obtained seats on Loyola's governance and on various department councils,[8] including that of the Department of Theology.[9] Though he was absent during the rally, Dechene saw himself and the issue surrounding his teaching contract as catalysts for the student movement and what it achieved.[10] He concluded that "Students should persist in questioning the Administration, until they produce evidence that academic freedom does in no way influence their decisions of policy."[11]

Dechene's contract ended despite student effort to save his career at Loyola. He would later complete a doctorate at Columbia Pacific University and then establish a teaching career at Austin Community College. Though he left Loyola, Dechene and the controversy surrounding his departure played an important role in the transformation of the Department of Theology towards openness and ecumenism. The department renamed itself the Department of Theological Studies in 1969 to capture this image of ecumenism and plurality, which they noted had been their policy for a number of years.[12] Theology also moved away from being compulsory, as it became optional for arts students beginning in the 1967–68 academic year. All students, whether Catholic or of other faiths, were likewise provided the choice between courses in theological studies and religious studies, the former focusing on Catholic theology and the latter focusing on a broader range of religious perspectives and traditions.[13]

## Theological Studies and the Department of Religion

The merger with SGWU in 1974 brought complications for the Department of Theological Studies. SGWU had its own programs in religious studies that were taught by its Department of Religion, and the original merger proposal recommended retaining a split between SGWU's Religion Department and Loyola College's Theological Studies. This split was recommended due to each department's unique approach to religion and because of Theological Studies' apparent preservation of Loyola's Catholic identity. Theological Studies objected to this perspective due to the department's ecumenical disposition. It saw itself as already teaching a plurality of theological and religious perspectives, and as such the department saw no need in retaining a separation between Theological Studies and the Department of Religion.[14]

In any case, SGWU and Loyola College merged in 1974 with separate departments of theological studies and religion. Leading up to the merger, Loyola sought to protect its Catholic heritage and unique philosophy of education.[15] Loyola and SGWU agreed to retain their own separate faculties of arts and science, with one faculty of arts and science located on the SGWU campus and another located on the Loyola Campus.[16] However, this separation did not last long. One year after Concordia

University was established, talks began to join the disparate faculties, a process that was not fully complete until 1986.[17] What would become the sole Faculty of Arts and Science included a continued separation between Theological Studies and the Department of Religion.

After the merger, Theological Studies marketed itself towards anglophone Catholics, seemingly acquiescing to the role of providing Catholic theology to a Catholic clientele.[18] The department needed to distinguish itself within the newly formed university, given that the Religion Department covered religious traditions beyond Roman Catholicism, a role that Theological Studies previously undertook at Loyola College. As a result, many theology courses became obsolete since the Department of Religion offered similar courses for several topics.[19] This was especially the case with courses that taught non-Christian and non-Catholic theology and religion. These developments led to Theological Studies losing several faculty positions and struggling during the immediate aftermath of the 1974 merger. In the same period, there was a sense of disunity among the faculty of Theological Studies.[20]

During the consolidation of the two faculties of arts and science, a merger between the Department of Religion and Theological Studies was considered in the early 1980s. This potential merger was met with opposition from the Department of Religion, which thought that further association with Theological Studies and its Catholic theologians would hinder its relationship with the Jewish community, a relationship that had been fostered since the late 1960s with the creation of its MA in Jewish studies. The Department of Religion also opposed the merger due to distinctions between theological and religious studies, where religious studies takes a comparative approach to religion rooted in methodologies of the social sciences, whereas theological studies approaches a specific religious context typically within the paradigms of that religion while applying methodologies from the humanities.[21]

Despite the tensions between the two departments, the Department of Religion provided space in its programs for Theological Studies to teach graduate courses for theology students towards an MA program administered by the Department of Religion.[22] The two departments also collaborated on the Theological, Religious, and Ethical Studies (TRES) program, along with the Department of Philosophy. This program provided religious, ethical, and philosophical education for teachers and lasted until the 1990s. The department also made several attempts to create its own MA program, including a proposal to create an MA through the Department of Religion, which Religion rejected. Efforts finally paid off in 1995 when Theological Studies successfully created its own MA program.[23]

### From the 1990s to the Present

The mid-1990s also saw Theological Studies weather another difficult period, after the university offered early retirement for professors and librarians, resulting in retirements of more than 20 percent of professors in the Faculty of Arts and Science.[24] Along with tight budget restrictions, this exodus of retirees further strained the department, reducing its number of full-time faculty to approximately two professors, one of whom was Pamela Bright.[25]

In the late 1990s, Professor Bright (who was chair at the time) rebuilt the department from this precarious situation, which also provided a much-needed opportunity to diversify the previously male and Catholic dominant faculty.[26] Over time, she added faculty members from Eastern Orthodox, Protestant, and even non-Christian backgrounds. This diversity of theological perspectives enabled the department to return to the ecumenical disposition it adopted during the transformative years before the merger, and this return to openness has lasted to the present day.[27]

The department has since continued to broaden its curriculum by adding perspectives from outside traditional theology. In 2018 a course in Indigenous spirituality was added as a core component of the BA in theological studies. This course provides students an opportunity to experience Indigenous practices, epistemologies, and axiologies, within the framework of humanity's relationship to the land. Another course in theology explores pilgrimage and encourages students to walk from Concordia University to Kahnawá:ke.[28] The walk represents an act of building bridges across cultures, which itself exemplifies the role of theology—which is to serve as a bridge between and among diverse perspectives as they relate to questions of mystery and meaning.

## Conclusion

The story of Theological Studies is that of a department that weathered the altered landscape of the 1974 merger to form a new and unique identity. The department has oscillated between the heritage of Loyola College and its ecumenical disposition. It has also retained an identity separate from the Department of Religion and Cultures and is in fact one of the last departments of theology in Quebec, given that many similar departments at other Quebec institutions have either been dissolved or folded into departments of religion.[29]

The Department of Theological Studies at Concordia is an echo of both the college within which it was formed and of the university through which it developed a unique and ecumenical approach to the discipline. The department is a place where students are provided space to reflect on their own traditions, which allows them to broaden their perspectives. Such an outcome is the result of a department and an institution that welcome different traditions and cultures, providing room for dialogue and interaction. Such a place is also where new ideas are fostered and where lives like mine are changed.

## NOTES

1   T.P. Slattery, *Loyola and Montreal – A History* (Montreal: Palm Publishers, 1962), 41; John Hodgins, "Loyola: The Beginning," *Jesuit Bulletin Anniversary Issue, 1943–1993*, 12.

2   *Academic News*, March 21, 1974, 2, I0005 Department of Theological Studies fonds, Concordia University, Records Management and Archives (hereafter RMA).

3   *History of the Department of Theological Studies 1964–1994*, 1, I0005 Department of Theological Studies fonds, RMA.

4   Charles H. Henkey, Acting Chairman, to Patrick J. Malone, President, Loyola College, February 28, 1966, Correspondence, I0147 Office of the President fonds, RMA.

5   Department meeting minutes, November 30, 1966, 1, I0005 Department of Theological Studies fonds, RMA.

6   "Dechene Status Uncertain: Administration Stand Clouded as Public Opinion Grows," *Loyola News* 43, no. 6 (January 17, 1967): https://archive.org/details/loyola-news-1967-january-17/mode/2up.

7   Allanah Murphy, "Protest Rally Set for Today," *Loyola News* 43, no. 27 (January 20, 1967): https://archive.org/details/loyola-news-1967-january-20.

8   Kathy Coughlin, "Faculty Judges Rally, Student Movement," *Loyola News* 43, no. 29 (January 27, 1967): https://archive.org/details/loyola-news-1967-january-27-incomplete/page/n7/mode/2up

9   Department meeting minutes, February 19, 1969, 1, I0005 Department of Theological Studies fonds, RMA.

10  Coughlin, "Faculty Judges Rally."

11  Coughlin, "Faculty Judges Rally."

12  See Department meeting minutes, October 20, 1969, I0005 Department of Theological Studies fonds, RMA.

13  See Department meeting minutes, March 1, 1967, I0005 Department of Theological Studies fonds, RMA.

14  Charles B. Paris, Secretary, Department of Theological Studies, to Patrick G. Malone, President, Loyola College, February 5, 1970, I0005 Department of Theological Studies, RMA, 3-4.

15  A 1972 historical survey of discussions between Loyola College and SGWU demonstrates the importance for Loyola of retaining its Catholic heritage. See *Historical Survey: Relations between Sir George Williams University and Loyola, Office of the Principal*, July 13, 1972, 4, RMA-SQW-Publications, RMA-Concordia-Publications, https://archive.org/details/1972-07-13-historical-survey-relations-between-sgwu-and-loyola.

16  The proposal to form two arts and science faculties was made in 1971. *Historical Survey*, 12–13.

17  For more information on the gradual move to join the disparate arts and science faculties, see Aloysius Graham, Vice-Rector, and Principal of Loyola Campus, to J. W. O'Brien, Rector, Concordia University, November 4, 1976, I0010 Office of the Principal fonds, RMA; see also Rodolphe Morissette, "Concordia: La structure académique dépendrait de trois vice-recteurs," *Le Devoir*, February 11, 1977, I0010 Office of the Principal fonds, RMA.

18  Prior to the merger, Theological Studies made no specific mentions to Catholicism when describing its programs. See *Department of Theological Studies – Report*, February 27, 1973, 1–9, I0005 Department of Theological Studies fonds, RMA. However, this situation changed by the 1980s where the department identified English Catholics as a primary clientele. See Michael Fahey, Chairman, Committee on Planning & Priorities and John Ryan, Chairman, Department of Theological Studies, memorandum correspondance re: Academic Directions, April 26, 1982, 3, I0005 Department of Theological Studies fonds, RMA.

19  For example, prior to the merger, Theological Studies taught courses in atheism and religious traditions outside of Christianity.

20  The dwindling numbers and the problem of disunity had been developing just prior to the merger, evidence of which can be seen in an external evaluation that occurred in 1973. See Fred E. Crowe, Charles E. Curran, and Jean-Louis D'Aragon, *Report of the Presidential Committee on Theology at Loyola, Office of the President*, December 27, 1973, 6–7, RMA-Loyola-Publications, RMA-Concordia-Publications, https://archive.org/details/1973-12-27-report-on-theology-at-loyola/mode/2up.

21  Michael Oppenheim, Chair, Department of Religion to C. Bertrand, Dean, Arts and Science Faculty, November 28, 1985, Correspondence, 1–5, I0097 Department of Religions and Cultures fonds, RMA.

22  Frederick Bird, Graduate Program Director, Religion to Charles Davis, Religion, November 18, 1974, Memorandum, 1–3, I0097 Department of Religions and Cultures fonds, RMA.

23  See Self-Appraisal Committee, *Self-Appraisal Report – Department of Theological Studies*, I0005 Department of Theological Studies fonds, December 2002, 3, RMA-Concordia-Publications, https://archive.org/details/2002-12-self-appraisal-report-department-of-theological-studies.

24  Ad Hoc Committee on Resource Allocation in the Faculty of Arts & Science, *The Allocation of Resources in the Faculty of Arts and Science: Process and Principles, Faculty of Arts and Science*, June 26, 1996, 1, RMA-Concordia-Publications, https://archive.org/details/1996-06-26-the-allocation-of-resources-in-the-faculty-of-arts-and-science.

25  See "Remembering Pamela Bright," *Concordia University News*, November 23, 2012, https://www.concordia.ca/cunews/main/stories/2012/11/23/remembering-pamela-bright.html.

26  Self-Appraisal Committee, *Self-Appraisal Report*, 19.

27  According to the department's 2002 self-appraisal, interfaith dialogue became an increasing feature of theological studies at Concordia. See Self-Appraisal Committee, *Self-Appraisal Report*, 30–31.

28  For more on the pilgrimage to Kahnawake, see Matthew Anderson, "From Old Montreal to Kahnawake: A 34-km pilgrimage to combat ignorance," *Concordia University News*, June 18, 2014, https://www.concordia.ca/cunews/main/stories/2014/06/18/from-old-montreal tokahnawakea34kmpilgrimagetocombatignorance.html.

29  For more information on the state of theology at higher education institutions in Quebec, see Jean-François Roussel, "SCT: Theology Today in Quebec: A Time of Transition," *Studies in Religion / Sciences religieuses* 50, no. 3 (2021): 356–64, https://doi.org/10.1177/00084298211036454.

**Holly King**
*Seascape and the Sublime,* 2005

Chromogenic print mounted on aluminum (410 cm x 350 cm)
Metro Entrance, Engineering, Computer Science and Visual Arts Integrated Complex, SGW campus

# THE THOUSAND AND ONE ADVENTURES OF FRENCH AT CONCORDIA UNIVERSITY

Françoise Naudillon

**BEFORE THE ARRANGED** marriage of Loyola College and Sir George Williams, both English-language institutions already offered French courses to their respective students. Several symbols bear witness to this and we offer, here, a few milestones from yesterday to today. In 1967 Loyola College student Lynn Ranger won the French Language Prize at the Seventy-First Convocation. For many years, Loyola College had been offering evening classes in French in their university courses. The same is true of Sir George Williams. In her article "Again the Air Conditioners: Finding Poetry in the Institutional Archive," Christine Mitchell recalls the experiment carried out as early as 1967 by French teacher Gilbert Taggart to produce a fifty-two-episode French course that combined video and language laboratory exercises, and could be self-administered by students at Sir George.[1]

Since then, the Département d'études françaises at Concordia has undergone many changes but remains the heir to the original experiments conducted by the two institutions that preceded it. Those who lived through it will remember that the integration of Sir George Williams and Loyola teachers was not easy. For a long time, until the late 1990s, the Département d'études françaises was geographically divided, with some professors retaining their offices on the Loyola campus and others downtown. Similarly, some of the library's French-language collections were still only available for consultation on the Loyola campus.

Today, the Département d'études françaises comprises three areas of teaching and expertise—literature, French language instruction, and translation—and it has continued to build up its identity year after year. It sees itself as an open window on the Francophonie worlds and cultures that share the French language. In literature, for example, in collaboration with the Simone de Beauvoir Institute, of which Maïr Verthuy was its first director, several courses devoted to women's literature were

---

**FRANÇOISE NAUDILLON** is a Professor in the Département d'études françaises at Concordia University specializing in francophone literatures and paraliteratures and their reception. In particular, she works on discourses of reception, popular literatures including comic strips, and Afrofuturist narratives.

44.1 Loyola French Studies student, Lynn Ranger, winner of the French Language Prize, 1967, awarded at Loyola College's 71st annual convocation.

created. Women's literature studies have constituted the department's reputation. With professors teaching in both Département d'études françaises and the Simone de Beauvoir Institute, bridges were quickly established and a number of critical studies on Quebec women authors were published. Courses in French literature also included literary history, literary and cultural panorama courses, and, of course, special topics on contemporary French authors. Quebec literature courses are particularly popular with students. For many, they are the anchor and reference point for knowledge of Quebec culture. Finally, the Département d'études françaises has developed, and continues to develop, courses in the French literature of Africa and the Caribbean.

Continuing in the tradition established at its birth, the department also offers courses in French linguistics and French as a second language. This is one of its essential missions within an English-speaking university. True to its history, the department uses

44.2 A Language Laboratory at Loyola College as seen in circa 1969. Both of Concordia' founding institutions had language labs in the 1960s and 1970s. At Sir George Williams University curriculum coordinator James Whitelaw founded the first language lab. He continued to promote French at the university while serving as Concordia's first associate vice-rector, academic from 1974 to 1984.

original learning methods and trains numerous cohorts of students each year, offering them a wide range of francization activities. The programs attract international students who also appreciate paying the same tuition fees as Quebec students.

The department's reputation is undoubtedly built on its translation studies programs. In Canada, with its two official languages, French and English, and in an increasingly interconnected world, translators are indispensable. Professors Jean-Marc Gouanvic, Sherry Simon, and Judith Woodsworth have made translation studies and professional translation programs one of the department's key assets. All the more so as it is the only university program offering training in translation from English into French and from French into English. As one can see, the Département d'études françaises has evolved considerably over the years. At the heart of the university, it represents not only an opening onto Montreal and its teeming cultural life, but also a gateway to other cultures that share the French language.

### NOTE

1   Christine Mitchell, "Again the Air Conditioners: Finding Poetry in the Institutional Archive," *Amodern*, no. 4 (March 2015), https://amodern.net/article/again-air-conditioners/.

# A HISTORY OF THE EARLY CHILDHOOD AND ELEMENTARY PROGRAM, 1971–2021

Ellen Jacobs and Nina Howe

**HOW DID TEACHER** education at Concordia start and how did the university become the pioneering leader in Quebec with an emphasis on the early years? The Early Childhood Education (ECE) program began at Sir George Williams University (SGWU) in fall 1971 with the mission to create a play-based, social-constructivist educational program. Building on North American and European initiatives that focused on the growth and development of preschool children (e.g., US Head Start [1964], Italian Montessori [1906], Scandinavian childcare [1970s]), the Concordia program was the pioneer and leader for early childhood education in Quebec. At that time, in Quebec, only private, half-day nursery school programs were available for three- to five-year-olds; public kindergartens were available for five-year-olds, but attendance was not required for grade one entry. To teach in a public school, teacher certification for kindergarten was required. In the early 1960s, BEd certification was obtained either at McGill University or Saint Joseph's College, Montreal. Neither training program was geared specifically to the preschool period of development or for teaching pre-kindergarten or kindergarten children. The lack of a preschool focus was the impetus for SGWU to develop an ECE teacher education program.

The BA major in ECE (a three-year ninety-credit major), created to respond to educational and community needs, required a two-year CEGEP diploma for admission.[1] Certification to teach was limited to preschool and kindergarten programs in the public and private sectors. The first two faculty members, Donna White and

---

ELLEN JACOBS is Distinguished Professor Emeritus in the Department of Education. She is co-author of the School-Age Care Environment Rating Scale (SACERS). She is the founder of the Concordia University Observation Nursery and founding editor of the *Canadian Journal of Research in Early Childhood Education*.

NINA HOWE is Distinguished Professor Emeritus, Department of Education, and held the Concordia University Research Chair in Early Childhood Development and Education. She taught in BA (early childhood and elementary education; child studies) and graduate (MA in child study; PhD in education) programs.

Ellen Jacobs, were responsible for designing the unique philosophy of the program with child development (zero to five years of age) at the core of all the courses. This approach distinguished the Concordia program from all other Quebec teacher education programs, which took a more traditional curriculum-based approach. Our social constructivist philosophy, which is a developmental, child-centred approach to teaching and learning and the creation of new knowledge, was the program's guiding principle. One unique aspect of our program was the three internships (one per year) every student was required to take. Another unique aspect was the development of a lab school, the Observation Nursery, where students observed best practices of the highly qualified teachers and developed their teaching skills under the watchful eye of a faculty member.

In 1979 the BA major in ECE became a specialization in ECE with certification for graduates to teach pre-kindergarten to grade three. A major curriculum change reflected the need for a broader coverage of issues related to ECE and resulted in more focused foundations courses and the addition of methods courses for teaching language arts, math, and science. In 1983 another significant curriculum revision involved the development of a seminar for each internship course.

In the early 1990s the Quebec government announced a reform to the Quebec Education Plan and restructured the school system from religious-based to linguistic school boards. The reform embraced a social-constructivist curriculum (kindergarten to grade eleven) along with a competency-based, cross-curricular approach.[2] According to an anecdotal report from a committee member of the group reviewing teacher education programs across Quebec universities, our philosophical approach influenced the ministry's redesign of teacher education.[3] This philosophical approach reflected a meaningful and appropriate model of early childhood and elementary education as advocated by international experts and in comparison to the ministry's prior more traditional curriculum. The reform increased the length of all education programs from 3 to 4 years (90 to 120 credits) to accommodate the increased number of hours of school-based internships. In Concordia's case, the reform also added a focus on grades four through six and resulted in the creation of our BA specialization in early childhood and elementary education (ECEE).

From the early days, research has been an important focus of our ECEE faculty. According to Richard Schmid, the former chair and long-time member of the Department of Education, the unit has been highly respected for the research its faculty has conducted over the last fifty years. The international reputation of the ECEE unit is evident in several metrics. Three faculty members have been awarded Concordia University Research Chairs (Nina Howe, Senior Career; Helena Osana, Mid-career; Holly Recchia, Early Career). The success of our ECEE faculty can be measured by the many external grants, extensive number of publications in high-quality and top-tier journals, numerous presentations at international scholarly conferences, and workshops for teachers, educators, and parents. Our faculty have also been active on editorial boards of journals and as grant, manuscript, and media reviewers. Ellen Jacobs founded the *Canadian Journal of Research in Early Childhood Education* (1985–2001) and in 1995 Nina Howe joined as co-editor. In conclusion, Concordia's program has been recognized as the foundational early childhood education program in Quebec. A more detailed history of the ECEE program has been placed in the university archives.[4]

### NOTES

1   CEGEPs are Quebec's system of pre-university college and vocational education.

2   See Michael Weiner, "Quebec Teachers: Submerged in a Sea of Reform," *McGill Journal of Education* 34, no. 3 (1990): 261–80; and William J. Smith, William J. Foster, and Helen M. Donahue, "The Transformation of Educational Governance in Quebec: A Reform Whose Time Has Finally Come," *McGill Journal of Education* 34, no. 3 (1999): 207–25.

3   William J. Smith and William F. Foster, "Educational Restructuring in Quebec: The Third Wave of Reform," *McGill Journal of Education* 34, no. 3 (1999): 201–5.

4   See Ellen Jacobs and Nina Howe, "History of Early Childhood and Elementary Program (1971–2021)," July 2020, I0022 Department of Education fonds, Concordia University, Records Management and Archives.

46.1 End-of-year performance at the Concordia Theatre, April 2019. Choreography: Mark Durand and Eva Myers. Dancers (*left to right*): Olivia Jaen Flores, Eva Myers, Mark Durand, Jaeli Anik Vialard, Camille Mougenot.

# LEAPING ACROSS TIME: FOUR DECADES OF CONTEMPORARY DANCE AT CONCORDIA UNIVERSITY

Silvy Panet-Raymond

**MONTREAL ENTERED** the 1980s driven by a new generation of artists and cultural workers. Sensing the zeitgeist, Alfred Pinsky, then dean of fine arts, solicited Australian-born, visionary dancer Elizabeth Langley to craft the modern dance program, followed by myself, Silvy Panet-Raymond, who went from part-time instructor to department chair, piloting the program solo in 1986 and transforming it into the Department of Contemporary Dance. I was an award-winning interdisciplinary choreographer/performer who had recently co-founded Tangente, the first organization to specialize in dance presentation in Quebec, now housed at the Wilder Building in Montreal's Quartier des spectacles. Initially, there were few suitable premises for dance at the university. Teaching happened in two vacated classrooms on the top floor of the Victoria School annex with performances in the large gym below. Aptly named Informals, the showings of student works attracted an audience that freely came and went, some with picnics and pillows. In the late 1980s, both Departments of Contemporary Dance and Theatre moved into Loyola's TJ Annex, not far

---

SILVY PANET-RAYMOND's curiosity about the myriad forms of mobility connects her imagination to worlds beyond. She has charted vast territories with students, built structures for future generations, and won prizes as a choreographer. She works across various media, collaborates on art in/through public space, and tends to be nomadic when not sedentary.

from the music department. Maintaining visibility and connections with the downtown cultural milieu was more challenging, though it fostered a different kind of proximity. In 2009 the department moved into the new John Molson Building (MB) downtown, and space planners considered dance's needs to have state-of-the art, versatile facilities, easily adapted for both classes and shows.

As one of the only university dance programs in the world where professors and guest artists do not choreograph on students, ample room is given for the artistic autonomy of students to take root and grow. The program's original mission shaped by Langley remains to this day: to provide students with the conditions to evolve their own choreographic vision while acquiring performance experience, technical skills, critical thinking, and hands-on production know-how. Same mission, new momentum, broadening horizons.

The MB studios provide students with opportunities to apply stagecraft skills while gaining academic credits to organize, curate, and present Studio 7 (previously called Informals), the monthly pluridisciplinary platforms. Much of these developments would not have been possible without Professor Michael Montanaro, who joined the department in 1995 after successfully directing his own dance company. His knowledge of artistic and technological production, coupled with a keen sense of creative inventiveness, encompasses two of Concordia's mottos of the time: "give wings to your imagination" and the subsequent rebranded "real education for the real world."

Collaborative projects foster partnerships that, in many cases, continue beyond graduation. For the second edition of Concordia's first Art Matters festival, I teamed my capstone choreography class with music students to compose works shown at Oscar Peterson Hall. For many, the festival continues to act as a springboard into a professional career. The yearly *60 x 60* show is a popular public event featuring one hour of sixty-second compositions by music, theatre, and dance students with lighting designed by scenography students with guidance from Concordia Theatre's technical production staff along with faculty from the three departments and funding from the Evenko Foundation. In addition to opportunities for live performance, experiential learning takes a wider variety of forms both inside and outside Concordia, including an immersion into Montreal's renowned annual Festival TransAmériques, and an intensive summer course initially taught by Associate Professor Angélique Willkie, a performer/dramaturg and a Prix de la danse recipient, who joined the department in 2015. Over the years, a number of off-campus creation residencies have taken place, such as at the Monument National Theatre with the National Theatre School's lighting design students and faculty; film and choreography collaborations with graduate studies from the School of Cinema that explore fiction, documentary, and virtual reality; and collaborations with studio arts student exhibitions in the FOFA Gallery; there are outreach workshops in underprivileged inner-city schools and community

46.2 Contact sheet. Students rehearsing in the Victoria School Annex gym and studios, 1982.

centres, as well as numerous internships with professional organizations. The wide-ranging experience that continues to be imparted to students by professionally active part-time and full-time faculty since the department's inception benefits students who learn to craft dance in its many forms, through low-fi or new media, to reach technical excellence, hone critical skills, make more and better choreography, and distinctively become agents of social transformation.

Alumni have shaped the immediate cultural milieux as creators, producers, and thinkers in various fields. Amongst them are Wants&Needs dance co-directors Andrew Tay and Sasha Kleinplatz, producers of Short&Sweet, who sell out events in major cities, featuring an eclectic roster of artists. As Toronto Dance Theatre's new artistic director, Tay is injecting bold ideas carried by a greater diversity of talent in the metropolis. Dana Michel, first dance artist in residence at Ottawa's National Arts Centre, reaps rewards from the Venice Biennale and other festivals for iconoclastic performances that embrace the complex intersections of Blackness.

Langley retired in 1997, but remains active as a dance dramaturg even in her ninth decade. The department's two senior faculty members, Professors Emeriti Montanaro and I recently retired and are respectively engaged national and international projects. Building on the original mission with new partners, Willkie, who chaired the President's Anti-Black Racism Task Force, is featured in a number of performance projects. She is joined by Professor and Department Chair Jens Richard Giersdorf, a critical dance scholar (formerly at Marymount Manhattan College, NYC), and Lilia Mestre, an experienced performance maker, writer, and curator who was artistic coordinator of a.pass (Advanced Performance and Scenography Studies) in Brussels. Sustaining change through movement.

*The author thanks Elizabeth Langley and Michael Montanaro for their valuable insights.*

# ELECTROACOUSTIC STUDIES AT THE DEPARTMENT OF MUSIC

Kevin Austin

**A MAJOR MILESTONE** was reached in 2000 when the Faculty of Fine Arts' Office of the Dean brought the major in electroacoustic studies to Faculty Council for formal recognition. Designed thirty years before in 1970–71, "sound from a loudspeaker"—electroacoustics—became a major area in the Department of Music. The electroacoustic studies area focuses on the individual, creativity, and perception, which removes the program from being "about" the technology. The orientation and objectives of the electroacoustic programs parallel the vision of the founder of the Department of Music in 1974, Professor Phillip Cohen.

The university's first electronic music studio was hand assembled from found and borrowed tape recorders, speakers, and wooden tables. Only the very young and very adventurous wanted to spend time with this new aesthetic that formed a basis of the discipline of sound design. Sound design in film had been called sound effects or foley, and in the mid-1970s the term began turning up in the credits of films. Electronic music had been around since the earliest days of the talkies, dependent upon the invention of the vacuum tube and loudspeakers, and the experimental work of film animation artists who drew the waveshapes onto the film. Dancers and theatre people loved to work with sounds shaped to their creative desires.

The number of students in the classes grew from fewer than ten to more than thirty by the mid-1980s, spurred and supported by the music industry that built the first synthesizers. The numbers of interested students grew, a second-year course, a second and third studio, a small project recording studio, and a third-year course were added. Concordia's audio-visual departments helped every step of the way. With the introduction of the major in electroacoustic studies in 2000, the area already had a notable history and national and international recognition, including twenty years

---

Professor **KEVIN AUSTIN** has taught continuously at Concordia since 1970. He self-describes as a composer, educator, and artistic animator. He has composed occasionally in most musical idioms, and written course curricula in electroacoustics, ear-training, and music theory. He gives no possible retirement date.

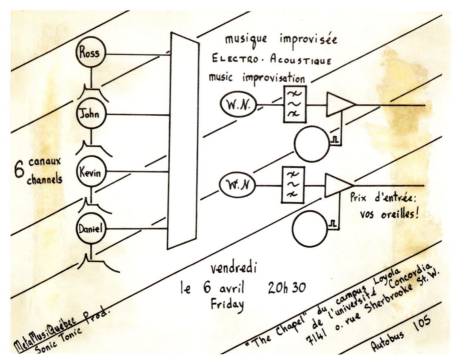

47.1 The Electroacoustic Composers Group hosted many concerts at Loyola beginning in the 1970s. Here a map helpfully directs would-be-attendees to the concert's location.

of electroacoustic and multimedia concerts; the founding home of the national electroacoustics association, Communauté électroacoustique Canadienne / Canadian Electroacoustic Community in 1984; a second full-time faculty member; the professional recording facility in the Oscar Peterson Concert Hall built in 1989–90; and sporadic interdepartmental collaborations with film, animation, theatre, dance, multimedia, performance art, and studio art installation practices.

The curricular core of the major in electroacoustic studies has remained rather constant for over five decades. It is not that the program has fallen behind the times, mostly because while the program adopted the technology for manipulating and building sounds, it was, and remains, the individual creative spirit that guides growth. This individual creative spirit is based on models of perception and the human mind. The materials consist of all sounds, the art of sounds, presented in their dominant distribution system, through loudspeakers.

The move of the department in 2008 from seventy-year-old cramped, often moist spaces to a near state-of-the-art facility on the eighth floor of the John Molson Building (MB) was another sign of recognition of the place and importance of the electroacoustic studies programs at Concordia. With support from the Faculty of Fine

# UNIVERSITÉ CONCORDIA

Music Department

Concordia Electro-acoustic Composers' Group      Series I Concert 2

1982-x-04

## Programme

*WAIT !                    KEVIN AUSTIN
                           DAVE LINDSAY
                           JAMES TALLON
                           JOHN WELLS
                               text: KEVIN AUSTIN

DOSWA                      ROBERT SCHERTZER

SUSPICIOUS                 DANIEL FEIST

— BREAK —

THE SNEEZE                 DAVE LINDSAY

ROCK IN THE WATER          JOHN WELLS

SELECTIONS                 JOHN WINIARZ

\* FIRST PERFORMANCE

(All composers are CAPAC)

47.2 A concert program from the early 1980s announcing the Electroacoustic Composers Group's upcoming live performance.

47.3 Kevin Austin (*second from right*) and friends before a live show on campus, circa 1982.

Arts' Centre for Digital Arts, today's electroacoustic studies program is now equipped with three multi-speaker studios and a classroom with nine channels, and features an historical tape archive of some 3,500 original pieces. Four full-time faculty members, along with nine part-time instructors, oversee the program's teaching load. Meanwhile, applications to the program are currently three to four times greater than the admissions quota. Along with an active student presence through the Concordia Electroacoustic Studies Student Association, the program boasts more than five hundred graduates to date, offering nine academic awards to students. All told, program growth continues to emphasize the importance of sound in the arts. This success would not have been possible without the aid of the hundreds of students, staff, faculty, and administrators who showed and have maintained their belief in and support for the development of electroacoustic studies.

## ORAL HISTORIES: Formations

### STEVEN APPELBAUM, FOUNDING OF THE EXECUTIVE MBA

*Piyusha Chatterjee: The Executive MBA program, tell me a little more about it. I'm wondering what kind of relationships did you build locally, through the program?*

Good question. Good question. So, when we started, we had an MBA program. It's basically: you pay your $3,000 for your fees, or whatever it was, and you take your courses. But it takes four years, five years, whatever it is, to graduate. The Executive MBA, you're done in two years. You come one week on a Friday; you take four courses. Eight o'clock to ten; 10:15 'til 12:15; 1:15 to 3:15; and 3:30 to 5:30. So, we designed it like that. Then you come on Saturday the next week. You basically lose one day of work, but if you're good, it doesn't matter with your boss. What we did was, one of my key associate deans named Roland Wills, who's now ninety-three years old and somebody I absolutely adore. And, we email each other every day. We've been friends forever. He did a survey in Montreal of what companies would pay for the students. I said to him, "Let's get the companies to pay." So, we'll have a tri-partite agreement: the company, the university, and the student. The company will *pay* for somebody, for the tuition. I think it was $20,000 then or something like that, way, way back. The student comes here, so they have one week, they don't work on Friday. Next week they give up their Saturday. So, in two years, they have sixteen courses. Yeah, they have sixteen courses, and they're done. But the courses, instead of being two and a half hours, are two hours, and the other half hour will be made up of a research paper that would constitute the other two hours that were

---

**STEVEN APPELBAUM** was a Professor of Management in the John Molson School of Business at Concordia University who started teaching at Concordia in 1979. A former Dean of the Business School, he helped found the Executive Master's of Business Administration program. This interview took place on Zoom on October 29, 2022.

**IRA ROBINSON** is Distinguished Professor Emeritus of Judaic Studies in the Department of Religion at Concordia University. He is also Chair and Director of the Concordia Institute for Canadian Jewish Studies and began teaching at Concordia in 1979. This interview took place at University Communications Services Studio on November 3, 2022.

**LINDA DYER** is Professor and Chair of the Department of Management in the John Molson School of Business at Concordia University. She has also served on the President's Task Force on Anti-Black Racism. This interview took place at the Centre for Oral History and Digital Storytelling on December 12, 2022.

different from the MBA. So, the companies were happy, the students were happy, the government approved it, and we got on the map.

And we got revenue. I was able to renovate rooms in the Guy Métro Building for the MBA program. We had nothing. We got rooms, and we tiered them, and we had kitchens, and we had breakout rooms. Nothing like we have now, in the MB Building. And we had students coming in from Ottawa. The University of Ottawa did not have an Executive MBA program. So, we had people from the government who came in on Friday night, stayed at a hotel, had classes on Saturday, or came in on Thursday night for the Friday classes ... In our classes, we had forty students in the classes. It would be forty students multiplied by sixteen or twenty thousand dollars. The money would go *right* into the faculty here, and I was able to renovate rooms. And that was one of the arguments I would have with the rector then: "It's not your money! *I'm* paying for the rooms; *I'm* paying for the renovations. I'm not taking any funding. I have to pay for the faculty members teaching this," because it was extra, so we had to pay them for overloads. "Had to pay for food. You can't take the budget away." His answer was: "I can do anything I want." And my answer was: "No, you can't." That was part of the battles. And I thought it was so *absurd* ... that the program would die. Well, the program didn't die, and the program is continuing to move along, and it has been successful, and it has been, as I said, thirty-seven years.

## IRA ROBINSON, RELIGIONS AND CULTURES

Well, back forty-plus years ago, the discipline of the study of religion was in the process of emancipating itself from the idea that there is a central major religious tradition and everybody else is somehow compared to it. This is how the study of religion got its start in North America, and it was very much a Christian-centred perspective with accommodations, if you will, for the study of Judaism, Islam, Buddhism, or whatever, but with the kind of idea that the main thing, the main game is Christianity. The Department of Religion at Concordia is the immediate descendant of the Department of Religion at Sir George Williams University, which was founded in 1959 by a professor named Boyd Sinyard. And Sinyard had a vision of decentring Christianity and introducing Judaism not as an appendage or Islam not as an appendage, or Buddhism not as an appendage to the study of Christianity, but as subjects in their own right. At that time, 1960s and 1970s, the designation Department of Religion was fairly standard for departments that were not heavily involved in Christian-centred study.

As opposed to that, for instance, at Loyola College, which is the other founding institution of Concordia University, there was a department of theology, which is the way Christian-centred departments were designated. And the Department of Theology maintained its Christian centrism, which meant that when Sir George and Loyola merged to form Concordia, with whatever degree of difficulty, history departments merged, physics departments merged, *études français[es]* departments merged, but the theology department at Loyola and the religion department at Sir George never merged. And historically there has always been, at Concordia, a department of religion, which, as I said, recently changed its name to Religions and Cultures, and a department of theology. And relations with, between the two departments were often collegial but sometimes a bit strained.

But the bottom line is that neither group wanted to merge. Each group maintained its principles. And, you know, these departments came by their principles honestly. And theology remained theology, though it did institute courses in other religions, but Christian theology, and more specifically Roman Catholic theology, was centre stage. And Sir George's religion department, which became Concordia's religion department, maintained its principle of decentralization of Christianity within the study of religion. But the evolution of thought, which led to the change, is, well, using religion in the singular still made people think, "Well, there is a possible standard religion" ... So, religion was not as good as religions. And "religions," by itself, was not as descriptive as "religions and cultures." A lot of thought and an evolution of thought went into the name change.

## LINDA DYER, "PEOPLE DON'T REALLY KNOW THE COLLECTIVE AGREEMENT"

When I started out, I was asked to join a [faculty union] negotiation side table. I don't know *why* they asked me, but whatever [*laughs*]. I did it. And then a bit later I was asked if I could join the negotiating *team*, and so I *sat* on the team, so I saw how it worked, et cetera. That was interesting. And then several years after that, I was asked to be chief negotiator, and I agreed [*laughs*]. So I did that. Then I was asked to be the grievance officer. And *that* has been *very* difficult, *very* difficult. Well, because, you know, it's people who are in trouble, not *always* because of something that they were aware of doing or that they did or whatever. I can't say much about that, but it's—it's—it's hard; it's been hard, very hard. And then very recently I was asked to be chief negotiator again. And I said okay, so that I didn't have to be a grievance officer anymore [*both laugh*] ... So, I guess I've been involved in the union for a long time ... I think it's important, because I think very many people don't really know the collective agreement. And when you don't know the collective agreement, you sometimes [*pauses*]—you sometimes end up doing things either the hard way [*laughs*] or the incorrect way, and *that* can be troublesome. You know ... I keep saying to others at the union; I say, you know, "We've got to get people fairly early on, and get them *involved*, and get them to *understand*, you know, not only what are the duties and responsibilities, but what are your *rights* as well." And one of the things that has concerned me is that people become department chairs, and they become department chairs because they are kind of pushed into it. "Okay, it's your turn, it's your turn; you've got to do it." And they do it without really understanding fully how the university operates.

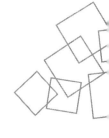

Futures

49.1 Kahérakwas Donna Goodleaf launches her five-year strategic plan to decolonize pedagogy and curriculum, September 8, 2023. *From left to right*: Provost Anne Whitelaw, Kahérakwas Donna Goodleaf, Director of Indigenous Directions Manon Tremblay, and Vice Provost Sandra Gabriel.

# REIMAGINING CONCORDIA'S FUTURE: A KANIEN'KEHÁ:KA PERSPECTIVE

Kahérakwas Donna Goodleaf

*Dr. Kahérakwas Donna Goodleaf has been the director of Decolonizing Curriculum and Pedagogy at Concordia since 2018. Her Indigenous Decolonization Hub on Concordia's Centre for Teaching and Learning website provides Concordia faculty members and staff with tools and encounters to support decolonizing and Indigenizing their courses and pedagogical practices. In March 2023 Dr. Goodleaf and Monika Kin Gagnon discussed the future of Concordia and university education from Dr. Goodleaf's Kanien'kehá:ka vantage point. Monika asked her to consider three questions: What is the value of universities today? What does your future university look like, given the kind of work that you're doing at Concordia? How can we get there?*

**WHEN I THINK ABOUT YOUR QUESTION** about what "my university looks like in fifty years," I think about a bigger context. My thoughts turn to the role of settler-colonial universities today and their histories, and I ask myself these fundamental questions: What was and continues to be the function and vision of these settler-colonial education systems? Who benefits from this system and who doesn't? I think about the colonizers and their descendants who came to Turtle Island with their laws, their institutions, their belief systems, values, their attitude and behaviour towards each other and the natural world. My thoughts turn to my ancestors and the oral stories that were passed down from generation to the next about the creation and purpose of the Two Row Wampum Belt Treaty known as Tekani Teiotha'tá:tie Kaswéntah. My ancestors created this wampum belt which served as a tool to navigate and to build relationships with all the incoming colonial settlers like the Dutch, the French, and their descendants known as Canadians and Americans today in how they were and are today, to conduct themselves living in the lands of Rotinonhsión:ni Confederacy.

---

KAHÉRAKWAS DONNA GOODLEAF is Turtle Clan and is a citizen from the Kanien'kehá:ka (Mohawk) Nation, Kahnawake Territory, which is part of the Rotinonhsión:ni Six Nations Iroquois Confederacy, and author of *Entering the War Zone: A Mohawk Perspective on Resisting Invasions* (1995).

I am reminded of the principles of the Two Row Wampum Belt in terms of the behaviours, in terms of the non-interference, the message that we always have to impart. I reflect and draw upon the Two Row as a metaphor to explain my existence in these two worlds—meaning having one foot is in my community, and the other foot is in these academic institutions. And so I have to use the Two Row Wampum Treaty as a political/social/cultural metaphor to explain the positions, our worldviews, and what we have been through as Rotinonhsión:ni peoples with the invasion of the settlers. My ancestors observed how they were very destructive to each other, the land, to the earth. We had to come up with a way to establish a relationship and communicate with these people who were and continue to be different, foreign to our lands. How do we do that as Onkwehón:we people, meaning "as the real people," as human beings? I think about the Two Row in that sense—we observed in the past and look at society today—at the destruction of the natural world, the environment that is still ongoing. We have to look at the development of the institutions that were created on our lands, these Western educational institutions that were constructed for a purpose: to destroy us as Indigenous Peoples, to annihilate us so they can steal our lands and our natural resources. And when I think about the critical time we're in today, the climate change that's happening, we didn't cause these destructions!

When I think about Concordia University, I think about these academic institutions as extensions of [colonial] residential schools that have been built on Indigenous lands, created to privilege settler-colonial society, their philosophies, their worldviews. And they're set up in a way to ensure the erasure of my people's voices, our histories, our stories. They're set up to perpetuate and maintain Eurocentric canons of thought across the academy. And for me, that's a huge issue we need to look at because when you look back at this history of the whole education system, who did it serve? What was the philosophy and the values that these institutions were built on? And how has it contributed to the ongoing destruction towards the land, the natural world, and its impact on the human family today? So, for me, when I think about what this vision for Concordia looks like in fifty years, I'll tell you, something has to change. The mindsets, the values, the belief systems that cause harm to people and the natural world has to change. When I think about my people, my community, I think about those little babies that we have, those little children that are coming up, and I think about how we're lucky that we have our own education systems in our communities. We have our own language programs that are grounded in our language, our young people are getting stronger in who they are as Kanien'kehá:ka people. But what happens when it's time for them to pursue post-secondary education? I have a huge responsibility, and my people are the number one that I think about. I see what these university systems are like, I've worked in them, I've been through them, and I will be honest, I don't want the little ones to go through the systems that currently exist right now. We have to reimagine and create an educational system that reflects democratic processes in structure and process, grounded in love and caring for each other and the natural world, and everybody is equal, and everybody is loved and cared for. And what students learn is grounded in a critical history of colonization, about who we are as Indigenous Peoples before colonization happened and learn about the brilliance and intelligence of our people today.

Scientists are coming to us now, needing our help, because they see the destruction that is occurring in this world. We've had delegations going to the United Nations trying to reach out to the world community and tell them about the dangers if they keep going on this path of destruction, we're not going to have a future. So, what are we going to do? What's the role of universities to ensure that the students, the children, humanity, and the natural world have a future? For me, I want to see my community flourish and grow stronger in who we are as Rotinonhsión:ni people and contribute to creating a society where we can coexist peacefully, where we can live in peace, where there's no violence, there's no racism, there's no hatred towards us as Indigenous Peoples. And I believe academic institutions need to impart these values, belief systems, and model this in how we treat each other in the hallways and truly giving back to the Kanien'kehá:ka nation whose lands the university is built on. When reflecting deeply about what I just mentioned, I am also very clear that Concordia is not ready. They are absolutely not ready to shake their foundations because it will require hard conversations, deep critical self-reflections about self and the complicity in the existing university structural policies and practices that, in my view, need to collapse so that we can reimagine and rebuild an education system that truly embraces all peoples and promotes the protection and sustainability regarding the natural world. This university needs to uphold responsibilities to ensure that the natural world is protected and ensure that the truth of our history is being told. They have to look at themselves and their complicity in perpetuating a false history. And they have to look at themselves and look at their positionality, their power and how they're contributing to these structures, how the policies that are created, the structures that are in place, protect the power of the institution, they protect patriarchy, protect institutional racism and erase our voices as Indigenous Peoples. And so, for me this work is Indigenous decolonization. What does that mean? It's very specific. It's grounded in who I am as a Rotinonhsión:ni woman and my world. I think about the Two Row as a metaphor, where we are to come together and travel this river of life based on these principles of peaceful coexistence, of friendship and trusting relationships. That we will travel this river of life grounded in truth and also transformation.

We have to have the power and the energy to reimagine what the future will look like for those faces that are piercing from the earth. They're the ones that I think about. I want to have a place ready for them so they can take their place and not have to lose their cultural identity at the door when they step into these halls of academia. I want them to be respected, value their worldview, their voices and histories, and recognize and see them as leaders who will take their rightful place in our communities as leaders to our people.

Universities have a huge responsibility to transform and critically reflect on this question: What are you for? Do you continue the path of perpetuating Eurocentrism, institutional racism, and harm towards Indigenous Peoples and other oppressed peoples? In my view, universities more than ever need to be bold and be courageous and take risks to really look inside of themselves and ask, What are we doing? How are we complicit? How do we turn it around? In my view, we need to become very action oriented. The work I do with faculty regarding decolonizing and Indigenizing curriculum and pedagogy is so critical and necessary because education is a powerful tool. And it requires faculty to look inward and examine their positionality, their power, and privilege they hold as instructors in the classroom, and their belief systems and misconceptions they have about Indigenous Peoples and how that has informed or shaped their course design and pedagogical practices in relationship to their students in the classroom. It requires faculty to examine and critically reflect on the messages that they impart to students because faculty are very powerful. Faculty have a very powerful role because they're educators. We need to look at how we can give students a better understanding of who they are, validating their complex social and cultural identities and validating their stories and let that be the centre.

When the Honourable Senator Murray Sinclair talks about truth and reconciliation, it's not enough to learn about the history of residential schools and be like, "Oh, my God!" You have to be very action oriented. You have to be able to move out of your comfort zone and that zone of guilt. You're either walking and cultivating a body of ignorance, and the *unknowing* you're cultivating and perpetuating is a lie, and for whose benefit? Or you walk alongside of us, with us supporting Indigenous Peoples, and you reimagine with us a new way of learning, a new way of creating and changing an institution. For me, we're at a very critical time, and you can't sit on the fence. You have to make a decision. You have to stand with us because it's your children, too, that are impacted. It's your future generations. And what do you want for them? What kind of society do we want? What kind of values will you pass on as educators? And what is it that we want to arm them with so that they're ready and that they're able to live in a society where we value each other, where we're friends and we have a common vision, where we lift each other up and support each other for the sake of our future, for our humanity. It's not only cultivating a critical consciousness, but also a relational consciousness that is needed. One of our chiefs, Robert Antone, an Elder who passed away, imparted words of wisdom about how we need to take responsibility to build better relationships with ourselves as people and with Mother Earth. We need to build a relational consciousness that is grounded in the principles of the Two Row and build relationships that empower the people and ensure that all of humanity and all of life's creation have a future. It's a call for people to wake up. It's what I hope for Concordia.

I don't know what Concordia will look like fifty years from now. I can only just reimagine where we need to go, but, you know, I have to believe that there's like-minded people that truly want to listen and to build respectful and trusting relationships with us and transform the university system in ways that centre the voices, the stories, the histories of Indigenous Peoples across all academic units in the university.

Because of climate change and because of COVID, we have had all these external events that were out of our control. It makes us step back and realize that we can't continue on this path; we have to look at other ways of being and creating. For us, it's a resurgence back to our ways of reconnecting with the land. And so, how do you create these land-based education systems that take students out of the classroom and get reconnected to the land? This has a much deeper impact in terms of understanding who they are, their responsibilities to the land and also to the community. I think and deeply believe that that's where we have to go—the future direction of Concordia. I'll be honest with you, we can't keep going the way we're going right now with classes. Students are wanting more out of the classroom, and we need to put them out on the land and to be able to experience these immersive connections to the land because it changes their philosophy, their understanding, and it grounds them in our philosophy, in our relationships to the natural world. They learn different skills of survival. They learn the spiritual, philosophical meanings about the Ohén:ton Karihwatéhkwen, the words before all else or the Thanksgiving Address to the natural world and why we do that, and our responsibilities to the land and why we need to protect the natural world. To me, that is a really good education model Concordia has to expand and build on. And we're seeing it emerging across Canada where Indigenous communities across Canada are taking their kids out of the school systems and returning to the land and offering immersive land-based educational experiences for Indigenous students. Universities are trying to partner up with Indigenous communities to build these land-based education systems. I believe we're going to see more of that because that's where Indigenous Peoples are going. And I think that the university has a role to play because for me, it's not just embedding students in our knowledge, in our history, in our land, but also, I think that faculty need to experience being out in the land as well to get grounded and make connections and develop deeper under-standing about who we are as Indigenous Peoples and our relationship and responsibilities to the natural world. Because if we're going to build a society where we have to live with non-Indigenous peoples in our world, then we have to also look at how we can also tap into these other knowledges that non-Indigenous educators have. For instance, we need to develop technologies around water. Water is so critical today. Our Rotinonhsión:ni scientists need to work with the Western scientists and learn from each other in respectful ways; educate them in terms of our protocols, but also share the knowledge base that they have as well as with ours. How can we bring both knowledges together? It's possible. So again, I'll go back to the metaphor of teaching as a tool, because, to me, I think we also need to be open and not be afraid to learn and explore these other knowledge systems that can contribute and help us in terms of building up our communities. How do we come together? Sitting in a circle and leaving your position at the door, leaving your hat at the door and coming as a human being and just being on the land and just let the land really embrace you and coming together and just share the stories. We have an intergenerational learning process where children are learning the stories, the oral stories. And in our world, everybody is equal. Everybody has an equal voice. And so, how do we bring that into the university system that nobody's better than the other? They all have stories to bring, and it's about validating those stories, creating and reimagining what we want.

The university institutions and knowledge systems have produced people that created the atomic bomb and machinery that is killing the natural world, the pipeline technologies that are poisoning our waters. People need to understand that and see how we're having a hard time with water. Perpetuating these knowledge systems only benefit the corporate world, which is bringing destruction to the natural world and to the environment. Do they think about their grandchildren and what they're going to grow up in? Are we going to walk around with gas masks for the rest of our lives? How are we going to deal with that? We can't be afraid to engage in hard unsettling conversations around what it is that we need to change and how do we do this in a way that brings about change that ensures the land, the people, and all elements of the natural world have a future. I want to believe that there's a future for our children, for those babies whose faces pierce from the earth waiting to take their rightful place in a society where there is peaceful co-existence and all of humanity and the natural world have a future. To my allies at Concordia University, I ask you, What are you for?

# AFTERWORD

Anne Whitelaw

**I WRITE THIS AFTERWORD AS THE PROVOST AND VICE-PRESIDENT**, Academic, at Concordia, a position in which I have served since 2019. Yet my association with the university goes much farther back. My father, James H. Whitelaw, came to Sir George Williams University in 1954 to head what was then the Department of Modern Languages and family lore has it that he did a backflip when he got the call that he had been hired (an image I admittedly have a hard time believing). Over the ensuing years my father held a number of senior administrative positions at Concordia, so many of the events and individuals described in these pages are familiar because of our dinner discussions or from our conversations as I grew older. He served as curriculum coordinator from 1967 to 1971, associate vice-principal, Academic Planning, from 1971 to 1974, and associate vice-rector, Academic, from 1974 until his retirement in 1984. Reading *Concordia University at 50: A Collective History* has filled me with joy and pride as it feels both so recognizable and so quintessentially Concordia. Indeed, when former University Librarian Guylaine Beaudry and I first discussed the publication of a volume to mark Concordia's 50th anniversary, it was clear that this could not be the traditional single-authored chronicle of the emergence and maturation of an institution. Rather, we wanted to hear the multitude of voices, views, and experiences that built the university: the personal narratives of determination and resilience; the stories about trying things out and succeeding despite the obstacles; and through almost every chapter, the clear sense of Concordia's strong links to Montreal's communities.

I began my BFA in art history at Concordia in 1984 (the year my father retired) and attended classes in what was then the brand-new Visual Arts Building that Catherine MacKenzie describes in her history of the Faculty of Fine Arts. A former parking garage (there's a photo you can see in that chapter), the tiered lecture classrooms were the original car ramps to access upper floors, but the renovated interior housed an amazing array of talent and creativity. The Concordia of the mid-1980s looked very different from the one we know today—as can be seen in the

---

ANNE WHITELAW is Concordia University's Provost and Vice-president, Academic, since 2021, having held the position on an interim basis since 2019. She joined Concordia's Department of Art History in January 2011 after serving for eleven years as a faculty member in the Department of Art and Design at the University of Alberta.

chapters chronicling the first twenty-five years of space planning, the acquisition of the Grey Nun's Mother House, and the recent construction of the state-of-the-art Science Hub at Loyola. During my undergrad, I worked evenings in the Art Education Print Library, and was also one of several research assistants hired by Professors Catherine MacKenzie and Reesa Greenberg to develop their resources for feminist art history. I returned to Concordia after completing my MA in the UK and worked for a year doing clerical work for Beth Morey at the Simone de Beauvoir Institute's women's resource centre (see her oral history excerpts in this collection), as well as in Rector Patrick Kenniff's office. Returning to doctoral studies in 1989, I remember the shock that reverberated from the tragic deaths that Johanne Sloan's visual story memorializes, and Donna Whittaker describes in her oral history. I was present for the Lesbian and Gay Friends of Concordia dances described by Gregorio Pablo Rodriguez-Arbolay (and their low-budget flyers), as well as the student mobilizations around Oka and the demonstrations following the Sex Garage police raid, including the kiss-in in front of Station 25. I also remember graduate student Carolyn Gammon's fight to adopt non-gendered degree nomenclature—the baccalaureate, magisteriate, and doctorate degrees we award today. Overall, I recall the pride I felt to be at a university that saw itself at the centre of major social issues and understood the importance of bringing the real world into the classroom and engaging its students in thinking about their place in that world. That pride informed the research I did in partnership with Danielle Comeau for Concordia's first recruitment video, launched in 1996.

As the current provost and vice-president, Academic, I have the privilege of being in a position where I can ensure that the values and approaches that defined my earlier experiences of the university continue to guide us as we expand our activities and enhance our global reputation. The numbers from just the past twenty years tell part of the story: in 2003, Concordia had slightly less than 30,000 undergraduate students and around 6,000 graduate students; in 2023, we had 35,400 undergraduates and more than 10,000 graduate students—that's an overall increase of 39% enrolment over a twenty-year period! In line with the important links we have forged with universities beyond our borders, including pioneering collaborations with China in the 1980s, our international student population has grown by over 300% over the past two decades—from 2,400 in 2003 to 10,400 in 2023. Concordia is now host to students from over 150 countries. Over those twenty years we have also increased our faculty complement by 45% and have introduced a wide range of programs at the undergraduate and graduate level as well as pioneering training through the D3 Innovation Hub in order to give our students the tools to be prepared for the labour market and to make an impact on society.

From a research standpoint, as Jean-Philippe Warren's chapter visualizes in part with data and Lynn Hughes describes in her oral history, we have morphed from a university focused largely on teaching to a research-intensive institution that has established strengths in a wide range of subject areas. The fine arts have always been an area where Concordia shines, but recent years have seen new strengths in the digital arts and in research creation with the establishment of the pluridisciplinary Milieux Institute for Arts, Culture and Technology. Media production and analysis has also garnered recognition through activities in the Departments of Communication Studies and Journalism and the Mel Hoppenheim School of Cinema. In science and technology, our strengths in synthetic biology were cemented with the opening of the Genome Foundry in 2018, while the Concordia Institute of Aerospace Design and Innovation (CIADI) has been a driving force behind aerospace research and teaching that has allowed the students of Space Concordia build a rocket that will be launched into space. More recently, Concordia researchers are making their mark in the emerging fields of applied artificial intelligence, software engineering, and cybersecurity, partnering with industry and the innovation ecosystem to position the university at the forefront of digital futures we can only begin to imagine.

As so many of the chapters in this book confirm, Concordia has long been interested in work that is grounded in social justice and activism, from the feminist work of the Simone de Beauvoir Institute and the more recent explorations of women and leadership in the John Molson School of Business, to work on mobility and migration. The stories and successes of Black community organizations are featured in chapters by Dave McKenzie and Annick Maugile-Flavien and Désirée Rochat, as well as being preserved in the library's Special Collections. Stories from these and other communities are held by the Centre for Oral History and Digital Storytelling, whose contribution to *Concordia University at 50* has been so formative to this volume's multiplicity of perspectives. More recently, we have demonstrated our research leadership in the sphere of sustainability with our Canada Excellence Research Chair in Smart, Sustainable, and Resilient Communities and Cities in 2019, expanding that leadership to include sustainable energy, with a $123 million Canada First Research Excellence Fund award in 2023 for Electrifying Society: Towards Decarbonized Resilient Communities. A hallmark of both these major grants is the interdisciplinary nature of the projects they support, weaving together the findings of engineers, philosophers, designers, and multiple industrial, community, and government partners. Indeed, a commitment to interdisciplinary approaches may be the thing that unites so much of our research activities, whether it is the work at the engAGE Centre for Research on Aging, or gaming at Technoculture, Art, and Games Research Centre, or the Indigenous AI of Abundant Intelligences that Jason Edward Lewis and Skawennati present in this collection. The creation of our School of Health in 2021 is a further testament to the value of Concordia's unique interdisciplinary pursuits, investigating the social and cultural dimensions of health as experienced within communities in ways that are distinct from the singularly medicalized approach favoured by so many other universities.

That an emphasis on communities characterizes the new School of Health should not be a surprise to anyone who knows Concordia. Throughout our fifty-year history, we have served as an anchor institution within the city of Montreal, forging connections with community organizations, businesses, and industry. As this collection highlights, this orientation to the outside world—this engagement with community—is part of the DNA that comes from our heritage in both Sir George Williams University and Loyola College and continues to guide our collaborations in the present. These are the values and the principles that have attracted and sustained students, faculty, and staff at Concordia for five decades and that keep our alumni so closely connected to the university. The memories and perspectives contained in this collection offer a powerful testament to the grit and creativity that is Concordia and a clear indication of the sustained educational leadership we have maintained over the past fifty years. As I look to the future—a future that has been marked by shifts in pedagogy accelerated by a global pandemic and increasing suspicion of higher education—I know that Concordia will continue to experiment, to challenge the status quo, and to develop innovative responses to the difficult questions of a rapidly changing world; and it will continue to prepare generations of students to make a significant impact on Montreal, on Canada, and on the world.

# ACKNOWLEDGEMENTS

**EVERY BOOK IS A PRODUCT** of many labours, and this book is no different. We begin by thanking the writers who responded to the call for proposals, the artists who gave their permissions to reproduce their work, and the many staff and faculty who provided consultation and support at the book's many stages. We thank all those who participated in the numerous consultations of 2019–20 on how to best mark the 50th anniversary of Concordia University and through which this edited volume first emerged. Fittingly, some of the participants became book contributors while others were interviewed for the oral history collection that is excerpted here and now fully housed at Concordia's Records Management and Archives (RMA).

Institutionally, this project originated in the Concordia University Library and received support from its staff throughout. The former lead editor and Concordia's previous university librarian, Guylaine Beaudry, deserves special mention for commencing the consultations and initiating this book. We also thank Concordia's new university librarian, Amy Buckland, for her ongoing support, as well as former interim university librarian, Pat Riva, and members of their staff, including Sandra Biron, Nadia Pecora, Maria Battaglino, and Luminita Florentina Draia.

The oral histories that appear in the following pages add texture and richness that few university histories have attempted to incorporate. We thank Piyusha Chatterjee for conducting these interviews in the fall of 2022, as well as Emma Haraké for her initial work on the ethics framework. We also extend thanks to the interview transcribers Allison Penner, Kelly Livingstone, and Lina Shoumarova, as well as our two creative videographers, Naakita Feldman Kiss and Shin Ling Low, for their contributions.

Meeting and working alongside Concordia's many departments and their friendly and energetic staff has been one of this project's joys. We would like to thank University Communications Services (UCS), especially UCS's chief communications officer Philippe Beauregard for ongoing consultation, as well as helping to arrange use of the UCS studio for our oral history team to film interviews. Special thanks to studio manager Veronique Verthuy and technician Salvatore Barrera for their assistance. We also thank Angela Polyzogopoulos and Christopher Alleyne who helped access specific images.

Deserving very special thanks is the team from RMA who, as Concordia's memory keepers, became virtual collaborators, and without whom this project would not have been possible. We thank RMA's director Marie-Pierre Aube and her team for lending their expertise and assisting our authors and us in our archival visits. We thank former technician Caroline Sigouin for providing a wealth of sources for authors on a range of topics; archivist Eric Côté for his tireless research into historical questions, both big and small; digital archivist John Richan for handling the deposit of our oral history collection; and archives and digital preservation assistant Olivier Bisaillon-Lemay, for tracking down and scanning what must have seemed like endless images that appear throughout this book. The more detailed captions were researched and written by Brandon Webb with the help of the RMA. We also thank RMA's interim director, Julie Daoust, for making this team available to provide sources, verify information, and look up esoteric institutional facts and figures, all of which is essential for any community-led public history project.

At Concordia University Press, with whom we worked over the past year, we thank Ryan Van Huijstee for his rigour and guidance, Meredith Carruthers and Saelen Twerdy, as well as copyeditor Joanne Muzak. We thank Colby Gaudet for excellent fact-checking. Associés libres's Rodolfo Borello and Jennifer de Freitas made this book come alive with their creativity and design wisdom. We are also grateful to Isabelle Cardin-Simard and Nathalie Charland for skilfully translating this book's range of voices for the French edition.

Our final gratitude goes to the book's editorial committee, Steven High, Catherine Wild, and Jason Camlot, who unreservedly provided guidance and support throughout the book's many stages, commencing with their initial selection of authors and chapters for this collection. We also thank Steven High for his oversight, organization, and expertise of the oral histories. And for editorial support of the French edition, we thank Jean-Philippe Warren. They all travelled the torques and turns of the project with us and this book is a result of their wisdom, advice, and continual guidance.

Finally, Provost Anne Whitelaw lent crucial institutional support to the project at key junctures. We thank her and her staff in the Provost's Office, as well as President Graham Carr. As scholars and historians, we deeply appreciate the trust, support, and interest that both President Carr and Provost Whitelaw showed in us throughout this project.

We conclude by thanking each other, without whom this project would not have been quite as much fun as it was, and our partners, Scott McFarlane and Fizza Jafry for their patience and interest.

*Monika Kin Gagnon and Brandon Webb*

# ILLUSTRATION CREDITS

## Abbreviations

### Archives

LAC – Library and Archives Canada
RMA – Concordia University Records Management and Archives
UCS – Concordia University Communications Services

### Publications

*CTR – Concordia Thursday Report*
*CU – Concordia Magazine*
*LN – Loyola News*
*TG – The Georgian*
*TL – The Link*
*TR – Thursday Report*

### Figures

1.1 Notice of name change, P0139 Concordia University Alumni Association fonds, RMA.

1.2 Charter Day at Sir George Williams College, I002-02-1510, Public Relations Department fonds, RMA.

1.3 "Malone Denies Talks," *LN* September 22, 1971.

1.4 Shuttle Bus, P0150-02-0096, *The Link* fonds, RMA.

3.1 Hall Building construction, P0184-02-0001, Jack Bordan fonds, RMA.

3.2 Loyola campus aerial, Archives de la Ville de Montréal, VM166-R3080-2_Ouest_7141-017.

3.3 SGW plan, 1974, File "New Buildings, 1974-81," Principal's Fonds, RMA.

3.4 Loyola plan, 1976. Marc-Cinq Mars / Larose Laliberté Petrucci, architectes, "Concordia University, Loyola Campus: Planning Study," January 1976, box HA 47, RMA.

3.5 2000 campus plan for Loyola, I0135 Facilities Management fonds, RMA.

3.6 2000 campus plan for Sir George Williams, I0135 Facilities Management fonds, RMA.

4.1 Bread and Roses benefit poster, RMA.

6.1 Grey Nuns Mother House, UCS.

6.2 Fort Qu'Appelle residential school, Item 3623706, LAC. Photo credit: Oliver Buell.

6.3 *The Extended Goodbye #1* (2009), courtesy of Suzy Lake.

7.1 Chemistry lab, I0069-02-0035, Faculty of Arts and Science fonds, RMA. Photo credit: Brian M. McNeil.

7.2 "A&S Divisions II and III chairmen oppose new A&S structure," *TR* 7, no. 27, April 12, 1984.

7.3 SCPA Board of Advisees first meeting, I0100-02-0004, School of Community and Public Affairs fonds, RMA. Photo credit: Brian M. McNeil.

7.4 Physics lab, I0069-02-0047, Faculty of Arts and Science fonds, RMA. Photo credit: Brian M. McNeil.

7.5 "Ad for Septemberfest talk," *TR* 6, no. 4, September 23, 1982.

7.6 Jane Stewart in her lab, I0002-02-7509, Public Relations Department fonds, RMA.

7.7 Faculty in Communication Arts, I0104-02-0024, Department of Communication Studies fonds, RMA.

7.8 Drummond building, I0049-02-0245, Records Management and Archives fonds, RMA.

7.9 Science Pavilion, I0185 University Communication Services fonds, RMA.

7.10 Journalism television studio, UCS.

7.11 Working class public history, courtesy of Steven High. Photo credit: David Ward.

7.12 *B/OLD: Aging in Our City* event, courtesy of Ageing + Communication + Technology (ACT).

8.1 Dance dress rehearsal, UCS.

8.2 Announcement for 1977 exhibition, P0273 Frank Barry fonds, RMA.

8.3 Art Matters poster, courtesy Fine Arts Student Alliance.

8.4 Visual Arts building, 1977, I0002-02-1830, Public Relations Department fonds, RMA.

8.5 Afterlife group exhibition, UCS and courtesy Raymonde April.

8.6 *Alfie* (1984). Collection of the Leonard & Bina Ellen Art Gallery, Concordia University / Collection de la Galerie Leonard & Bina Ellen, Université Concordia. Purchase/Achat, 1984. 984.42. Image: Denis Farley.

8.7 Year End Screening Programme 1986, I0062 Mel Hoppenheim School of Cinema fonds, RMA.

8.8 Cinema open house, UCS.

8.9 Art Hives, UCS.

8.10 Performance, UCS.

8.11 Charles Ellison class, UCS, with the permission of Charles Ellison.

8.12 Barbara Layne, I0040 Marketing Communications fonds, RMA.

8.13 *Les fées ont soif,* I0072-02-0009, Department of Theatre fonds, RMA.

8.14 *Disconnecting the Dots*, UCS.

8.15 Encuentro Manifest! UCS.

8.16 *Icebreaker* performance, UCS.

9.1 YMCA headquarters, P0101-02-0014, Fraser F. Fulton fonds, RMA.

9.2 "PhD Administration Program 10 Years Old," *TR* 9, no. 27, April 25, 1986.

9.3 "Peruvians take the gold at MBA Case Competition," *CTR* 23, no. 9, January 28, 1999.

9.4 "Women and Work Symposium," *CTR* 22, no. 16, May 28, 1998.

10.1 Dave McKenzie. Photo courtesy of author.

10.2 Clarence Bayne, *CTR* 22, no. 14, April 23, 1998. Photo credit: Christian Fleury.

11.1 EV building, UCS.

11.2 Aerospace and aviation engineering lab, I0040 Marketing Communications fonds, RMA.

11.3 Rooftop experiment on top of the Hall building, I0040 Marketing Communications fonds, RMA.

11.4 Patrick Kenniff at engineering event, I0040 Marketing Communications fonds, RMA.

11.5 FutureCars Challenge, I0040 Marketing Communications fonds, RMA.

11.6 Troitsky Bridge Building Competition, I0002-02-9451, Public Relations Department fonds, RMA.

11.7 Robokeith guitar, photo courtesy of authors.

11.8 Women in Engineering, I0185 University Communications Service fonds, RMA.

11.9 Women in Engineering, "WIE Inspire, WIE Empower," event, courtesy of WIE.

11.10 Gina Cody with a group of students 2018, courtesy of WIE.

11.11 Gina Cody at Spring Convocation 2019, I0018 Office of the Registrar fonds, RMA.

14.1 "School of Graduate Studies," I0040 Marketing Communications fonds, RMA.

15.1–15.7 Graphics provided by the authors.

16.1 Research plan, courtesy of Indigenous Futures.

16.2 *Face-Off* (2010), courtesy of Skawennati.

16.3 *Quartet* (2019), courtesy of Jason Edward Lewis.

17.1 Student and library catalogue, I0002-02-1280, RMA.

17.2 McConnell Library Building, 1988, I0135-02-0379, Facilities Management fonds.

17.3 Statue of David, P0050-02-0331, Association of Alumni of Sir George Williams University fonds, RMA. Photo credit: Paul Hrasko.

17.4 Cover of *TR* 13, no. 9, November 1988.

17.5 J.W. McConnell Building inauguration, I0200-02-0012, Office of the President and Vice-Chancellor fonds, RMA.

17.6 Webster transformation, UCS.

17.7 *Bibliofile,* Fall 2003.

17.8 Presentation of books at the Vanier Library, I0002-02-1253, Public Relations Department fonds, RMA.

19.1 "Course syllabus," I0049 Records Management and Archives fonds, RMA.

20.1–20.3 Poetry Series posters, provided by the author.

21.1 Poster for talk, "Crime, Protest, Punishment," P0009 George Rudé fonds, RMA.

21.2 Portrait of George Rudé, P0009-02-0002, George Rudé fonds, RMA.

22.1 Bird's-eye view on computer centre cards, P0116-02-0698, Loyola Alumni Association fonds, RMA.

22.2 List of student demands, I0074-02-0121_29, Office of the Vice-Rector, Administration and Finance fonds, RMA.

22.3 Group arrest of students, P0116-02-0696, Loyola Alumni Association fonds, RMA.

22.4 Exhibition poster, RMA.

22.5 *Protests and Pedagogy* exhibition at 4$^{TH}$ Space, provided by the author.

22.6 *Protests and Pedagogy* exhibition at Media Gallery.

24.1–24.4 Photos courtesy of the authors.

26.1, 26.2 Photos courtesy of the authors.

27.1 Men's football, I0034 Department of Recreation and Athletics fonds, RMA.

27.2 Women's Rugby, I0034-02-1822, Department of Recreation and Athletics fonds, RMA.

27.3 Women's hockey, I0034 Department of Recreation and Athletics fonds, RMA.

27.4 "1962-63 Loyola Warriors Basketball team," *Loyola College Review*, 1963, RMA.

27.5 Stingers fans, I0185-02-0206, University Communication Services fonds, RMA.

27.6 *CIAU Football,* 1995 issue, I0034 Department of Recreation and Athletics fonds, RMA.

27.7 C.I.A.U. National Soccer Champions 1976, I0034-02-0232, Department of Recreation and Athletics fonds, RMA.

27.8 Men's hockey, I0034-02-0518, Department of Recreation and Athletics fonds, RMA.

27.9 Concordia women's basketball yearbook, 1985–86. Department of Recreation and Athletics fonds, RMA.

29.1 Oscar Peterson at Victoria Hall, P016-02-016, Johnny Holmes fonds, Concordia University Library, Special Collections.

30.1 CUSA agenda cover 1991–92, P0263 Concordia Student Union fonds.

30.2 Dean of Students Awards, UCS.

32.1 "Gay Issue," *TL* 8, no. 22, November 17, 1982.

32.2 Poster, *Super-danse Hollywood,* Concordia Archives Private fonds, RMA.

33.1 Film event, courtesy of the authors.

34.1 Sir George TV, P0024-1-02-0004, CUTV fonds, RMA.

34.2 CIRL radio, P0150-02-0108, *The Link* fonds, RMA.

34.3 TV Sir George, P0024-1-02-0005, CUTV fonds, RMA.

34.4 Sound and Vision II poster, Concordia Archives Private fonds, RMA.

34.5 *TL* 8, no. 17, November 13, 1987, P0150 *The Link* fonds, RMA.

34.6 *TL* 8, no. 18, November 18, 1987, P0150 *The Link* fonds, RMA.

36.1 *CU* 1, no. 1, April 1975. Poster design credit: Peter Lanken.

37.1 Pamphlet for Centre for Continuing Education, Loyola, 1974, I0098 Centre for Education fonds, RMA.

37.2 Centre for Continuing Education, UCS.

38.1 University of the Streets, UCS.

38.2 University of the Streets, UCS.

39.1 *CU* 27, no.3, September 2004.

40.1 Photo of Tom Waugh in *TL* 9, no.9, March 20, 1989, P0150 The Link fonds, RMA.

40.2 Posters for the HIV/AIDS Lecture series, I0031 Concordia HIV/AIDS Project fonds, RMA.

41.1, 41.2 Photos courtesy of the author.

42.1 Manon Tremblay, I0002-02-9189, Public Relations Department fonds, RMA.

42.2 Beading Workshop, I0002-02-9188, Public Relations Department fonds, RMA.

43.1 Advertisement, courtesy of Department of Communication Studies.

44.1 Portrait of Lynn Ranger, I0002-02-0411, Public Relations Department fonds, RMA.

44.2 Language lab in the 1960s, I0002-02-0247, Public Relations Department fonds, RMA.

46.1 Dance performance, courtesy of the author.

46.2 Dance contact sheet, I0040 Marketing Communications fonds, RMA.

47.1 Electroacoustic Composers group, I0040 Marketing Communications fonds, RMA.

47.2 Concert Program, I0040 Marketing Communications fonds, RMA.

47.3 Kevin Austin, courtesy of the author.

49.1 Decolonizing presentation, photo: Lisa Graves, UCS.

51.1 Zoom screen capture, courtesy of the editor.

# PUBLIC ART COLLECTION AND CREDITS

Sandra Margolian

**CONCORDIA UNIVERSITY'S PUBLIC ART COLLECTION**, a unique amalgamation of public artworks and artifacts, was brought to life over fifty years ago when Jean McEwen's glass windows were integrated into the newly built Henry F. Hall building at Sir George Williams University, one of Concordia's founding institutions. The Public Art Collection is on permanent display and can be enjoyed free of charge, year-round, inside or outside many buildings in public areas on both campuses, and is accessible in person or online. As Concordia's Public Art Policy of 2023 describes:

> "Public art" means an original artwork that is owned, commissioned by, or loaned to the university that is located in a space accessible to the public, that has aesthetic qualities, and that can represent the public interest. Public art engages the public and includes artworks of different typologies, durations, and media, from temporary and ephemeral to semipermanent and permanent installations. Public art can be object or non-object-based, such as sculpture, media art, sound or light art, performances, socially engaged art projects, and art that uses digital technologies. It can be interactive, accessible online, or in other forms yet to be identified. It engages with the contemporary artistic period when it is produced. Typically, the creation of public art considers site and context as part of its process.

The current collection is a compilation of donations, commissions, and works acquired during the university's rapid expansion that began in 2000. Thanks to Quebec's Ministère de la culture et des communications and their "Intégration des arts à l'architecture" program (also known as the 1% program), Concordia benefitted from provincial funds for the creation of nine large-scale public artworks by renowned Quebec artists, all of which are featured throughout this publication as they directly relate to the university's physical growth over the last fifty years.

Also included in this publication are a memorial installation commissioned by the university that speaks to the complicated and tragic history of the downtown campus, historical artifacts, and a donation by the university's chancellor in honour of Montreal's 375th anniversary and Canada's 150th anniversary.

SANDRA MARGOLIAN is the Public Art Lead at Concordia University.

In recent years the University has invested in the long-term care of the collection by creating the Public Art Lead position to ensure that collecting practices align with its current and future vision of pedagogy and values of equity, decolonization, diversity, inclusiveness, accessibility, creativity, and sustainability.

In 2023, the University adopted a Public Art Policy and created a long-term initiative called Honouring Black Presence at Concordia University to celebrate the histories, presence, and futures of Black Concordians through the creation of temporary public artworks. In 2024 the University appointed an advisory committee to support the Public Art Lead in maintaining open and transparent processes, ensure equitable and respectful practices, and address the inconsistencies and omissions in the current collection.

For further exploration of the collection, Concordia's public art website provides maps for self-guided walking tours of each campus and three self-guided thematic audio tours created by Concordia Fine Arts graduates.

For more information, see https://www.concordia.ca/arts/public-art.html

**Credits**

Page xi
Marc-Antoine Côté
Intégration des arts à l'architecture, Ministère de la Culture et des Communications

Pages xii–xviii
Kamila Wozniakowska
Intégration des arts à l'architecture, Le ministère d'alors, appelé ministère de la Culture, des Communications et de la Condition féminine

Page xix
Jean McEwen
Commissioned for the Hall Building at the time of its construction

Pages 50–51
Pierre Blanchette
Intégration des arts à l'architecture, Le ministère d'alors, appelé ministère de la Culture, des Communications et de la Condition féminine

Pages 106–107
Geneviève Cadieux
Intégration des arts à l'architecture, Le ministère d'alors, appelé ministère de la Culture, des Communications et de la Condition féminine

Pages 146, 148–151
Eduardo Aquino, Johanne Sloan, and Kathryn Walter
Commissioned as a dedication to the memories of four professors who were shot and killed in Concordia University's Hall Building on August 24, 1992. Photos: UCS

Page 167
François Houde
Intégration des arts à l'architecture, Ministère de la Culture et des Communications
Restored in 2016 with the assistance of the Ministère de la Culture et des Communications

Page 168
Marie-France Brière
Intégration des arts à l'architecture, Le ministère d'alors, appelé ministère de la Culture, des Communications et de la Condition féminine

Pages 188–89
Effets Publics – Rose-Marie Goulet, Alain Paiement, Randy Saharuni, Guy Bellavance
Intégration des arts à l'architecture, Ministère de la Culture et des Communications
Restored during the renovation of the Webster Library with the assistance of the Ministère de la Culture et des Communications

Pages 222–23
Nicolas Baier and Cabinet Braun-Braën
Intégration des arts à l'architecture, Ministère de la Culture et des Communications

Pages 276–77
Adad Hannah
Intégration des arts à l'architecture, Le ministère d'alors, appelé ministère de la Culture, des Communications et de la Condition féminine

Page 307
Kenneth Hensley Holmden
Recovered and restored from the York Theatre and reintegrated into the EV Building, located on the former site of the York Theatre

Pages 332–33
Lintels from the Thomas D'Arcy McGee House
Donated by Eli, Cecil, and Victor Hill

Page 367
Anthony Howe
Donated by Susan and Jonathan Wener

Page 376
Holly King
Commissioned by Concordia University's Part-Time Faculty Association (CUPFA) for the union's 30th anniversary

Editors' Note: The Ministère de la Culture et des Communications was named the Ministère de la Culture, des Communications et de la Condition féminine between 2004 and 2012.

51.1 Concordia President Graham Carr and Chief of Staff, William Cheaib visit student representatives, faculty and staff of the Department of Communication Studies at a department meeting held on Zoom on February 12, 2021. When COVID-19 public health isolation and social distancing measures commenced on Friday March 13, 2020, the nature of teaching and work radically and irrevocably transformed.

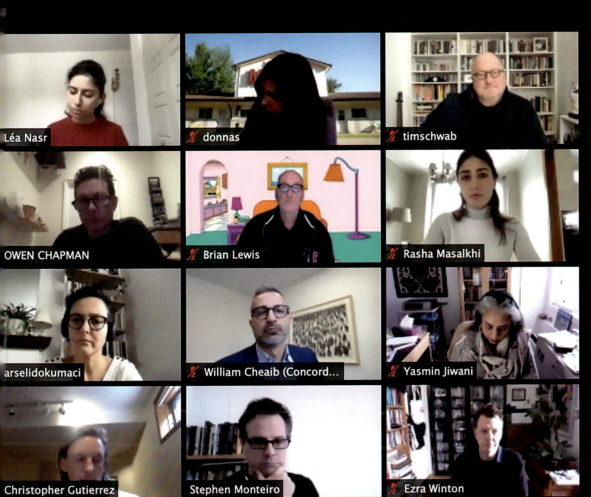